EXOTIC NATIONS

Renata R. Mautner Wasserman

EXOTIC

NATIONS

Literature and Cultural Identity in the

United States and Brazil, 1830–1930

CORNELL UNIVERSITY PRESS

ITHACA AND LONDON

First published 1994 by Cornell University Press.

Printed in the United States of America

♾ The paper in this book meets the minimum requirements of the
American National Standard for Information Sciences—Permanence
of Paper for Printed Library Materials, ANSI Z39.48-1984.

Library of Congress Cataloging-in-Publication Data

Wasserman, Renata R. Mautner (Renata Ruth Mautner), 1941–
    Exotic nations : literature and cultural identity in the United States and Brazil,
1830–1930 / Renata R. Mautner Wasserman.
        p. cm.
    Includes bibliographical references (p.) and index,
    ISBN 0-8014-2877-7 (cloth)—ISBN 0-8014-8205-4 (paper)
    1. American literature—History and criticism.   2. Literature, Comparative—
American and Brazilian.   3. National characteristics, American, in literature.
4. National characteristics, Brazilian, in literature.   5. Literature, Comparative—
Brazilian and American.   6. Literature and society—United States—History.
7. Brazilian literature—History and criticism.   8. Literature and society—Brazil—
History.   9. Exoticism in literature.   10. Indians in literature.   I. Title.
PS159.B6W37 1994
809'.93327—dc20   94-20368

to my parents

Hans and Erna Mautner

Contents

Preface

As a first-generation Brazilian and later as an American citizen, I have always lived in more than one culture, always had before me an amalgam of nationalities, cultures, and beliefs. Long ago I recognized that identity is necessary but contingent, a construct, but so made as to seem inevitable and "natural."

This book grew out of my observations about identity, necessity, power, contact. I hope it does justice to the virtues of those among whom I grew up, from whom I learned: my argumentative parents and their friends; Vilém Flusser, in whose house all ideas were welcome and none taken for granted; Antônio Cândido, whose pioneering course in literary theory at the University of São Paulo shaped my thoughts about literature in general and about Brazilian literature in particular.

I thank all who listened to my ideas while they were a-shaping, read the early versions of various chapters, and gave me encouragement and advice: Rolena Adorno, Charles Baxter, Henry Golemba, Michael Giordano, Marisa Lajolo, Arthur Marotti, Walter Mignolo, Michael Palencia-Roth, Ross Pudaloff, Roberto Schwarz, Elizabeth Sklar. They did much to show me the right direction and save me from blunders.

I thank the English Department and Wayne State University for leaves of absence and grants that allowed me the time to complete this work. And I thank the Newberry Library for its help and the National Endowment for the Humanities for the grant that allowed me to attend the Newberry's invaluable Summer Institute on Transatlantic Encounters in 1986.

Earlier versions of portions of this book have appeared as articles.

Parts of Chapter 2 appeared as "Travelers' Tales about Brazil: Variations," in *L'esprit créateur* 30 (Fall 1990): 15–26; parts of Chapters 6 and 7 appeared as "The Red and the White: The 'Indian' Novels of José de Alencar," in *PMLA* 98 (October 1983): 815–27; "Re-inventing the New World: Cooper and Alencar," in *Comparative Literature* 36 (Spring 1984): 183–200; and "The Reception of Cooper's Work and the Image of America," in *ESQ: A Journal of the American Renaissance* 32.3 (1986): 130–45, an early version of Chapter 8 appeared as "Preguiça and Power: Mário de Andrade's *Macunaíma*," in *Luso-Brazilian Review* 21 (Summer 1984): 99–116. I thank the journals for permission to use these materials.

Unless otherwise noted, all translations in this book are my own.

Finally I thank my husband, Rick, and my children, Sarah and Daniel, for advice, patience, encouragement, and joy.

RENATA R. MAUTNER WASSERMAN
Ann Arbor, Michigan

EXOTIC NATIONS

1

Introduction:
Designing Nations

Despite the attending noise, recent shifts in the distribution of political and discursive power between men and women, whites and nonwhites, First or Second and Third or Fourth worlds reveal how closely the contending sides are interconnected and how interdependent are their interests and even their identities. Alliances among women, among minorities in the United States, among Latin Americans, have been strained as contests for power have redefined interests and hierarchies, as attempts to describe the characteristic traits of a collectivity have become the means of opening rifts within it, as new boundaries have been drawn around subjection by class, gender, or ethnicity while time, history, and opportunity redistribute power among them.[1]

These realignments have prompted new readings of materials from the past, of writings by Phillis Wheatley and Frederick Douglass, by Harriet Beecher Stowe, Charles Brockden Brown, and James Fenimore Cooper; of captivity narratives, and reports of the early encounters

---

[1] Without elaborating, I mention the arguments about the relevance of mainstream feminist demands to working-class or black women; the dissolution of the African-American–Jewish alliance of the sixties; the identification in Angel Rama's *Ciudad letrada* or Frantz Fanon's angrier *Wretched of the Earth* of a split in the "developing," or Third World, between governing elites and masses. Gayatri Chakravorti Spivak discusses some of the class and culture rifts within feminism in "French Feminism in an International Frame," in *In Other Worlds*, pp. 134–53.

between Europeans and Amerindians.[2] These readings, which treat matters of power and identity at some length, refer as much to conditions of the present in which they are constructed as of the past they study. In the past, as in the present, issues of power and identity brought a strong emotional and ideological charge to works of the imagination, but time has removed much of the original urgency, and it is possible to gain new profit from their study.

Important shifts in political and discursive power took place in American nations just after they won independence in the late eighteenth and early nineteenth centuries. The literatures of the new nations set themselves the task of contesting the legitimacy and power of the former metropoles, determined to disentangle distinctive national selves from the cultural ties that still bound them to Europe. Yet different former colonies took different ways toward political and cultural independence. Here, I want to compare Brazilian and (North) American writings to understand how these ways, which have come to be seen as necessary and almost "natural," were in fact, to a certain point, contingent, nondetermined.[3] Both nations produced complete "literary systems"—a concept on which Antônio Cândido builds his study of Brazilian literary

---

[2] See David Leverenz, "Frederick Douglass's Self-Refashioning"; Frances Roe Kestler, comp., *The Indian Captivity Narrative*; Frederick Drimmer, *Captured by the Indians*; David Grimstead, "Anglo-American Racism"; Ross Pudaloff, "One Subject at a Time"; Mitchell R. Breitwieser, *American Puritanism and the Defense of Mourning*; Rachel Bowlby, "Breakfast in America"; Jane P. Tompkins, "Sentimental Power." Drimmer's book is a reprint whose new title, changed from *Scalps and Tomahawks* (1961), marks a discursive shift in the argument about the relationship between colonizer and original inhabitant of the Americas. Drimmer's introduction speaks with some gusto of the hardship and bad treatment suffered by the captives, though it also indicates that at times they married or were adopted into a tribe. Ross Pudaloff is doing important work on the role of captivity narratives in the formation of early national American literature.

[3] In chapter 3, "*Beyond the Positivity of the Social: Antagonisms and Hegemony,*" of *Hegemony and Socialist Strategies* (esp. pp. 115–19), Ernesto Laclau and Chantal Mouffe build a subtle and complex picture of how a discourse constitutes for itself certain categories that must seem essential but, insofar as they are discursive, must also participate in the nondetermined, contingent character of discursive constructs. Installing notions of discourse and contingency (even if it is via Antonio Gramsci) in socialist theory is in effect a complex task, but the author's sense that it is needed illustrates the destabilizing effect of non-European conditions on European interpretations of the world. In quite a different key, A. J. R. Russell-Wood, in "Preconditions and Precipitants of the Independence Movement in Portuguese America," surveys different characteristics of independence movements in the Americas, noting common elements and disparities in the policies of metropoles toward their colonies, before settling on the particular case of Brazil.

history.[4] Both were, or are, marginalized. I am particularly interested in the initial marginality of the literature of the United States and the present marginality of Brazilian literature because they indicate that marginality may be a function of time and because they offer what Roberto Schwarz has characterized as the built-in critical stance of the margin toward what the center takes for granted in values, culture, politics, literature.[5]

Because we are now distant in time from all the American independence movements and distant from many in space or culture as well, we can easily "estrange" for study what every grade-school mention of Washington in the United States, Bolívar in Spanish America, or Dom Pedro I in Brazil endeavors to "naturalize."[6] But those of us who live on the western side of the Atlantic are also close to the history of how the New World sought political and cultural independence, for we remember learning to think of our nations, and of ourselves in them. We can recover what was tentative and contradictory in school explanations of how we became independent, of how our nations defined themselves and how they endeavored to inscribe themselves in a world where history was dominated by the colonial powers.

At the core of concepts of nationality in the New World is historical and ideological material encompassing, first, the encounter between the very different cultures (later identified with races)[7] of Europe and the Americas; second, the awareness, almost within memory, of a time when national history began; and third, the consciousness of establishing a culture, of marking the boundaries between nature and culture. If we isolate these components we defamiliarize the sense of cultural

---

[4] Antônio Cândido follows Angel Rama's analysis in "O olhar crítico de Angel Rama," p. 145, and uses the concept of literary system as a basis for his *Formação da literatura brasileira*. Both authors deal with South American, not North American, literatures.

[5] See *Ao vencedor as batatas*; "Cuidado com as ideologias alienígenas"; etc.

[6] Victor Shklovsky thought of "estrangement" (or defamiliarization) as a "procedure" by which "what we call art" justifies its existence, "producing a sense of life, . . . so we can feel that a stone is made of stone, . . . producing the sense of the object as vision and not as recognition." It operates by "increasing the difficulty and the duration of perception" and combats the "automatization" of everyday life ("L'art comme procédé," pp. 82–83). I give the term a meaning close to the original one to indicate a process, not necessarily artistic, of casting doubt on something generally taken as given. As the opposite of "estrangement," I use not the Shklovskian "automatization" but the more Foucauldian "naturalization," since it implies not only the habitual but also that which seems to be determined by nature.

[7] In "One Subject at a Time," Ross Pudaloff traces the beginnings, in the United States, of a discourse of race in the sense of inherent biological characteristics of cultural groups to Mary Rowlandson's narrative of her captivity among Indians.

identity, the notions of history and nature which are so powerful while they are taken for granted. If America is all nature, as it was so often depicted, its inhabitants could be neither partners nor adversaries of Europe, defined as civilization. If American nations wanted to retain a difference defined in terms of nature, yet enter into a civilized relationship with the metropoles, then the line separating nature from culture had to be redrawn, and in being redrawn, it could not be taken for granted.

The questions of identity, nature, history are not always posed in the same terms, but they are repeatedly answered in the literature of nationality and its criticism. Myra Jehlen, for instance (in *American Incarnation*), finds attempts to connect concepts of national identity with American nature and to merge notions of civilization and nature. Peter Hulme finds that the early accounts of Euro-American contact resolve that problematic connection with an erasure, as when Europe justifies exploration and conquest by insisting on the need to inscribe civilization on an "empty" continent, and ignoring the contradiction of its own complaints about the difficulty of overcoming the resistance of inhabitants, who had, at first, fed and sheltered the invaders (cf. *Colonial Encounters*, pp. 128, 156–57). The question reappears in eighteenth-century European thought about the origins of society, which in turn provides some of the concepts on which definitions of American national character were based. The difficulty of reconceiving nature and civilization accounts for the tension and sometimes the interest of the new American literatures.

Similarly, the notion of historical origins is defamiliarized if the new nations can decide where national history begins, if origin is chosen rather than given. Preoccupied with the question of historical continuities and discontinuities, the new literatures acquired the deconstructive force of a built-in critical view of themselves and their objects.

Questions about nature, culture, history were encoded by means of writing, the fourth problematic category in an American "literature of nationality,[8] whose conscious and deliberate aim was to define national identity and to assert cultural parity with the former metropoles. Writers and public considered this literature of nationality a necessary complement to political independence, and it resisted metropolitan "cultural

[8] With *Foundational Fictions* Doris Sommer offers a longitudinal study of the literature of nationality in Iberian America, stressing parallels among the new American national literatures, rather than continuities with the discourse of the exotic elaborated since the discoveries.

power" with a certain thematic consistency. Generally through marriage plots it tells of implanting civilization in the American natural world, weighs the appropriateness of joining the opposites of nature and culture, European and non-European. It also tells stories about origins and history and considers the role of writing in the constitution of identity. These themes cannot be ordered hierarchically or causally, nor do they have constant or equal importance in all the works I discuss, but some of them at least are always present in the literature of national consciousness, and they form the kernel of chapters on specific works.

The epic poems, essays, lyrics, and novels comprised in this literature do not necessarily defend independence directly; rather, they aim to create a new cultural environment by using autochthonous material cast in traditional forms that both copied and contested metropolitan forms and values.[9] Commentators of that time, readers as well as authors, took it for granted that literature would serve nationality.[10] Present-day critics make a stronger, though related, claim. Central to Benedict Anderson's *Imagined Communities*, for example, is the argument that writing for mass circulation, specifically the newspaper and the novel, "provided the technical means for 're-presenting' the *kind* of imagined community that is the nation" and became the secular replacement for the "sacred" languages binding together the earlier complex communities, feudal or ecclesiastic, which were weakened or dissolved by intense pressures at the end of the eighteenth century (pp. 30, 25). Similarly, the title and the introduction of Homi K. Bhabha's *Nation and Narration* posit a necessary connection between writing and nationality. This association can appear, however, without being central to the argument; in *Novels, Readers, and Reviewers* Nina Baym addresses the specific link between American novel and national identity only in her last chapter; she cites British critics who consider the American love of "romances" a sign of cultural primitivism (p. 226) but does not contradict American reviewers who accept the abundance and popularity of the American novel as signs of cultural progress and of the democratic orientation of their country.[11]

[9] Stephen Railton believes the success of Cooper's first novels depended on their traditional English form as well as their American material (*Authorship and Audience*, pp. 4–5).
[10] According to Benjamin Spencer, "scarcely a native author of any importance before 1900 failed to engage in the inquiry [into national character] and to declare himself publicly on its issues" (*The Quest for Nationality*, p. ix).
[11] Increased reading is a sign of "the diffusion of education," and novels mark "an advanced state of society." Baym is quoting from the *North American* and the *Democratic Review*; see *Novels, Readers, and Reviewers*, p. 29.

Novels of nationality generally declare themselves so by choice. Added to their preoccupation with and denaturalization of history, nature, and culture, this choice gives the literature of nationality a slightly strained edge, revealing the operation of the will at the very moment when creation should result from what romantic literary theory, from Johann Gottfried von Herder on, saw as the inevitable coincidence between nation and literary expression.[12] The element of will is probably what leads critics to read literature of nationality as allegory, defined, in Schopenhauer's words, as "the purposeful . . . use of a work of art for the expression of a concept."[13] Fredric Jameson, in "Third World Literature in the Era of Multinational Capitalism," analyses two works from the "Third World" as representative "allegories of nationality," characterized by preoccupation with history and out of step with the First World, for which history is no longer such a problem. Mutatis mutandis, Jameson, like Schopenhauer, finds that these allegories cannot be received as art by a First World reader, whose most empathetic reaction would be to imagine that their stale material and manner must seem original and meaningful to a Third World public. One cannot argue about taste. One can dispute Jameson's evaluation of allegory, however, as Walter Benjamin did Schopenhauer's, by defining it not as an artistic technique but as a form of expression, like writing or speech, which arises in a discursive transformation of history into nature (pp. 178, 203). It may then be possible to oppose a literature in which the transformation has become invisible to one in which it is on display. The preference of one to the other is a different matter; it implies a relationship, which Jameson does not stress, between the national alle-

[12] Inasmuch as the relation between novel and nation was established in the nineteenth century, contemporaneously with the independence of the American nations, Benedict Anderson notes, it is not surprising that it should have become important to writers and other citizens. Anderson maintains that the countries of the western hemisphere were the first to emerge "which self-consciously defined themselves as nations" and therefore "provided the first real models of what such states should look like" (*Imagined Communities*, p. 49). This conclusion may be forced. Portugal had been a self-contained political and administrative unit since the twelfth century; Spain's unification dates from the end of the fifteenth; periods of turmoil had not seriously threatened the core unity of England. Their rebellious colonies did not have to invent nationality from scratch. Luiz Costa Lima says that in the nineteenth century "the study of literature derived its legitimacy from the idea that literature was the expression of nation-states" (*The Dark Side of Reason*, p. 111).
[13] Schopenhauer, *Die Welt als Wille und Vorstellung*, pp. 279–81, quoted by Walter Benjamin, *Ursprung des deutschen Trauerspiels*, p. 177. Benjamin disagrees with Schopenhauer's disqualification of the work as art when it is so used but not with the definition of allegory.

gories he devalues and the cultural matrixes they implicitly address as they attempt to transform *their* history into the "nature" in whose guise readers from another world see their own history. The aim of these fictions, then, is not to create but to exorcise allegory so as to be included in history as written by that more powerful world.

Doris Sommer characterizes as inexact and anachronistic Jameson's contention that Third World literature is allegorical and First World literature is not (*Foundational Fictions*, p. 42). Taking her definition from a "clue" by Benjamin, she describes the "allegory in Latin America's national novels as an interlocking, not parallel, relationship between erotics and politics" (p. 43), which links together the central characters' "desire for union and for nation" (p. 48). This definition does not require the traditional structure of levels of signification in ascending degrees of abstraction; it makes allegory less "static,"[14] but also more difficult to recognize, and this difficulty is part of the definition of these works and of their reception.

Instead of attempting to redefine allegory, it may be useful to speak not of allegorical novels but of allegorical readings. When the literature of nationality calls itself a representative of national identity and declares its aim to be the creation of the cultural equivalent of political independence, it invites an allegorical reading. Its characters and their interactions, its settings, its opinions stand for a population, a country, an ideology. In order to signify cultural equivalence to the metropolis or to their formerly colonial public, however, these allegories must also allow themselves to be read as novels. Their characters and their interactions, their settings, their opinions must be individual and particular as required by romantic and then realistic conventions. In his reading of Third World fictions as allegorical, Jameson reestablishes a cultural distance those fictions are trying to bridge.[15] Speaking in "Third World Literature" from a position of cultural authority (though with a regret that colonial authorities did not usually show [p. 65]), Jameson reacts to a bid for cultural parity by reasserting the ability of the dominant discourse to define and to bestow identity.

If an allegorical reading of the literature of nationality is not only a

[14] See Jameson's exposition of medieval allegory, which he uses as a basis for his description of a Marxist allegorical reading of realist texts, in *The Political Unconscious*. The first chapter, "On Interpretation," is an extended discussion of various definitions of allegory and their modes of operation.

[15] The chagrined tone of Aijaz Ahmad's response to Jameson's "Third World Literature" bears me out. See Ahmad, "Jameson's Rhetoric of Otherness and the 'National Allegory.'"

response to its declared intent but a distancing move, then instead of defining or exhausting this literature, it can single out recurring structural elements of bids for control over discourse or the channels of communication, over the power to assign value or the right to self-definition and self-evaluation. An allegorical reading also implies that the terms of identity and value are still those of the powerful discourse whose domination is being contested. Those who accuse Mario Vargas Llosa or Chinua Achebe of being excessively "Europeanized" are reacting negatively to a particular attitude toward this entanglement between the contesting discourse and the one being contested.[16] An allegorical reading can be a strategy to deny either the entanglement or the claim to cultural parity, but this is not its only possible goal.

Many of us will also remember a nonallegorical, nondistanced reading of some work of the literature of nationality when we met, in adolescence, noble Indians who fought against perfidious whites and cruel savages to protect fair maidens or chivalrous young men in the New World wilderness. These fictions were fixtures on lists of books considered appropriate for the amusement and edification of young persons. And we may have read them more or less as Jane Tompkins remembers reading Cooper's *Deerslayer*, "at age nine, in a large uncomfortable chair, in a dark house, on a long summer vacation" (*Sensational Designs*, p. 99). Those were formative years, when we were less interested in the structure and function of a novel than in the rattling good tales we expected from that combination of characters. If we were growing up in Brazil, we might have met José de Alencar's Indians before we met Cooper's, and then have gone on from *The Last of the Mohicans* to Chateaubriand's earlier validation and Karl May's later appropriation of exotic American themes. Later still we might have relegated the entire genre, with its primitives and its wilderness alternately threatening and sheltering the admirable, though incompetent representatives of a more refined civilization, to a personal protohistory of reading, unworthy of our newer regard for works we had come to think more complex and more deserving of serious study.

But the memory of being isolated from friends, from the outside world in the dark and silent house, dislocated from workaday activities in the hiatus of summer vacation, reading simple yarns, is misleading. If

---

[16] Antônio Cândido's blunt statement that there is no such thing as an absolute specificity of (Latin) American literatures usefully clears the ground ("O olhar crítico," p. 141). See also Kwame Anthony Appiah, "The Myth of an African World," in *In My Father's House*.

we were of the New World, we were privately engaged in the collective assertion of cultural identity for which those emblematic Indians were an important building block. If we were of the Old World, we might be imagining, in private, the alternative and complement to our own excessively determined surroundings. The American authors of those novels were assembling the elements of what Tompkins, alluding to the psychological "dream work" that forms and reveals personality, calls the "cultural work" of defining a characteristic national identity. Tompkins connects Cooper with Harriet Beecher Stowe and Charles Brockden Brown. If we connect him instead to Chateaubriand and Alencar, we see not only the internal cultural work of a nation but also how that cultural work intersects with, draws upon, influences, and distinguishes itself from the work of other related cultures and nationalities. Like Philip Fisher, who also analyses Cooper's "cultural work," we can say that Cooper has been forgotten because he performed it too well, making it obsolete; that he "invented" the American wilderness so convincingly it was no longer necessary to read him in order to know it: it had entered the language of its culture (*Hard Facts*, pp. 7, 10–12).

Representative works by Chateaubriand, Cooper, and Alencar form the core of this book. The differences among the two Americans and the Frenchman who made the American wilderness into a legitimate setting for popular fiction tell us much about the role of imported cultural forms in the establishment of cultural independence. The differences between the North and the South American authors indicate the possibility of different roads toward cultural independence and introduce an intra-American relation of dependence, prompting even further cultural work.

This cultural work is difficult, sometimes repetitive. The literature of nationality faces the task of asserting a national self against an externally imposed definition as other, posits an independent history that obeys local, not alien standards in the valuation of events, and provides a written record that defines and validates its own culture. The forms in which these tasks are performed—combinations of the historical novel, the adventure story and the marriage novel—are furnished by contemporary European literature; the materials—the natural setting of the New World, its original inhabitants, its discovery and settlement, the establishment of new communities—tend to be autochthonous; the relationship between plot and material is at times strained. On the whole, the literary relations between European and American texts, and among texts of various New World nations illustrate the complex process by

which cultural power— the power to define and evaluate cultural characteristics—is distributed.

Cultural power is a notion rooted in an anthropological definition of
culture as a system of practices and values, and in Michel Foucault's
argument that power is not a matter of "constitution, sovereignty, etc.,"
or of "the state apparatus," or invested just in "the economic instance
and the system of interests which this serve[s]," but is exercised and
makes itself felt in the organization of daily life, functioning under rules
naturalized as common sense (*Power/Knowledge*, pp. 56–58). Economic
and political power are easier to recognize, in part because they drama-
tize themselves; cultural power is a somewhat slippery category, its
operation more readily perceived by those who lack it than by those
who have it. Foucault also speaks of it as the "regime of truth," where
"'truth' is linked in a circular relation with systems of power which
produce and sustain it, and to effects of power which it induces and
which extend it" (*Power/Knowledge*, p. 74). Paul Bové glosses it as "the
interwoven connections of incommensurable and interwoven power effects in discourses and in institutions that produce 'the truth'" (p. 9).
The concept has diffused through the disciplines dealing with how
informally enforced and incompletely articulated systems of ideas and
values determine actions and judgments.[17] The importance of the literature of nationality for its original readers lay in its resistance to a cultural
power that qualified political independence by continuing to control
the image of the newly independent nations. It reveals national selves
in the process of construction, assimilating for self-definition material
used till then to characterize otherness, and stumbling over the uncer-
tainties and disjunctures in the newly formed identities.

Such literature is, however reluctantly, reactive. The title of Robert
Weisbuch's *Atlantic Double-Cross* implies the reciprocity between English
and American letters even a century after the American declaration of
political independence. At the same time, by stressing (perhaps even
exaggerating) the effects of American letters on the literature of the
former metropolis, the book carries into its third century the effort

---

[17] Appiah uses the phrase to name the pressure of non-African definitions of Africa
which need to be avoided or exorcised with every reference to Africa and in every
encounter between it and what is outside of it. Edward Said's *Orientalism* sees European power as inescapably informing and deforming the "orientals'" very vision
of themselves.

to affirm an American cultural power still rooted in resistance to the former metropolis.[18]

Just as problematic as resistance to a cultural power located outside the new nations is the relationship between their European and non-European components. On one hand, it is necessary to ascribe positive value to the non-European component, because it handily signifies a positive difference between former colony and former metropolis; on the other hand, choosing the non-European component as an identifying trait risks a judgment of barbarism by a metropolis arrogating to itself the title of civilized. This relation of difference is often treated indirectly in stories about contact and intermarriage. In their more developed form, such tales of kinship and difference construct systems of oppositions in which extreme endogamy, or incest, opposes extreme exogamy, or marriage between European and American, to which value, positive or negative, is assigned.[19] This valuation can either reproduce

[18] Since Weisbuch adopts Harold Bloom's paradigm of the "anxiety of influence," he stresses the confrontational aspects of the literary relation between England and the United States, "the savagery characterizing the American debunking of imported British wisdoms" (*Atlantic Double-Cross*, p. xvii); he lists statements made from 1832 to 1869 complaining that American literary works copy the English (pp. 4–5) and derogatory remarks about American literature published in British literary magazines (pp. 12–13); he explains that though "American literary nationalists . . . argue[d] that Britain had been superseded, like the claims of separation and superiority to which it is related, this American-aggressive version of the myth falls prey to anxiety" (pp. 72–73). The continued scholarly interest in the subject is one indication of its centrality to the cultural history of the United States, as is its repeated translation into contemporary critical terminology. The extended and fascinating discussion of the often unacknowledged influence of American literary works on important British ones shows cultural parity between former colony and former metropolis still at issue. Andrew Ross, in "Uses of Camp," places the question of relation in an even less likely context when he finds that British acceptance validates American "lowbrow" culture: "For Britons, the importation of American popular culture, even as it was officially despised, contained and controlled, brought with it guaranteed immunity to those traditional 'European' judgments of elitist taste to which it was structurally oblivious. By the early sixties, the 'success' of this wave of American exports among British taste makers was such that they were able to set the final seal of approval on the formation and acceptance of Pop taste in the U.S. itself. Thus, the British version of Pop (always an *imaginary* relation to a foreign culture . . .) was somehow needed to legitimize American pop culture for Americans" (p. 5). One should note that though the process of legitimation is homologous with that of the early nationalist period, it now takes place in relation to a marginalized subculture within the larger American cultural landscape, which no longer depends on recognition from Britain for itself but is open to British validation of differentiated forms of discourse within itself.

[19] Weisbuch observes, for an instance, that in Herman Melville's *Pierre* a semi-incestuous romance refers in a critical way to Wordsworth's and Byron's relations with their respective sisters (p. 14), but he sees that reference as part of the discourse

or arrest the slide toward "naturalizing" a social regulation of marriages across class, religious, or national boundaries. If the prohibition of incest is, as Claude Lévi-Strauss maintained, the threshold between nature and culture, one should expect it to hover, as it does, over these tales of contact. And the literature of nationality then finds models in European works that specifically associate exotic settings with the treatment of marriage between social classes (such as *Paul et Virginie* by Jacques Henri Bernardin de Saint-Pierre) or between cultures (such as *Atala* by the vicomte de Chateaubriand). Their international popularity shows how close they were to the interests of readers on both sides of the Atlantic.

These works, in which marriage is a metaphor for contact with the exotic other, could be lined up with American stories of marriages that mediate between the New and the Old worlds and make conquest and settlement possible. The evaluation of enabling contact differs between colonizers; João Ramalho, who made it possible for the Portuguese to penetrate into territory beyond the first coastal settlements, is a Brazilian hero. Cabeza de Vaca, who as Richard Slotkin notes, aided the efforts of conquest and settlement by the perilous method of going native (*Regeneration through Violence*, pp. 35–36), was excluded from a U.S. national pantheon ruled by a Puritan fear of dissolution in contact with American otherness.[20] To the extent that this fear imposed itself on notions of an American self, it kept the story of Cabeza de Vaca out of the repertory of available national narratives and branded Thomas Morton of Merrymount, who advocated the inclusion of Indians in the

---

of national superiority and national identity; he does not discuss the literary fashion for brother-sister incest as a metaphor for the union with the perfectly appropriate other—the one closest to the self—which is the object of frustrated desire in such blockbuster novels of the beginning of the century as *Renée* and *Atala* by Chateaubriand. Nor does he establish a direct connection between the incest theme and the theme of difference treated in works about national identity, including Melville's. J. M. S. Tompkins, in *The Popular Novel in England*, documents the popularity of the incest theme in the European novel at the turn of the century of American independence (pp. 62–66), noting that it is used, often "casually," as "the unexpected obstacle suddenly thrown in the course of a plighted pair to the altar" (p. 65). It is the more interesting to see the theme appear in the literature of nationality, adapted to the consideration of questions of cultural identity and of the creation of new social or cultural entities.

[20] Capistrano de Abreu's swift, nervous history of colonial Brazil, *Capítulos de história colonial, 1500–1800*, mentions Ramalho, the first colonist established where São Paulo was then founded, without further comment or explanation; he assumes that everyone will know about this adventurous person, whose huts, together with those of "his half-Indian, half-Portuguese sons and relatives, . . . announced the victory over the coastal forests, obtained earlier here than anywhere else in Brazil" (p. 85).

process of settlement, a debauched villain (Slotkin, pp. 58–60). Peter Hulme shows how the story of Pocahontas was rewritten into a "foundational" (to use Sommer's term) narrative that turned an equal exchange into voluntary subjection of Amerindians to Englishmen. And the evaluation of Marina, the Indian woman who served as an interpreter to Hernando Cortez and bore him a son is still not settled in the Mexican debate on the conquest of Montezuma's empire.[21] Slotkin sees the Puritans' rejection of contact as central to their concept of their colony's identity and of the relationship between colony and metropolis: they were as afraid of intermarriage as of cannibalism—two forms of merging with the wild. This rejection of a relation that must take place is mythified as a system of negations, as for instance in Cooper's elegiacally titled *Last of the Mohicans,* in which the autochthonous population, whether aggressive like Magua or protective like Uncas, is intrinsically dangerous and must be destroyed.

But even though Magua and Uncas die, they introduce a characteristic difference in Cooper's novel, to which American readers respond with self-recognition and European readers with the recognition of an American otherness. They too can recognize Mohicans and Hurons, having been prepared for them by centuries of European texts on American difference beginning with the accounts of discovery and exploration, continuing with the incorporation of that information into the philosophical discourse of the eighteenth century and flowing into the early texts of French romanticism. The legibility of an American literature of self-definition depends, thus, on familiarty with the literature that views it as other; its otherness can be intelligible only if it is not complete, if it is translatable.[22]

The exotic, for centuries a mode in which strangeness is translated for the West, constitutes such a mediating entity. The exotic arises as a sign of interest on the part of the self in that which is not self. It is not, however, the complete other; it is the acceptable, complementary,

---

[21] Fernando Coronil, however, states that "most contemporary Mexicans view [Marina, or 'la Malinche'] as a symbol of cultural betrayal" ("Discovering America Again," p. 322).

[22] In a different context, and for a different purpose, Laclau and Mouffe define the interrelation between self and other, explaining that neither can exist entirely in itself when both are present: "If language is a system of differences, antagonism is the failure of difference; in that sense, it situates itself within the limits of language and can only exist as the disruption of it—that is, as metaphor" (p. 125). Neither the other nor its relatively benign form, the exotic, can exist in isolation from the self, the nonexotic.

renewing other. The exotic mediates between the defining self and a more radical otherness, which at the limit would fall outside the grammar of the defining discourse. Edward Said identifies one eastward-looking form of the European discourse of the exotic, which he calls Orientalism. It is, he says, not a mediating discourse but a form of cultural domination, a "discourse of power," which takes up "a position of irreducible opposition to a region of the world [which Europe] considered alien to its own" (*Orientalism*, p. 328). Said claims that Orientalism "produce[s] the Orient" (p. 3); he also documents certain ways in which Orientalism contributes to produce Europe. And of course, his book is itself a chapter in the constitution of an independent "Orient," still on the basis of resistance.[23]

The totalizing and demonizing strains that Said isolates in *Orientalism* have a parallel in the mythologies of or about the Americas: it is the image of the American other in the form of the cannibal. But even this image arises, as Hulme explains, in fears made ideologically unspeakable to Christian Europe,[24] and can be shown to represent not the ontologically alien but the ethically abhorrent. In that form even cannibalism can be adopted as a positive representation (as Michel de Montaigne comes close to doing) by a newly critical discourse of the exotic which unmasks the earlier euphoric exoticism as an ideological construct.[25] Thus, the members of a Brazilian movement of resistance to an official culture perceived as alienating happily term themselves Anthropophagists.[26] In 1971 Roberto Fernández Retamar adopted Shakespeare's Caliban, whose name is an approximate anagram of cannibal, as the patron of a Latin-American culture in opposition both to Europe and to the United States, seen as heir to the metropolitan role.[27] A journal of "New

[23] Said objects to Dante's placement of Mohammed in the eighth circle of hell, which seems to me a normal, though ungenerous consequence of a political war exacerbated by religious differences, corresponding (for example) to a less artistic Iranian Satanization of the United States. Dante's placement of Avicenna, Averroës, and even Saladdin in the same privileged space as Socrates (*Orientalism*, pp. 68–69) looks to me more like a recognition of "Oriental" merit than a denial of "Oriental" autonomy.
[24] Hulme believes that Europe creates the cannibal, eater of human flesh, out of its unspeakable horror of the implications of the Eucharist. We shall see that the similarity presented itself to the Brazilian novelist José de Alencar.
[25] Antônio Cândido discusses these ideological transformations at greater length and depth in "Literatura e subdesenvolvimento," esp. pp. 140–43.
[26] This literary, cultural, and artistic movement of the 1920s is a radicalization of Brazilian modernism as introduced by the "Modern Art Week" of 1922; it will be discussed later.
[27] Roberto Fernández Retamar begins "Caliban: Notes Toward a Discussion of Culture in Our America" with a question asked of the author by a "European journalist"

World Thought and Writing" founded in 1975 in the United States called itself *Caliban*.[28] And the Yoruba trickster figure Esu-Elegbara of West Africa, who exists to subvert all rules, including those of the culture that created him, turns up as a theoretical term that Henry Louis Gates applies to African-American (and, by implication, to any non-Euro-American) literature ("The Blackness of Blackness"). These examples show the other as translatable, and implicit in this translatability, as in that of the exotic, is not only the incomplete otherness of the exotic term but also the relative receptivity of the term constituted as its opposite self. Those who read and write the exotic as otherness can nevertheless regard it as embodying often-idealized alternatives to the self. Then the exotic becomes associated with desire, with a sense of the imperfect or the incomplete self. But the mediation of the exotic also opposes extreme solutions to the confrontation with otherness. It thus throws into doubt the integrity of a self that strives to assert its identity and its ability to judge by separating itself completely from that which, from the outside, judges and defines it.

Those who aimed to formulate a definition of national identity in the Americas had to develop the notion of the self so to speak from the point of view of the other, to incorporate an exotic identity into the definition of the self. It is both an advantage and a disadvantage that the exotic does not constitute a complete opposition to the defining self. Insofar as the successful assertion of a national self depends on acceptance beyond national borders (just as the successful definition of

---

about whether there exists a Latin-American culture (p. 3). The reaction is as indignant as was that of Americans to the English question about who would read American literature.

[28] Michael Palencia-Roth, in "Cannibalism and the New Man of Latin America," unlike me, believes that "the cannibal represents the New Man at the point of greatest difference from the European . . . the extreme Other" (p. 2). Nevertheless, he also shows Montaigne using the *cannibales* as relatively positive models whose actions and motives allow him to criticize European shortcomings. As for the journal *Caliban*, it began publication in the winter of 1975, edited by Robert Marquez, with David Arthur McMurray and Hortense Spillers; an editorial statement identifies its contributors as "heirs to the combative spirit of the Antillean slave who is [their] symbol, and whose name [they] take as [their] own"; it takes a stand "against the eurocentric, capitalistic, hierarchical vision traditionally imposed upon who and what we are, upon how we view ourselves and our history," and affirms "authenticity and singularity" (p. 4). Its assumption of the oppositional name is explicitly associated with claims to self-definition and self-revaluation and to the appropriation of a history of the self that is independent from an extraneous discourse of power. It proposes to achieve this revaluation well within the discursive structures of that power, however, as an academic literary journal, legitimated by a passel of respected writers and scholars signed on as advising and contributing editors.

psychological selfhood depends at least in part on acceptance by others), the European other's identification of the exotic with desire, with the complement, ensures initial recognition; that form of recognition, however, must itself be rejected in time. The first American writers could be read in the metropoles and often made their careers there, combining their mastery of metropolitan rules of behavior, thought, and expression with their knowledge of exotic customs and landscape and sometimes relying on their own exotic appearance as well. European acceptance placed them at the inception of the creation of national literatures in the colonies.[29]

Later, however, this very ability to be recognized by the defining (metropolitan) self seems to block the development of the exotic as its own self. Opposition becomes desirable as a guarantee of identity, and writers admired for their success during colonial times come to be derided for their excessive dependence on the language and the values of the oppressive metropoles.[30] This desire for difference prompts an embrace of the exotic as defined by the colonizing power and, at the same time, a rejection of the mediating function of exoticism. But the rejection, too, is vitiated. Caliban is defined from the outside: to identify with Caliban is at the very least to acknowledge that definition. Athens defines the barbarian, who is to that extent dependent on Athens, as becomes more evident when the more benign exotic must decide be-

---

[29] The Brazilian Gonçalves Dias, graduate of the University of Coimbra, author of some of the first "national" Brazilian poetry, "immensely popular" and "praised . . . by leading Portuguese critics," is one example (David Haberly, Three Sad Races, p. 19). Washington Irving is another, writing in a "strange land," which Railton sees as the presence of the reader in the writing but which can also be taken more literally, as a reference to where Irving was writing and to his consciousness of the metropolitan reader, prompting the "provincial cosmopolitanism of his allusions" (Authorship and Audience, p. 4).

[30] Sacvan Bercovitch's rehabilitation of the Puritans as legitimate ancestors of an independent America, like Weisbuch's after him, and like Antônio Cândido's placement of the Vila Rica poets on the Brazilian rather than the customary Portuguese side of the development of a national literature (in Formação da literatura brasileira, vol. 1, chaps. 2, 3) and Rolena Adorno's recuperation of Guaman Poma for the Americas from a judgment of excessive hispanicity which had so far disguised the subversive elements in his work (in Guaman Poma), is more than the rehabilitation it would at first seem to be. Such restorations are symptoms of greater assurance in affirming the independent identity of the Americas, and they oppose the less secure strategy of defining writers from colonial times by only that part of the contents of their work which depends on European models.

tween acculturation and barbarism, both conceptualized within the discourse of cultural power.[31]

Like the power relations in which it arises, self-definition is not static. Lisa Lowe's identification of various European Orientalisms in different nations at different times and directed at different regions of the East fragments the Orientalist juggernaut (Critical Terrains). In the Americas self-definition becomes less urgent as the new nations acquire political, cultural, and economic power in internal or external markets. They go from defining themselves in relation to an external power to conducting the discourse of national identity with reference mainly to internal conditions. Those parts of their heritage which had till then been used to mark estrangement, and the ascription of a fundamental identifying importance to that estrangement, begin to be spoken as an inherently national identity without necessary reference to outside validation. For Cooper the newness of American institutions is a valued sign of difference from metropolitan oldness; for William Faulkner, F. Scott Fitzgerald, or Thomas Pynchon the value of American newness is not separate from but neither is it dependent on European tradition.

In time cultural power became contested among American nations. As the political and economic power of the United States grew, it developed a regionalized literature of the exotic which explored internal power relations between North and South, East and West, descendants of old settlers and new immigrants, slaves and slaveholders. At the same time, certain elements of an exotic discourse of nationality were reconceptualized. For instance, the term *Indian* came to be seen as inaccurate and excessively charged with a history of distortion by nineteenth-century exoticism. Although "Indian" stereotypes persist in stories of the Wild West prepared for internal and external mass consumption,[32] a separate discursive trend tries to reclaim for populations descended from the original inhabitants of the continent a measure of

---

[31] The need for opposition becomes even clearer when one considers the difficulties occasioned by the acceptance of exotic categories within the dominant discourse. If Esu were adopted into general critical discourse, for instance, as a shorthand sign for Mikhail Bakhtin's carnivalization, he would become useless as a marker of African-American difference.

[32] These stories are examined in Henry Nash Smith, *Virgin Land*. His revaluation of that study, "Symbol and Idea in *Virgin Land*," is a rare and interesting document of change in the attitude toward the discourse of American (U.S.) exoticism in terms of an empty land inhabited by tragic Amerindians.

conceptual independence from which could be derived an independent demand for recognition.

Helen Tanner's recovery of an Amerindian history (as she investigated claims to territory) in the interstices of customary American history is valuable in itself—as we value information— but the perception of a vacuum for this information to fill develops as the discourse of power is rearticulated. Tanner's documentation of Indian trail networks and portage routes counters the European disparagement of Native American populations as incapable of far-flung and purposeful movement of people and goods (though, characteristically, colonial discourse also justifies European occupation by the mobility of Amerindians, who roam upon, and therefore do not own, the land).[33] Tanner's revaluation uses the same index of value— purposeful mobility—but though it serves the integration of cis-Atlantic elements into the dominant system of values, it simultaneously indexes an instability in the allocation of power within the nation.[34] Similarly, Rolena Adorno's recuperation of the split Inca-Spanish address of Guaman Poma to the king of Spain posits a relation between discourses of power and disempowerment which breaks up the customary dichotomy between self and other, colonizer and colonized, by introducing a diversity of interests among the colonized.[35]

Though they often speak in terms of bipolar systems of opposition, recent studies of the "subaltern" address the variety of interests that can oppose colonial (or neocolonial) domination and arrive at the apparently disconcerting recognition that the mantle of national liberation is large enough to cover, within a "liberated" nation, the subjection of one

[33] Helen Tanner, *Atlas of Great Lakes Indian History*, p. 4. In addition to the network of water and land travel routes, Tanner documents the ability of Native American people to communicate in more than one language, belying the stereotype of an insular, immobile population confined within limited cultural variations.

[34] Robert E. Berkhofer, Jr., remarks that "as fundamental White ways of looking at themselves changed, so too did their ways of conceiving of Indians" (*The White Man's Indian*, p. xvi). Berkhofer traces these changes even though, as he states in the preface, the main purpose of his book is to stress continuities, one of the most important of which is the persistent dichotomy between the white "we" (or self) and the Indian "they" (or other) (xv). In his account power relations do not play a role, for they are not seen as changing.

[35] See Adorno, *Guaman Poma*, especially the introduction and chapter 4. The application of modern and sophisticated techniques of discourse analysis to the long-devalued text Adorno's work recovers, is also an example of how certain forms of the exotic become visible once the dominant discourse acquires new tools for scanning the cultural materials around it, and of the usefulness of their difference whenever the dominant discourse is challenged from within its own sphere.

class or gender by another. The notion of the subaltern hypostatizes the dichotomous structure of the relationship between dominator and subject and generalizes the operation of colonial power till it applies everywhere and absorbs the mediating term of the exotic. While it stresses the role of writing in relations of power, it refuses the three-way relationship—for example, among European, Euro-American, and Amerindian—within which power shifts do not necessarily destroy one of the contending entities.[36]

Like other theories of difference, that which defines the subaltern reflects changes in the distribution of power. Similarly, reconsidering the factor of nativism in the Americas no longer serves to differentiate America from Europe, as it did in the nineteenth century. Just as American nativism marks the transfer of political, cultural, and economic power from Europe to the Americas, twentieth-century "ethnicism" is part of a rearrangement of the internal influence of certain populations in the United States and the modification of United States power abroad. Preoccupation with ethnic and national identity or consciousness coincides with the attempt of certain populations to be self-sufficient and with claims of originality for their literatures, formerly seen as derivative. It is a revaluation that takes place in an often-acrimonious dialogue between the dominant discourse and that defined as other, but also within the dominant discourse as it changes and as it comes to revise its own self-definition. The need to affirm cultural or national identity arises in reaction to a denial by a more powerful culture and also acknowledges ties with that culture. Similarly, Europe provided not only the opposition against which the assertions of national identity were made in the nineteenth century in America but also the terms in which that assertion could be made.

Proponents and creators of the national literatures of the Americas unanimously declare them to be indispensable to the expression of national identity and cultural independence from Europe. Just at the time

---

[36] Spivak, in "A Literary Representation of the Subaltern: A Woman's Text from the Third World" (*In Other Worlds*), raises the problems implicit in this division, similar in many ways to those one encounters when looking for the trace left by Native American populations in the records of conquest. It is difficult to recover an otherness that has not been overwritten by colonial discourse into a mere boundary for the self. In this respect, the literatures of nationality simply use the rhetoric of otherness; making it originate in some American essence identified with American nature or culture is a discursive maneuver that allows the colonists to take over any discourse that could have so originated. The point is that the takeover cannot be complete; however elusive the trace of otherness, it has to be there for the discourse of liberation to become possible.

of the American independence movements, a coalition of European—mostly German—historians, philosophers, and critics was developing the theory that the expression of nationality is a legitimate and even necessary element of the work of art.[37] Hans Robert Jauss begins his study of the interrelation between written works and their readers by reminding us that according to the influential German cultural and literary historians of the late eighteenth and early nineteenth centuries, the main function of any literature is to define national identity; great and recognizably German poetry, drama, and fiction would justify German claims to political prominence as well as to the cultural and political heritage of ancient Greece ("Literaturgeschichte als Provokation" p. 147).

Americans who traveled to Europe in search of "culture" brought back and disseminated these ideas, calling on them to support American aspirations to independence from and intellectual parity with Europe. Benjamin Spencer documents the influence of Mme de Staël's German-inspired writings about how autochthonous elements stimulate and legitimate national literatures (pp. 35, 91) and the role of young American cultural pilgrims to German universities, who rejected "Old World modes" but saw "that certain critical principles and literary developments currently dominant in Europe afforded silent reinforcement for their designs and aspirations." They were "impressed, as [George] Ticknor enthusiastically reported, by the autochthonous expression of popular feeling in Germany and in Spain" (p. 90). It seemed reasonable to press American material—natural and cultural—into service as a complement to or even a replacement for ancient Greece, and still to claim conformity with European values.

At the same time autochthonous American materials appeared in French novels of sensibility as a sign of literary rebellion against classicism and the cultural dominance of the aristocracy. Even so, a society in political disarray found reassurance in the appeal to unspoiled nature—human and botanical—on the other side of the Atlantic. Thus Europe, in a process at once necessary and problematic, offered the new American literatures a repertoire of forms they could adapt to their own pre-

[37] Henry Steele Commager, *In Search of a Usable Past*, p. 4. Commager also mentions Giuseppe Mazzini, Joseph Renan, and John Stuart Mill as proposing the study of the oral record in old stories and poetry, as well as documents, in the search for an authentic ancestral spirit to explain and justify the more recently constituted American nations (p. 4). Germans, however, such as August Wilhelm von Schlegel and the brothers Grimm were probably the most influential proponents of such restoration of the past for the purpose of anchoring a definition of nationality.

occupations with rebellion, self-affirmation, and independence from Europe. Benedict Anderson confirms the importance of that idea by turning it on its head and suggesting that these historians, philosophers, and novelists, by arguing that nation produced narration, made it possible for narration to produce nations.

As consistently as they define a national self in terms of American nature and humanity, literatures of nationality ground their claims to parity by aspiring to what José Matos Mar calls "historical density" ("Dominación," p. 8). One of the ways Europe denied its former colonies cultural parity was by asserting that they had no past.[38] Even in the earliest European accounts the Americas are described as empty, in part because the inhabitants are seen as lacking writing and therefore as lacking history. Dirceu Lindoso finds this absence actively inscribed from the outside on "archaic peoples," such as Amerindians, who "became the object of the history of the other, which imposed on them a compulsory destructurization. Theorizing about this process, colonial ethnography concluded that history did not exist in an archaic context," though such ethnography always saw itself as observer, never as an agent of this "privation of history in an archaic context" (*A diferença selvagem*, p. 35). Similarly, Hulme observes that "prehistory . . is always and everywhere ended by the colonial encounter" (p. 56) between Amerindians and Europeans, whom Roberto González Echevarría characterizes as compulsive scribblers (*Myth and Archive*). Thus, the new nations discovered that in claiming Americanness they were infected by insufficient historicity, which interfered with their assertion of parity with the colonizers, whose definition of history and whose preference for a long history they accepted. The new nations therefore searched for a way of affirming the depth of their own time. They found it, according to Commager, either in the wholesale appropriation of the European past or by embracing the future and asserting that the past is irrelevant (pp. 9, 7). Another strategy was to accord sufficient weight to the American past since the discovery to make it covaluable with Old World centuries.[39] A variant of that tack was to appropriate the pre-

---

[38] Weisbuch notes that Melville and his generation were constantly hearing the British taunt that they had no history, and without history they could have no literature (p. 53).

[39] "It is difficult," says Commager, "to exaggerate the impatience of the transcendentalists with the past. . . . they found it irrelevant" (p. 7). George Santayana sees in Whitman the variant of this strategy which valued the American over the European by deemphasizing the past altogether and declaring "that what was vital in America was only what was absolutely modern and native, to the exclusion of anything that

Columbian past, adopting its myths and stories to perform the grounding function of those of ancient Europe.[40] Insofar as it implies the possibility of choosing a past, the process of defining national identity
estranges history by highlighting the difference between meaningful
time and the natural sequence of moons and seasons.

But the logic of this estrangement, which, if pursued, would deprive
contemporary notions of historicity of their authority, is apparent in
hindsight. At the time the more useful strategy was to accept a European notion of meaningful time and turn to American advantage its
identification with progress. Progress, said the new European historiography, marched westward, and therefore American aspirations to historical respectability could be satisfied in that inexorable process. In the
United States, John Adams could say that "there is nothing, in my little
reading, more ancient in my memory than the observation that arts,
sciences, and empire have travelled westward; and in conversation it
was always added since I was a child, that their next leap would be over
the Atlantic into America."[41] In France, Alexis de Tocqueville saw in the
United States the continuation and possible fulfillment of the historical
march toward an ever greater degree of democracy, a continuation, thus,
on Atlantic shores of a specifically European history.[42] The idea was
even older than Adams indicates: Jacques Cartier had observed that
Christianity traveled from east to west, from the Mideast to Europe,
and that it was, just as he wrote, poised to cross the Atlantic and alight

---

might have been transplanted to this country ready-made, like the Christian religion
or the English language." This belief, however, says Santayana, is a "mistake," for
"after all, the future often belongs to what has a past" ("Genteel American Poetry,"
p. 149). Whitman's effort and Santayana's analysis and criticism are among the many
signs of the pervasive preoccupation with the relation between writing and history
in the consideration of American letters: it seems that the more "American" a
nineteenth-century author is considered, the more pressing the question becomes.

[40] One of many examples of this strategy can be found in Matos Mar's examination
of ten thousand years of Peruvian history, the last four hundred of them continuous
in many ways, he says, with the first ninety-six hundred. The strategy tends to appear
in conjunction with other forms of valorizing autochthonous American material,
and will be discussed later. See Matos Mar, "Dominación, desarrollos desiguales
y pluralismos."

[41] Quoted by Weisbuch, to make a slightly different point (p. 71); Weisbuch gets the
quotation from Benjamin Spencer (p. 22).

[42] Alexis de Tocqueville, Introduction to *Democracy in America*, 1: 3 – 16. Incidentally,
Democracy in America further illustrates the use of American material in the analysis
of European phenomena. Phillips Bradley's "Historical Essay," appended to Tocqueville's text notes that it was not written "only for the benefit of Americans . . . [but]
in order to show how and to what extent democracy was applicable to Europe and
especially to France" (II:405).

in the New World (Quinn, *New American World* 1:305). Adams and Tocqueville secularized the march of history, replacing religion with "civilization." They also turned the argument around and in claiming parity, claimed the superiority of the New World over Europe.

But the validation Adams asks for, and Tocqueville grants, was not always forthcoming, the strength of the resistance an indication of the importance of the claims. Recent studies have found Hegelianism pervasive in the American discourse of national identity, attributable, Henry Sussman writes, to a fortuitous congruence, when "the seminal deliberations on the nature of an American national identity coincided with certain structuralist alignments of historical material effected by Hegel" ("An American History Lesson," pp. 35–36). Or Hegel's presence can be iconic, as in Bainard Cowan's narrative of the attempt to introduce his thought to America through an "unreadable translation" by the "St. Louis Hegelians," who "saw the historical dialectic as culminating in the American nation state" ("The Unreadable Translation," p. 3). More important, according to Cowan, a Hegelian view of history informed the interpretation of historical events, from the Civil War, in which through a "labor of the negative" a "higher unity was formed and a greater freedom achieved," to Frederick Jackson Turner's "frontier theory of American society" (p. 4). And as Gregory Jay writes, the idea that America would perfect European institutions can also be derived from the teleology of Hegel's "dialectic of materialism and idealism . . . in which Spirit achieves Freedom through History," developed in the *Philosophy of History* ("Hegel and the Dialectics," p. 89).

In the next four chapters I illustrate the selective use of American material for European cultural purposes. The use of Hegel documented in these studies gives an example of the selective adoption of even recalcitrant European material for national American purposes. For in the same *Volesungen über die Philosophie der Geschichte (Philosophy of History)* that supported American claims for historical continuity with Europe, Hegel specifically dismisses its possibility. His (Rousseauean) notion of an instinct (*Trieb*, p. 74) of human perfectibility, which would differentiate a historical from a purely cyclical, or natural—and meaningless-sequence of changes (p. 72), could justify what Myra Jehlen sees as the American impulse to anchor the definition of man and history in nature (*American Incarnation*, pp. 3–7). Hegel views historical development as a movement toward freedom, defined as the coincidence between the will of the reasoning individual and that of the state, which is more than a political entity and embodies the spirit (pp. 30,

32, 36, 56). Such a view could be and, as we have seen, was used to buttress the claim that freedom had been served in American history. But one of Hegel's aims is to justify German claims to cultural and (therefore) political legitimacy. His great hierarchical and diachronic ordering of moralities and religions shows that the admirable Greeks are the predecessors of the still superior contemporary Europeans, among whom the Germans stand out, and that Protestantism is superior to the Catholicism that surpassed paganism (pp. 71–77). Applied to the New World, Hegel's scheme preempts Adams's use of a similar historicism: "The world is divided into an old one and a new one, and the latter is so called because America and Australia have only lately become known to *us*" (p. 107, my emphasis). Conflating pre-and post-Columbian America, Hegel emphatically denies the new nations any participation in the history that bears the burdens and benefits of meaning and civilization. "We have news of America and its culture, particularly of Mexico and Peru, but all they tell us is that it was *entirely* natural and that it had to go under as soon as the spirit came near it. America has always shown itself physically and spiritually impotent and still does so. . . . all that happens in America has its origins in Europe" (p. 108, my emphasis). In the Americas even Protestantism is no longer one of the highest cultural and ethical achievements in history but "falls apart into sects whose observances are expressed in the form of possession and sensual license" (p. 113), that is, into a depraved form of the natural. Finally, the very land of the New World is immature and cannot give rise to properly historical cultures, for its rivers are just huge masses of water, which, not having found well-regulated beds for themselves, seep away into formless, chaotic, irrational marshes (p. 107).

These passages attack all the strategies thus far discussed as useful in formulating an affirmation of American identity: American history is derivative or meaningless (not history); the American population is either behind times or in decay; even American nature, which, like the bass line in a piece of music, anchors and shapes the discourse of nationality, cannot rise out of chaos. The peculiar denial of civilizational potential to American waterways constitutes an early example of the conceptual difficulties facing later discussions of New World civilization as determined by natural environment; it also highlights the problems inherent in the acceptance of American geographical and geological features as guarantors of individuality or value.[43] Hegel's argument

[43] Roberto Ventura, in "'Estilo tropical,'" says that in the New World nature became one of the features in the definition of national culture; it is a concept fraught with

breaks the connection between European and American history, denies at their roots any American claims to covaluable existence within a European system of values, and thus brings into clear light the strategies for self-definition and evaluation used in the Americas. Ernest Renan, referring to historical injuries, says that "it is good for everyone to know how to forget," and he implies that even a definition of nationality is arrived at by systematic inclusions and exclusions.[44] Thus, Hegel's rejection of American parity can either provoke indignation or simply be forgotten, and Hegel can continue to underlie a discussion of identity in terms of the weight of history, the composition of the population, and the role of nature.

Arguments about the influence of Hegel or Herder on the American literatures of nationality imply that they would as a matter of course refer to those texts we recognize now as central to the development of European thought of that time, that these literatures, if not original, would at least be up to date. But though Renan would probably bridle at the suggestion,[45] if a nation needs to forget certain things, then perhaps national consciousness has something of *bricolage* about it, is assembled, that is, from assorted images, odd bits of theories. The following chapter details some of the facts and judgments out of which Europeans and then Americans constructed notions of the Americas. The criteria

---

fruitful contradictions, one of which is that it can stand Hegel on his head and attribute to American nature both value and the power to grant cultural identity. But this subversion of Hegelian negative judgment is fragile, since it accepts his geographical and geological determinism. Hegel too, however, writes within a tradition of the representation of the New World, and the form of geological determinism he displays appears often in the literature of the exotic. William Boellhower notes that in novels set in the Americas, "place defines character; climate evokes a political order and a way of life," and "if habitat is all, only the New World is all habitat" ("New World Topology and Types," pp. 156, 160).

[44] Ernest Renan, "What Is a Nation? " p. 18. He also states, further on, that "man is a slave neither of his race nor his language, nor of his religion, nor of the course of rivers, nor of the direction taken by mountain chains," and that what "we call a nation" is a "kind of moral conscience" (p. 20). Thus he stands in opposition to the racial and geographical determinists whose theories worried a later generation of artists and scholars trying to define national character in Latin America. See Nancy Stepan, *The Hour of Eugenics*, especially chaps. 1 and 2. It is important to attend to Renan's words, since they could at least be used against that kind of determinism, even if one agrees with Martin Thom that in view of his earlier writings and French politics (international, intellectual, and other), it is likely that "Renan . . . was less committed to the 'voluntaristic' argument than his lecture suggests" ("Tribes within Nations," p. 23).

[45] He wards off randomness by specifying that the idea of nation would be created by a "large aggregate of men, healthy in mind and warm of heart" (p. 20).

of selection and combination are not entirely determined; they can be culled from the center or the margins of the dominant discourse, which would still be called upon to legitimate that selection.[46] As Benjamin Spencer notes, almost in passing, "Inasmuch as the question of nationalism was of little moment in the literary principles of seventeenth-and early eighteenth-century Europe, it would not be surprising to find the small band of colonial writers ignoring the issue entirely" and, more in keeping with the general preoccupations of their time, portraying their efforts—as some did—as the "realization of dreams and designs from the Old Testament, or from Milton, or from Locke" (p. 3). Asserting independence and defining a separate national self are to an extent the results of choice and strategy that may process elements not yet or no longer central to the culture against which the assertion is made.[47] The disagreement between Spencer's and more recent analyses of the relation between European thought and American nation alerts us to the impermanence of all such analyses.

This disagreement should also remind us that the more powerful culture is not monolithic. There may be differences between its center and margins, or access to the center may be oblique. Thus the novels of nationality can reach into history to deny that their demands are a form of opposition, arguing that they are simply the dues of an alliance. In *The Last of the Mohicans* Americans and Englishmen face the French and Huron enemies together. In José de Alencar's *O Guarani* the old nobleman placed in the position of fictional ancestor to the new nation's new population is loyal to the Portuguese dynasty when Spain claims the Portuguese crown; his loyalty should make him acceptable even to the Portuguese.

In this appeal to an older unity, the American search for a separate identity proceeds by counteracting the sense of radical discontinuity in the European view of the discovery, conquest, and settlement of the Americas.[48] Carrying with them their politics, their religion, and their

[46] Robert Weisbuch documents the importance of these criteria to American writers and the American public.
[47] Centrality could be disputed; a decision would depend on an extensive study of the diffusion of German romantic philosophy and literary criticism, but would not affect my point that justifications for American claims of legitimacy do not have to resort to the central tenets of European thought of the time. I will add that most of the articles on Hegel's role in the development of American thought and literature collected by Bainard Cowan and Joseph G. Kronick in *Theorizing American Literature* deal with authors from the American Renaissance to the modernists.
[48] Even Francis Jennings, who in *The Invasion of America* discusses (in a vein of criticism) the continuities between European history in Europe and in the Americas,

diseases, conquerors, settlers, and colonizers arrived at an utterly unfamiliar New World. In their reports they struggled to describe the taste of new fruit, the look of new animals and people, the sound and sense of incomprehensible languages; the very smell of the coast looming up before their ships surprised them. The strangeness did not shake their belief in their right to occupy the land or their obligation to impose their religion; they did not doubt they were human and civilized, whereas the humanity of American populations had first to be decreed and their civilization was often a matter of argument. Unlike the difference of the Orient, that of the Americas constantly escaped European comprehension, conquest by the power of discourse. The travelers' comparisons fall short and attempts to describe tastes, smells, customs falter, subsiding into Columbus's refrain, "It is a marvel." Counteracting this sense of difference is as important for the development of literatures of nationality as their appeal to it.

In one form of this counteraction, the Americas recall their own infiltration of Europe. From the beginning, the spoliation of America is well documented; the history of European activity in the Americas in the first two centuries after the discovery is mostly a tale of conquest, exploitation, and destruction. Yet something like a counterinvasion by American difference appears in its interstices, in the European adoption of new elements in everyday life, making it more practical or more comfortable without changing its structure, or in the creation of new, hybrid forms of eating, dwelling, speaking, thinking, or being.[49] Ameri-

---

begins the first chapter, "Crusader Ideology—and an Alternative," at the point "when Europe *burst* its bounds in the late fifteenth century" (p. 3, my emphasis).

[49] Sometimes the adaptations appeared first among groups that were eccentric to begin with, in the sense of existing on the periphery of the culture, the place where it necessarily comes into contact with other cultures. For instance, J. H. Parry, in *The Age of Reconnaissance*, casually mentions that during the first voyages of discovery the Spanish, Italian, Portuguese, and other sailors of the Atlantic had to sleep on hatch covers and coiled rope, for the hammock, an Amerindian invention, was adopted only after a few voyages; and casually too he explains that the cassava, the tropical staple he calls "dreary," became widely distributed mainly because of its durability and suitability for long sea voyages (chap. 4, "Seamen and Seamanship" esp. pp. 70, 72). In the two first volumes of *Civilization and Capitalism*, Fernand Braudel documents the penetration of European life by the epiphenomenal and structural consequences of the great voyages of the fifteenth and sixteenth centuries, from the introduction of Mexican chocolate (1:249–50) to the vast trading networks that integrated the discoveries into a world economy (vol. 2, esp. chap. 2). The development of characteristic building styles and cuisines in the Americas, showing the influence of all the peoples who adapted to local conditions rather than simply transplanting themselves from the metropoles, demonstrates the accommodation to the new environment on

can strangeness slipped unnoted into European custom and discourse under cover of preexisting structures of meaning such as the fabulous stories about travel and exploration popular from medieval times through the sixteenth century.[50] Adapting, adopting, or translating, Europe absorbed quietly while conquerors appropriated by force. Both methods, in practice and in discourse, bridged the discontinuity that had confronted travelers upon their arrival; they did not always notice that strangeness was invading their invading certainties

A further development blurred the cultural boundary between former colony and metropolis: as discoverers became settlers, and conquerors established governments, their interests began to diverge from those of the metropoles. This separation of interests was unlike the estrangement within the same culture which characterized the first reports of the encounter with the Americas. It placed the colonizers, so to speak, on the other side of the process of definition and, while preserving their claim to power over the soil and the original inhabitants of the Americas, complicated their function as conduits of colonial power. It is in this sense of distance from a kindred culture that the American exotic is most commonly defined, both by Europeans and by Americans. In the struggle for power—political, economic, and cultural—the definition of the exotic as representing the American self wavers between acceptance and rejection of an American otherness. The novels that at the time of political independence became the models for a literature of nationality attempt to validate the exotic, by definition dis-

---

the level of practical life, even when the ideological superstructure—politics, economics, or religion—strictly enforced separation from it.

[50] David B. Quinn, in *New American World* reprints Saint Brendan's mythical *Navigatio*, which circulated in Europe in the last quarter of the fifteenth century; the islands where he was said to have landed appeared on maps into the fifteenth century (1:54). Parry observes that "nothing illustrates European geographical ignorance better than the long inability of the reading public to discriminate between [Marco] Polo's eyewitness accounts and [Sir John] Mandeville's lying wonders" (p. 8), at least where extra-Mediterranean navigation was not politically and economically important; when such travels got seriously under way, "the value of Marco Polo's Travels as a reliable source of information came to be generally recognized," first, presumably, among serious students: both Henry the Navigator of Portugal and Columbus owned copies (p. 8). Pierre Chaunu, however, while acknowledging that because of Marco Polo thirteenth-century Asia became contemporary with Christopher Columbus in the imagination of Europe (*L'expansion européenne*, p. 85), also notes that the *Travels* were read for the pretty picture Marco Polo paints of the khan in a Europe enfeebled by plague and famine. Carlo Ginzburgh in *Il fromaggio e i vermi* tells the story of a miller from a small village in northern Italy, who was burned by the Inquisition for his heresies, some of which consisted in his acceptance of the validity of non-Christian cultures and religions he had read about in Mandeville's *Travels*.

continuous with the original European experience, while maintaining
continuity with that same European experience and with a historical
sequence whose origins and meaning are on the other side of the
Atlantic.

Another thematic field organizes the literature of nationality: writing
itself. Benedict Anderson has shown how important it was for the literature of nationality that colonial independence movements followed
upon the growth of the reading public, the rise of the novel, and the
birth of journals and newspapers. It was equally important for the diffusion of information about the discoveries into European discourse that
they coincided with the invention and diffusion of print. Through print,
the logs, diaries, letters, and reports, the sea of writing that from the
beginning washed over the contact between Europe and the Americas,
became widely available as a repertoire of images out of which grew
the various strains of the European discourse of the exotic. The importance of print made the absence of writing among American peoples
all the more striking to the travelers. This perception that Amerindians
had no writing, and so no history or culture, was perfectly able to
coexist with the admission that some had books—a sign, says Walter
Mignolo, of "conflicting ideas associated with the book in two cultures
at different stages of their technological development" and "an example
of the function of the book in the process of colonization."[51] India,
China, Islam were other to the European self, but they wrote, and they
were recognized as civilizations; unwritten, the New World fell outside
the known opposition between Christian and either heretic or infidel.[52]
Infidels had rival books and monuments; recorded law, theology, and
history; palaces and temples. American populations did not. Although
Mexico and Peru later strained this perception, the very obvious monuments of the Incas and the Aztecs disproving this lack, what predomi-
nated in the image of the Americas was the model of the first tribes
encountered, those that lived along the Atlantic in what might be called
a limbo of visible or recognizable history, an "absence of civilization"
that later became useful in a European discourse of the exotic. Similarly,
Columbus's conclusion, based on a few signs exchanged with the people

[51] Walter Mignolo notes the non sequitur: "Castilians readily conceded that the Aztecs
had books, even though they knew they did not have writing" ("Signs and Their
Transmission").
[52] See Parry on the religious definition of the conquest under Isabella and on its
relation to the Catholic reconquest of the Iberian Peninsula: if the inhabitants of the
new continent were not Christian, at least they were not Muslims; this was one of
the logical openings to catechization (p. 30).

who met him on the American shore, that "they have no religion whatever" fosters this image (*Diários*, 11 October 1492). So does Pero Vaz de
Caminha's Letter to the king of Portugal about the discovery of Brazil,
describing a people who walk around naked and without shame, like
Adam and Eve before the Fall. They are, he states, without religion,
ready to be cultivated by the church; their land, too, is without cultivation, but "if you plant, anything will grow" (*A carta*, p. 240).

The fiction of emptiness was as necessary to conquest as its factual
falseness.[53] The writing of conquest inscribes it. Francis Jennings bases
his indictment of this falseness on the idea of the "cant" of conquest,
that is, on the linguistic operations that shaped the New World and its
inhabitants for the use of Europeans. One can see its work in John
Locke's notion of the tabula rasa, which picks up and generalizes the
idea of a humanity in the New World open to inscription.[54] In the discourse of origins which rethought European politics, psychology, and
education, the perceived cultural emptiness of the New World made it
possible to envisage in secular— ethnographic—terms a stage preceding history and social organization, just as the perceived continuity
between American nature in its benign aspect and its gentler human
inhabitants had made it possible to assign geographic coordinates to
an earthly paradise.

By the time of the movements for independence, the New World
had become, as Pierre Chaunu writes of the history of discovery and
settlement, "a part not only of the flux of an economic reality . . . but
[of] the only truly essential history, which is that of thought" (p. 6).

The example of a slip shows how much so. In one of his best-known
sonnets, John Keats, upon first reading George Chapman's translation
of Homer, felt "like Stout Cortez when with eagle eyes / he star'd at
the Pacific." Keats nodded then (like Homer), mixing up his conquista-
dores and his explorers. It is the sort of nod noted with amusement in
literature classes: of course we know it was not Cortez who stood silent
upon a peak in Darien, discovering the wishfully named Pacific Ocean
and an endless horizon of possibilities, and of course the mistake does

[53] Francis Jennings reminds us that "European explorers and invaders discovered an
inhabited land. Had it been pristine wilderness then, it would possibly be so still
today, for neither the technology nor the social organization of Europe in the sixteenth
and seventeenth centuries had the capacity to maintain, of its own resources, outpost
colonies thousands of miles from home" (p. 15).
[54] The same expression was used by the Jesuit missionary to Brazil José de Anchieta
to describe the people he had been sent to catechize: they were "tamquam tabulae
rasae" on which it would be easy to inscribe Christianity (*A província do Brasil*, p. 43).

not affect the real meaning of the poem. The nod and its dismissal do mean something, however. The poem associates the discovery of new imaginative and intellectual realms with the discovery of the New World; the discovery of the New World stands for any kind of discovery. At the origin of new powers of the intellect and the imagination Keats places, interchangeably, the empty lands beyond the sea, waiting to be written, and the poem poised precisely where song becomes writing and myth shifts into history. Homer, the bard who never wrote, stands outside of writing but provides the foundation of literature. His proper name denotes not a person but a double function, of discovery and conquest, like the figure on the peak. In this sonnet, once again, the New World is covered with the written word; it is made intelligible to and usable by the Old World by being associated with a mythical European past continuous with the historical European present. When Keats's slip is skipped in the New World, however, the New World implicitly accepts Europe's appropriation of its history, Europe's assessment of the role of writing, Europe's vision of the beginning of history and its relation to myth.

Keats's association of Homer and the New World is not uncommon. The voyage of Ulysses can easily be seen as prefiguring and validating the expeditions of discovery, exploration, and settlement, providing a language that assimilates the strangeness of the new land and its inhabitants to better-known categories of strangeness. Thus the Yara, a water spirit of the Tupi, becomes a siren, and Amazons inhabit the banks of a river that takes their name: literature covers the strange with a veil of familiarity that falsifies it while making it knowable. The exchange of names on the peak in Darien falsifies but regularizes history.

By the time of Keats's sonnet, the literature of nationality was already established in the new nations. Like Keats, it had drawn upon the writings of settlement and exploration, transformed and placed in the service of European art, science, and philosophy. The information in those writings had to an extent cut loose from its sources to build a composite, generic, and sometimes muddled image of the world across the Atlantic. Hobbes, Locke, and Rousseau, Chateaubriand and Bernardin de Saint-Pierre drew on that bank of information and images, entirely absorbing it into a European discourse from which American writers in turn drew them back, legitimated, though changed, by their life abroad.

Convinced of the importance of a written record and of the impossibility of finding an autochthonous model for it, the writers of the first period after independence set out to complete the record of settlement

and to provide sufficient written matter to ground historical existence
and shore up cultural identity. The role of writing as a sign and guarantee of an independent identity was acknowledged by the metropoles as
well as by their American colonies. During most of the colonial era,
Portugal prohibited printing in Brazil as potentially subversive. Benjamin Franklin as printer and founder embodied the association between
writing and a separate American identity. With its own periodicals and
novels, the new nation could not be associated with the primitivism
that had for so long been the only imaginable difference between European and American; the new American difference used European criteria of identity and value against European strategies for exclusion and
cultural domination.

That this absence of culture was a matter of convenience could be
seen later, when the process of settlement, itself amply documented in
relations, edicts, and records, eliminated even the traces of the presence
of the original inhabitants of the land, except as translated into the
justification of whatever action the colonists decided to take against
them. Jennings is forever reconstructing the events that led to various
wars of colonists against Indians because the original agreements and
treaties have disappeared and because from the negotiation meetings
between colonists and tribes only the original complaints of the colonists but neither the Indian responses nor the results of the conferences
survive on record.[55] Here too the written word serves to build and
control an image of the independent American self which manipulates
the elements it uses to construct itself at the same time as it is manipu-
lated by them.

The following chapters trace the development of certain discursive
elements that came to represent the New World, starting with their first
appearance in accounts of voyages and settlement, then examining how
they became organized into a language of otherness used to conceptual-
ize cultural change in Europe and were transformed in turn into a language of national identity as the European colonies achieved political
independence and strove for a commensurate cultural independence.
These developments occurred in texts that circulated widely in their
time and functioned well within the "horizon of expectations" of the
culture that produced them. The accounts of exploration and settlement
from the sixteenth and seventeenth centuries; the works of Rousseau,

[55] See, for instance, chap. 13, "We Must Burn Them," on the buildup toward war
against the Pequods.

Bernardin de Saint-Pierre, and Chateaubriand; the novels of James Feni-more Cooper and José de Alencar, and the modernist text *Macunaíma* by Mário de Andrade (Alencar and Andrade being Brazilian authors) carry my argument. They show that ideas of the New World were formed and changed in accordance with the distribution of power among the collectivities holding and using them, that the boundaries within which these ideas shifted were set on both sides of the Atlantic, and distortions occurred in the crossing, that these ideas gained in importance when power was in the balance, and lost when power was established.

The texts are examined as they illuminate the problem of American national identity; I establish continuity and coherence in the considera-tion of such different works by returning in each instance to how they address history, contact, writing, and what Rolena Adorno, following Michel de Certeau, calls the "boundaries limiting cultural fields"—that is, the definition of the territory of culture as against that of nature.[56] The obbligato in this discussion—to change metaphors—is the interre-lation between ideas of self and other in any consideration of cultural power and the reaction it invites. I intend to examine the necessarily self-contradictory process by which cultural identity is defined and modified and, by using the concept of exoticism, to mediate between notions of self and other, to show that interaction can have results other than isolation or destruction. And by showing the connection between exoticism and power, I propose to add a historical and distancing di-mension to a question of national or group identity—so compelling when it arises that both the clarity and the assurance necessary to confront it fall victim to the heat of immediacy.

[56] Adorno discussed that in "Arms, Letters, and the *Mestizo* Historian in Early Colo-nial Mexico." The reference is to Michel de Certeau, *Heterologies*, p. 68.

2

First Accounts:
The Building Blocks

The encounter between European explorers, conquerors, missionaries, and settlers, on one hand, and the peoples and land of the Americas, on the other, produced a complex discourse from which European thought and fiction of the eighteenth and nineteenth centuries built a variety of images of the "original," the "natural," and the "barbaric." Having become acclimated in Europe, these images recrossed the Atlantic and, in the nineteenth century, became indexes of American difference from the colonial powers in an American discourse of political independence and cultural identity. But the accounts of the first contact do not form a master narrative; rather, they provided a repertoire of often conflicting images, available for both a colonizing and a decolonizing discourse.

A random dip into nineteenth-century European fiction gives an idea of how images of the Americas and Americans had become naturalized. In Gustave Flaubert's *Madame Bovary*, the platitudinous pharmacist Homais berates his wife for making their children wear padded headgear that might impair their mental development and "make them into Caribs or Botocudos" (p. 83). Neither Homais nor Flaubert bothers to gloss the reference, which for Homais denotes mental inferiority and for Flaubert connotes Homais's prejudices. In *Hard Times* Charles Dickens describes Coketown as "a town of unnatural red and black like the painted face of a savage" (p. 65); the image of natural man unnaturally painted simultaneously brings up the absence and the excesses of civilization.

The protagonist's dining room in Benito Perez Galdós's *Doña Perfecta* is decorated with copies of French drawings of Columbus's voyages, a satirical portmanteau that attacks Spanish bad taste, Spanish backwardness unredeemed by ancient glory, and Spanish reliance on French prestige to validate that glory. Mary Shelley's *Frankenstein* opens with Walton's attempt to discover the Northwest Passage and uses sixteenth- and seventeenth-century explorations of the Americas as a type for nineteenth-century scientific advances, of which Dr. Frankenstein is perpetrator and victim and which his story implicitly condemns, causing Walton to turn back. These texts assume a common and widespread (not necessarily accurate) acquaintance with the discoveries and the Americas, and each mention bears a little ideological charge against the sum of which an American image of Americanness would have to prevail.

This common knowledge rests on all the accounts and pictures of the encounter between Europeans and the New World, from Columbus to Alexander von Humboldt. At the time when the New World colonies were seeking political and cultural independence, European views of the America were, on one hand, incorporated in American definitions of the American self and, on the other, rejected and resisted as instances of European scorn and domination. Now, as the literature of the encounter is being reexamined, it may tell us something beyond itself about the workings of such a process of definition. In the awareness of current prejudgments, Peter Hulme's close reading of Columbus's diaries and his letter to Ferdinand and Isabella relating his third voyage (see *Diários*, pp. 133–47), or of the story of Pocahontas, attempts to reconstruct how these documents shaped new knowledge to the interests and preconceptions of European history. Wayne Franklin's *Discoverers, Explorers, Settlers* begins by examining just one of Columbus's sentences, where he finds *in nuce* a complex set of judgments and attitudes of Europe toward America, as well as the record of an implied American contribution to European discourse about the New World (p. 1). But even as one watches old judgments become established through iteration and selection, one can see present-day critical discourse fall into the classic metaphors of America: Hulme regrets the disappearance of an Edenic America; Franklin would like the dispersed accounts of the encounter to be collected and published as a "wilderness of books," a "swamp" teeming with life (p. 204), like an America of uninscribed nature.

Franklin sees how early accounts of the Americas informed the acquisition, transformation, transmission, and use of knowledge about the New World on either side of the Atlantic; other critics tell us how these reports figure—or prefigure—the character of "Americans." In *American Incarnation* Myra Jehlen begins her analysis of eighteenth- and nineteenth-century literature in the United States by identifying William James's "embrace of the factual by which [he] located himself in the wilderness" as "an impulse from the heart of his American identity." James has chosen between the two paradigmatic attitudes toward the Americas: Amerigo Vespucci's practical one, "acknowledging [America] as a concrete fact"; and a "theoretical" attitude, "one of the innumerable versions of America's primal scene, Columbus arriving on an unknown shore" and unable to make sense of what he saw. For Jehlen, in either case, "the drama of America's discovery describes an archetypal conjunction of personal identity and national identification coming together in the very earth of the New World" (pp. 2–3). Like other critics, Jehlen derives her distinction between American and non-American from the record of discovery, combining notions of (American) nation, (American) nature, and (American) humanity in accordance with a long history of the discourse of the New World. Yet Jehlen is unusual in pushing the models for a United States discourse about origins back past the English Puritan landing to the first Spanish encounter (p. 237 n. 1). This dislocation of the origin of North American (specifically, U.S.) identity to include Spain manifests both of a love of accuracy and a contemporary shift in perspective: the record of the encounter still responds to the interests of its time and public.

On the other side of the Atlantic, Tzvetan Todorov sees in Columbus's and Cortez's letters not only the traces of a conquered New World but also the roots of a divided, totalitarian Europe; *La conquête de l'Amérique* recontextualizes the history of the discoveries for a time when the boundaries between Europe and non-Europe were under question once again. He says he chose his subject because "the conquest of America announces and founds our identity" (p. 13), without explaining the reference of the pronoun "our." It could mean "European" or "non-American" and thus implicitly criticize the imposition of one culture on another. It could mean "French" (the language of his book), or "non-Spanish," "non-Portuguese," "non-English" (the languages of those who colonized most of the Americas and, according to the French, fairly botched it). It could also refer to unequal power relations between Eastern and Western Europe contemporary with the writing, and allow Todorov to claim the authority of both marginal (Eastern,

Bulgarian, homologous to Amerindian) and dominant discourse (Western, French). In any case "our" does not refer to the Americas, the object and result of European conquest; the history Todorov retells is likely indeed to be "closer to myth than to argument" (p. 11). His statement that "we are all the direct descendants of Columbus" (p. 13) may express European guilt; yet it preserves Europe's status as the active subject of American history.[1] It is not likely that he or his readers would accept the cheerful view of the (South) American scholar Germán Arciniegas, who, in *America in Europe*, traces the American roots of European science, humanism, democracy, and freedom and recommends that they be enjoyed, not regretted, by Columbus's progeny, originators of European virtue and happiness.[2] All three critics show that even in America the question of America has never been a question only for America. They also reveal an element of randomness in both the production and reception of these accounts.

Nevertheless, each reading of the French, Spanish, English, and—if it is considered at all—Portuguese discovery and conquest attempts to see it as a more or less coherent inventory of reasons and justifications for the substitution of cultures and populations in the Americas. Such readings can express both the traditional horror of its means and a more modern horror of the substitution as such. The older horror is in fact contemporaneous with the more encomiastic and exegetic accounts of conquest: Bartolomé de las Casas, credited with first articulating it, was seconded by Jesuits, who, because their own form of conquest and substitution depended on garnering souls, defended the persons of their "charges." The Enlightenment then enlivened its opposition to the institutions of church and state by reviving a condemnation of conquest and developing a new kind of benevolent interest in Indians, east and west. The horror in modern analyses of the discourse of conquest, for all that justifies it, may predominate once again because it correlates with a critical view of the civilization where it arises, a disgust not only with its past but also with more recent developments within it.

The references to the Americas in these examples address different audiences. Jehlen and Todorov speak to academics; the novels, to the

---

[1] For a similar and extended critique of *La conquête d'Amérique*, see Coronil.

[2] It is amusing to read Archiniegas's work against G. V. Scammell's "New Worlds and Europe in the Sixteenth Century." Scammell denies that the navigations, discoveries, etc., made more than "some impression" (p. 389) on European civilization, whose rhythm of development, he says, went on pretty much as it had before all that overrated colonial drama.

general public. The academic analyses revalue and re-estrange; the novels show how familiar the Americas had become in European discourse by the nineteenth century. That familiarity allowed for incoherence, for positive views of American innocence and for negatively valued ideas of savagery in the Americas or hybris in the conquering European powers. Though Walton is relieved when Dr. Frankenstein on his ice floe turns out to be civilized and not "a savage inhabitant of some undiscovered island" (p. 23), Frankenstein's creature is later described positively as a "natural man" made savage by the underlying savagery of European civilization. With the creature's attempt to learn language, history, reading, and writing, Mary Shelley restates the notion that the savage New World differs from the civilized Old in lacking a history and a written language. In the attempted correction of this lack, she raises all the ethical and ontological problems in the discourse of otherness.

Even in the cursory examples I have given, neither this discourse nor that upon which it is built is simple or uniform; they record different attitudes toward and evaluations of the New World, just as the early accounts by explorers, conquerors, and settlers differ according to the time, circumstances, audience, and purpose of the writing, according to the things described and the character of the writer. Their effect differs according to their public, the time of dissemination, the uses to which they were put. Together, the accounts form a repository of narrative fragments that, like the bits of glass in a kaleidoscope, fall into different patterns as the tube turns. They are, in any case, not simply the reiterated statement of an opposition between civilizing European and savage American.

Thus, the choice of Columbus as originator of the discourse of the Americas is already the beginning of an interpretation: Jehlen, after all, chose Vespucci. But as Peter Hulme shows, an analysis of Columbus's diaries and letter can also yield the germ of a discourse of the American other. Philology and a history of the anthropology of Amerindian populations show how its meaning was constructed in the service of the European economic and ideological exploitation of the continent. Hulme refuses to settle the question of whether Amerindians "really" ate human flesh and concentrates on verifying the truth of assertions that they did; by implication, he thus demands a critical and distrustful reading of the entire written record of the encounter (chap. 2, "Caribs and Arawaks"). Such a reading retains the validity of that record but makes it release a different knowledge: in "Pocahontas," Hulme recovers the "other" side of the encounter with John Smith and reinterprets English accounts of that interaction by reconstructing or reimagining the *mentalité* of Pocahontas's people (chap. 3). For Hulme the documents of the encounter must be read aslant and all in concert.

No account, then, is sufficient. Though Columbus was the first to encounter and record American otherness, even Todorov considers his view eccentric. And this meeting between a fifteenth-century Genoese and Caribs leads to meetings between sixteenth-century Spaniards and Mexicans,[3] between Jesuits and the Amerindians of Brazil or Canada, between new Christian[4] merchants and pagans, between Portuguese colonists and enslaved Tapuias, between the ill-humored Martin Frobisher and the Inuit, between an intrigued and delighted Pero Vaz de Caminha and the apparently no less intrigued inhabitants of the northeast coast of Brazil, or between French or Dutch Protestants and Brazilian tribes. And if the monsters and marvels of Pierre d'Ailly, which Columbus kept in his library and carried in his mind, colored his view of the Caribbean, Vespucci's Italian Neoplatonism was no less of a European-constructed lens trained on the New World (Arciniegas, pp. 60, 63–65).

New World otherness is not fixed, then, but looks different to different viewers and to different periods. By the eighteenth century the Americas, no longer a theater of immediate, heroic action, had become a reservoir of concepts and examples for the expression of new and politically significant European notions of culture, origin, and history. Like Todorov's, the Enlightenment's resort to the American record responded to its own time and preoccupations. But the more timely this use of the historical record, the more inevitable seemed its conclusions. This impression of inevitability grounds the plausibility of interpretive discourse; it makes history appear as a self-justifying system, events determined and explained by ideological necessity: history as a highway. In the welter of accounts, however, history is a random net of forking paths and detours. Without the background of randomness, the concept of determination would be unnecessary; it is as essential to the tragic reading of the conquest presented with ample justification by Todorov as it is to the triumphalist reading that preceded it. Both im-

[3] A centerpiece of Hulme's argument is the shift in meaning from the term "Carib," used at first to designate a population, to "cannibal," and Columbus's role in effecting it. I am using the term imprecisely, to mean the original inhabitants of what we now know as the Caribbean.
[4] "New Christian" is a literal translation of the Portuguese term for Jews who converted to Christianity in response to early modern persecution.

pose order with an implicit appeal to the ahistorical category of truth, but the approach to any such truth has to be asymptotic, deflected by differences and discontinuities.

Todorov stresses the tragic misalignment between European categories and the nature and cultures of the Americas, the misunderstandings and the unequal power relations between Columbus and his hosts or between Cortez and Montezuma. This account of fatality and responsibility becomes ideologically more complicated when one factors another line of inquiry into the means of conquest. It had long been known that the original population of the Americas was decimated by Europeans in wars and massacres, but new studies changed the meaning of this "decimation": it is not that one in ten original inhabitants died; more likely only one in ten survived the epidemics brought from Europe, Asia, and Africa by the conquerors. But for the aid of smallpox, which in the 1520s spread from Hispaniola to Mexico and then to Peru, killing peasants, merchants, leaders, and warriors of the Aztecs and the Incas, the handful of adventurers under Cortez and Pizarro might have been unable to subjugate the two great American empires. Similarly, a handful of missionaries might have been unable to achieve their mass conversions of American peoples had they not conceivably felt as abandoned by their gods as the Europeans felt favored by Providence. The horror of this demographic catastrophe can only partly be resolved into responsibility.[5]

In addition, an analysis of the documents which stresses ethics and responsibility may neglect the constraints of interest and even genre informing them. Stephanie Merrim reminds us that Cortez was not only reporting his deeds; he was also writing an apologia for himself, an autobiography, according to established discursive rules. His account is filtered through these rules; it does not give transparent access to the facts of Spanish-Aztec misunderstandings ("Ariadne's thread").

Genre conventions also left their traces on travel accounts that grafted themselves on a classical or medieval tradition of marvelous voyages. This tradition lives in Columbus's scattered references to fabulous animals, in his bemusement about the existence of pleasant lands in the torrid zone, and in his speculation, in the account of the second voyage, about whether he had found earthly paradise. It fleshes out his description of the banners and their bearers as they first set foot in the New

[5] See William H. McNeill, *Plagues and People*, esp. chap. 5; Henry F. Dobyns, *Their Number Become Thinned*, chap. 2, pp. 34–45; and Chaunu, pp. 60, 365.

World, more circumstantial than his account of the island, where "they saw very green trees, many waters and fruits of various kinds" (11 October 1492). With similar lack of detail, the ship "entered a very beautiful river . . . full of trees, covering its banks from end to end, lovely and green, and different from ours, with flowers and with their fruit. Many birds, large and small, singing with the greatest sweetness" (28 October 1492). Instead of describing the dress and appearance of the islands' inhabitants, he speculates about their potential for conversion or their knowledge of gold mines.

Almost every entry of the diary of the first voyage mentions conversion or gold: Columbus was funded to outflank the Portuguese in their access to the wealth of the Orient. Commentators have consistently noted the promise of increased accumulation of capital with which Columbus's writings prefigure mercantilist domination. But his endeavor also connects with medieval protoscience; he does not see or seek gold for mercantilism, metallurgy, or civilization; he speaks of it as if he hoped to find in the new lands a geographical philosophers' stone. It is the theme of religious expansion that sounds a new note: in its contacts with Islam, Christianity had tried to eradicate or replace a religion it recognized as a rival; Columbus proposed implanting Christianity where he discerned no religion at all. His stance prefigures the importance of missions and missionaries in the colonial project and, more significant, speculation about whether it is possible to recognize humanity in the absence of what can be recognized as culture. The question underlies not only Christianization but also political and psychological theories that in the next two centuries would justify the colonists' resistance against the colonial powers.

Columbus's diaries and letters sometimes mediate and sometimes simply veer between medieval "fancy" and early modern "fact." In his account of the first voyage he clutches at any indication that he has reached the Orient and records hearing the islanders mention Cipango (Japan) or the great khan (24 December, 23 October [when he identifies Cuba as Cipango], 28 October). By the second voyage, when Columbus had still not found the land or the riches described by Marco Polo, his letter to his sponsors, Ferdinand and Isabella, speculates on whether he had not come close to the earthly paradise of balmy climate and luxuriant vegetation shining atop the raised stem end of a pear-shaped Earth, so unlike the dry, torrid lands at the same latitude east (*Diários*, "Third Voyage," p. 145). The substitution of an eschatological goal— the earthly paradise—for the initial economic one is a regression to earlier fabulous explorations, an attempt to conflate the old world, in which the unknown still functioned as an appendix to Christianity, with the new one, which had to be won for religion.

The fiery lands and balmy islands of medieval voyages are themselves reread in the light of the discoveries. David Quinn, Alison Quinn, and Susan Hillier imply such a rereading when they place Saint Brendan's *Navigatio* at the beginning of their great anthology of early modern travel accounts. In the *Navigatio* the saint and his followers discover an island that "shyned as bright as the sonne" with flowers, fruits, and precious stones—a generic description not unlike Columbus's. The voyagers delight in the vegetation and promise riches gathered without toil in the contradictory conjunction of value and availability characteristic of a paradisiacal economy later sought in the New World. But they also land on a volcanic island of hell, whose hairy "feendes," forges, and balls of fire show the negative, hostile, and evil face of unknown places, and they state a third great topos of the later tales of discovery, with the theological and allegorical dimension of their voyage. Its parts coincide with the divisions of the canonical year; the islands illustrate states of the soul; their availability to humanity depends on the conversion of the world, for they will become manifest when all nations are "brought to subjection" under Christianity (Quinn, 1:65). The "feendes," however, are moral, not ontological, others, and the conflation of these two realms of difference is at least as important for the operation of American otherness as the question of otherness itself.

The differences among the tales of Saint Brendan's, Fernão Mendes Pinto's, and Mandeville's voyages and later accounts are important too. As J. H. Parry points out, it was only in the late fifteenth century, "as the search for India by sea got seriously under way," that the *Travels* of Marco Polo began to replace those of Mandeville as sources of accurate information (p. 8).[6] This shift to the "factual" signals a more general discursive turn from tradition, authority, and faith to empirical evidence and experience as guarantors of the accuracy of fabulous-sounding fifteenth- and sixteenth-century accounts by discoverers and explorers.[7]

[6] Hulme discusses the fabulous elements in Marco Polo's tale and argues that, given contemporary knowledge about the rest of the world, readers would understandably find one as believable as the other.

[7] Even Mandeville's accounts served to destabilize old certainties and could be used to oppose established authorities. Recall Ginzburg's miller from an isolated village in Italy, who derived in part from Mandeville the heretical idea that alien customs were equivalent to Christianity, for which he was eventually condemned to death by the Inquisition.

Yet it is significant that an old dichotomous and eschatological structure persisted under these empirical claims.

This epistemological shift did not take place unawares, as we can see in Giovanni da Verrazzano's Letter to the king of France. Verrazzano measures coasts and routes for the sake of science as well as conquest and defends his observations as true because they are scientific, even if they contradict Aristotle and centuries of church-sponsored, church-sanctioned explanations of the world (Quinn, 1:288). But Verrazzano applies the scientific model only to the natural world; when he describes morals or manners, and finds the Amerindians friendly, sweet, and gentle, he compares them to the ancients (1:283), establishing an epistemological distinction between morals and science: the ancients' authority validates morals but cannot confirm science. In knowledge Europe has surpassed the ancient authorities, but in behavior his sailors are inferior to the savages, who live in a golden age from which Europe has fallen. Jacques Cartier, too, corrects by experience a traditional geography based on authority. The ancients are wrong to have believed that only two of the five zones of the world are inhabitable: "They formed that opinion from some natural reasonings, whence they drew the basis of their argument, and with these contented themselves without adventuring or risking their lives in the dangers they would have incurred, had they tried to test their statements by actual experience" (in Quinn, 1:305). Cartier has taken the risk, tested the reasoning, and he knows better.

Slowly, the newer accounts supplant the older tales. They give specific information about navigation, about the geography of distant coasts, about the fauna and flora of the New World; they inform and entertain a public with new interests. Convinced that the new lands were not the Orient, the expeditions' sponsors needed to learn what was there and how to get it. The Spanish and Portuguese wanted to safeguard their new possessions; other nations wanted to justify their attempts to share in the bounty; the general public found interest in the pageant of religious and national rivalries brought to light by rapidly multiplying printed matter. As we define various interests, some of the entwined strands of Columbus's diaries and letters are untangled. His repeated assurances that "these Indians are docile and good for receiving orders and making them work, plant, and all that which will be necessary, and for building villages and learning to go dressed and follow our customs" (16 December 1492) reappear in the letters of missionaries and settling companies. His thirst for signs of gold—an old man said "there were many islands around, a hundred leagues or more way, as far as it could be understood, where much gold grows, and on others, saying there was one of pure gold" (18 December 1942)—reappears in the accounts of explorers. Though the fabulous and mystical elements survive into the next centuries, they began to be overshadowed by a demand for the newly important category of empirical fact.[8]

At least this distinction between medieval fable and modern report, the orderly progress from former to latter, seems widely acceptable as a reading of the written record of the navigations, supported by the political, cultural, and economic power of Western European— French, English, German—cultural discourse. Even here, however, an alternative reading is possible, illustrating the unexpected difference of a view from the margin. A Luso-Brazilian version of the encounter between Old and New Worlds by the Brazilian historian Sérgio Buarque de Holanda, based upon Portuguese documents generally ignored among travel accounts, offers the properly eccentric argument that the Portuguese present few signs of the Italo-Spanish excesses that Todorov, for instance, finds in Columbus's letters. In Portuguese accounts cupidity is kept in (relative) check by the scarcity of mines or even signs of gold, while the fabulous and the marvelous tend to be clearly identified as hearsay and outweighed by a sober and matter-of-fact reporting of New World strangeness (*Visão do paraíso*, p. 3). Holanda also reverses customary notions of medieval and Renaissance turns of mind; he finds Portuguese accounts archaic in style and matter, medieval in attitude; they look upon secular matters with a cold, almost "objective" or scientific eye, while relegating the marvelous and the fabulous to the separate realm of the spirit (or, more prosaically, of rumor). It is the Renaissance, Holanda believes, which, by transferring the foundation of all knowledge from the supernatural to the natural, located in the world of the senses all phenomena, including the most countersensical; it is in the world of the Renaissance that everything is possible in general and most things are probable across the Atlantic. Thus the "Portuguese exploration of the west coast of Africa and then of the distant lands and seas of the Orient could, in a way, be compared to a vast enterprise of exorcism" (p. 15), compensating with its refusal to fantasize for its small contribution to the formation of the "so-called myths of conquest" (p. 10).

[8] The fabulous creatures of early travel tales live on, in fantasy and children's literature; C. S. Lewis's *Voyage of the "Dawn Treader"* revives some of Mandeville's curious entities. See especially chap. 11, "The Dufflepuds Made Happy," pp. 137–62.

Holanda's shot from the sidelines reminds us that even within the play of oppositions between medieval and modern, fantasy and knowledge, the data can be organized in more than one plausible way. It is not necessary to choose medieval over modern to introduce a slight shift in the allocation of discursive power; that small deflection toward Portugal could begin to reposition an argument. G. V. Scammell's interpretation, by contrast, works to prevent such a shift; he too notes the sobriety of Portuguese accounts but attributes it to the influence of Italian and Netherlandic humanism in Iberia, whose youth studied at Louvain, Bologna, and Florence and whose universities, Alcalá, Salamanca, and Coimbra, "were in varying degrees centers for the dissemination of humanist doctrines" ("The New Worlds and Europe," p. 398). Buarque de Holanda wants to argue for Portuguese—and, by inheritance, Brazilian—difference from a generic "European" colonial experience; Scammel wants to argue that European culture was little affected by colonization. Though the readings of the original material converge, each argument feeds a different interpretation.

In turn, the early writings from the New England colonies give another spin to the dichotomy between sober account and embroidered fantasy. Long after Renaissance rationality was agreed to have superseded medieval suprarationality, these writings describe a religious pageant in which "providences" take the place of secular causality, fiends reappear in the shape of Indians, and monsters are born to women of doubtful doctrinal orthodoxy.[9]

In time more, and more accurate, information about the New World became part of common European knowledge, but it was not disseminated in an orderly way. Hulme disentangled from all others the thread of logical and ideological arguments leading from Columbus's first mention of rumors about people who ate human flesh to the fully developed image of the fearsome American cannibal. Other threads took their own long and circuitous routes to common knowledge. The information in the letter of Pero Vaz de Caminha to the king of Portugal about the voyage to Brazil was buried as Portugal looked east and its power waned before that of Spain. That in missionaries' letters, such as the Jesuit *relations*, reached a large lay public. The letter from the Chevalier de Villegagnon to John Calvin on the attempt to establish a Huguenot French colony in the bay of Guanabara and the disputatious reports of

[9] Stories of such monsters and "providences" appear with doctrinal force in Cotton Mather (*Magnalia*, 2:404–5), Increase Mather (*Remarkable Providences*, pp. 252–55), and John Winthrop (*Journal*, 1:266–68), for example.

the Calvinist preacher Jean de Léry (considered foundational by de Certeau) and the friar André Thévet, who accompanied that expedition, were widely available in multiple editions and translations. Some letters to kings, such as those of Columbus or Verrazzano, influenced policy as well as ideology.[10] Verrazzano's description of the New World as a *locus amœnus,* a pleasant place, endowed with "a sweet fragrance" (Quinn, 1:282) and inhabited by gentle people lacking social organization and even idols, who could easily be shaped by the colonizers, informed the Edenic view of the Americas. These images of pleasure provided a consistent and durable counterpoint to images of distaste and fear which led to the rise of the cannibal, and at times even softened the image of the anthropophagi.

Because of vagaries of distribution the influence of some documents was not contemporaneous with their writing, and such disjunctions affected the weight of variously important texts in the "canon" of discovery and settlement documents. There does not seem to be a good reason for the different publication histories of the two perfectly conventional works of Pero de Magalhães Gandavo on Brazil, but the *História da província de Santa Cruz* appeared almost immediately after it was written, three years after *Tratado da terra do Brasil,* which was suppressed for more than three hundred fifty years and was brought to light only over the objections of the Portuguese crown by the French historian H. Ternaux-Compans in 1837.[11]

More noteworthy is the story of the letter from Pero Vaz de Caminha to the Portuguese king Dom Manuel on the voyage to Vera Cruz, now Brazil. The king used this first official document about Portuguese occupation of transatlantic lands to inform the king of Spain that Portugal was taking possession of what it had been awarded by the Treaty of Tordesillas.[12] After this one political use, however, the letter disap-

---

[10] Their circulation was often determined by style of government: Henry Kamen finds that the "Portuguese exercised strict control over information about their trade, but the Spaniards were never so secretive and allowed free exchange of ideas" (*European Society,* 1500–1700, p. 11).

[11] See the introduction by Capistrano de Abreu to the edition of both works by the University of São Paulo Press. Apparently the *Tratado* was written around 1570 although first published only in 1837; the *História* was written and published in 1576.

[12] This treaty was signed between Spain and Portugal to settle conflicts arising from Columbus's first voyage. In 1493 Pope Alexander VI drew a line running from pole to pole a hundred leagues west of Cape Verde, all lands to the west of which would fall to Spain. King João II of Portugal complained that too little space was left for Portuguese exploration of the African route to the east, and on 7 June 1494, the Portuguese and Spanish negotiators met at Tordesillas and, while reaffirming the idea of the division of the world, moved the line to 370 leagues west of Cape Verde,

peared, deemed, according to Jaime Cortesão, important but not of general public interest.[13] Thus the letter had no part in forming a European discourse of the New World, but it became important when, after a couple of mentions in the eighteenth-century account of the discoveries by the Spanish historian Juan Bautista Muñoz, it reappeared in the 1817 *Corografia brasílica* of Father Manuel Aires de Casal (pp. 21–27, n. 11). At the time, the Portuguese empire was being governed from Rio de Janeiro, João VI of Portugal and his court having fled there to escape Napoleon, and the colony had begun to enjoy its new power. Rediscovered, the letter was seen no longer as an official certificate of Portuguese domain (Cortesão, p. 71) but as an invitation to Brazilian autonomy; its language and its content were immediately recruited for the formulation of a national identity politically affirmed only five years later in the Declaration of Independence by the king's son, Pedro I of Brazil. The "archaic" plainness that, according to Buarque de Holanda, is typical of Portuguese writing about the discoveries, became a sign of the letter's objectivity; three centuries after being written, it was readable in contemporary terms; instead of Columbus's islands of monsters and fables, it describes a mild and friendly world that pleases a more modern imagination and whose birds and plants are recognizable as an early, positively valued, desirable version of the new Brazil.

Just as the image of cannibals helps to confirm the justice of colonization, Caminha's letter confirms the romantic patriotism of the first expressions of Brazilian national consciousness. The new nation seemed to like the idea of originating from a generous land and a people of childlike virtue and simplicity (and the letter also intersected with an early romantic positive valuation of the child). Caminha answered the need for a positively valued national difference with his delight in the strange, many-colored birds and in the friendly men, painted like checkerboards, something like a chess rook embedded in their lower lips. All he saw was healthy and clean, and the air, as Verrazzano also says, was sweet. The people, eating fruits and roots, accustomed to life in the fresh air, were stronger and more robust than the grain- and meat-eating Portuguese, and the new nation was pleased, for it wanted

---

from the mouth of the Amazon to where the city of Santos is at present, including almost the entire coast of Brazil; unlike the first line, it gave the Portuguese a foothold in the New World. Papal approval of the new line came in January 1506, almost six years after the voyage of Pedro Alvares Cabral which officially "discovered" what became Brazil.

[13] Jaime Cortesão published an edition of the letter in 1943.

better people, not just more wealth, than the former metropolis. The women too were new in a positive way, showing their bodies with the same innocence with which they showed their faces, described with a curiosity and delight that at times seem to mirror their objects' unself-consciousness; that curiosity and delight, so different from lust, colors the reports of the sexual encounters between the Portuguese and the original inhabitants of the land and allowed the new nation, in some moods, to claim it arose from innocence.[14] Not that the letter contradicts accepted values of its own time. It shows no awareness that the women it describes might live within a cultural economy marked by signs other than European clothing or European shame. It never forgets the advantages of Amerindian gentleness for the political, economic, and religious domination intended by Portugal. And in an ominous note, sounded twice, it reports how eagerly the Indians helped to carry and erect the cross with which the expedition imposed the double conquest by king and church and muses that they were better friends to the Portuguese than the Portuguese would be to them—a note of regret that speaks well for Caminha but does not resonate in Brazil's first formulation of a discourse of independence. It is the account of the good waters and the friendly inhabitants, the promise of plenty, since "the land is so good that, if you plant, anything will grow here," the prophecies of prosperity, which made the letter a useful document in the creation of Brazil's new image of itself.

The initial suppression of Caminha's letter did not affect Portuguese possession of Brazil, and the image of the colony as a pleasant place was constructed in other documents too, but texts could be kept from circulation for weightier political and ideological reasons than the automatic secretiveness of an Iberian crown. Rolena Adorno notes that José de Acosta's descriptions of native Mexican culture were accepted and diffused, but Bernardino de Sahagún's were suppressed—at first by the Inquisition—till the twentieth century. According to Adorno, though both convey similar information, Acosta is careful to frame it—particularly the descriptions of human sacrifice and cannibalism—in Christian apologetics, using it to justify the conquest that put an end to such

[14] David Haberly notes Caminha's use of the same word for "shame" and "genitals" and claims that "pious zeal" and "a strong but repressed . . . sexuality" coexist in the letter. He also calls attention to another weighted element in the physical description of the people: Caminha stresses that the men are uncircumcised, which "he took . . . as fundamental proof that Brazil's inhabitants had not been sullied by contact with the circumcised enemies of Iberian Catholicism, Moslems and Jews" (*Three Sad Races*, p. 10).

barbarism. Sahagún, however, does not offer such guidance, leaving open a potentially subversive reassessment of European culture in contact with an internally coherent otherness.[15] At present, in a new ideological climate, Sahagún is preferred, the absence of a frame around otherness being congenial to contemporary reassessments of the relation between Europe and the non-European cultures with which it came into such traumatic contact.

Historical vagaries, deliberate suppression, carelessness, lack of interest—all could keep serious texts out of the cultural repertoire, while opportunistic nonsense could enrich it with inaccuracies. A purported 1780 German translation of a Spanish document describing Portuguese America opens with an almost parodic discussion of whether the place names Maranjon and Grand Para refer to Señor Maranjon y Grand Para or to a Señor Maranjon and a Señor Grand Para and continues with equally ludicrous speculation about his, or their, adventures; it comes with a preface, annotations, and an exegetical essay and reminds us once again of the disorderly formation of a discourse of the Americas (Cudina, *Beschreibung des portugiesischen Amerika*, p. 12).

But the disorder can also be political. Reports from the New World were part of the contentious politics of conquest and were pirated, intercepted, or corrupted as more or less competent informers acquired, understood, and transmitted them. David Quinn reprints intelligence reports from Portuguese archives, such as the letter from a Portuguese agent, intercepted by a Spanish agent, about Cartier's voyage. It reports accurately on Cartier's trip up the St. Lawrence and on Indians he took back to France with him, less accurately on the value of skins he acquired, fancifully on the fabulous animals he had seen; and it fabricates the news that Cartier had found natives living underground and brought back a ship full of gold.[16] Such letters reveal more about the

[15] Rolena Adorno, in "Literary Production and Suppression," discusses José de Acosta's books *De procuranda indorum salute: Pacificación y colonización* and *Historia natural y moral de las Indias,* comparing them to Fray Bernardino de Sahagún, *Historia general de las cosas de Nueva España.* One should note, in the context of the confrontation between the European and a suspect otherness, that Sahagún also wrote admiringly about the Chinese; such tolerance might have made his description of Mexico unacceptable to Catholic authorities (cf. Scammell, p. 380).

[16] The instance is a letter from Fernando Lagarto to King João III, from St. Malo, where the Cartier expeditions originated, reprinted in Henry Percival Biggar's compilation *A Collection of Documents relating to Jacques Cartier and the Sieur de Roberval,* pp. 75–81, and kept in the Arquivo da Torre do Tombo, Lisbon, corpo cronológico 3/14/37. See Quinn, 1:328. The letter from the Portuguese agent indignantly identifies Roberval as a marauder who is attempting to invade the lands of the king of Portugal (Quinn, 1:334).

economic and political rivalry among the three kingdoms they connect than about Cartier's expedition. They document the misinformation that circulated about the new lands or even, in some cases, provide purposeful disinformation. Quinn notes that Ralph Lane's account of his expedition is imprecise and possibly doctored so that Spain would not learn the location of the colony, settlers would not learn about the dangers of settlement, and Walter Raleigh, to whom the letter is formally addressed, would not learn of Lane's mismanagement (3:295).

National interests impelling colonization also color the accounts. Those of the Portuguese and the Spanish aim to confirm possession; those of the French dispute it. A French attempt to found a colony in Brazil challenged the Iberian and Catholic monopoly over the New World, at least in Villegagnon's initial intention to create a place of religious freedom, where Huguenots could live in peace, profit themselves and the crown, and stop making and attracting trouble in France.[17] Villegagnon planned to enlist tribes inimical to the Portuguese (identified for Brazilian schoolchildren as brutal savages) in a region he saw as "inhabited by some Portuguese, and by a nation at war to the death against them, with whom we have an alliance." He was optimistic, for the Indian nations "indicated, in their language, that we were welcome, offering us their goods, lighting joyous fires, for we had come to defend them against the Portuguese and other mortal and capital enemies of theirs" (Villegagnon, pp. 17, 18). The resistance against the French invasion is an important episode in the story of the formation of a Brazilian (and Portuguese-speaking) nation, but what mattered to Villegagnon were the political and economic rivalry between France and the Iberian nations played out in the southern part of the New World and the religious rivalries within France. He saw Amerindians, independent actors in the Brazilian narrative, as pawns in European games. He cared neither for the land nor for its inhabitants in themselves.

Villegagnon's colony in Rio de Janeiro fell to internal dissension[18] and

[17] See Jean de Léry, *Viagem à terra do Brasil*. Paul Gaffarel's is the recommended French edition; the Brazilian edition is translated and annotated by Sérgio Millet, and includes a bibliography from Gaffarel as well as Plínio Ayrosa's "Colloquium in the Brazilian language and notes on Tupy," with information on language apparently provided by Léry himself. Villegagnon was in direct contact with Calvin, through whom Léry became interested in traveling to the planned new French colony; in chapter 6, Léry describes Villegagnon as initially sympathetic to reformed worship and ideas, but later as "tilting" toward Catholicism (pp. 94–102). In any case, this was a rare expedition including people of both persuasions.

[18] Léry accuses Villegagnon of treachery and ill will; between the lines one reads of a man who may prefer arguing about religion to believing in it and who seems

to the fortunes of another of the many wars among the English, the French, and the Spanish in North America, the Portuguese, the Spanish, the French, and the Dutch in South America. These rivalries gave rise to another class of texts, to propaganda less concerned with the difference between Amerindian and European than between various colonial powers: between the two Iberian nations, between Catholics and Protestants,[19] and parenthetically, between different Amerindian tribes as potential allies or enemies of contending Europeans. Cristóbal de Acuña's history of the Spanish exploration of the Amazon region, culminating with the expedition of 1639, expresses the usual hopes for gold and precious stones, while sniping persistently at Spain's competitors. The area is rich enough, says Acuña, to profit whoever would investigate its fish and plants, but it also has gold in deposits surely richer than Potosí, much gold at the Putumayo River, and the "immense treasure that the Majesty of God has in keeping, to enrich that of our great King and Lord Phillip IV" (*Descubrimiento del Amazonas*, pp. 40, 51, 74, 52). Sadly, though, the vile Portuguese enslave "los pobrecitos indios" (the poor little Indians); they plant crosses in all villages, and if these are damaged, they abduct the inhabitants; Acuña himself, not being Portuguese and wanting to prevent idol worship of the crosses, refuses to plant any (p. 58). For Acuña, the difference between conquerors was more important than their common religion. Yet religion transformed the fruit of conquest from American soul into Spanish gold; the misdeeds of the Portuguese became simply a shifting mechanism.

Reports were also written and published to foster national policies. Gandavo's treatises are neither militaristic nor religious. Part memoir and part propaganda, they aim to garner settlers for the new colony, so the king will profit, and the land will be safe from his Spanish, French, or Dutch rivals. Thus, unlike Columbus or even Caminha, Gandavo does not promise quick riches or speak of gold—he mentions mineral wealth only in the last chapter of the *História*—but praises the

---

annoyed that the opponents of a rigid Catholicism can be just as rigid in support of their own dissenting beliefs (chap. 6).

[19] See Gaspar Barleu (or Caspar Barlaeus, or Caspar Baerle), *História dos feitos recentemente praticados durante oito anos no Brasil*. The Dutch humanist and historian of Count Maurice of Nassau's governorship of the Dutch West India Trading Company colony in northern Brazil is much concerned with the religious competition for the souls of the neighboring Amerindians and with religious rivalries between the Dutch and the Portuguese. The University of São Paulo Press has published a facsimile of the classic Brazilian edition (Ministério da Educação, 1940), with translation and notes by Cláudio Brandão. Barleu's *History* was first published, in Latin, at Amsterdam in 1647.

mild climate, the fertile land, the sweet exotic fruits, the abundant game
and fish, the pure waters, and the healing flora of the colony.[20] The
riches he promises are pastoral and bucolic, and the ideal behind them
is neither golden Eldorado nor the orderly and clean trade center of
Bernal Díaz's Tenochtitlán in Mexico;[21] he foresees a prosperous and
virtuous polity, where the poor will not come "begging at the door as
in this kingdom here" (p. 94).[22] Gandavo's New World is rich in cultivated land rather than in gold.[23]

Similarly, Thomas Harriot's book of 1587, apparently written to attract
settlers to Virginia, taken up by Richard Hakluyt and then by Théodore
de Bry, and circulating widely in English, German, Latin, and French
(Quinn, 3:139), deals almost entirely with the animal and vegetable

[20] Gandavo does not forget the religious purpose of colonization; he describes the
Indians as lacking religion or laws (though observing also that women are faithful
to their husbands and that the Amerindians "live justly and in accordance with the
law of nature" [p. 128]), and he promises conversions in addition to happiness,
health, and prolonged youth.

[21] "And when we saw all those cities and villages built in the water, and other great
towns on dry land, and that straight and level causeway leading to Mexico, we were
astounded," or "We were astounded at the great number of people and the quantities
of merchandise, and at the orderliness and good arrangements that prevailed, for
we had never seen such a thing before" (Díaz, Conquest, pp. 214, 232).

[22] The comment is pointed. Henry Kamen notes that "no century had been so conscious of the poor as the sixteenth. Commentators agreed that the number of poor
and the problem of poverty were both of unprecedented size. In Rome, Sixtus V in
1587 complained of vagrants who 'fill with their groans and cries not only public
places and private houses but the churches themselves; they provoke alarms and
incidents; they roam like brute beasts with no other care than the search for food,"
(p. 167). The early seventeenth century saw significant changes in the administrative
response to poverty, with the creation of hospitals and other institutions to care for
the poor and sick—or, according to Foucault, to control them. Foucault dramatically
connects forms of control imposed—beginning in the seventeenth century—on the
sick, the poor, the young, the mad, in the chapter "Panopticism" of Discipline and
Punish, pp. 195–228.

[23] Gandavo makes clear that this prosperity is made possible by slavery, and, as is
common, accepts African slavery quite casually: "Anyone who, after arriving in the
land, manages to acquire two pair [of slaves], or a half dozen (even if he owns nothing
else), soon has the means to support his family in an honorable way" (História, p. 93).
Missionaries vigorously opposed colonists' enslavement of Amerindians, whom they
wanted to gather in their own "missions." Africans were beyond the reach and definition of such missionary projects. Several missions were able for a while to shield
Amerindians from the colonists, who actually benefited from this opposition since
these settlements supplied them with the food that their extractive export economy
discouraged them from cultivating (see Abreu, pp. 95–96, 144, 207). The juxtaposition
of missionary activities and Gandavo's invitation is one more of the ideological disjunctions upon which much historically significant action rests: not all who are attracted by the description of a bucolic idyll will be content with the material rewards
it can actually offer.

kingdoms. Harriot promises a wealth of spontaneously growing "merchandisable commodities"—for example flax and hemp, 3:141)—as well as plentiful medicinal plants, dyes, and wood, especially hardwood for shipbuilding, sorely needed then in England (3:143, 149), and rich, easy harvests of tobacco and sugarcane (3:143, 145); he also promises abundant fish and game, maize, beans, edible roots, and European grains (3:144–48). When he finally mentions mineral wealth, gold is notably absent from his catalog of alum, nitrum (niter), and copper (3:142–43). The resident population, he writes reassuringly, is harmless and unarmed, living in ill-defended towns, friendly, disposed to love, and amenable to conversion to the true religion (3:150, 151).

The reports I have mentioned so far stress the physical characteristics of the new lands, suitable for exploitation or cultivation, easy to reach or live in, rich, and empty. Yet, without a sense of contradicting their description of an empty land, these and other reports also provide divergent information about its original inhabitants. Some of the divergence is part of the propaganda one would expect to issue from military alliances between certain tribes and the European powers disputing the new territories. Jean de Léry, for instance, speaks sympathetically of those he calls "our" Tupiniquins, even though he remembers at times that they are heathens and cannibals (he writes of witnessing cannibalism; the nineteenth-century editor Paul Gaffarel collated his reports with Hans Staden's). "Their" (Portuguese) Tupinambás, however, are treacherous and bloodthirsty. Peter Hulme observes that the Spanish named the peoples of the Caribbean not according to their tribal affiliation but by their "response" to the Spanish (p. 72), but the two images of Native Americans as "the guileless and the ferocious" (p. 42) also needed internal European rivalries to become established in European consciousness.[24] Politically, Léry's account classifies Native Americans according to disputes involving four, not two, contenders. Like the Spaniards, the French and the Portuguese entered what Hulme describes as a fluid situation with occasionally intense hostility between villages. The negative image of the Amerindian is thus an instance not

[24] Michel de Certeau places Léry's account at the origin of several cultural and discursive developments: the history of history, ethnography, the view of the savage Other ("At the end of his journey . . . the Savage is invented"); he also sees it as filling out what in "a long medieval tradition of utopias and expectations . . . was already marked [as] the locus that the 'noble savage' would soon inhabit" (*The Writing of History*, pp. 213, 212). Reading Hulme together with de Certeau, one realizes once again that the creation of the complex image one recognizes as the New World was a cooperative European endeavor.

only of the power of discourse to define a resistless otherness but also of war propaganda that implicitly recognizes the separateness and freedom of the denigrated opponent.

Another source of information about Amerindians, documenting yet another form of their contact with Europeans, is the letters of Jesuit missionaries. They describe the customs and languages of many different Amerindian peoples in both North and South America, attempt to understand beliefs, are often the only remaining records of cultures disintegrated by contact with European settlers, conquerors, and diseases. Though generally addressed to the fathers' superiors or companions, they were also at times, like the seventeenth-century Jesuit *relations*, aimed at a wider public and used as fund-raisers for missions. This vast documentation, despite its primary concern with the Christianization of Amerindians, became an important source of information and anecdotes about the American other. It also became one forum for a long, deep, and finally unresolved debate upon the justification of conquest and settlement. Like the travel accounts, individual letters reveal differences between the agents and the subjects of the conversion attempts. Recent studies argue that the contacts documented in the *relations* did not result in the simple imposition of one religion and one culture on another but in a complicated semiotic negotiation that, if it changed Amerindian cultures, also challenged the certainties of the missionaries.[25]

In the letters of the Jesuit José de Anchieta the challenge appears indirectly as occasional irritation with his charges; it takes another shape in the Tupi grammar with which he recorded and legitimated their language and in the plays and poems in which Portuguese, Spanish, and Tupi coexist equally in a hybrid form that makes him (for some scholars) the founder of Brazilian literature.[26] Anchieta documents the

[25] In "Toward a Semiotics of Manipulation" Paul Perron argues that learning the Hurons' language affected the missionaries' ability to teach them orthodox Christianity; as an example, he discusses the difficulty of explaining the Trinity in a language in which the concepts of father and son make no sense on their own, for every father has to be the particular father of a particular child, and "'relative nouns' always take on the meaning of one of the three possessive pronouns" (p. 152). Perron also touches on the problem of disease in cultural analysis, noting that missionary work suffered when the Hurons associated baptism with death from European disease. Disease was probably the most powerful European weapon in the American continent, but it does not fit easily into a morally oriented tale of the conquest. Significantly, Tzvetan Todorov hardly mentions it in *La conquête de l'Amérique*.

[26] For an edition of Anchieta's poems and plays in Portuguese, Spanish, Latin, and Tupi (the last translated into Portuguese), see José de Anchieta, *Poesias*. For the argument on Anchieta's role in the formation of Brazilian literature, see Antônio Cândido,

conflict between the secular colonists, who wanted Indian slaves, and the Jesuits, who wanted subjects for their theocratic society, in the colonists' idiom of ambition, pleading with the king to curb the colonists, who snatch his devout and submissive converts into forced labor, killing the Christians and scaring away the pagans (*A província do Brasil*, pp. 37, 39, 33).[27] Anchieta's hope that "there should come the law . . . , that they should not be captives, and neither should anyone be able to brand or to sell them" (p. 43) marks one of the breaches and cross alliances within the forces of colonization, whose congruence was also contingent. Such contingency is a necessary but seldom noted part of the discourse of American identity, which could arise in some of these fissures of the metropolitan project.

José de Anchieta's discourse is paradigmatic in being mixed, opening a field for the operation of difference. He opposes the secular colonizers and applies their language of ambition to the garnering of souls. Yet he compares the grammar of Amerindian languages to that of Greek and sees Amerindian eloquence as parallel to that of the Romans (*Província*, p. 40); his remarks are echoed in later attempts to provide an American past for the new American nations by assimilating Indians to the ancients and finding in the Americas an earlier, correctable model of European history. Without adverse judgment Anchieta describes Amerindians who dressed up in nothing but a hat, a pair of shoes, or a shirt (p. 30), separating elements of European culture from codes of class, gender, or morality. As instances like that naked, painted Indian in a hat accumulated, the connections between the elements of culture

---

Formação da lateratura brasileira, vol. 1; Ronald de Carvalho, *Pequena história da literatura brasileira*; Afrânio Coutinho, *A tradição afortunada*; José Guilherme Merquior, *De Anchieta a Euclides*; José Osório de Oliveira, *História breve*; and Sílvio Romero, *História da literatura brasileira*, vol. 4.

[27] Merquior (pp. 6–10) notes the antagonism between colonists and the Jesuits, who intended to establish, with the cooperation of converted Indians, an organization that opposed the seignorial, mercantile polity the crown was encouraging; they were, he says, "rowing against History" (p. 7), and the literature they produced, propagandistic and mystical, owed more to the Middle Ages than to the Renaissance. Still, he declares that Anchieta was "the first great literary figure of colonial Brazil, even if not its first great writer" (p. 8). The Jesuits' acquiescence in the enslavement of Africans has been explained as a compromise: assured of a labor supply, the colonists would keep their hands off the Indians (Merquior, p. 7). Merquior contends that the Jesuits were not interested in racial differences as such; they saw Africans as already historically marked by the imposition of slavery, from which Indians were still free. Manuel da Nóbrega, Anchieta's predecessor and, for a time, superior, did not object to slavery either. See "Cartas," in which Nóbrega asks for slaves from Guinea and says it would not be proper to use Indians (pp. 25, 67–68).

ceased to be taken for granted; their recontextualization became an essential tool for the new American nations' claims to cultural independence.

Anchieta had to try to transform "demon"-worshiping Indians—morally—into Europeans, but he recognized them as possessed of their own coherent culture. In documenting this culture, he was seeking an entry for the spread of Christianity; nevertheless his efforts produced the kind of hybrid artifact that came to exemplify the desired characteristic of an independent Brazilian culture. His plays, with their mixture of languages, and his preaching of Christian concepts in Indian languages are cultural composites. His work is a witness to conflict among Europeans and respect for, if not acceptance of, autochthonous cultures, and it records complex patterns of contact. Even if some of his letters seem hostile toward some of his charges, Anchieta was later read and taught as an early codifier of a hybrid Brazilian civilization.

The "Cartas" of Manuel da Nóbrega, Anchieta's predecessor as provincial of Brazil, use the language of political and economic conquest for spiritual matters. The souls available in the new land for the church are a more accessible and valuable treasure than all the gold and dye wood desired by king or colonizer. The congruence between the language of economic exploitation and that of religious conversion addresses an ideological disjunction among the colonizers: the missionaries oppose both the bishop, representative of the secular church, and the settlers. Bishops and missionaries dispute spiritual authority over the colonies and tailor their strategies to their constituencies. The bishops almost condone unregulated consort with Indian women; the missionaries denounce it. They offer a buffer between Europeans and Amerindians which does not interest the bishops. This triangular argument, though conducted in terms justifying conquest, opens the possibility of criticism.

But among Jesuits, too, there were differences. Father Pierre Biard, in his "Relation of 1611" shows a bemused curiosity about his territory and its inhabitants and a good-humored acceptance of their oddities and even the hardships he endures. Though cold and hungry, he says, he and his brethren are seldom sick, probably because of the healthful air and waters of the Americas; he is sensible on the topic of American abundance, pointing out that it is useless from a commercial point of view because of difficulties in transportation; most important, he tries to see himself and his fellow Frenchmen as those he calls "our Savages" see him and is quite ready to consider their mockery of the physical deformities of the French a corrective against excessive self-satisfaction.[28] In contrast, Father Charles Allemant is reduced to tautology in his disapproval of Canadians: "As for the habits of the Savages, it is enough to say that they are entirely savage." He sees the inhabitants as greedy, mercenary, and dirty and recognizes only misguided pride where others had seen dignity.[29] His is also the first account in the *Relations des Jésuites* of torture and cannibalism practiced by Amerindians against their prisoners (p. 8).[30] Other letters and *relations* corroborate both the more benign and the more gruesome views of the inhabitants of the wilderness: any general view of the full collection must necessarily result from choices made according to the reader's as well as the Jesuits' interests.

One can also find in the Jesuits' accounts early examples of the use of alien custom to criticize European civilization. Father Jean de Brébeuf thinks that if, like the Hurons, Europeans had to transfer their dead from temporary winter burials to permanent cemeteries, they would be less likely to forget their mortality.[31] Such observations make it possible to conceive of European self and American other as aggregates of characteristics that can be freely modified and transplanted, possessed of beliefs that can be reformulated and adapted to new circumstances. Neither rigid nor infinitely modifiable (the limits of change trouble the writers studied by Paul Perron), self and other can accommodate rereadings as they cross and recross the Atlantic and as moral, political, economic discourses on both of its shores contribute personal, social, historical, or ideological twists to their definition.

Territorial disputes between the Spanish and the Portuguese and between the Iberian nations and the French, English, and Dutch; between missionaries and colonists; between missionaries and the secular clergy; among Amerindians whose interests became entangled with those of the conquering Europeans; among individuals with different

[28] Biard, "Relation of 1611," in *Relations des Jésuites*, 1:3–9.
[29] Father Charles l'Allemant, letters to Father Hiérome l'Allemant, his brother, 1626, *Relations des Jésuites*, 1:3.
[30] Descriptions of cannibalism were a staple in accounts of South American Amerindians. Léry gives a graphic but detached account (chap. 15), for which Milliet reprints Gaffarel's annotations, with corroborative references to Gandavo, *História;* Ulrich Schmidel, *Voyages curieux;* André Thévet, *Cosmographie universelle,* Joseph François Lafitau, *Moeurs des sauvages américains;* and Hans Staden, *Wahrhaftige Historie.*
[31] Material like this from the "Relation de ce qui s'est passé dans le pays des Hurons en l'année 1636," from Iean de Brebeuf to Paul Le Jeune, superior of the Jesuit mission in New France (p. 133) appears, as we shall see, in Chateaubriand's musings on history and mortality in the Americas.

visions of the Americas and how they should be approached were the perceptible signs of such twists. So were the activities of expedition organizers looking for investors; missionary houses looking for novices, donations, or leeway from the Vatican; geographers and navigators looking for information. Along an axis of political action, all these goals and interests coalesced into conquest and settlement but did not necessarily become congruent with ideas about European self or American other; a reservoir of ideas always remains available to be drawn upon for any necessary shifts in direction or action.

The awareness of difference is set off by a desire for coherence, evident in the cross-referencing that took place as authors of new accounts refuted the previous literature of exploration or used it to legitimate their own observations and as readers collated or confused them. Thus Cartier compares Canadian and Brazilian Amerindians—they all plant corn (1:313) and live with everything in common (1:318)—extending the themes of abundance and community to the Americas in general and helping to create a generic American otherness. Highlighting common elements mitigates the operation of chance and error, the conflicts of powers and interests within and among the conquering nations. It becomes possible to find a discourse of colonization among cultural differences and tensions in the worlds of both colonizers and colonized.

Once again the eccentric position of Portugal in Europe offers a different perspective on the discourse of conquest. Without contesting Buarque de Holanda's analysis of Portuguese language and culture as archaizing or medieval, Raymundo Faoro argues that Portugal's development of a centralized government and a mercantile economy in advance of the rest of Europe created a disjunction between language and politics reflected in its administrative relationship with its colonies.[32] The disjunction appears in the contrast between the long Portuguese indifference to its American colony, where it implanted feudal fiefdoms, and its interest in the East Indian trade, which then seemed the safest bet for the future, since it was so clearly continuous with the past business of medieval and early modern Europe.[33] Thus also the elegiac tone of

[32] See Faoro, Os donos do poder, esp. chaps. 1 and 2. Chaunu makes a much stronger argument for the importance of the margin: for him the entire "maritime adventure" of discovery and conquest was, for a long time, an "affair of the margin, a germination on the borders" (p. 65).

[33] See A. J. R. Russell-Wood, "Preconditions and Precipitants," esp. p. 7. One can note that many of the first trading posts in Portugal's American colony were established by new Christians, possibly as a compromise between expulsion and subjection and perhaps an indication of official indifference to these new lands.

Luís de Camões's *Lusiad* seems to regret rather than glorify the discoveries, as marking the end of a period of advancement. Thus also, though interests clashed in Brazil as in other parts of the Americas, the conflicts produced a variant reaction to American otherness in the repertoire of representations of the New World. Illustrating the discourse of colonization by a power that was politically and economically peripheral to European history acting in a land that remains on the periphery of world powers, the accounts of Portuguese colonization both confirm and fragment the universality of that discourse.

One last factor contributing to fragmentation and indeterminacy is seldom taken into consideration: personal idiosyncrasies affect not only the tales of voyages but also the actions undertaken. It is an uncomfortably random factor and might suggest that even the modern view condemning expansion and making of conquest a tale of culturally rather than divinely determined fatality simply reverses Sir Francis Drake's smug opinion that the "Inglishe God" was showing a preference for the conquerors with the epidemic they had sown among the "wilde people" (Quinn, 2:306). In all, it becomes clear that the story of conquest and settlement was not the work of a monolithic Western or European or even a more parochial English or Spanish control of discourse or events. One need only read one after another the contradictory mixture of fact, fancy, and mysticism in Columbus's letters; the pettiness and lack of imagination of Frobisher; the precise, supercilious, but interested and alert urbanity of Jacques Cartier, who assumes his interlocutors have their own agenda and who finds the political where Columbus sees the fabulous and Frobisher the monstrous.

Cartier and Frobisher had different interests and sponsors; they landed in different spots and dealt with different populations; but these factors do not fully explain the differences between their impressions. Frobisher's is one of the most disagreeable accounts of the Americas. The Inuit he meets disgust him, and he immediately classifies them as "anthropophagi" for eating raw, unsalted, animal meat (Quinn, 4:212). Cartier's account, by contrast, is larded with descriptions of abundant and delightful new foods—dozens of birds salted, smoked, roasted (Quinn 1:294), new fruits, new roots, and eventually new medicines for his men.[34] Both Frobisher and Cartier sought treasure, but whereas

[34] In passing, and at the risk of engaging in national stereotyping, I will note that French reports brim with delight at new foods. Léry devotes whole sections to the wonderful fish of the Atlantic crossing and of the Brazilian coastal waters, thinks pineapples are the best thing he has ever tasted, and almost apologizes for not participating in a feast centering on human meat, or for not really appreciating the

Frobisher forces indications of gold from indifferent stones—just as he had forced indications of cannibalism from the inhabitants' diet—Cartier learns Amerindian languages for use in commerce, even though at first he thinks little of his hosts, because they "own nothing of value" (Quinn, 1:295, 301) and seem unlikely trade partners.

In the interstices of these accounts there also emerges a response by the original inhabitants, who seem to be adopting the defensive technique of groups before a great danger (what Henry Louis Gates calls "signifying")[35]—from negotiating with Cartier to fleeing from Frobisher. Even indirectly, the accounts show that the Americas did not suffer the imposition of European civilization passively, that otherness did not simply bow into oblivion. Different tribes signified that gold could be found inland, southward, northward, anywhere but where they were being asked about it. In Cartier's difficulty at getting taken to Hochelaga one recognizes a defensive hospitality: his guides suggested indispensable side trips and visits till the season was too far advanced to complete the voyage. And it was not just one side that brought divinity into negotiation: Cartier reports that through messengers dressed as devils, his hosts' gods instructed him to stay away from Hochelaga, but he responded in kind that through *his* priests Jesus conveyed approval of the plan.

Even Frobisher lets us see a—desperate—resistance, though he himself cannot understand it. He hates the people he encounters, despite their courtesy, and destroys their villages but is puzzled that they flee him or throw themselves to their deaths from a cliff at the sight of him; he takes a couple of women and is puzzled that their companions are upset; his men examine the feet of the older women for cloven hooves and, unable to prove them witches, decide they must be anthropophagi (4:222).[36] Like other explorers, Frobisher took back to London a man and a woman to exhibit. The man went deaf and died, having unreasonably refused to be bled when sick; the postmortem determined that he also had a perforated lung and a concussion. The woman died too after the man's funeral, where she was shown his body placed in a hole in

---

fermented drink of his hosts. Certeau, forgetting Frobisher, says that pleasure is a remainder of the encounter with the other, which cannot be recovered or transmitted, which exceeds the writing (*Writing of History*, p. 220).

[35] See Gates, "The Blackness of Blackness."

[36] One should note that Frobisher's bile is not directed only against the Eskimos his and their misfortune brings together: on the way out he stops in the Orkneys, and has little good to say of its people, who "live in huts with their cattle," "dresse their meate very filthily," and follow the Reformed religion (4:208).

the ground and not eaten, the English not being cannibals as she might have feared, in case she was one herself (Quinn, 4:212–18). Frobisher is oblivious to the cruelty of his tale, but we are not, and by misreading him, we hear a dialogue where he heard only silence. Frobisher's consistent obtuseness almost forces a judgment on his actions triggering what one could call a "Dowell effect," after the narrator of Ford Madox Ford's *Good Soldier*—that skeptical, ironic reading of historical documents which, as denizens of our time, we learned from all the pointedly unreliable narrators of late realistic or early modernist fiction.

Frobisher's report, one of the first on North America to circulate widely in Europe, sounds a single negative note on the New World; Cartier's is subtler and feeds more complex notions of American difference. What he observes of Amerindian economic activity would eventually require a revision of such basic notions as property and profit; they live with everything in common (Quinn, 1:301) and, in Gabriel Archer's words from the Virginia colony, have "no respect of profit, neither is there scarce that we call meum at tuum among them" (Quinn, 5:275). On such astonished remarks about a fundamental difference in social and economic organization other writings build a picture of prelapsarian American innocence, which, however, is not developed to its most logical consequence; this truly different view of property leads their hosts, in Archer's terse note, to "steal everything" (Quinn, 5:275) and makes Cartier complain that they are "wonderful thieves, and steal everything they can carry off" (5:301).[37] The American peoples, then, can be admired as living examples of Edenic innocence and biblical hospitality or punished as thieves. In either case they challenge basic assumptions upon which European society is built; they could be called upon when these assumptions were later challenged from within.

Different interests and interpretive structures led to different explanations and evaluations of Amerindians' relations to objects or property,

[37] This Amerindian view of property—it could be called the lack of such a view—is still used to mark the difference between a natural innocence and the corruption of civilization as understood under the European or Euro-American definition. Waichee Dimock discusses later uses of these differences in the definition of the relation of goods and people: invoking Locke's notions of the connections among individualism, labor, and property, the new North American nation declared that Indians had no right to their lands; they did not "own" them according to the proper definition; furthermore, that difference made them into barbarians (*Empire for Liberty*, pp. 33–36). In *Mad Maria*, the Brazilian novelist Márcio Souza introduces an Indian who "steals" because he simply does not understand the distinction between *meum* and *tuum*. There are dire consequences that serve as severe criticism of a culture that does not understand and cannot imagine the benefits of not knowing such a distinction.

even within the same texts. Even more clearly than individual texts, the aggregate of accounts of the New World constitutes a catalog, without necessary synthesis, of a necessary cultural incoherence in readers and writers for whom consistent and coherent explanatory schemes might become an impediment to action or even to understanding. The incoherence can also show that the unity of the conquering culture is another projection of desire, not the result of observation. Although there is justification for identifying what is called Western or European culture, Portugal, Spain, England, France, and Holland each had its own particular America and its own enterprise of conquest, as did Protestantism and Catholicism. Each could be in turn self or other, for self and other are not only concepts in opposition but also "shifters," whose meanings necessarily change with context. Todorov's seemingly universal ethical matrix—"my main interest is . . . that . . . of a moralist" (*Conquête*, p. 1a)[38] is in fact culturally based, for it regularizes the other so the self can be consistent, once again placing American innocence in the service of European conscience.

These inconsistencies indicate that the triumphal reading of the encounter was contested almost from the start. The view that America fell victim to the misdirected, dishonest, inhumane, and destructive energies of conquering Europeans appeared early, and is present as a solemn obbligato even in the most optimistic readings of European expansion and Amerindian collapse. In the different tellings and readings it is possible to trace how generations of accounts began to merge into fiction, how they could anchor Rousseau's theories in fact or could supply later fictions of nationality. As we regularize the accounts, we should remember that readers were so open to fantastic possibilities that Gulliver's adventures had to be almost outrageous if Jonathan Swift was to convey that his book was meant to be satirical, not informational.[39] And we can be wary of Todorov, who, though sensitive to the idiosyncrasies of Columbus's letters, writes as if they were the model of reports of the New World and a seed of the subsequent relation between Old and New, rather than part of a repertoire of images and ideas.

[38] Todorov begins by stating that he will tell "une histoire exemplaire," an exemplary story, which "never forgets what the interpreters of the Bible called the tropological, or moral, sense" (*Conquête*, p. 12).
[39] Patricia Hernlund has shown that Swift used contemporary speculation and knowledge of the world to make geographically correct satirical points, locating his imaginary countries on contemporary maps in accordance with contemporary cosmology, which he was both using and mocking ("The Maps in *Gulliver's Travels*").

In effect, if the discourse of otherness is a construction, then, though one cannot assume it to be either consistent or reliably accurate, one can see it as a privileged example of how such construction might work. It can be expected then that "Americans" will appear in contradictory terms, as innocent and cunning, as monstrous cannibals and childlike hosts, as shiftless nomads and prudent cultivators of the food that permitted the visitors to winter over across the Atlantic—the contradictions expressed sometimes in the same sentence, as in Gabriel Archer's information that Indians "are naturally given to treachery, however we could not finde it in our travell up the river, but rather a most kind and loving people," and that "they are a very witty and ingenious people, apt both to understand and speake our language" (Quinn, 5:276).[40] More commonly, like Columbus, the commentators mix spontaneous and coded reactions: "They are all of good build. They are a very handsome people: the hair is not curly, but straight and thick, like the mane of horses, and all have wider faces and features than any generation I have seen so far, with beautiful, not small eyes" (11 October 1942)[41]— ready for time- and interest-bound interpretation. The first ill-favored man Columbus sees becomes involved in an incident in which the Spanish wound some "Indians," beginning a series of references to homely "Caribs" or anthropophagi (13 January 1492). Only later would this dichotomizing of the inhabitants of the New World be normalized.

Such normalization can also obey something like market forces. As Percy Adams notes, public demand encouraged a supply of fables: the giant Patagonians inspired by Antonio Pigafetta became staples in the literature if not in Patagonia (*Travelers and Travel Liars*, pp. 21–29). Some of this fantasizing could simply be due to imaginative exuberance, but some was more specifically political. Robert Berkhofer notes that the Dutch publishing house of De Bry favored the gorier accounts of the New World, for stories about Spanish atrocities toward savage cannibals fed Holland's enmity against Spain and Catholicism and supported its

[40] Hulme uses the same letter to argue that such documents do not aim at coherence or respect what is usually termed evidence (p. 47).
[41] The reference to straight hair is coded, and repeated in several other accounts, to indicate the difference between the populations of the Americas and those of Africa. This coding is a pivot for their differential treatment: the enslavement of Africans was common enough at the time to have been specifically sanctioned by the Catholic church through Pope Nicholas V, in an agreement signed in 1454 with the Portuguese crown by which the papacy received commissions on the receipts of the existing traffic in Africans, but Indians had not yet been classified in the master-slave structure and were, in fact, consistently difficult to subject to it. (See Julio José Chiavenato, *O Negro no Brasil*, p. 112.)

attacks on Spanish ships and territories (chap. 1). In general, Northern Europe preferred the more sensational tales of warfare and cannibalism, such as the *Wahrhaftige Historie* of Hans Staden. Its public was not directly involved in colonization or with the moral and economic problems confronting the French, the English, the Spanish, and the Portuguese. The colonizing countries produces not only the kinds of reports necessary to prepare and send out colonists and to convey what to expect of the venture but also discussions of the humanity of the newly found peoples, necessary for deciding whether they would be treated as slaves or coadjutors, whether they would be separated into reservations or employed, if that is the proper term, in the new plantations, whether they would be guides to be cultivated or enemies to be exterminated.

The genre of Hans Staden's *Wahrhaftige Historie* came to underlie a negative, Hobbesian view of the populations of the Americas and, by extension, of humanity at its origins. Conversely, reports of hospitable, generous innocent Amerindians, unspoiled by civilization as understood in Europe, were used by other theorists to postulate an originally gentle humanity. Locke says that "in the beginning all the World was America," integrating the Americas into a European discourse of origin and showing the completion of the process by which, as Berkhofer says, the "Indian . . . moved from the contrasting descriptions of explorers and settlers to the ideological polemics of social philosophers."[42] Thus the tales of explorers roasted by giant American cannibals fed a taste for the sensational and a propaganda campaign embedded in European politics and economics while also buttressing the political, cultural, and economic power of those whose view of the other as savage provided a convenient embodiment of the negative components of the European self or justified European atrocities in America.[43] When Roberto Fernández Retamar embraced Caliban/cannibal as the incarnation of an American (more specifically, a Latin-American) self opposed to and redemptive of European history (which includes the United States and excludes Eastern Europe), he once again appropriated otherness, this

---

[42] Berkhofer (p. 22) quotes Locke from the *Two Treatises*, p. 319.
[43] This is part of the argument of Michael Palencia-Roth, for whom the image of the Amerindian as cannibal predominates in the European iconography of the Americas. See "Cannibalism and the New Man," pp. 2, 5, 15–19.

time to defend a Cuban revolution in search of a newly redemptive autochthonous primitive.[44]

In the end, the differences and incoherencies in and among accounts of the New World are not reducible to regular patterns of interpretation. The only thing Todorov's view of their characteristically destructive European arrogance has in common with Germán Arciniegas's sense that they brought about an explosion of knowledge and an opening of ethical and epistemological vistas in Europe is the implication that voyages and accounts had a destabilizing epistemological effect on established world views. Certeau says that the image of America in which "the other returns to the same," reassembled with elements of the self, also established a break, marked by the Atlantic, between the "over here" (though Certeau is over there) and the "over there" (though the Amerindians are over here) belonging to a *"new* world" (*History,* pp. 218–29). The break was then "transformed into a rift between nature and culture" essential for the elaboration of a new cultural identity. The game of identity and difference that characterizes this elaboration began as soon as it was possible to think that "nature is what is other, while man stays the same" (p. 220).

But that distinction is not stable either; it can be reelaborated in different ways. Explorers had practical reasons to bring back to Europe samples of savages, like specimens of the exotic flora and fauna (were the Amerindians curious too? Rousseau, as we shall see, says they were not): to court a sovereign, to prove the success of one expedition and solicit financing for the next, to show Amerindians the advantages of civilization and win their alliance for the work of conversion (see, for example, the Letter of Paul Le Jeune to Father Barthélémy Jacquinot, provincial of France, April 1632, *Rélations,* 1:14). But otherness, like the self, does not define itself in isolation, and these "savages" often seemed to exist beyond familiar oppositions, such as, for example, those of religious beliefs. The scandal of such otherness is apparent in attempts to deny or regularize it: Rolena Adorno tells of the inquisitor of Granada, who, upon becoming archbishop of Lima in 1580, tried to govern Amerindians as he had governed the "morisco" (imperfectly Christianized Muslim) population of Spain and found that familiar dichotomies no longer worked. Neither did tips gleaned from de las Ca-

---

[44] See Theodore S. Hamerow, "Exotic Revolutionism and the Western Intelligensia," esp. p. 210, where he refers specifically to the history of the conquest.

sas's catechization of Amerindians work to make new Christians of the Jews in Valencia ("*La ciudad letrada*," p. 5): knowledge was suddenly not transferable. In the end, the Americas prompted a review of the notions of origins and the relation between humanity and nature, but the revision soon became so thoroughly naturalized that it lost its own origins and its initial critical force.[45]

Images of the New World became naturalized as they were used in a critique of European polities and culture. It is because the discourse of the first accounts is polyvocal that it could be woven along the centuries into a discourse of otherness with which, in the literary and intellectual movements of the eighteenth century, Europe rethought origin and history and the legitimacy of established forms of social, political, and economic organization. This streamlined discourse of the New World then became part of the discourse of American nationality at the time of the independence, recrossing the Atlantic to justify opposition to the metropoles and eventually to be integrated into the images of the new nations for internal and external consumption.

Normalizing the discourse of discovery and conquest involved choices, as did normalizing the "colonial discourse" that followed it when writing became rooted in the colonies, or normalizing the discourse of the independent nations originating from these colonies. This dialectic of opposition and emulation continues, as we see when Angel Rama defines a unified Latin America against the more powerful North American nation in ways reminiscent of those that had once defined it against powerful European metropoles; it is extended in the opposition he identifies between the literate center and the disempowered margins within Latin America (see *A cidade das letras*). Stressing the continued resistance to synthesis which allows differentiation, explication, and redifferentiation to continue as discursive power shifts, Rolena Adorno

---

[45] In chapters 2, "The Prose of the World," and 3, "Representing," of *The Order of Things*, Michel Foucault states that at the beginning of the seventeenth century a radical epistemological shift in European thought occurred, affecting the ideological structure of ordinary life and common assumptions and persisting to the present day. Before the shift, "nature, like the interplay of signs and resemblances, is closed in upon itself in conformity with the duplicated form of the cosmos" (p. 31). After the shift, nature extends itself, knowledge is based no longer on resemblance and contiguity but on origin. Could not the discovery of new forms of life on land that was not even supposed to exist have helped destabilize the earlier structures? Foucault does not mention the discoveries. In this omission at least his subversive discourse once again naturalizes the events of those two centuries and becomes continuous with Scammell's conservative denial of Europe's debt to the age of discovery and conquest.

asks her readers to remember that even in Rama's universe, "ideological harmony and unanimity characterize neither the sphere of the dominant society, nor that of the dominated one." Neither forms "one single ideological discourse; they are polyvocal" (*"La ciudad letrada,"* p. 4). Normalization, then, identifies the operation of a discourse of power; differentiation identifies the claim to discursive power. Polyvocality and even incoherence open the field where discursive power can be reclaimed.[46]

It is also because the discourse of otherness is polyvocal that certain alliances are possible in apparent contradiction to the customary notions of the distribution of power between the conquerors and the conquered. Thus, persecuted Amerindians look for support to the highest officials of the metropoles, up to the sovereign him- or herself (Adorno's *Guaman Poma* shows the Inca chronicler addressing Philip II of Spain over the heads of colonial authorities). The argument of these appeals is conducted in the discourse of the conqueror (often depicting local tyranny as detrimental to royal revenues), but it also attempts to fracture the discourse of power and turn it against itself. The subjugated other protests subjection within the discourse of domination, and on the conquerors' terms, asserting a separate self despite subjection. This contradictory movement appears in arguments for the congruence between Christianity and Amerindian beliefs to preserve them from destruction and for the incongruence between Christian action and belief. Christianity is contested in its own rhetoric, which is the best available means of communication with the seat of power (Adorno, *Guaman Poma*, p. 13).

[46] The argument between Fredric Jameson and Aijaz Ahmad in the pages of *Social Text* is almost too pat an illustration of this relationship between a dominant discourse and discourses it would like to dominate more completely. Jameson uses one Chinese and one "African" text to characterize the literature of the Third World and the category of history to differentiate it from that of the First World. Turning Hegel on his head, he declares that the Third World has too much history, rather than not enough, that it is still mired in the political and the social, which the First has already left behind ("Third World Literature in the Era of Multinational Capitalism"). Ahmad points out that "there is no such thing as a 'third-world literature' which can be constructed as an internally coherent subject of theoretical knowledge," that literatures commonly lumped together as Third World are all different, and that if there were such a literature, Western critics would know nothing about it because they don't know the languages ("Jameson's Rhetoric of Otherness," pp. 4, 5). He almost says that the distinction resides not in the essential character of the Third World but in the power relation between reader and writer, noting that within the United States feminist and black writing can be just as allegorical as African writing or that Urdu literature, written for internal consumption by a sophisticated culture, can be nonallegorical (pp. 15, 18). Kwame Appiah's argument, in *In My Father's House,* that the term "Africa" has meaning only in a homogenizing discourse from outside the continent also asks for attention to difference.

Similarly, American claims for independence and recognition are often based on arguments developed in the metropoles; attempts to define national identity through difference often resort to the repertory of characteristic traits made available in the early accounts of the Americas. There are limits to how much it is possible to manipulate those materials, but that it is possible at all should caution us against a nostalgia of essences and against metaphors of depth and remind us that resistance, difference, and criticism can be planted in the very discourse of conquest.

For centuries the New World validated theories of European progress and provided terms for criticizing European institutions. It verified theories of history which maintained it lacked history. It gave rise to new populations for which it was devalued. But by stressing difference, the new nations reminded Europe of its doubts about its own legitimacy. Theories of American primitivism and backwardness argued American innocence, European exhaustion, and a historically necessary transfer of power from Europe to America.[47] The evolutionary interpretation of history which declared a pure European population superior to the mixture of races and peoples in the New World also implied a new humanity that would revitalize a depleted European stock. The absence of writing led to an investment in education and a revaluation of literacy which allowed Americans to claim civic maturity and the right to political emancipation.[48]

In the end, the image of the New World constructed from the accounts of the first travelers and explorers falls into the "complex order" that Fernand Braudel finds "at the very deepest levels of material life," with its "strange collections of commodities, symbols, illusions, phantasms and intellectual schemas," which constitute civilization and to which civilizations contribute (*Structures of Everyday Life* 1:333). As "strange collections" rather than determined structures, these schemas can shift allegiances and change their meanings as they tumble about in the current of history.

[47] This is what Robert Weibsuch identifies as the opposition between European "lateness" and American "earliness."

[48] In this matter it is interesting to read various missionaries' reports on young Indians' talent for Latin. Fray Toribio de Benavente o Motolinia, in *Historia de los Indios de la Nueva España*, praises the great "ability" of the Indians, who could confound a newly arrived Spanish cleric by arguing a point in Latin, then cap it with an observation on Latin grammar (p. 390).

3

Jean-Jacques Rousseau
and the Discourse
of the Exotic

In order to elaborate notions of national and cultural identity, the new American nations could draw on accounts of discovery and conquest as rich sources of images and information, but in most cases they did not go straight to those accounts. Instead, they turned to cultural artifacts from contemporary European art and thought, to romanticism and political theory as elaborated in eighteenth-century England and France. These European theories, as a matter of course, used information from the Americas, by then incorporated into a discourse of justification of European conditions or opposition to them. This interaction between American images and European concepts can be traced in many ways, but since Jean-Jacques Rousseau's works articulate many of the terms in which the American struggle for independence was formulated and codify important aspects of the transposition of a discourse of otherness into European politics, especially in hypotheses about the origin of political and social organization, they can be examined as representative of that interaction.

Rousseau's influence on the language and thought of the eighteenth and early nineteenth centuries was so pervasive that it is hard to pinpoint. At the same time, his thought is so steeped in the intellectual cross-currents of his time that he can also be seen as a spokesman, and "influence" seems the wrong term for the endless ripples created by his writings. His work gave intellectual weight and general currency to a system of terms that, like the term "discourse" in our time, escaped its first user's control, acquired its own meanings and value, and infiltrated the languages of politics, economics, morals, and literature.[1] Even at a quick glance, accounts of his influence appear as likely to list those who attacked him as those who followed him, and his ideas spread despite intense private and official opposition and despite the banning and burning of his books. *Du contrat social,* published in Amsterdam in 1762, was immediately both forbidden and pirated in France; it was banned in Geneva, after it had about a dozen editions between 1762 and 1763.[2] *Emile* was burned in Holland, Paris, and Geneva; in 1762 it was placed on the Catholic index of forbidden books, and Rousseau was forced to flee Paris and shun Geneva.[3] Nevertheless, the book became the most influential treatise on education in France and left its mark on theories of education in Germany and in England, where it was translated at least twice despite English dismay at the French Revolution, for which Rousseau was counted at least partly responsible.[4] Just as his writings were credited with inspiring political positions from the extremes of totalitarianism to anarchy, so they were refuted at the beginning of the nineteenth century by traditionalists such as the vicomte de Bonald, or liberals such as Benjamin Constant, positivists such as Auguste Comte, or socialists such as Pierre Proudhon, serving as a stimulus for dissent and for discussion and debate where they did not serve as inspiration (Robert Derathé, "Les réfutations du *Contrat social,*" p. 90). In Spain although Rousseau's friends met regularly to study his works despite prohibitions by church and state, one of the main instruments for the dissemination of his ideas was the heated refutation

[1] Jacques Derrida makes a complicated case for Rousseau's role in the establishment of the very notion that is now called "discourse," its sign-centeredness, its self-reflexiveness, its dependence on a sense of "desire," and its concomitant—as it is put in German—*Bodenlosigkeit* (see "Introduction to the 'Age of Rousseau,'" in *Of Grammatology*). There is an implicit claim of discursive synchronicity in Derrida's analysis, as if he were talking with Rousseau rather than about him from a distance of the two centuries in which political developments and scholarly commentaries have affected the semantic context and content of Rousseau's writings. I do not aim at this synchronic effect, but it confirms the sense that Rousseau pervades (and many still say that he perverts) even our thought.

[2] See Ronald Grimsley, Introduction to Rousseau, *Du contrat social,* pp. 3–5.

[3] Maurice Cranston depicts the Geneva in which Rousseau grew up as stern in morals but relatively free in ideas (*Jean-Jacques,* chap. 1, esp. p. 27): the banning of his works there is a strong indication of the shock they provoked.

[4] François and Pierre Richard, Introduction to Jean-Jacques Rousseau, *Emile, ou De l'Éducation,* pp. xxix, xxx.

of his *Discours sur l'origine et les fondements de l'inégalité* by Benito Feijoo de Montenegro (Jefferson Rea Spell, *Rousseau in the Spanish World*, pp. 45, 20–22). In Argentina, on the other shore of the Atlantic, the Colegio Carolino offered a whole course to combat Rousseau's ideas, ensuring that at least some version of them would be available to impressionable young minds (Boleslao Levin, *Rousseau y la independencia*, p. 24).

Rousseau's works became central to Enlightenment discussions of liberty, equality, political representation, and property from which the European colonies in the Americas derived theoretical and moral justification when, one after another, they began to declare their independence. The effect of his thought was not always direct, just as the intellectual and political processes leading to independence were not uniform throughout the hemisphere. Unlike the former French and Iberian colonies, the United States received French political theories in part indirectly, through the debate in England which blunted their radical edge; as the first to achieve independence, moreover, the United States itself became a model for revolutionary movements on both sides of the Atlantic. Brazil, unlike all other former colonies, won independence as a monarchy. One can trace the influence of both the French Enlightenment and the theorists of American independence in its earlier insurrections, particularly those of 1789 in the provinces of Bahia and Minas, which did demand national independence in terms of European and U.S. ideas of social and economic justice derived either directly or through their detractors and interpreters from Rousseau, Guillaume Raynal, and Gabriel Bonnot de Mably.[5] By the time the nation

[5] E. Bradford Burns, in *A History of Brazil*, chap. 3, traces the development of intellectual justifications for independence: improvements in schools brought about by the marquess of Pombal's expulsion of the Jesuits; the founding of academies dedicated in particular to the study of European and North American scientific and political ideas; the kinds and quantities of books imported (he notes the emphasis on learning foreign languages and the visits of foreign intellectuals for lecture tours and study periods as instrumental in establishing direct contact between Brazilian intellectuals and foreign—mainly French and German—ideas). He notes that leaders of independence movements owned copies of the American Declaration of Independence and of works by Thomas Jefferson and Thomas Paine. Kenneth R. Maxwell, documents a meeting at Montpellier between Jefferson and some Brazilian students at the university desirous of Brazilian independence ("The Generation of the 1790s," p. 107). He also remarks on the books by and about figures of the French Enlightenment and the North American independence theorists to be found in the libraries of the Minas conspirators. Court documents listing books confiscated from the conspirators also indicate that those intellectuals who defined the aims of Brazilian movements of independence had found inspiration in the French thinkers of before the French Revolution. Eduardo Frieiro discusses one such list of confiscated books, which is

adopted a republican government, almost a century later, it did so in the vocabulary of positivism; it is in the effects of the second emperor's francophilia, as well as in his interest in the United States, that one finds the mark of Rousseauean ideas.[6] In Mexico, by contrast, portions of *Du contrat social* found their way into constitutional drafts.[7] In general, as Horst Dippel shows, the formulation of early modern concepts of the state, of the place and origin of laws, of the possibility of different forms of property ownership, of the formation of national wealth, of the relation between the individual and the state, which were essential in the establishment of the new American nations, arose amid an intense interchange of ideas between English and French thinkers to which the United States contributed intellectually and also by functioning as a kind of socioeconomic laboratory.[8]

The degree to which Rousseau's thought affected various American movements for independence is a politically charged question; it is also

---

also a snapshot of the intellectual climate in Ouro Preto, capital of the province of Minas Gerais, at the time of the 1789 insurrection, known as the Inconfidência (*O diabo na livraria do Cônego*). Kátia M. de Queiroz Mattoso finds key concepts from important speeches of the French Revolution in pamphlets and posters of the uprising in Bahia (*Presença francesa no movimento democrático baiano de 1798*). Given the paucity of the documentation—three lists of books resulting from the government's investigation of the movement and a number of pamphlets that had been posted in prominent places around Salvador—and the difference in conditions between prerevolutionary France and colonial Bahia, however, the data point to the use of a vocabulary of the French revolution to lend legitimacy to the Bahian rebels, rather than an influence of French political events upon the dynamics of the Brazilian uprising. David Haberly, "The Mystery of the Bailiff's List, or What Fagundes Varela Read," illustrates that foreign books were common in Brazilian libraries, but also that intellectual influence is serendipitous, quite likely to give equal weight to works by authors we now consider most important and others now sunk in complete—and presumably deserved—obscurity. The necessary assumption, if one wants to explore the influence of ideas on political movements, is that the "great" authors exercised an ineffable force that impressed itself on lesser luminaries who ended up as something like "carriers" of their ideas.

[6] Thomas Skidmore, in *Black into White*, documents the persistent cultural influence of France over Brazil, even into the twentieth century, and the effects of positivism on both abolitionism and republicanism. See esp. chaps. 1–3. He documents the emperor's interests in "Brazil's American Illusion: From Dom Pedro II to the Coup of 1964," esp. p. 73.

[7] The essays collected by Mario de la Cueva in *Presencia de Rousseau* trace the influence of Rousseau on the independence movements of Argentina, Mexico, Colombia, etc.

[8] See Horst Dippel, *Individuum und Gesellschaft*, esp. chap. 3. David Cameron's thesis of the comparability of Rousseau's thought to Edmund Burke's rests on a more general view of an intense interchange of ideas between England and France in the second half of the eighteenth century. See specifically *The Social Thought of Rousseau and Burke*, p. 36.

unnecessary to answer. The purpose of the present discussion is to examine how Rousseau's vocabulary of origins, legitimacy, and opposition to established power structures was used to justify the American nations' political separation from the European metropoles and to define their separate national identities. I also want to investigate the degree to which Rousseau's vocabulary is itself constructed from elements furnished by Europe's experience of the American exotic. When the new nations began to work seriously at affirming cultural independence and defining national identity, Rousseau's writings furnished some of the necessary concepts and vocabulary. There, Rousseau's influence was once more pervasive and less direct than in the political arena, operating on the formulation of concepts of national identity through a European view of the Americas, traceable in his use of American elements at the foundation of his arguments.

The *Discours sur l'origine et les fondements de l'inégalité* repeatedly refers to American examples as it theorizes the origins of society and of humanity; the terms of these references illustrate the characteristics accorded to "Americans" and fix them in the discourse about the Americas. They recur in *Du contrat social*, which uses Amerindians as examples of presocial man and which influenced the wording of new constitutions in South and Central America; in *Emile*, which provided the basis for a rationally planned system of education to produce appropriate citizens for the new republics, and in *La nouvelle Héloïse*, which not only defined the proper place of the domestic sphere in the economy of the state but also, together with the second part of *Emile*, proposed a proper assignment of functional and psychological roles to men and women, husbands and wives, so as to constitute the family as the breeding ground of a sturdy citizenry. Thus, the examples Rousseau adduces from what was known of so-called primitives constitute themselves into a language of opposition to European social structures which is grounded in the societies of the New World and later shapes their image. Its terms, however, escape any determination of accuracy or truth. They are exempted, on one hand, because of the scandal of opposition and, on the other, because of the familiarity conferred by centuries of repetition. Rousseau's ideas may be questioned but not his "Americans"; noble or brutish, they persuade, embedded in a common knowledge careless of contradictions.

Of course, the language that here presents as "roles" the positions of male and female, weak and powerful, child and well-intentioned adult, citizen and outsider, is foreign to the system of Rousseau's thought. Nor are exoticism and power part of a Rousseauean vocabulary. I use these concepts to estrange Rousseau's discourse in order to weigh the consequences of its acceptance into the vocabulary with which new polities were established and with which they defended the legitimacy of the redistribution of power effected through independence and nation formation—events contemporaneous with the violent redistributions of power within Europe at the end of the eighteenth century.

I am interested here not in how Rousseau shaped a discourse of the creation of the state but in the echo of Rousseau—something like the harmonics his concepts provide to the tone of his times, that which is recognized as Rousseauean. It is not the structure of Rousseau's arguments that I address but their effects, acknowledged even among his fiercest detractors in the conviction that his ideas led to action, to the establishment of structures of government, courses of study, attitudes toward authority, and most important here, concepts of the relation between past and present, politics and history, class and education which informed the discourse of the New World.

Rousseau never wrote specifically about the Americas; he was not interested in the politics or the anthropology of non-European states and peoples, and he did not contribute to the literature of the exotic that flourished in the middle of the eighteenth century.[9] In *Frêle bonheur*, Todorov hints that Rousseau was uninterested in otherness because he was too absorbed in constructing a personal and cultural self.[10] But it is precisely because his works are not *about* the exotic that they show its acculturation so clearly: they use the exotic as a given.

Rousseau illustrates theoretical assertions about human nature and the conduct of politics by frequent reference to accounts of the New World. In the seventeenth century, notes Hans Günter Funke, particularly in France, these accounts had "fused the traditions of the Renaissance utopia and the authentic travel report" to create a widely read genre that used observations about real or fictive non-European lands and peoples to criticize European mores and societies. These alternative perfect societies were presented with all the discursive markers of truth; formally, they were not to be distinguished from the travel accounts

[9] In *Tristes tropiques* Lévi-Strauss calls Rousseau the most ethnographic of all the philosophers but refers only to his extensive use of ethnographic accounts available at the time, acknowledging his lack of any firsthand experience of cultural otherness (p. 451).
[10] *Frêle bonheur* examines the causes and consequences of viewing Rousseau as a pioneer in the exploration of the self.

circulating since the discoveries (Funke, *Die Utopie der französischen Aufklärung*, p. 42).[11] The otherness of the New World was thus quite consciously made to occupy an intermediary space between truth and fiction, and it became available as a formal tool for social criticism and political speculation. As Rousseau wrote, this transitional function of the discourse of otherness had been deeply absorbed into the literature of criticism; it did not necessarily mark a difference. Rousseau's predecessors had buttressed theories about the origin of society or property with examples from the new worlds, just as they had attributed to foreign visitors or captives in Europe an outsiders' perspective from which to discuss and criticize aspects of European politics and mores. Montesquieu's *Lettres persanes* exemplifies such a use of the outsiders' perspective, as does Swift's device of sending his hero to outrageously "exotic" places for a clearer view of what was amiss in England. But Rousseau's use of the exotic marks a further development. Hottentots, Caribs, and Hurons figure in his arguments about the origin of humanity and society as ancestral figures, remnants of what Europeans must have been sometime in the past. They become the evidence in a protoevolutionary discourse not as objects of astonishment or fear, as in the writings of the explorers, settlers, and scientists, or of admiration, as in the utopias, but as providing something like the historical equivalent of introspection.[12] Primitives are thus englobed in the European self, made into illustrations not of what is alien to Rousseau's civilized readers but of what they ought to recognize as existing vestigially in themselves. Primitives illustrate the past and explain the present; in a corollary, they give hope for the future.

This is Rousseau's imprint on the discourse of the exotic. It became a validation and a rejection of European civilization, axiom and argument

---

[11] Funke's aim is to define the Enlightenment utopia in terms of genre; some of his observations are suggestive in other contexts too. For instance, unlike the utopian writings of classical antiquity or the Renaissance, which take the form of dialogues, those of the Enlightenment are most often travelogues. They operate a shift from the encounter with another self to an encounter with an other (p. 41).

[12] Arthur O. Lovejoy notes that Rousseau's originality does not lie in his treatment of the "state of nature" as such, which owed much to thinkers such as Samuel von Pufendorf or even Denis Diderot, but in his "early formulation and diffusion of an evolutionary conception of human history" ("The Supposed Primitivism of Rousseau's *Discourse on Inequality*," p. 25). Bernard Gagnebin and Marcel Raymond, editors of the Gallimard edition of Jean-Jacques Rousseau, *Oeuvres complètes*, compile a long list of sources for Rousseau's notion of the primitive, including travelers and other philosophers, and comment on his importance as a protoevolutionarist (*Discours sur l'inégalité*, pp. 1304–5).

about the foundations of society, actively debated blueprint for the establishment of new non-or counter-European polities, and quietly accepted characterization of the human substratum of these polities—a realized language and virtual grammar. Thus Rousseau's definition of something like a zero degree of human social and political organization embodied in the American exotic justifies claims of legitimacy based on the correct application of the first principles he deduces. Antipathy to Rousseau as one of the ideologues of the French Revolution did not prevent acceptance of the idea that it is possible to deduce the moment before the origin of social and political organization and return to it to choose a new form of community.

Searching for the origins of legitimate political power, Rousseau speaks not only to opponents and reformers of contemporary regimes but also to preservers of the state. Thus, as the American colonies declared themselves independent of European metropoles and sought, on one hand, to legitimate their rebellion against the colonial powers and claim recognition in the concert of nations and, on the other, to write the rules of law within their borders, Rousseau's theoretical exposition of society could be referred to as a blueprint. Not that Rousseau's were the only ideas then current and influential; they coexist in a passionate dialogue with and against Locke, Hobbes, Montesquieu, and Voltaire. But insofar as Rousseau proposed the systematic constitution of a new form of social organization, rather than an analysis of the existing one, he presided over the establishment of a discourse of independence even more than over the establishment of the particular articles that legally founded that independence. Though his influence was muted in the United States, possibly because of the articulate opposition to his ideas in England, Rousseau left his imprint indirectly. Henri Roddier shows that in England Rousseau's ideas permeated the arguments about the power of government and the role of the people's will in the various crises of George III's reign, and that they continued to worry the English as they formulated their reaction to the French Revolution and constructed a national educational policy (see *Rousseau en Angleterre*, esp. chap. 6). As frameworks for ideology and policy, these debates in turn affected American political thought before and after independence. At the same time, the American discourse of opposition to metropolitan power and of difference from the metropolis used the terms of a European discourse of opposition in which the original inhabitants of the Americas figured as difference. Appropriating that discourse, the new nations reincorporated into their definition of nationality a European definition of their difference, filtered through the ideas of a European proponent of opposition to contemporary forms of power distribution in Europe.

But Rousseau's primary importance for the establishment of a discourse of the American exotic is his incorporation in his theory of the origins of social organization of a theory of the ontogenesis of man: the "natural man" he posited, this "savage," was mostly American. Rousseau's construct drew on knowledge current at his time, and his arguments were acceptable within the expanding language of intellectual and then political opposition to established power. Thus, even though many of his readers and the authorities of church and state found his conclusions disagreeable, his works could nevertheless become the basis of both political opposition and intellectual respectability, both identity and difference, origin and future, in the more nebulous reign of a discourse of national consciousness. The traces of his thinking are found not only in political discourse but also in the discourses of identity, nature, and history by means of which the new nations claimed cultural autonomy. Whether Rousseau reached the New World directly through his books, indirectly through his detractors, or even once more removed, through the debates around his ideas, the traffic marks a new phase in the exchange by which American raw materials—goods or concepts—came back to be reintegrated in national cultural or political economies.

The materials that inform a discourse do not determine its import, however. In the seventeenth century Europeans fused American material into the form of the pastoral golden age and noble savage, on one hand, and the antipastoral figure of the "wild man," on the other.[13] In the eighteenth century Rousseau's works gave rise to both a "romanticizing" and a politically oriented view of the aboriginal populations of non-European lands in general and the Americas in particular. The romanticized Americas appeared as apolitical repositories of the moral virtues and physical endowments that European civilization (identified with civilization as such) had lost. The political America was the laboratory where a new political order would be created under known and controlled circumstances. There the promise of *Du contrat social* could be fulfilled, legitimating the writing of all the "social contracts" that affirmed the independence of American states, any or all of which

---

[13] Peter Weston, in "The Noble Primitive as Bourgeois Subject," notes the various uses and transformations in European cultural history, of the notion of primitive man, derived from accounts of the New World (see esp. pp. 60, 61, 65).

might realize Rousseau's dream, overcoming both the primitivism of savages and the corruption of civilized Europe.

Critical of established political authority and privileging the point of origin of social organization, Rousseau's terms were used to justify the transfer of established power from the metropolis to the new nations and to legitimate new power relations. But the same new nations became uncomfortable with these same terms when they found themselves striving for acceptance among established countries. As the literature of the new American nations set for itself the aim to complement political with cultural independence, the echoes of Rousseau in the discourse of the New World changed: his language was used less for political purposes than to elaborate a concept of nature identified with the Americas, for with that identification, his language established, at the origin of the new nations, a substratum and guarantee of virtue, a corrective against the cultural pressure of a (European) civilization that had evolved crookedly from just such origins. This notion of nature separated the Americas from the politics of the European states, no longer "natural" in the sense of divinely ordained and uniquely fitting within the proper order of the world. Nature now preceded and opposed social organization; though it included some essentially human qualities, it excluded products of human activity. The original inhabitants of the New World, then, dwelled in a realm of nature from which Europeans had fallen away in the course of their history. In this reading of Rousseau, New World otherness is no longer defined in political terms; it is characterized not by its potentially redeeming historical function but by the fortunate absence of history.[14] Thus the New World can turn the charge that it lacks history against the Old World and at the same time justify its claim to its own, redemptive historical weight.

But a discourse on otherness is always in some way adversarial, so that the new nations' claims to historical depth and to the role of redeemers of a botched European history are not necessarily taken seriously. Europe never devalues its own sense of historical weight; if it accepts the notion of a redemptive primitivism, it is only to make opposition confirm the weight of its history. Marie Antoinette valued her pastoral theater, and the crowds that came to the reconstruction of a jungle scene in Rouen were delighted with the opportunity to meet

---

[14] Bronislaw Baczko, *Rousseau: Solitude et communauté*, traces Rousseau's notions of history and otherness to an existential crisis generated by his alienation from the society of his time, which he made many attempts to describe and theorize.

face-to-painted-face with what they regarded as nature, but neither the queen nor the crowds made their homes in these representations of a world more innocent than their own. These theatrical constructions derived their value from being framed by a city and a palace, themselves the scenes of real history and real power. Nature unframed, as in the Americas, continued to be only an invitation to intervention, and the literatures of the Americas still struggle now, as they did more clearly at the origin of the American states, with the problem of preserving the values of the natural, which had at first defined their independence, while claiming the legitimacy of history, which would protect them.

The positive value Rousseau gives both the original substratum of nature and the creation of a legitimate structure of government and social organization promised to solve the dilemma of ahistorical legitimacy. His work allowed the new nations to define themselves as embodying the virtues either of nature or of a new state, as opposing the corrupt society of contemporary Europe or exemplifying progress from the insufficiencies of primitivism to the fulfillment of a state of civilization that Europe had been unable to achieve.

In time the first part of his argument, proposing a return to origins in nature, overwhelmed the second part, which operates the transition from nature to civilization. When that happened, the new nations had to buttress their claim for cultural parity by denying their "lack of history," a lack that implies crude, rather than virtuous and uncorrupted primitivism. The link with Rousseau, useful for a while, was repressed. It emerges in occasional movements back to nature or in attempts to rediscover a Native American past, often colored by the contradictory desires to deny history and to assert historical depth, to atone, if that past is covaluable with that of Europe, for its destruction. Then the new nations were forced to digest their contradictory heritage as "native" and destroyers of "the natives."

It is for his concept of the "noble savage" that Rousseau is most commonly associated with a New World discourse of cultural independence. Like many shorthand terms, this one is neither clearly defined nor easy to find in that precise form in its author's writings. But its very imprecision expands its meaning and creates a good feeling of understanding between interlocutors before the rigors of definition set in.

The idea of the nobility of the American native did not originate with Rousseau;[15] it was part of the repertoire of attributes assigned to the

[15] Lévi-Strauss attributes its formulation to Diderot, stressing that "Rousseau never fell into Diderot's error of idealizing natural man" (*Tristes tropiques*, p. 451).

peoples of the new lands from the earliest days of conquest. One could argue, as Todorov has for those days, that a characterization of the savage as noble is as likely to arise from ignorance, misunderstanding, and lack of imagination as the picture of that same savage as cruel and treacherous (*Conquête*, chaps. 1, 3), but since it was not the aim of the more benign characterization to justify political domination and social intervention, it acquired an aura of innocence and impartiality which made it ooom an appropriate vehicle for the American claim to a positive otherness.

Thus the noble savage entered a system of arguments and, misinterpreted, became an aim of desire (Baczko, p. 137); the concept's *adaequatio ad rem* became less important than its role in that system of arguments, as one can see in Claude Lévi-Strauss's assertion that "the study of these savages . . . helps us to build a theoretical model of human society, which does not correspond to any observable reality," and in his assessment of the usefulness of such otherness: "Other societies" provide us with "a means of distancing ourselves from our own" (*Tristes tropiques*, p. 453). As for Rousseau, he relegates primitive man to footnotes, where primitivism founds a potentiality, a predisposition in the very nature of humankind strong enough to carry philosophical statements about authority and about the relation between individuals and the social system in which they exist. The "nobility" of this original human being is a function not of his obedience to moral rules but of his potential to create and obey them.[16] The noble savage is not yet virtuous and does not yet live either in society or in history but is capable, as he falls into history, of creating a virtuous society[17]—the process of forming a society constituting, in an analogy Rousseau did not seem able to avoid, something like a fall. In raising radical questions about and voicing radical objections to the governments of this time and the societies over which they presided, however, Rousseau is not addressing only a particular political organization. Combining the political and the psychological, one can also argue, with Bronislaw Baczko, that Rousseau was driven to radical criticism of his society because he saw it as entirely alienating and alienated, so that, for the health of its

[16] My consistent use of masculine nouns and pronouns accords with Rousseau's usage rather than with present rules of gender neutrality in public expression.
[17] This potentiality is what Rousseau calls *perfectibilité*, a distinguishing characteristic of humanity, which, it must be remembered, implies a positive valuation of the social state and also the ability to decay to a negatively valued state (*Discours*, p. 142); decay could turn the citizen of a good society into the accomplice of a corrupt one, like that which Rousseau criticizes in the *Discours* as well as in *La nouvelle Héloïse* and *Emile*.

members, it had to be rebuilt from first principles. To help himself and his readers imagine a human being not yet alienated by the fall into history which produced that corrupt civil society, Rousseau refers, in comments scattered throughout the *Discours sur l'inégalité*, *Du contrat social*, and *Emile*, to the common and readily available stock of varied information about the "savages" of the New World.

But that corrupting history is what Europe wrote and, in due course, imposed on the Americas; it conditions the Western imagination. Rousseau's attempt to go back to origins is an attempt to unimagine Western history and, thus, is productively contradictory at its inception.[18] It hovers between imprisonment in the language in which it must be spoken and a free fall into the emptiness that separates the noble savage from the Indian of the Americas. The "emptiness" of the Americas, in all its factual inaccuracy and cultural suggestiveness is yet again metaphorically extended to its original inhabitants, still outside of systematically organized societies and devoid of history and once again made ready for the intervention of forces that create history. If emptiness was necessary for the European conquerors to justify their intervention and their possession of the land and souls of their inhabitants, it was reasserted by the creators of the independent political entities of the New World. The Rousseauean reformulation of American emptiness gave credence to their claim that they were creating societies anew. Although historical depth was sometimes asserted by including the Amerindian past, moral legitimacy tended to be justified by claiming structurally conditioned virtue rather than by accepting the authority of historical continuity. Thus the claim to the right of rebellion stated in the U.S. Declaration of Independence, which applies criteria of extrahistorical right to a political problem, justifies the transfer of power by a break with history and from a point of judgment outside history.[19]

---

[18] The notion of the fundamentally paradoxical nature of Rousseau's thought has been productive in recent criticism. In particular Felicity Baker, in "La route contraire," considers the paradox at the beginning of *Du contrat social* ("one will force him to be free") as paradigmatically generative of Rousseau's discourse. John Charvet sees the same characteristic but, less tolerant than Baker, judges that Rousseau meant to "return to nature in the sense of refounding society on nature and this project creates a paradox which lies at the center of Rousseau's ultimate incoherence," destroying the credibility of whatever else he has to say (*The Social Problem*, p. 2).

[19] Henry Steele Commager considers that one of the defining characteristics of American law is its reliance on a system of values above those that institute it, present from the beginning and as useful for the organization of the American state as for its initial struggle with England ("Constitutional History and the Higher Law," in *In Search of a Usable Past*, pp. 28–55).

Rousseauean thought appears, then, at the center of the transatlantic debate on history, precisely because, as Baczko points out, Rousseau himself is not a historian, having left no account of a historical period and having shown himself to be as ignorant and fanciful in his discussion of Greeks and Romans (p. 106) as in his views of Hurons. Because Rousseau does not write history, it is possible to disconnect origins from history, to affirm historical depth independent of chronology or the succession of historical facts. Thus the European argument against American cultural parity—namely, that the new nations have nothing to look back on which was not provided by Europe—can be countered by finding in the Americas, where history is beginning again, autochthonous structures and sequences noncontemporaneously analogous to European historical developments.

Since they need not be "historical," Rousseau's American primitives are never completely defined: at times they are the Indians, at times the European settlers. All are reduced to the homey, shocking, or amusing details of intelligible human lives and common human abilities, allowing Rousseau to give form and habitation to what he himself denies has historical truth, in a curious game of hide-and-seek with his sources. The primitive he invents does, however, combine the integrating function of model and the estranging function of critic; it is an otherness that makes imaginable a way of being that is human and yet structurally different from all that his readers commonly think of as human. At the same time and inevitably, this creation contradicts its premises by participating in the structures of contemporary imagination. It is like the partly adolescent and partly mystical attempt to "think of nothing": the structures of ordinary thought and imagination invade the attempted nothingness. In other words, the travelers' account provide Rousseau with welcome signifiers for the central signification of his criticism of society, opposing and comforting his alienation with a vision of integrated otherness. And since signifier and signified are not separable, Rousseau's theoretical construct absorbs the available images of the New World as emptiness and potentiality and also transforms them into a useful otherness that can reoriginate the culture in which its concept arose.

Perhaps because it is difficult to imagine and to express in intelligible terms the true otherness of a nonsocial man, the image of New World "savages" is not consistent throughout Rousseau's work. In the *Discours* and in *Du contrat social* they live in an exemplary closeness to nature original to man and lost to Europeans, but in the justly forgotten play

La découverte du nouveau-monde the original Americans are akin to the Romans, Greeks, or Spaniards of French classical theater and suffer the same exasperations of love, honor, spite, and jealousy, though stripped of classical fullness and reduced to the allegories of an age that no longer believes in them. At the end of the play an "American" declares, "No heart is savage that is conquered by love"; Columbus tells the Indian chief, "I want you for a friend, be Isabella's subject"; a Spanish lady sings, "Discovering new worlds is offering new myrtles to Love"; and the chorus concludes, "Let us spread over the universe / Our treasures and bounty. / Let us unite, in our Alliance / Two worlds separated by the abyss of the Ocean." The contrast between the classically noble Americans of the play and the keen-nosed Canadians of the political writings shows not only the contradictions between the various images of the original inhabitants of the New World but also the kinship between the concepts of a nobility homologous to that of a braver European past and of a virtue dependent on its distance from the foundations of present European civilization. In one passage of the *Discours sur l'inégalité*, Rousseau seems to bridge the opposition between primitive and ancient, so marked in his play, by making it into a question of misreading: noting that ancient reporters never speak of orangutans or mandrills, he muses that perhaps those were what the ancients called satyrs or fauns, seeing gods where modern man sees only beasts (p. 211).

This oscillation between considering the original inhabitants of the New World as primitives, precivilized tabulae rasae, and considering them as ancients, carriers of human and civic virtues long lost to Europeans, appears in their definition by Europeans as well as in the first American writings on them; it is one of the many traits imported from European discourse on the New World which are used to distinguish the New World from Europe. Like other transposed elements of European discourse about the Americas, it both classifies and evaluates. It is useful that savages can be called upon to represent a desired American difference, while they also, as ancestors, stand at the origin of identity in European civilization; it is possible through them to articulate the equivalence in value of the humanity underlying all differences. At this point also, the universalizing tendency of eighteenth-century philosophical theories coincides with universalizing tendencies in the Christian churches and works to justify the changes imposed on the New World and its original inhabitants by the process of settlement. The explanatory usefulness of these ancestral, primitive, ahistorical, innocent, virtuous, and ultimately abstract Indians is independent of their or their cultures' continued existence: they would serve it as well by becoming civilized or by ceasing to exist. It is only later that romantic nostalgia would demand a different kind of authenticity for the recognition of the savage's otherness, would claim that once again the Roman virtues were about to disappear.

But Rousseau's use of American Indians is teleologically if not always semantically consistent: his Indians are an important part of his didactic project. Rousseau's reconstruction of the world takes for granted an already established tradition of the savage as critic. Anthony Pagden catalogs works widely read, widely respected, or both, which created the composite image of natural man to which Rousseau could refer without need for further definition and without fear of being mistaken. He notes that although "the savage comes always from a [remote] world, . . . if the normative values which he embodies are to be acceptable or indeed intelligible to the reader, his *moral* universe must in all important respects be a familiar one" ("The Savage Critic," p. 33).[20] This familiarity of the moral universe finally absorbs the remoteness of the "savage" world; discourse regularizes experience and tames otherness. Nevertheless, the disjunction operated by a discourse that criticizes European mores from the "outside" reinstitutes difference, forcing an imaginative estrangement of custom and belief, showing a rift between them, destroying the illusion—only then discovered to be such—of their seamlessness. In his role as critic of European society, the savage makes it possible to say, like Pagden, that Christianity and European laws result from the work of imagination; they distort reality and displace reason (p. 41). But it must be remembered that the possibility of this critical formulation also depends on rifts within Christianity and widespread opposition to certain forms of European law. The notion of a

[20] Pagden's list of works in many languages attests to the diffusion of these notions of the savage within Europe and to the relatively small role played by national boundaries and language differences in the formation of that image; unlike the variety of images in reports of the encounter, this image seems relatively independent of the particular political and economic conditions of the various colonizing nations or of the scholars, thinkers and writers who examine government, society, morality, the origin of social structures, or the treatment of "savages." The "fictitious Mexicans of Dryden (in *The Indian Emperor: or the Conquest of Mexico*), Sir William Davenant's Peruvians, the Huron and the Incas of Voltaire, Diderot's Tahitians, Denise Vairasse d'Alais's Australians, the Huron of the Baron de Lahontan," the *Arlequin sauvage* of François Delisle de la Drévetière, mentioned by Rousseau in "Lettre à d'Alembert," or "*Tombo-Chiqui: or the American Savage*, of John Cleland," are very much alike ("The Savage Critic," p. 33).

"natural reason" with which John Dryden's Moctezuma confutes the priest who visits him while he is on the rack is not alien to European thought; the savage king's arguments are intelligible in reference to it (*The Indian Emperor*, act 4; see Pagden, p. 35). Thus, a discourse of American national consciousness, if it is to assert difference and achieve intelligibility, must begin by finding the interstices, the faults, in European discourse; the most visible and most easily inhabitable of these faults are already associated with images located in the Americas, in the utopias (or dystopias) to which the discoveries had given a geographical position (cf. Pagden, p. 34).

Examples from the Americas are thus used to inform and to criticize or instruct. The eighteenth-century European discourse of American exoticism mediates between the worlds of facts and of values. In Rousseau facts are subordinate to values; his discourse on values mounts a radical criticism of European society both diachronically, with hypotheses about the origin of societies, and synchronically, with proposals for the reconstruction of the political self. Formed or reformed in accordance with the directives of Rousseauean pedagogy set forth in *Emile*, that self would want and be able to create a self-sufficient household like that of *La nouvelle Héloïse* and a civil society like that of *Du contrat social*. The realms of self, family, and state appear in Rousseau as concentric circles, all based on the well-formed individual, who has acquired proper socialization but not lost primitive virtues and capabilities. In *La nouvelle Héloïse*, this is how Julie describes the organization of M. de Wolmar's household: "The order that he has created in his house is the image of that which reigns in the depths of his soul and seems to imitate, within a small household, the order established in the government of the world. . . . he has ordered its first arrangement so well that at present all works as if by itself, and we enjoy, at the same time order and freedom" (pp. 371–72).[21] One of the important functions of this rational organization is to perpetuate itself: "One does not marry in order to think exclusively of one another but in order to fulfill jointly the duties of civil life, to govern the house prudently, and to raise children well" (p. 372). In this argument any reference to the primitive or the original seems contained in an ancient European image

---

[21] Felicity Baker notes how similar the proposed relations between child and physical world as developed in *Emile* are to those between citizen and social world as developed in *Du contrat social*, both built on the paradoxical interdependence of freedom and obedience (pp. 137–38).

of the garden as the place where divine nature and human order meet in harmony.

Yet even in this entirely European novel and argument, the Americas hover on the periphery as a point of comparison and a place of refuge. When Saint-Preux crosses the ocean to forget Julie, his description of what he sees over there summarizes the ways in which the new lands are imagined and used. They are sign and victim of European greed: "I have seen the shores of Brazil, where Lisbon and London draw their wealth, and where the miserable inhabitants step on gold and diamonds without daring to touch them." Or they are a place where untouched nature affords unfallen man the conditions to live virtuously: "I have seen from afar the land of those so-called giants [the Patagonians], who are outsized only in their courage and whose independence is better assured by their simple and frugal life than by extraordinary stature. I sojourned for three months at a deserted and delightful island, a sweet and touching image of the ancient beauty of nature, which seems confined to the ends of the world for the express purpose of serving as a refuge to persecuted love and innocence" (Saint-Preux to Mme de l'Orbe, letter 3, pp. 412–13). The positively valued land of the Patagonians, free from the strife, confusion, and immorality of the rest of the world, forms a parallel to Julie's peaceful garden of reason; the negatively valued shores of Brazil show the effect of European vices transplanted to the New World. The brief passage bundles together several of the significations clustered around the facts of the New World and assigns them their places in Rousseau's political and moral discourse. Meanwhile, as Saint-Preux finds in the New World "a refuge for persecuted love and innocence," *La nouvelle Héloïse* becomes a precursor of the fictions of Bernadin de Saint-Pierre and Chateaubriand.[22]

In *Emile*, Rousseau fashions not the society but the person, not the setting but the character who, Baczko says, offers the "suggestion to try again to realize missed possibilities, to transcend the present state of things" (pp. 141–42). The individual's return to origins parallels society's return to origins, envisioned in the political treatises, just as the concept of childhood in *Emile* parallels their proposed notion of natural man. Peter Weston, linking Rousseau's idea of childhood with the image of

[22] To bolster a different argument—that the Leather-stocking tales "retain sentimental characteristics"—Ines Tetley-Jones documents the knowledge of Rousseau in the United States: "*The New Eloisa* became, between 1761 and 1764, . . . the most widely read novel in the colonies" ("Sentimentalism versus Adventure and Social Engagement," pp. 15, 5).

an American natural man, contends that in *Emile* "childhood takes over from Locke's America as the philosophical ground of the myth of the free subject" ("Noble Primitive," pp. 67–68); childhood, nature, America take turns as the empty locations for an innocence that precedes present corruption and originates future virtue. Childhood thus corresponds in the development of the individual to the primitivism of natural man in the development of societies, but it makes intervention more intelligible and more palatable, by justifying it through association with the ideologically respectable process of education which had already served to justify colonization. *Emile* shows how the children of civilization can be educated into remaining simple and moral so that as adults they can form a new, redeemed society. As it shows how to build a new human being, *Emile* describes the traits that would make the new citizens of the Americas models of what Europeans might have been had they not been corrupted. It is not exactly proof of these assertions, but it is a nice historical touch that Simón Bolívar, the liberator of Spanish America was brought up by a tutor who used precisely the techniques advocated in *Emile*.[23] And it probably helped Benjamin Franklin in his conquest of French society that he was seen, in his simple overcoat, as the embodiment of the sober, straightforward, truthful, able, independent, democratic man Emile would have been. Franklin and the new nation profited from his—probably conscious— embodiment of the image of the virtuous and natural American. Close to nature, protected from the vices of civilization and yet able to correct the shortcomings of the state of nature, he presented a living example of American perfectibility.[24] Such alluring images shaped the data provided by chroniclers of the New World into a system of values and significations with which Europeans spoke of the New World and which Americans could use or had to fight when they proposed to fashion their own language for their own purposes.

[23] Jefferson Rea Spell discusses Bolívar's childhood under the tutelage of Simón Carreño Rodriguez, who taught him physical endurance before any academic subjects and, just like the tutor in *Emile*, made him read *Robinson Crusoe* when the child showed an interest in books (*Rousseau in the Spanish World before 1833*).

[24] A. Owen Aldridge notes that in Paris Franklin worked quite consciously "to create the impression that he was a rural philosopher or primitive patriarch" (*Franklin and His French Contemporaries*, p. 13). He was trading on his abilities in the practical world and on the image of simplicity, virtue, and wisdom which often led to an association of "Americans" not only with the uncorrupted origin of society but also with the ancients who were at the historical origin of contemporary societies. He was seen, says Aldridge, as a modern Socrates (p. 12, citing Hervé, *Madame Toussaud's Memories*, p. 56).

As Franklin also understood, the new man (like Emile) is not exceptional: he is the average man of nature prepared to live in society, but
he has to be carefully prepared to be natural. For Rousseau the natural
is not a given but a theoretical construct; the need for re- and deeduca-
tion from birth indicates that the corruption of society starts operating
on the individual before consciousness develops. But as one follows
Emile from birth and from nature, certain logical (some onto-, and some
epistemo) problems come to the fore from which the warm glow of
natural virtue had deflected attention. Rousseau has to posit an order
of individual development to be followed by the ideal educator; this
order has to describe the general inclination of individuals and also has
to accord with the needs of an ideal society. Rousseau assumes, to begin
with, that reason and imagination, defining attributes of humanity, are
to be developed only after the physical body and the practical mind have
been strengthened and secured, qualities primary for the definition of
humanity are secondary in the order of nature.

Emile is to be strong; he is to develop the physical endurance of a
primitive, deprived of sleep or food in long walks and rides. Rousseau
privileges physical prowess as exemplified in an image of the uncorrupted body of the savages, whose strength, he says, is "subtle (*Emile*,
p. 118), especially in comparison with the clumsiness of European peasants.[25] Rather than devalue the mind, these passages attempt to show
it at one with the body: savages still think with their bodies; they are
not alienated from nature or from themselves by the critical, divisive
faculty of intellect and its tool, language. This savage integrity of the
inhabitants of the New World constitutes for Rousseau a living illustration of his theories and makes it possible for him to imagine the regeneration of the society he despises, but the dissatisfaction he despises is
precisely what led to knowledge about these savages. To the explosion
of energy that carried Europeans across the ocean, Rousseau opposes
the curiously negative virtues of a "natural" integration in the world as
it is: "Of all the men in the world, the savages are the least curious and
the least bored; all is indifferent to them: they do not enjoy things, but

---

[25] In the whole passage Rousseau grapples with what looks like the very modern
problem of social man's dissociation from his senses and his body; he attributes this
self-alienation to the encroachment of society on freedom: peasants are clumsy because their work, though physical, is compelled from the outside, whereas savages,
being free, decide upon each act by themselves: "The more their bodies are exercised,
the more their spirits are enlightened: their strength and their reason grow together."

themselves; they spend their lives doing nothing and are never dull" (*Emile*, p. 271).

The constant activity with which the tutor manipulates Emile's surroundings seeks to restore savage repose, but what it teaches is further activity: the pupil must learn how to cultivate the land, fix a clock or a pair of shoes, shoe a horse, and find his way by the stars, acquiring these abilities at the level at which idealized "Americans" have them and learning to value them like people at an early point of development.[26] Gradually the model American changes; he is no longer the Canadian who lives by his senses in unmediated contact with nature (*Emile*, p. 174). Civilization slips in, and he now looks like one of Jean François Marmontel's noble Incas, who, like Rousseau, prize agriculture and manual labor and cannot understand Europeans' aversion to them. The moral point masks the shift in the point of origin, the difference in the definition of American natural man; yet natural man is still American.

A similar shift takes place in Emile's moral education. The virtues of generosity, obedience, trust, and love of honor which should govern the citizen, the man of nature who lives in society, cannot be acquired naturally but must be taught by means of exemplary situations staged by the tutor. More important, Emile also has to be carefully taught compassion, that necessary pivot upon which, in Rousseau's theory, the isolated, independent presocial, and prehistorical savage turns into social and moral man. He has to learn last and from a (socialized) teacher that quality which logically comes first and upon which human society depends. This circularity is important not because it falsifies Rousseau's educational project but because it characterizes his theory of origins as a language, a tool for knowledge, which presents itself as knowledge itself, culture once again passing for nature.

Jean Starobinski claims that Rousseau's enclosed spaces—all these tended gardens in *La nouvelle Héloïse* or *Emile* where men and women live uncorrupted—hearken back to the story of the Fall and constitute a "transcription of the theological theme of the fall into the language of natural causality" ("La mise en accusation," p. 23). But even if these ideal spaces begin by transcribing the fall into nature, and as if inno-

---

[26] The presence of the clock in this list is amusing. The development of accurate clocks made navigation possible and facilitated the conquest and savaging (in the ignoble sense) of the New World. The clock, moreover, became one of the more commonplace symbols of a mechanized humanity. Does clock repair as a basic skill subvert Rousseau's idea of a "natural" upbringing?

cence were still not enough, Rousseau introduces into each of these figurations of innocence a secular source of almost absolute power dedicated to halting or preventing alienation: the husband, the tutor, the prince. Their right to that power resides in their moral qualities and demands the reasoned, willed acquiescence of their subjects. Wholeness and harmony follow from the proper exercise and due acceptance of this power and determine the quality of life in these enclosures, from physical health to linguistic univocity. Rousseau absorbs into his picture of an unalienated society the desire for an "original" congruence between man and nature and between word and thing whose loss leads immediately to the lie and is the first result of the Fall. As Montaigne maintains in "Des cannibales," savages do not have words for treason or lie and since for them words are still identical with things, do not betray and do not lie.[27] Thus, to reestablish innocence, to cure the disease of the Fall, it is necessary to regulate language by curtailing some and imposing other forms of discourse. Rousseau attempts to create a discourse, within civilization as he knows it equivalent to that of "savages" as that civilization imagines them. In the process he defines a discourse *for* exotics, as well as for Emile, functioning in accordance with European notions of exoticism.

Thus, so that he can live in truth and in nature, Emile is kept away from any sort of book knowledge, especially works of the imagination, until his body and character are strong enough to resist them. The semantic and ethical ambiguities of even the simplest fable by La Fontaine are enough to trouble the clear and simple morality upon which Emile's virtues are based and to charge the language of his daily life with resonances that confound its directness and cloud its transparency. In *Emile* the aim of education is to remove the separation not only between man and nature but also between word and thing. Thus it bans metaphor, following the example of "savages" who live either completely within metaphor—so that it does not function as image but as thing—or completely without it—so that their words correspond directly to things. They also live outside of history, which, like fiction, introduces between word and thing a distorting opacity that impedes

---

[27] Michael Giordano shows Montaigne's efforts to imagine himself out of his own culture and language ("Re-reading *Des Cannibales*"). In a way, Rousseau was attempting to write the laws for achieving such a retreat into the entirely different. Much of the difficulty in reading Rousseau may be due to the essential contradiction within the task he set himself.

the perception of truth.[28] This opacity is what Cooper, for instance, tries to erase when he switches from the fictions that made him famous to the transparent account of his nation in *Notions of the Americans.* This book avoids metaphor; the Leather-stocking tales steep in it the characters who are in closest contact with nature and represent the original American substratum of the nation.

Rousseau, however, refuses to allow for this opacity when he restricts Emile's library to a copy of *Robinson Crusoe,* which he must read repeatedly, in an abridged edition—"unencumbered by all its claptrap"— which includes only the period from the shipwreck on the desert island to Crusoe's rescue (*Emile,* p. 221). Part of that "claptrap" is the story of Robinson's compulsion to travel and disobedience to his father, his commercial adventures, and his readiness to engage in the slave trade. It is as a story lifted out of history that *Robinson Crusoe* supplements the reality of the environment the tutor has created for the education of his pupil. Yet it is read as if it were a historical account of survival in nature, completely and accurately mimetic, as if nothing set in a world as yet deprived of a fictional overlay could be fiction.

The programmatic exclusion of fiction from the laboratory-garden where Rousseau conducts his experiment in natural education is one step in the re-creation of that world. But though the tutor draws his views of where to begin the construction of a new man for a new society from what he knows of Hurons and Hottentots, the society into which he educates his pupil is that of small, independent landholders who ideally would not want to leave their bit of soil. Emile is not allowed human contacts that would lead to speculation; he is limited to those that bring unmediated, practical benefits: a wet nurse for the human milk and cuddles necessary to his infant health; a laborer to teach him that work is the foundation of property; a shoemaker and a smith to teach him their trades; selected urchins to teach him to compete in races

[28] Anthony Pagden, in "The Savage Critic," reminds us of the philosophical and ethical conclusions at which European thinkers arrived on the basis of the assumption that "savages" had no words for lie, treason, avarice, envy (Montaigne, "Des cannibales," p. 243), or even God (Manuel da Nóbrega, "Cartas," p. 62). The editors of Rousseau's *Oeuvres complètes* quote Charles Marie de la Condamine's *Relation abrégrée du voyage fait à l'intérieur de l'Amérique méridionale* (Paris: Pissot, 1745), pp. 51–54, to the effect that the languages of the Amerindians lack the words for time, duration, space, being, substance, matter, body, as well as for virtue, justice, freedom, recognition, ingratitude. Here the point seems to be that they lack the means for abstract thought, rather than for the expression of particular vices. The general idea however is that the lacunae in the vocabularies of savages are proof of their moral or intellectual capacities, of their difference.

and to be as magnanimous in victory as is appropriate for his social class, and Crusoe to teach him to survive in pure nature. In this glide from nature through property to class one can see at work the process that transformed savage Hurons into noble Incas, that makes morality wander from the unalienated body into unalienated language, that always defines noble savagery according to an unacknowledged base of civilization. With writing, however, distinctions seem at first clearer: the savage is literal, and Emile must avoid La Fontaine's "Fox and the Raven," ethically as artificial and distorted as its syntax; a child has no business understanding either because understanding is already a sign of corruption. La Fontaine makes the child clever instead of good and teaches that moral corruption is inevitable, that the idle exercise of the imagination is laudable, that words have multiple meanings, and that the relation between the text and the extratextual is mediate.[29] But a transparent *Crusoe* is not a text, and its transparency confers the same status on *Emile*; it can thus uphold the authority of *Emile* and elide the manipulations of the tutor, Rousseau's pedagogical self. The primitivism described by Daniel Defoe (whose name Rousseau never mentions) is presented as ontologically equivalent to the civilization for which Emile is being prepared. At least at this point in Rousseau's argument, however, primitivism is also instrumental and temporary. Emile should learn from Crusoe how to be practical and from the primitive world of the book how to be self-sufficient for as long as self-sufficiency is practical. *Robinson Crusoe* is given to him at an early age because its lessons are basic: it teaches Emile to value a hardware store more than a trendy boutique (p. 213) and by limiting his experiences, it serves, like the Hurons, as an introduction to thinking about the origins and perfection of language, society, and writing.

In Defoe's island Rousseau sees a precedent of his own laboratory for civilization. Though he constantly reminds his readers that Emile's pedagogical garden is as fictional as the pupil and the tutor, Rousseau uses *Robinson Crusoe* to blur the line between fiction and documentary, to mediate between his own text and the extratextual world. What matters for the present argument, however, is that the New World becomes the space of his laboratory, the medium in which his theories will grow strong enough to be transplanted into the corrupted world of civil society without succumbing to its vices. In using Defoe's fiction as if it were

[29] Joan DeJean analyses Rousseau's quarrel with La Fontaine's fables mainly in psychological terms, focusing on the pedagogical relationship, rather than on the question of language ("The Law(s) of the Pedagogical Jungle").

one more travelogue, Rousseau constructs a relay over which the initial discourse of the New World changes registers from factual to moral and is readied for retransmission to the New World.

Criticism of Rousseau's notion of natural man has shown the ambiguity of both its definition and its valuation, but even if it is no longer read as ethnographically and archaeologically accurate or as an ethical model for members of a civil society, it can still be seen as the index of how civilization thought of itself and a compendium of the virtues it would be prepared and equipped to preserve.[30] But the misunderstanding of Rousseau is as much a fact in the history of ideas as is his reasoning well understood.[31] The conventional image of the noble savage, documented in fiction and in what today we call "faction,"[32] acquired the status of extraliterary reality and shaped that reality. When Chateaubriand disavows the noble savage (*Atala*, Weil ed., p. 8), he shares his misreading of Rousseau with his audience; despite his criticism of Rousseau, his depiction of Amerindians both in his fiction and in his memoirs fixes that image and gives it a denser reality than the cliché could otherwise have achieved.

Primitivism, however, that state of potentiality preceding the actualization of civil society, is a condition defined not only ontologically and juridically but also ethically and genetically. Asocial man, as Rousseau

[30] Jean Terrasse lists the characteristics of what he calls the *contenu* of the "myth" of natural man in a clear and concise discussion (*Jean-Jacques Rousseau et la quête de l'âge d'or*, pp. 59–60). Cranston characterizes the "man of nature," or "original man," of the *Discours sur l'inégalité* as Rousseau's response to social and political realities of his time, to the ideas of Locke and Hobbes, and to his own life experiences—that is, as criticism conditioned by the world in which Rousseau lived (chap. 15, "On the Origins of Inequality").

[31] Lovejoy believes that "the notion that Rousseau's *Discourse on Inequality* was essentially a glorification of the state of nature, and that its influence tended wholly or chiefly to promote 'primitivism' is one of the most persistent of historical errors." He rectifies this misreading by reference to specific passages in the *Discours* and to its relation to contemporary writings of Hobbes, Diderot, Locke; he also quotes an extended passage of W. A. Dunning, *History of Political Theories*, 3:8–9, to document the persistence and respectability of that misreading (p. 14). Jean Terrasse discusses some of the internal reasons for the multiplicity of readings, since "nature . . . [is] at the same time the collection of historical manifestations of human consciousness and the principle which produces them, and the knowledge of which allows the philosopher to fill in by conjecture the lacunae of history" (p. 69).

[32] Marmontel, whose *Incas* was part of Rousseau's intellectual environment, claims for his work the truth of facts as they were reported by Bartolomé de Las Casas, the authority of a proper ethical stand, and the persuasiveness of a complementary imagination: "It is therefore less the tissue of a fable than the thread of a simple account, of which the entire substance is historical, and to which I have added a few fictions compatible with the truth of facts" (*Les Incas*, pp. xxiv–xxxv).

sometimes conceives of him, is also amoral.[33] His desire cannot meet with judgment or resistance, because it is all directed toward the satisfaction of basic needs for food, shelter, and occasional sexual contact.[34] For the Rousseau of the treatises, sexual contact itself is simple and direct, and since individualization appears only at the moment of socialization, any female is good for any male: only the function of reproduction matters and the complex of social rules governing the proper choice of males is unnecessary Thus Rousseau disposes of the entire charged matter of sexual morality in the early stages of individual or social development, with consequences, as it must happen, for the view of morality in "primitives" as encountered in other climes. Sexual amorality is difficult to imagine: it tends to flip into immorality, into license, for much of the complex of regulations governing the life of social groups revolves around the allocation of sexual partners, and many of its strongest laws (according to Lévi Strauss, precisely those that constitute the foundation of societies and separate culture from nature) detail forbidden pairings.[35]

It is a testimony to the importance of regulations for the proper allocation of partners that in the fiction of the New World, whether written by Europeans or by the first writers of the newly independent nations,

[33] Marc Plattner wrestles with the ethical implications of Rousseau's possible assumption that "natural man is just another animal" (*Rousseau's State of Nature*, pp. 63–64). In his introduction to *Du contrat social*, Ronald Grimsley states that, for Rousseau, primitive man was animallike, nonmoral, happy, innocent, independent (p. 9). Grimsley then follows the logical process by which arose morality as well as the alienation consequent on the development of society as it came to be in Europe. But Rousseau himself explains: "It seems at first that since men in that state [of nature] had among themselves no kind of moral relationships nor any common duties, they could be neither good nor evil and had neither vices nor virtues except insofar as one considers vices in the individual those qualities that can harm his survival and virtues those that foster it" (*Discours sur l'inégalité*, p. 152).

[34] "L'homme sauvage" desires only food, woman, and rest; he fears hunger and pain; he knows no death, having neither prescience nor memory (*Discours sur l'inégalité*, p. 143).

[35] One of the intriguing aspects of Rousseau's discussion of the relation between sexual morality and social organization is his separation of the natural function of procreation from the social institution of marriage. In the *Second discours* he quotes a long passage from Locke's *Second Treatise of Government* (1619), which argues for the "naturalness" of the institution of the family (chap. 7, sec. 79–80). Rousseau objects that in the state of nature a male is not aware of either conception or gestation, that neither male nor female need be aware of the connection between cohabitation and gestation; forming a family is a consequence of choice, conditioned by freedom, not natural necessity (*Discours sur l'inégalité*, pp. 214–18). For Lévi-Strauss's discussion of the relation between the incest taboo and the origin of culture, see *Les structures élémentaires de la parenté*, p. 9.

these regulations, whose absence had been one of the more dramatic traits of Rousseau's characterization of the state of nature, became pivotal points in the formulation of national consciousness. The fiction of the New World almost invariably touches on the problems of either incest or extreme exogamy (in marriages between original inhabitants of the Americas and European settlers and conquerors), as if it were mapping the boundaries of a definition of culture. On one hand, it tries out the extremes of primitivism and decadence which touch in the theme of incest, the act that affirms the absence of marriage rules; on the other hand, it posits extreme cases of exogamy, which mark the possibility of association with what appears as an absolute other, a partner who shares with the European protagonist only those traits defined as independent of cultural condition, as "natural." The incest plot questions the morality of conquest by charging the conquering culture with a breach of rules fundamental to its very classification as a culture, before matters such as its right to action and its superiority are even raised. The exogamy plot touches on the process of conquest, raising the possibility that European mastery of the New World is conditioned upon the embedding of the conqueror in the conquered and the blurring of a difference that affirms European identity and should continuously signal and validate conquest.

From the beginning, the discourse of sexuality had been part of the discourse about the New World, and when he informs his readers of the correlation between the state of savagery, on one hand, and early puberty and strong sexuality, on the other, Rousseau picks up on information given by various travelers as well as following the logic of his own argument about the characteristics of "savages."[36] Like his assertion that sexual behavior in the state of nature is indiscriminate, his discussion of the sexuality of savages not only contributes an alluring color to the depiction of conditions in the New World, whence he takes most of his examples, but also defines its dangers for civilization, civility, and morality, which are based on the regulation of the libido and on the proper distribution of females.

Living for and by the satisfaction of simple desires coterminal with each individual's existence, man in Rousseau's state of nature has no memory and no history. His world begins anew at every dawn, and he is never separated from the needs and pleasures of one day by the

[36] Book 4 of *Emile* discusses sexuality in adolescence and in primitive peoples; see especially pp. 251, 247, 249.

memory or fear of another.[37] Like the implications of his thought in terms of the marriage plot, this savage ahistoricity can be made into a New World asset, but the assertion of value is seldom made upon a negation. As it developed in the New World, the choice was not whether to value the presence or the absence of history but which of two different histories to value. Just as Rousseau selected aspects of New World ethnography to validate his theories, so the New World selected aspects of Rousseau's theories to validate its self-definition and fabricate an identity and a history with bits and pieces of what was considered important in the metropoles, like Frankenstein fabricating a new man.

Since, like Rousseau, the New World saw itself as creating a new society and a new citizen for it, his works provided a manual and also an argument about what underlies the task. *Du contrat social* and *Emile* posit that society and man-in-society cannot be taken for granted: in searching for their origin, Rousseau also makes them subject to choice and thus contingent. Julie's and Emile's gardens result, by definition, from a return to nature by man formed within an alienating society. Like Defoe's island, Rousseau's gardens are the product of a salvage operation, a bricolage with bits of European civilization saved from shipwreck. For Rousseau too, nature does not in the end suffice as a fundamental value: in place of Robinson's Bible, he inserts in *Emile* the "Creed of the Savoyard Priest," the metasystem of beliefs that originate the moral certainty upon which he plants his garden. And thus Emile is prepared to become not a man in the state of nature but "nature as reconstructed by a rational being."[38] Emile is removed from society and history so he can occupy his rightful place in society and fulfill the historical obligations of his class as landowner and head of a family; his separation from history leads to his retrieval of authentic time and an authentic self.

One can see how Rousseau's transformation of the received discourse of the New World became useful when the New World prepared to establish a willed identity in the space between redemptive nature and productive civilization. Just as Rousseau furnished arguments for different political systems, he also furnished grounds for different and con-

---

[37] Baczko sees this animallike existence as another side of the new sensibility Rousseau introduces, a matter of psychological, rather than social or historical alienation (pp. 13–14). This may be, as Baczko himself suggests further on (p. 19)—an insight shaped as much by the circumstances of that critic's situation as by the thought he analyzes.
[38] The observation is that of Ingrid Kislink, whose view of these gardens differs from mine. See "Le symbolisme du jardin," p. 330.

tradictory approaches to the topics through which self-definition was sought. He returned the gift of the New World vocabulary enhanced in fiction, philosophy, and political science. In the forests of the New World, for instance, to seek man removed from history was to perfect Emile with Indians, whose ahistoricity did not have to be artificially induced, who did not have to be removed from society since they could be—and often were—defined as presocial. The figure of a noble savage, regardless of its fidelity to the Rousseauean concept, could be used to paint an American native most agreeable to European fantasies of Eden recovered and the golden age reconstructed. Some of his virtues— fidelity to friend, vengefulness to foe, capacity for constant love—were completely out of character for Rousseau's natural man, since they defined social relationships, but in the fiction of the New World, they combined freely and even necessarily with the more properly "natural" virtues of endurance, strength, and familiarity with the forest, which could also be read in Rousseau. The combination melded in fictional inhabitants of the New World the best qualities of unspoiled nature and a renewed social man. In this guise of examples of virtue and redemption defined by and external to European civilization the Amerindians of early New World literature came to function as a metonymy for all the positively characterized inhabitants of the colonies and to represent the possibility of creating there a redeemed society.

At the same time, Rousseau can account for the new nations' continued intervention in the original garden. The *Discours sur l'inégalité* implies the presence of an unnamed power lurking in the interstices of a discourse that purports to be entirely about neutral nature. Not only does Rousseau claim that he cannot imagine an unmediated process for the acquisition of language, the indispensable instrument for socialization (p. 151),[39] but he also introduces a telltale passive voice at the very point where he first proposes pity, or compassion, as the basis upon which it becomes possible to leap from the absolute freedom (resulting from the absence of desire) of natural man to the social organization that permits the creation of civilization. Compassion, he says, "was given" to man (p. 154) to soften the ferocity of self-interest which would have permitted neither the propinquity necessary for the formation of a society nor the more benevolent feelings toward others which he saw as the only positive justification for social life. The passive voice intro-

---

[39] At this point Rousseau gives up on part of the problem of language and invites others to decide whether it or socialization came first.

duces an unnamed actor into the impersonal field of rational discourse, an agent into the process of natural development. Although the primitives that for Rousseau exemplify man without society are specifically defined not as properly natural but only as closer to nature than the Europeans who study them, conquer them, and use them as examples, it is still logically necessary to posit an intervention by some more socially developed entity (in *Emile*, the tutor) before these natural men are able to reach full socialization. The passage is not necessarily a happy one. In fact, Rousseau sees the intermediary stage as particularly unhappy, a state in which a new system of uncontrollable and unquenchable desires is overlaid on an older, though primitive, contentment. It is very much like the state in which Chateaubriand shows Chactas of *Atala*, and it constitutes one possible justification for the construction of political entities on the substratum of a "natural" landscape and population of the Americas.

The "noble savage" as a shorthand for the ideal of the virtuous primitive persists in modern characterizations of early modern authors, shorn of its more complicated connotations and formed into a systematic and culture-bound misreading of Rousseau. Roy Harvey Pearce and George D. Painter title chapters of their studies of Cooper and Chateaubriand by that name, characterizing the national subject matter of the former and buttressing the authority of the latter. Nevertheless, a "correction" of this misreading would falsify, if not Rousseau's thought, then the common references to it. Rousseau speaks of the savages with nostalgia and values them positively; that he promises an even higher value for the restored naturalness of the ideal society was safely disregarded by those who used his terms to create a system of oppositions fundamental to the discourse of the New World.

The vocabulary-generating force of Rousseau's hypotheses defied the contradictions of his premises.[40] The mysterious capacity for socialization of his natural man, which permits the essential shift from the state of nature to that of society,[41] generated a space for the fiction of new

---

[40] In a somewhat different context, Baczko notes that history took charge of some of the meanings of Rousseau's work (p. 50).

[41] *Pitié*, or the capacity to put oneself in another's place, is the positive form of a basis for social relationships; it is a given. *Amour-propre*, or the undue preoccupation with the opinions of others, is the negative or corrupt form of attention to others. Rousseau opposes it to *amour de soi*, self-respect, which could be said to mark independence from the other. Charvet opposes it to *pitié* itself and considers this opposition one more of the essential contradictions at the root of Rousseau's idea of man's capacity for social life (pp. 12, 17–19). Charvet thinks these contradictions invalidate Rousseau's

polities. The indeterminacy in the definition of the man of nature provided a semantic space where a natural New World opposed and redeemed denatured Europe, and promised to cure, within society, society's ills. Thus the positive valuation Rousseau attributes to his imprecisely defined man of nature created, together with a denotative vocabulary, one of values. By marking the primitive as desirable and the worth of the social as, at best, doubtful, Rousseau opened the possibility for a positive valuation of the foundations on which the new American nations built their civil societies; but he also provided terms in which the new nations could couch their necessary attempt to leave the state of nature and, as fully constituted societies, claim the right to participate in the political, cultural, and economic affairs of a world economy of goods and ideas.

Rousseau's concept of natural man gives theoretical and philosophical density to the factual accounts of the early voyagers but places the peoples of the New World in the intellectual service of European thought. At the same time, natural man, without history or language, without society or desire, invites crowds of qualities into these empty conceptual spaces. A traditional iconography of New World inhabitants draws up his features and adornments; the ancients contribute civic virtues, and natural man, transformed into the noble savage, becomes also a starting point from which the discourse on origins questions European political institutions and allows power and morality to be seen as no longer "natural," as created and modifiable by human will.[42] And thus natural man travels back from the New to the Old World.

Rousseau's effect on an already established discourse on origins, history, power, and the limits of desire becomes clearer as one considers another well-received work that became the model for a treatment of the New World in its own time. Marmontel's influential book *Les Incas* recounted the conquest of Peru as tragic history. His Incas are as noble a people as were the ancient Romans. Theirs is a developed and reasonable society, whose institutions, though imperfect, are open to improvement by a virtuous representative of Christianity, a European aristocrat by birth and character. The civil war that erupts among the Incas just

---

thought, but they could also be seen as generating various forms of social and literary discourse, from autobiography to satire.

[42] Baczko notes the subversive character of the question about origins: "Whatever version it appears in, the search for 'origins' is equivalent to a call into question" of that which is taken for granted, whether in principles of government, justification for the distribution of power, or a definition of human nature which would explain them (pp. 61, 62–64).

at the time of the European invasion and the presence of bandits, rogues, and religious fanatics among the invading Spanish precipitate the tragedy of conquest and destroy the opportunity for mutual redemption by allowing the worst sort of European tyranny to replace the best of American indigenous civilizations.[43] But for Marmontel the tragic conflict does not pit nature against civilization; on the contrary, it exposes the breach that necessarily splits civilization—not savagery—into a virtuous and an evil side. The play of oppositions takes place within the field of civil society, which contains all recognizably human life. But the reformist impulse of Les Incas was abandoned, and despite its initial success, Marmontel's did not become the model for a fiction of the New World, which structured itself not around an opposition between good and evil within civil society but around the opposition between the social and the extra-or pre-social, characteristic of a criticism of society based on a meditation about origins. The return to origins implicitly promises regeneration, but the concept of the original flickers on the limits of the imaginable. The New World, then, furnished the images in which that concept could become conceivable, and the fiction that resulted from that use put the concept in motion and explored the consequences of the opposition between the cultural and the natural and the demands placed by culture on nature.

[43] Les Incas is dedicated to the king of Sweden and introduced with a diatribe against fanaticism in general and Spanish atrocities in particular, as described by Las Casas; it thus indirectly attributes errors in civilizing savages to the improper distribution of power among European states, which assigned the New World to an incompetent civilizer. That he does not doubt the appropriateness of the civilizing effort itself can be seen in his assertion, through an epigraph by Fénélon, that men should be led toward God and king by a "gentle persuasion," and in his definition of the Indians as "weak" and, in a Rousseauean turn, "without desires, almost without needs" (pp. xiv, xvi–xxii).

4

Love in Exotic Places: Bernardin de Saint-Pierre's *Paul et Virginie*

In Rousseau's philosophical novel and treatises the role of the exotic is marginal in two senses: though it grounds the argument, it is presented as incidental to it, and though it marks the boundaries of the solidly European, it is not seen as affected by the European. This marginality is significant because it shows that the exotic had become acclimated in European discourse; it was no longer so strange that it had to be given full attention when it appeared. But the exotic did not stay at the margins; it returned to the center in two of the most widely read European fictions of the turn of the nineteenth century, Jacques Henri Bernardin de Saint-Pierre's *Paul et Virginie* and René de Chateaubriand's *Atala*. These novels translate some of the political, ethical, and philosophical questions Rousseau addressed into the language of fiction and turn Rousseau's dramas of the intellect into tales of passion. But this exoticism, once more revisited, had once more changed. The two novelists continued the work of synthesis which made of the exotic a language in which to couch burning contemporary questions about a "normative," nonexotic self and society. Yet these novels exemplify the process through which New World strangeness, after it had guaranteed the universality of European writing, became available to found a writing of American difference. The two novels fashion a European language with which the New World could refer to itself as both different and legible.

Like Rousseau's works, these novels address origins and the formation of a new, counter-European society, but they displace them to exotic
surroundings that function as sites of experimentation. They compress
their preoccupations into terms of contact between difference, expressed in marriage plots whose weight overwhelms other plot elements; though both novels lead to an impasse, they became prototypes
of the love story in their time and thus placed the exotic at the center
of an important European cultural development. Both novels transplant
European history into the New World and, while sounding as if they
were not conditioned by history, absorb the historical events of colonization. Both are constructed as a vacation from history; both end tragically; both reveal the impossibility of leaving behind the cultural
baggage that prompted the choice of their exotic settings; both Europe-
anize the exotic and in the same gesture make it available for American use.

Paul et Virginie and *Atala* use the exotic New World as a setting, but
their operation naturalizes the exotic just as Rousseau had when he
used examples from the New World as a familiar language about difference. Offering the familiar in the guise of the exotic, the novels were
embraced with the kind of furor accompanying the modern marketing
of such cultural products as *Star Wars* or *Batman* (the movies), with
theme lampshades and coffee cups, with massive sales of engravings
that show drowning Virginie and dead Atala, and with the appearance
of a slew of novels and plays about the primitive, the naive, and the
exotic, transplanted back to Europe.[1]

Both Chateaubriand and Bernardin de Saint-Pierre held public office;
Bernardin was a scientist and director of the Paris Botanical Gardens.
Their writing was as firmly in line with their official patrons' sentiments
as with those of a vast public. Their fictional discourse came to be seen
as representative of their period; their characters became public models

[1] Hinrich Hudde tracks the progeny of *Paul et Virginie* both in Europe and in the
United States, mentioning, among the better-known followers of Bernardin de Saint-
Pierre, Chateaubriand, Balzac, Flaubert, both Dumases, and Poe (*Bernardin de Saint-
Pierre*, pp. 167–90). Jean-Marie Goulemot sketches out the publishing history of the
novel, noting that even if the number of editions was not exceptional (twenty-one
between 1788 and 1795), its diffusion was: there were not only Parisian but also many
provincial editions, a number of foreign editions, expensive illustrated editions and
cheap popular ones, expurgated editions for the use of children, and special Catholic
editions ("L'histoire littéraire en question," pp. 208–9). He also mentions the appearance of Virginie haircuts and of dinner plates and fire screens decorated with scenes
from the novel. Like Cooper's novels, *Paul et Virginie* was eventually consigned to the
shelves of children's literature.

of sentiment and behavior. Tearful sentimentality and *mal du siècle* are shorthand for the moods of the late eighteenth and early nineteenth centuries as well as for *Paul et Virginie* and *René* or *Atala*. Inasmuch as these works were set in a New World yet to be fully spoken by the discourse of fiction, however, they had the dual destiny of creating language appropriate for what Europe felt about itself, and for what Europeans saw as America. In turn the strength of this European discourse of the exotic also made it into a support and a challenge for American writers in search of cultural autonomy and a definition of national consciousness. In a curious reversal, then, *Paul et Virginie* and *Atala* suddenly became, as in Edmond and Jules de Goncourt's complaint, the epitomes of that romanticism which, like a "foreign" growth, invaded Europe,[2] and in which the otherness on the farther shore of the Atlantic became part of a canonical European discourse of alienation.

Paul et Virginie is set not in the Americas but on an island in the Indian Ocean. Its exotic setting is so carefully rendered, however, that it becomes a model of the detailed description of nature that will later be recognized as characteristic of a romanticism of the exotic. The felt accuracy of this description serves as a guarantee for the truthfulness of the plot, and yet the description is transposable. Despite his attention to local detail, Bernardin de Saint-Pierre's Indian Ocean comes to signify a generic tropical exoticism and to stand for all "empty" ultramarine worlds, untouched by what is implicitly defined as civilization. Its factuality, at least in the popular imagination, is both demonstrated and reinforced by such phenomena as the Paul and Virginie Room in the Musée d'outre mer in Paris.[3] It is extraordinary, in effect, how insistently this novel, whose announced historical content is much lower than that of any other fiction of the exotic under consideration here, is read as a

[2] See Hudde, pp. 109–12 for a discussion of the exotic component of French romanticism. Affonso Arinos de Mello Franco mounts an extended argument to show the effect of information about Brazilian Indians not only on Rousseau's theories but also on the political ideas and historical events of the French Revolution (*O Indio brasileiro e a Revolução francesa*). His book belongs in a long line of works that affirm the validity of American civilization by showing cultural influences crossing the Atlantic in both directions. American efforts to assert this mutuality are as characteristic as European denial of or hostility to the idea.

[3] For a description of this room, see Hudde, p. 108. Many of the essays Jean-Michel Racault has collected in *Etudes sur "Paul et Virginie"* take it as given that the novel accurately represents the island of Mauritius and makes the island known and valued in "world literature." Raymond Hein researches all the facts about the sinking of the actual ship on which Virginie was traveling back to her island home (*Le naufrage du St. Géran*).

history; it is as if a historical component were so necessary to such a fiction that it is added if it is not there originally.

The novel's argument tests out the possibility of building a new society free of specific, clearly identified European evils, and part of its analysis and implied recommendations are based on ideas proposed in Rousseau's *Emile*. Bernardin de Saint-Pierre, however, modifies Rousseau's proposal and makes it appear more extreme, while actually restoring it to a traditional image framework entirely acceptable even to a public distrustful of the philosopher's innovations. Bernardin transposes the experimental garden to an island, emphasizing the theme of isolation and retreat from society which Rousseau had intended to be temporary; he also removes the tutor, so that the task of educating the two young protagonists falls to nature alone, and he transfers from plot to narration the problem raised by positing a willed interference in the organization of society. Finally, he doubles the pupil into male and female, brought up together in innocence and according to the same principles, in a direct reference to the myth of the Garden of Eden, a part of creation neither made nor chosen by human will or reason. The island setting replicates Columbus's New World discoveries, both the island of the first landfall and the pear-shaped paradisiacal nipple afloat somewhere in the Caribbean (*Diários*, pp. 143–45); it appeals to the comfort of the now-familiar exotic, while taking advantage of the freedom granted by the strangeness that still defines it. Bernardin creates a new society to correct his own; the novelty he propounds, however, is at the same time guaranteed and mooted by the estrangement implicit in its setting.

The initial situation of *Paul et Virginie* is schematic. Two young women come to a tropical island. One is wellborn and rich but has been disowned for marrying a poor commoner; to make a fortune commensurate with her name, the young husband takes to the seas, and like so many adventurers of the great European expansion, he perishes. The other woman is a poor commoner who has been seduced and abandoned by a young aristocrat. Both women are pregnant. Both had attempted to marry outside their class, and both attempts were socially nonviable. In both cases the reader's sympathy is invoked for these marriages between unequals. For the women, the island is a refuge, the potential site of an alternative society, where "their children, happier than they, would enjoy at the same time, and far from the prejudices of Europe, the pleasures of love and the happiness that comes with equality" (p. 16). The women of *Paul et Virginie* escape from European power relations inscribed in class and gender codes. Their experience encourages the assumption that their new society will evolve a new code, built on a utopian impulse to demand justice, produce pleasure, invite love, and create happiness which fuels the novel and is part of its legitimating force. Another part of that force, however, is the reinscription of those codes in the new society. Both parts operate in the development of a literature of exoticism.

Slowly, *Paul et Virginie* frustrates its initial reformist impulse in ways that indicate ambivalence less about its viability than about its legitimacy. The consequences of that first removal of inequality, as well as its final reinstatement, attest to the difficulty of imagining a true, even a better, other to the cultural self under criticism. The society Bernardin imagines for the women on the island differs in essential ways from that which had caused their unhappiness. Their community is insulated from corrupting exchanges with the outside world, and this defensive isolation from the beginning casts doubt on the desirability of the exchanges from which the story originates. The community is also both matriarchal and asexual, eliminating, together with the males who would make acceptable mates for its ruling women, the possibility of sexual exchange even within the enclosure.[4] The two women are happy, however, removed from the social scrutiny that in *Emile* was one important source of alienation from the authentic self: the women "did not desire to have, in the outside world, a vain reputation that intrigue could grant them and calumny could take away from them. It was enough for them to be their own witnesses and judges" (p. 40). Their isolation is said to make them "more human" rather than "more savage," the two extremes conditioned not by social but by psychological factors (p. 42). Because on the island the women are no longer subject to the social scrutiny that enforces social rules, their transgressions cease to exist; the strictures that had unjustly defined them as deviant, are dismissed as arbitrary. In their isolation, the women and their chil-

---

[4] Marie-Claire Vallois reads the novel entirely in relation to contemporary French politics and culture and thus as part of a concerted effort to contain the power of women unleashed during the French Revolution. She discusses what happens to Virginie as an exotic and feminine other, restrained and contained through the novel by the force of a male self, just as the women of the Revolution were restrained by the Napoleonic Code ("Exotic Femininity and the Rights of Man," pp. 183–86). She does not quite fold into her argument the restraining role of Virginie's mother or the fate of Paul; she implies that the women were in fact among savages (p. 182). But in showing how tightly the text is interwoven with French culture, Vallois also indirectly indicates how carefully an adaptation to the former colonies' aims would have to navigate among its implications.

dren are subject only to nature, and the exotic, which is the nature of the island, becomes associated with fundamental, that is, natural values, opposed to the social, the oppressive, the nonnatural. But with sexuality the women also ban that element which the social order finds it most important to control. Matriarchal and classless, the community on the island is an experiment in a new form of social organization which corrects European shortcomings and excesses by restricting its semantic universe, rather than by modifying its grammar. As the consequences of these restrictions on relationship work themselves into the plot, they are shown to jeopardize the creation of the new meanings promised in the novel's first statements purpose and, finally, to question the viability of the new society both in the present and in a projected future.

In the details of Bernardin de Saint-Pierre's island garden reside those ingrained habits of thought which are taken for natural and which pierce even the most radical construction of alternatives; they indicate how this discourse of the New World arises in the interplay between new and old, in the space between model and opposition. The setting, for instance, in a natural enclosure brings into play the long tradition of gardens in the Western imagination; but the differences between Bernardin de Saint-Pierre's picture of Mauritius and the traditional representations of Eden indicate this novel's role in the creation of an exotic, alternative world. Bernardin refers directly to Eden (pp. 66–67), but he also redefines paradisiacal innocence, and the redefinition comes to play an important role in the discourse of the exotic. When he shows the two young people conversing, "at first, like brother and sister," he is not refiguring Genesis but prefiguring the virtue of sensibility and *mal du siècle;* when innocence is lost, it is not by disobedience to a father or murder of a sibling but by the presence of a perpetually deferred sexuality tinged with incest.[5] His construction of paradise, as Joachim Schulze notes, echoes Milton's, with its two numinously charged trees at the

[5] Jean-Michel Racault fits the novel into the popular eighteenth-century genre of the pastoral, noting its similarities to Marmontel's *Annette et Lubin,* which tells of the innocent love between a shepherd and a shepherdess who are cousins; she gets pregnant and cannot understand why everyone is so shocked and why the church prohibits their excessively consanguineous marriage; in the end they are granted a dispensation and live happily ever after ("Pastorale et roman dans *Paul et Virginie,*" in *Etudes,* ed. Racault, pp. 180–81). The differences, however, some of which Racault mentions, are important also: they show that on the formal level the fiction of the exotic adapts popular genres to its own purposes and that on the thematic level it treats matters too problematic for easy resolution by decree from a recognized authority.

center, as well as the restored garden paradise of *La nouvelle Héloïse*.[6]
But the addition of incest and social meliorism to the ancient gardens
opens them to the treatment of marriage and origin in terms of the
exotic and assimilates the exotic to a tradition with legitimating powers.

With these adaptations, unexamined assumptions invade the ideal
space. Though his novel society is ideal in being classless, Bernardin
de Saint-Pierre does not risk charging his wellborn heroine, or even her
humbler friend, with servile occupations; he assigns them a slave for
the practical details of survival in nature, such as planting edible crops,
channeling the waterways, terracing the mountain. When he is old
enough, Paul, the former servant's child, helps out, but only by introducing and caring for ornamental plants that carry affective meanings,
such as the flowers that symbolize Virginie: "Paul had embellished what
the Negro Dominique could but cultivate" (p. 42). We are thus left not
only with a separation of classes and occupations but also with the
"naturalization" of slavery and the reintroduction of the superfluous,
which Rousseau abhorred but which Bernardin depicts as the proper
sphere of the gentleman. Slowly, as we watch, the valley becomes less
of an alternative to the society that writes it.

The history of the valley and its small society is told at two removes;
the narrator tells the story he heard from an old man after the valley
had already been destroyed and its inhabitants were dead or dispersed.
The narrator, who keeps silent after the initial question that elicits the
tale, represents a decadent Europe, and he has much to learn from the
old man, an inhabitant of the island, who knows that paradise was
destroyed because it could not absorb the intrusion of history and civilization (Vasanti Heerallal, "Ouverture et cloture," p. 88). The reader
knows from the initial description of two ruined huts that the attempted
paradise did not survive and that only the power of writing can bring
it to life, that it exists only at the moment of reading, as an imaginary—
or a theoretical—construct. We know, then, from the beginning that the
enclosure where Paul and Virginie grew up in innocence was breached.
Innocence and enclosure play on images of the New World as paradise,
existing in pure time before it too was propelled into history. But two
modifications of the pattern are significant: first, that its inhabitants are

[6] Joachim Schulze, "Das Paradies auf dem Berge," p. 126. Schulze (p. 130) notes that
Paul and Virginie are compared to Adam and Eve before the Fall (*Paul et Virginie*,
p. 80) and also calls attention to Pierre Trahard's edition of the novel, which makes
reference to the garden in *La nouvelle Héloïse* (pt. 4, letters 11 and 17), as well as to
Les jardins, a didactic poem by Jacques Delille.

refugees from Europe whose innocence is not original but recovered and, second, in an odd displacement of responsibility, that a fugitive slave is the first intruder. When the children leave the enclosure to take the slave back to the plantation she had fled (their "natural" upbringing prompting them to respect property rights), they become aware of the injustices of colonization in other parts of their island, the cruelty of the exploitation of land and person upon which it is based, and the historical face of their own garden. Outside the valley, in the world of colonization, it is symbolically appropriate that the two children of nature are no longer fed and sheltered unproblematically by the land itself. Hungry and thirsty only a few feet from a fruit tree and a spring, they have to be rescued by a sortie from the valley. And thus ends their first contact with the rest of the world.

A visit from the governor of the island to inspect their settlement breaches their enclosure in a different way, indicating that their paradise can exist only insofar as it is sanctioned by the customary authorities. Though the novel treats these contacts as marginal to the argument, absorbed like a stone by a lake, it implies that the continuation of the idyllic life of the valley depends on the tolerance—or protection—of an external power aligned with the authority of history, not nature. On the margins of the tale, these contacts draw the boundaries of the two women's experiment and redraw cultural limits they had set out to exceed. The intrusions underscore, in addition to the valley's isolation, its fragility, on sufferance from other forms of colonization and finally at the mercy of the society around it.

But the problematic nature of the alternative society in the valley is clearest and its frailty in concept and execution is most evident when the absence that grounds it, rather than the authority that surrounds it, begins to insist on representation. Bernardin de Saint-Pierre can permit sexuality in his paradise only in characters who are excluded as carriers of culture, such as the slave and his wife, or he can allow carriers of culture to fulfill the function culturally ascribed to the sexuality of women—which is to produce and nurture children—while barring them from sexual expression. Just as the visits from the authorities draw the boundaries of the experiment from the outside, sexuality recalls the participants from inside the physical confines of the valley. Rousseau makes explicit provision for Emile's sexual development, offering information, exercise, and a wife at the appropriate times and acknowledging the role that controlled sexuality plays in the organization and preservation of societies (book 4); but Bernardin de Saint-Pierre tries to suppress the sexual, deflecting it into the perception of the landscape or the intensity of the relationship between Paul and Virginie.[7]

The crisis in the novel arrives when the sexual development of the two children reestablishes an explosive relation between time and history, held in abeyance during their childhood. The valley had attempted, almost successfully, to exist outside history, but the tale cannot evade time, since its argument is the development of two children who eventually must leave childhood, seen as asexual and therefore timeless, and come to the age when they can contribute to the physical succession of generations. At that moment the valley opens up to both culture and history, which ideally it had existed to oppose.

In particular, Virginie's maturation marks not only the beginning of her individuation but also the end of the paradisiacal state. It is presented as a dramatic event that shakes up the moral and causal presuppositions till then grounding the action. Full of vague fears and longings, uncomfortable in her skin, the adolescent Virginie goes to her mother, who, instead of enlightening her about what Rousseau might have recognized as the "natural" development of her body, recommends prayer.[8] Still restless, the girl goes to bathe in "her" fountain. As the cool water soothes her hot limbs, a fearful storm breaks over the valley, mixing earth and waters, tearing up trees, destroying terraces, sweeping away the work done in the time of the children's innocence, and returning the valley to a pre-Edenic state of chaos.[9]

Rousseau had correlated corrupting civilization with early puberty (*Emile*, book 4), and while praising the innocent ignorance that allows even physically mature rustic youths to play familiarly together without thought of sex, he is quite conscious that the capacity to generate chil-

---

[7] Hudde speaks of the "uterus- . . . like character of the space" the women occupy on the island (p. 41). Though his main argument tends in a different direction, Clifton Cherpak notes that the two women, "especially Mme de la Tour . . . prevent Paul and Virginie from living a natural life of work and sexuality," without, however, considering the cultural component of all definitions of what is "natural" ("*Paul et Virginie* and the Myths of Death," p. 251).

[8] Despite Rousseau's open references to and pedagogical interest in the sexual maturation of Emile, however, no parallel care is taken with the development of his assigned ideal mate, Sophie, who is left to sort out the vicissitudes of her maturation by means of an ethicoliterary infatuation with Fénélon's *Télémaque*.

[9] In all gardens, of course, including that of Eden, nature has already undergone at least one instance of mediation by culture; the reference to any garden as "natural" is by definition self-contradictory. Ingrid Kislink notes that the Elysée, Julie's garden in *La nouvelle Héloïse*, "represents nature as reconstructed by a rational being" (p. 330); it does not institute an opposition between nature and culture but is "a place where nature and culture . . . unite to form a harmonious whole" (p. 354).

dren introduces a child into the social world from which an educational garden could insulate him. Consequently, unlike the adult characters in *Paul et Virginie,* Rousseau provides for the onset of puberty in his pupil, determining that he be told the details of the "facts of life" by the age of nine (and if not, that they be kept from him until he is precisely sixteen). The tutor does not, as has been pointed out, try to make of Emile a pure child of nature (now in another sense of *pure*) but only to make sure that, prepared for life in civil society, he would not be deprived by a faulty, alienating upbringing of the advantages and virtues that had been enjoyed by humans in the hypothetical time, described in the *Discours sur l'inégalité,* before they banded together in a society that would regulate their impulses, including their sexuality.

Bernardin de Saint-Pierre modifies his master's scheme in two important ways: he posits the valley as the realm of nature rather than a controlled environment where the elements of civilization are introduced in a rational sequence for a certain end, and he adds the theme of fraternal love between the children. They nurse from both mothers, as if either could have given birth to either child; they sleep in the same bed, innocent as puppies. This very stress on their innocence, however, prepares the introduction of the incest motif, defined simply by contiguity, since the children are not in any way consanguineous; incest, then, overlies the theme of class exogamy of which they are the products and whose value and legitimacy their marriage would confirm. Thus Bernardin de Saint-Pierre endows their story with a double dose of prurience which is allowed fullest course and made even spicier by the continuous insistence of the text on the purity of the two young people, that is, their ignorance of both the sexual and the social taboo. Hinrich Hudde attributes a good part of the novel's popularity to an almost willful misreading, which concentrates on the "topos of an innocent, naive love, conditioned solely by nature," while it is perfectly aware of the "clear erotic representation of sexuality wrapped in the garments of a love between children" (p. 227).[10] One can note also that Virginie's "difficulties," as Schulze discreetly puts it (p. 132), marking the point where the perpetuation of the society in the valley becomes biologically possible, foreground the sexual, which had remained implicit between the children or been excluded for the mothers, and directly link the sexual and the social. It is when the children, whose existence and

---

[10] Hudde also calls attention to various bowdlerizations of *Paul et Virginie,* indirect proof that the public is quite aware of the novel's erotic, even "decadent" content (pp. 228–29).

whose presence in the valley are a consequence of the social evaluation of their mothers' choices of partner, come themselves to the point of possible choice that the valley is revealed as representing not nature but the establishment of culture. This redefinition changes the import of the first part of the tale, which now appears to deny sexuality itself rather than the taboos that an unjust society places on it or the arbitrary directions into which that society tries to force it.

Trapped between the denial imposed on the mothers and the immaturity to which it is condemned in their children, charged like the original inhabitants of the New World with representing the natural, an innocent sexuality appears as an obstacle to the establishment of the ideal society, rather than its vivifying principle. Moreover, insofar as "the natural" is identified with the New World, with its physical as well as its human landscape, the very promise of radical reconstruction of European society which is its principal ideological attraction is invalidated, hollowed out when the work of culture is obliterated as soon as it has to confront the forces from which it derives its redemptive charge, when the natural is revealed not as the redeemer but as the opponent of the cultural.

Incest appears under two guises in *Paul et Virginie*. In the first part, it is one of the possibilities of sexual combination in a presocial world where it could not yet have become taboo and culture forming; at the close, it is a sign of the decadence of a culture, of the end of a civilization (Hudde, p. 223). But the theme of incest in *Paul et Virginie* also stands in opposition to the socially exogamous marriages of the two mothers, their difficult attempt to wed difference. Such an oscillation between the poles of extreme endogamy and extreme exogamy, with their respective promises and perils, is one of the important legacies of *Paul et Virginie* to the New World literature of national consciousness. The positions taken regarding these perils and promises are often characteristic elements in the different literatures, correlating with ideologically important premises about the relation between colonizers and colony or colonized, between nature and culture, myth and history. They determine the definition of difference from the metropoles and play semantic games with the socially based notion of legitimacy.

The coincidence between the havoc in the elements and the sexual maturity of the two young people has further implications. The children do not quite know what is happening to them, but their mothers do. For Virginie's mother the change in the children produces a change in attitude: she who had tried to flee the bonds of class and property becomes, as she is of the higher class, the guardian of female virtue by which class and property are preserved and transmitted.[11] Previously, she has been content to do without money, status, and manners (defined as an artificial overlay on natural acts), the value-laden markers of distance from the natural immediately invoked in any discussion of social woman's (or man's) principled flight from the state of society. Suddenly, however, when Virginie reaches puberty, she decides that her daughter cannot marry the companion of her childhood because, of all things, he would not have enough money to keep her. The moral sanction for this strange preoccupation with money, than which nothing would have seemed less necessary in the enchanted valley, materializes with the arrival of a missionary carrying news of Virginie's inheritance: "God be praised! You are now rich" (p. 87). So it is determined that Virginie will be educated in the ways of the world at its center, Paris, and off she sails to claim her "place." That place is not the island refuge of the women and children who had been made unhappy in society but that same society, to be conquered by learning the languages of money, manners, and history.

The destruction of the valley makes it seem as if the world of nature itself were expelling Virginie. Like the writers of the first accounts of the New World, Bernardine de Saint-Pierre cannot conceive of the sexual as natural. The sexual must express itself in culture; it is a necessity that becomes indisputable, whose denial is unimaginable, if it is presented in terms of the sexuality of women. Thus it is Virginie who must leave the island. The novel, however, unwilling to abandon the dream of a new beginning, remains there. And as it continues to write the unlettered island, it makes Virginie introduce into the plot both the control of sexuality and the theme of writing in the form of letters from civilization. One of these offers, among expression of the girl's unhappiness, the trope of the inversion of values by which Paris becomes a "land of savages" (p. 97) and even a sketch of the recurrent theme of classical comedy, the unsuccessful wooing of the young heroine by an old suitor. The two themes identify Virginie, on one hand, with the clear-eyed New World critic of the decadent Old World and, on the other, with an even more traditional character in a characteristic Old World genre of social criticism.

Meanwhile, under the guidance of our narrator's informant, Paul too

[11] Ingrid Kislink remarks on the change in Mme de la Tour and its importance for the continuity of the valley community but describes it in moral terms as a "lack of sincerity" (p. 366).

is forcibly educated into civilization. While Virginie writes, he is advised to read. Reading, writing, history had been banned from the valley: "Never had useless sciences caused their tears to flow; never had the lessons of a sad morality filled them with boredom" (pp. 18–19). Now, however, Paul must read history and geography, which disgust him; fashionable novels, whose morality horrifies him; and also Fénélon's *Télémaque* and novels about the states of the soul, where he finds a model for behavior and the means to express the consciousness of self newly imposed on him by the shattering of his childhood world. Unlike Emile, whose book learning comes at a point when all his other abilities and experiences have prepared him to establish a critical distance beteen himself and the society of which they speak, Paul is made unhappy by these newly acquired lights, with which he prepares himself to be worthy of a finished and polished Virginie (p. 116).

But the intrusion of European civilized values is not limited just to the sudden necessity for literacy, history, and intellectual unhappiness on the island. With her letters, Virginie sends packets of French seeds and invades the very realm of nature. The flowers she sends are full of the meanings of European gardens and do not thrive in the valley, despite Paul's care. They languish, but they also displace the original flora and daub the valley with the worst of both worlds. Thus, reading and gardening, Paul prepares himself for the return of a sophisticated Virginie for whom the simplicity of their upbringing, initially presented to him and to the readers as sufficient for the renewal of society, is no longer enough. Bernardin de Saint-Pierre forces Paul to participate in the artificiality of Virginie's cruel and alienating Parisian education, as if he were not convinced, finally, that a truly human life is possible without Paris. And the reading, which takes too much of Paul's time and makes him miserable but with which he turns himself into a fit companion for the new Virginie, keeps him from the work that would assure their subsistence in the garden. In short, this part of the novel buries the arcadian vision of the New World and invalidates its image as Eden, as a place where the curse on work does not apply—a remission naturalized overtly by all the early reports on the bounty the New World awards to those who seek it and covertly by the slaves who produce that bounty, also noted in early reports of New World settlements.

Bernardin de Saint-Pierre handles the categories of nature and culture deftly, successively estranging and refamiliarizing emotions and activities in one or the other of them. Thus he rescues from the alienation Rousseau had diagnosed and decried the European project of domesticating the part of the world it had assigned to the realm of nature. The pleasure of shaping a garden, that innocent place between nature and culture, "naturalizes" the transformation of nature into culture. In other matters, however, the attempt to reconcile nature and culture runs into its own internal contradictions, evident in the choices and exclusions it must effect. The language in which the events are told is necessarily that of a culture, but the various relays through which they reach us veil the cultural foundation through translation, first from pure event into ordered narrative, operated by the old man who tells the story to the novel's narrator, and then from oral to written narrative, as the narrator transforms the tale into the novel we hold. The relays distance the audience from the event, but the chosen language neutralizes the distance, erasing the boundary between myth and history. First Bernardin refers us to a myth of origin sufficiently familiar not to call attention to itself, whose timeless terms are the circular garden, the innocence of two children, the bounty of trees and rain, the waters that make it fertile. At the same time, he writes the language of history, as in his re-creation of origins, of the point in the development of societies when an error—not a sin—crept in and skewed what should have been progress and enlightenment. The story thus blurs any distinctions between its references to myth and to history as it locates the origin of that error in a New World that occupied in European consciousness the place where nature, myth, culture, history—and fiction—separated themselves into distinct entities from a seeming unity.

Though criticism can point out these opposing terms of myth and history, culture and nature, work and pleasure, error and innocence as they appear in the creation of the island garden and in the development of its inhabitants, however, Bernardin de Saint-Pierre attempts to force the reading of his island as an instance of harmony and purity by avoiding the articulation of such terms as the Fall, sensuality, money, or redemption, whose presence denies island innocence but also mediates between that innocence and readerly experience. Silencing these oppositions still present in the text seems a costless way to avoid the perception of conflict and disharmony in a society invented to escape them. In effect, however, as with the silence on slavery, this absence makes it impossible to imagine survival in the terms in which the story is organized.

For instance, part of the novel's charm lies in its successful combination of myth and science—that emerging modern discourse of power over nature—embodied in the careful, precise botanical account of the

Garden of Eden, with the implied promise to actualize in a geographically identifiable locality the delights thought lost in an irrecoverable
past. But another part lies in the guarantee of nonactualization, which
is also a guarantee against disproof, introduced by the author with the
fault he places in the system: Virginie's puberty. Nature beckons with a
promise of abolishing alienating social rules, but the biological fact of
puberty carries along with it all the rules governing the exchange of
sexual partners and, implicitly, the transmission of culture. Up to that
point the myth of paradise is sufficient for the continuity and interest
of the tale, masking, because it is a structure so habitual, the mediating
role it plays between culture and nature. But that story, too, breaks up
at the irruption of sexuality, at the introduction, with the notion of
successive generations, of historical time. When the myth of paradise
explodes, the need for mediators, previously denied in the interest of
wholeness, becomes inescapable. At precisely that point money appears
in the valley, with Virginie's inheritance, perceived as good not only by
the governor of the island but also by Virginie's mother, Mme de la
Tour. Then books make their appearance too, presenting the continuity
of human culture in the form of history and the codification of human
social behavior in the form of manners.[12]

At this juncture in the progress of the love between the two young
people the tale shows again how difficult it is to write a human society
according to rules different from those that make the writing possible,
even if, according to the system of values expressed in the narration,
those rules are destructive. The attempt to imagine a "natural" coupling
abuts against two limit situations: either it brings to light the ultimate
meaning of absorption into nature, which is the loss of what makes the
characters human, and also implies the loss of identity and consciousness with which to tell the tale of a return to nature; or it leads not to
the absence of culture but to the rupture of necessary constraints, to
its destruction in the breach of the incest taboo, the brother-sister relationship between Paul and Virginie having been instituted as fundamental to the establishment of a paradise on the tropical island.

Virginie's return to marry Paul and to replicate on the island the
fundamental rules of the society from which it was to be a refuge threatens the validity of the definition of paradise established in the first part
of the tale as well as the fundamental rule against incest on which social

[12] Vallois shows that the irruption of letters is more literal still, inscriptions being
engraved directly on the natural world (p. 193). I shall return to this motif in the
next chapter.

life is based. Rather than allow that, Bernardin de Saint-Pierre sacrifices his protagonists. As Virginie's ship approaches the island, a terrible storm arises. In her long white dress, she stands on deck and looks up to heaven for help, refusing a sailor's offer to swim with her to shore if only she will disencumber herself of some of her garments. She'd rather die than dive naked into the elements, than divest herself of the dress that, by covering them, signifies taboo areas of the body and sanctions its division into public and private, social and natural. Virginie's refusal just to take off her dress and be saved like a sensible girl may seem overwrought,[13] but her shame signals the introduction of the social into nature, the consciousness of the eyes of the other upon the self, the need for the rupture that is a sign of the human.

This revelation of a deadly contradiction within the exotic troubles the novel's otherwise more cheerful approach to exoticism, its specific intention to create a fictional language capable of doing justice to the reality of unknown landscapes. In *Voyage à l'Ile de France*, Bernardin criticizes other travelers (I might mention Columbus) for their ineptitude at describing landscapes: they are too general; their mountains have nothing but foot, sides, and summit; there is no word about the specific shapes of those sides, their caves, their slopes, their rounded forms.[14] These foot-sides-summit descriptions are enough, of course, to recall mountains already known to the reader through a literary tradition in which the sketchiest indications suffice to evoke the appropriate images and meanings, but the mountains of Bernardin's tropical islands are as yet meaningless, and his rivals are simply preempting the emergence of a system of significations when they write in conventional signs, while the New World, a potentiality crying for actualization, needs these new systems. Bernardin's strategy, befitting a naturalist, is to use his botanical observations of the natural world of the tropics to create a general but precisely denotative vocabulary, which carries the sign of scientific truth and accuracy while documenting the unknown. His descriptions thus become a way of making the unfamiliar familiar while impressing readers with the accuracy and authenticity of his discourse on the unknown, so that critics can praise the fidelity with which

[13] Madelyn Gutwirth is not the only one to call that "apogee" of Virginie's life "ludicrous." She sees its uncritical presentation and enthusiastic reception as indications that it responds to some otherwise unspoken but fundamental bases of common belief, specifically, that female power must be contained ("The Engulfed Beloved," pp. 215, 216).

[14] See Bernardin de Saint-Pierre, *Voyage à l'Ile de France*, p. 254, cited by Wilhelm Lusch, in *Chateaubriand in seinem Verhältnis zu Bernardin de Saint-Pierre*, p. 153.

he describes something they have never seen. Thus he contributes to making the exotic into one of the available categories of common discourse.

But *Paul et Virginie* also functions as a modern novel of sensibility; it uses exoticism to express a contemporary, entirely nonexotic cultural condition. With delightful and tearful pathos the novel reaffirms social rules and reassures readers with its unacknowledged punishment for an unmentioned transgression. The delicacy of Virginie, her long, white, flowing robes, her birds and flowers, her semifraternal relationship with Paul—innocence veined with passion, the iridescence of incest offering forbidden fruit in the purest language—and finally the deaths at the end of the novel follow and modify European literary fashion and serve European needs. The incest theme, for instance, allows for a peculiar negation of sexuality: games between siblings must not be sensual, which means that they are not, in fact, sensual; the desire for innocence becomes a denial of sensuality which, in turn, opposes the ruleless sensuality of natural man, that which would be found at the end of the constant search for origins in which the century engaged.

The play on the limits of incest (forbidden endogamy) and marriage with the alien humanity that inhabits the other shore of the Atlantic (feared exogamy, which promises both conquest and dissolution) appeared first in the literature about the New World and then in the literatures of the New World as questions about the definition and valuation of the newly constituted nations as hybrid or alien. More immediately, however, the attention to botanical detail and the doomed love plot of the novel ground the exotic in scientific observation and wrap it in fictional cliché, containing it and limiting it on all sides like the liqueur in a bonbon. In the process, the tropical landscape becomes more than just decoration. An integral part of the meaning, it refers to the search for renewal which is an important element in the culture where the novel originates, and it brings into a fictional discourse received as attuned to the demands of the time, the possibilities opened for it in the New World. But it also shows the limits of the imagination confronted with a new world to be spoken in realistic terms. The scientific description of fauna, flora, and geology places these novels of the New World between the purely imaginary utopias to which the discoveries had given rise and the travel literature that, at least officially, concerned itself with the truth about the new lands.

Like the philosophical discourse of Rousseau, these fictions about the

New World naturalized its otherness. They made the exotic familiar and created a necessary language in which to speak of it, but at the same time, they robbed the new of the unfamiliarity that till then had been part of its attraction and its meaning. On their exotic island, Paul and Virginie promise that upon such as they a new society can be built. In their new world the ills of the old, its class divisions, its use of and devotion to money and possessions, and its education that distorts children for life in a distorted world can be corrected. At the same time, however, the exoticism of the island shades over into a primitivism that, through the incest theme, casts doubt on whether a new society built on these premises can be an alternative form of culture at all or simply the negation of culture. The determination of the plot by the irruptions into the valley of sexuality, class, money, and reading indicates that the specific forms of resource distribution in a society—its kinship systems, its social structure, its manners and morals draw the limits of their members' imagination, of what is speakable and thinkable within it, at least within discourse sufficiently disseminable to be able to modify its forms of thinking and speaking. It is a paradox expressed when eighteenth-century morality destroys the valley that promises it moral regeneration: however else, in decency, could a young woman have behaved?

Paul et Virginie is a European elegy for the possibility of establishing a renewed culture in an empty New World. Unfolding, as one critic has put it, from the suggestion of a pastoral at the beginning, it "modulates slowly into a triumphal funeral march celebrating the removal of the inevitable human corruption from a clean, green world" (Cherpak, p. 254). In this respect, it comes to express precisely the opposite mood from that which the New World deems appropriate to its own writing, while it also legitimates a literature about the not yet civilized. It is, in fact, this legitimation of the primitive as a proper subject for mainstream literature that becomes the heritage of the novel. As Hudde shows, its successors are set wherever the primitive is thought to be found—in the wilds of Scotland or in the inaccessible mountains of Switzerland (pp. 167, 105). In other words, though the novel makes it appropriate to value the primitive and to write of it and thus becomes a precursor of novels where the primitive is home rather than the exotic, it also demands that novels which are at home in the exotic operate a transvaluation; their task is to convince readers that the clean, green world can blossom into societies existing on their own terms and not in need of a Parisian education to cleanse their riches. Theirs is also the task of grafting onto new institutions the *Lumières* that had saddened Paul and, conversely, to introduce their writing into the history books whose accounts had made Paul unhappy. They could not, nevertheless, without cutting themselves off from their public, dismiss the happy valleys or invent another language of the plants and animals to be found there, for fear those strange shapes, colors, and sizes of the natural world would immediately overwhelm the senses and frustrate the public's imagination.

Once again, Marmontel's *Incas* offers an instructive contrast to the text under study, for it focuses directly on the work of Europe in the New World. *Paul et Virginie* is simply set on a tropical island; the valley is essentially a tabula rasa, where any form of social organization could in principle be set up and which in fact abuts on other, negatively valued new settlements. *Les Incas* however, by acknowledging the presence of the other in the conquered land, can deal with the moral problems of settlement. Bernardin de Saint-Pierre posits a new form of social and moral organization but is incapable of imagining one that does not either include or just directly oppose what he and his public know as the particular civilization of a decadent Europe in need of rehabilitation, which they take for granted as signifying civilization in general. But in *Les Incas* the civilization of Europe is given another chance on its own terms. Amerindians are assimilated to figures of a European past defined as politically, ethically, and socially—but not technically and religiously—superior to that of contemporary Europe. Yet for Marmontel the peopling of America is strictly a chapter in the moral and political history of Europe, and if he sees the new lands as offering redemption, he is under no illusion about the frailty of the chance, nor is he desirous of making that opportunity into a flight from European history or a negation of European civilization. He thus writes a political and historical drama to serve as a tool of reason in its war against fanaticism and against the darkening of the intellect by the subordination of religion to greed and to the lust for power. His appeal did not go unheard. Both Rousseau and Bernardin de Saint-Pierre mention *Les Incas* as a moral benchmark. But their own writings take an entirely different road, and theirs, not Marmontel's writings, became seminal in the formation of a discourse of the New World by the New World. Their probes of the "states of the soul," as in the books that Paul finally learned to enjoy, became dominant. Set in the New World, their works legitimated the use of the New World and made it possible for American successors to appropriate these "states of the soul" for a national exotic self. They presented American writers with the double challenge of reconquering the territory they had covered, recreating the people they had turned into exempla, and reshaping the language in which their lands had been spoken.

5

Chateaubriand's *Atala*
and the Ready-Made Exotic

Rousseau used the exotic as a background, not to be questioned or fully noticed but to enhance the foreground. Bernardin de Saint-Pierre foregrounded the exotic, only to reabsorb it into the familiar. René de Chateaubriand, however, in his most popular fictions, *Atala* and *René*, gives the exotic the status of a subject, seeming to speak for its own self. His New World exoticism addresses its European public directly and appropriates the language of the exotic for its own discourse of the self; Chateaubriand's interest legitimates this appropriation, but in lending his voice to the exotic other, Chateaubriand necessarily subjects that address to his own inflections and turns exotic discourse into a discourse of the exotic.

Chateaubriand too compiles his exotic characters from existing texts, and his too is a discourse of power over the exotic, but in asserting this power, his fictions open the definition of the exotic to challenge. By building his work, as Gilbert Chinard has shown, on the exotic, Chateaubriand legitimates American material and makes it available for literature that is both serious and widely disseminated; he popularizes a version of the Americas which will at the same time encourage and constrain its domestic construction by the Americas. The thought and plot structures of his "American" works also establish models for a literature of cultural identity by foregrounding the definition and role of history, the inscription of the signs of the self on a formless other, and the opposition between incest and marriage plots.

121

Chateaubriand's work is not much read these days, rejected in the light of our greater knowledge of, or different attitude toward, some of the subjects of his fictions.[1] His work has been marginalized in the great rereading of French literature by psychoanalytic, structuralist, and deconstructionist critics.[2] For decades now his books have encountered most of their public through truncated school editions.[3] As texts for young people, they are invested less by the culturally determined signs of "great literature" than by a pedagogical intent more likely to invite rebellion and rejection than revaluation. Yet Chateaubriand's novels on exotic America are instances of the role played by European discourse in an American bid for voice and power, presiding like a mask of Janus over the autochthonization of European culture across the Atlantic.

Chateaubriand had in himself the cultural authority to shape the image of exotics—American and others—on both shores of the ocean. Part of that authority was biographical: a member of the aristocracy, he lost family and friends to the Terror, fought in the counterrevolutionary wars, and after hard years of exile in England, returned to parlay the huge success of *Atala* into public office under Napoleon's patronage.[4]

[1] Edward Said, for instance, is very annoyed by Chateaubriand's account of the "Orient" but acknowledges his importance in creating an image of the Near East for the European imagination. He also claims that Chateaubriand helped create the image of the romantic writer in particular, and of Middle Eastern civilization in general (*Orientalism*, pp. 172–75).

[2] He is neither entirely ignored nor widely glossed. In the preface to Chateaubriand's *Vie de Rancé*, Roland Barthes discusses only the aging genius, omitting any reference to the young literary revolutionary ("La voyageuse de nuit"). Pierre Barbéris applies the newer critical tools to readings of *René, Atala, Les Natchez* (*René de Chateaubriand; A la recherche de l'écriture;* and *Chateaubriand*). Chateaubriand, however, did not undergo the rescue operation performed, for instance, on Sade or Poe. A revision may now be under way, by an approach unlikely to have pleased him—feminist historicism, which sees his early works as part of a postrevolutionary construction (and repression) of femininity. See, for instance, Naomi Schor, *Breaking the Chain: Women, Theory, and French Realist Fiction,* and the articles by Schor, Gutwirth, Vallois, and Waller in *Rebel Daughters*. Waller distinguishes between *Atala*, which she sees as a cautionary characterization of the feminine, objectifying and distancing, and *René*, seen as inviting identification with the male. All see these texts—and *Paul et Virginie*—only as they function in postrevolutionary French culture.

[3] Richard Schwitzer, for instance, bemoans the "fate of *Atala* as a beginning French reading text" whose effects at that level can be "disastrous" (*Chateaubriand*, p. 90). Barbéris proposes that the "taming of the text" by "scholarization" and by cutting selected passages effectively counteracts the ideological danger of a "free and savage reading of the text" (*René de Chateaubriand*, pp. 15, 19–20); in this reading Chateaubriand is sufficiently subversive of the nineteenth century for acceptance in the canons of the late twentieth.

[4] Margaret Waller finds that the prescriptions and implications of *René, Atala*, and the volume from which they were excerpted, *Le génie du christianisme*, fit in precisely with

He saw himself as a combination of Samuel de Champlain, Pierre Charlevoix, and (later) Napoleon, defending France and Christianity in exotic places. Combatant and exile, political maverick and literary innovator, he was both outsider and representative.[5]

Another part of his authority came from his works, which stand at the foundation of French romanticism; they make exoticism into the language of the romantic interest in rupture, desire, nature, and the self and provide continuity with the past greatness of French voyagers and travel writers, with Rousseau's meditations on the primitive and on the sources of political power, and with Bernardin de Saint-Pierre's literature of sensibility.[6] His *René* replaces Werther's German crags with the forests of the New World, where it cries out the boundless longing and desire, the alienation and ennui the *mal du siècle*. For a time Chateaubriand was, as he says of Shakespeare, one who "invent[s] words and names that increase the general vocabulary of men," one whose "fictional characters become real" (*Essai*, p. 138).[7] René and Atala escape the mediation of texts; they seem permeable and congruous with the extratextual. The combination of permeability of the text and cultural authority of the author allowed Chateaubriand's view of the Americas to impose itself on the New World and direct its literary experience.

Chateaubriand used previous discourse about the New World for a

---

Napoleon's plans to turn back the French Revolution (p. 158–59); Naomi Schor says that *"Atala* helped pave the way for the Napoleonic Code, first promulgated in 1804" ("Triste amérique," p. 144); there is a precise fit between Chateaubriand and his time.
[5] Chateaubriand's energetic life and multiple loves have inspired many biographies and his voluminous autobiographical writings are another endless source of information (or disinformation) about his life. I refer most often to George D. Painter, *Chateaubriand: A Biography,* which covers the period up to the publication of *Atala* and seems accurate on the facts.
[6] The introduction to one collection of excerpts from Chateaubriand's works begins by stating flatly that "Chateaubriand is more or less unanimously considered the founder of French romantic literature," as if it were merely repeating undisputed facts (Emile Faguet, Introduction to Chateaubriand, *Atala, René, Le dernier Abencérage.*) Intertextuality between *Atala* and *Paul et Virginie* is also taken for granted. See, for instance, the essays in Sara Melzer and Leslie Rabine's collection *Rebel Daughters.*
[7] This wording appears in the extended section on Shakespeare in the *Essai sur la littérature anglaise* (pp. 124–38) and is repeated in *Mémoires d'outre tombe* (1:504). One should also note Chateaubriand's contribution to the view of Shakespeare as a naive genius: "Fortunately, he knew almost nothing, and escaped, through his ignorance, some of the infections of his century" (*Essai*, p. 108). Chateaubriand's view of an innocent Shakespeare (such innocence more likely in a British than in a French genius, the British being less civilized than the French) mirrors his creation of Chactas as a savage of the Enlightenment, and shows his consistent attribution of value to what, in either system of significations, occupies the slot of the exotic.

revolution in French literature and gave to the familiar the newly important prestige of the new. The overall authority of his writing legitimated the American elements it encodes and readied them in turn for use in an American discourse about the Americas. After the political rupture of independence, New World writers found in Chateaubriand autochthonous material as part of an authorizing European discourse that itself carried the marks of innovation and rupture with the past. Recent criticism has accused Chateaubriand of complicity with his times. I do not dispute it: it is not clear that anyone can escape such complicity. I contend, however, that Chateaubriand presented his works as innovative and, to an extent, oppositional and that they were so accepted by his readers. At the inception of French Romanticism, Chateaubriand's writing, according to Pierre Barbéris, "constitutes a rupture with received texts" (*René de Chateaubriand*, p. 11); as it became influential, however, and generated other texts, rupture itself became canonical and a mark of value, a condition for the acceptance of a text as culturally significant.[8] But the rupture is tame, since Chateaubriand breaks with literary tradition in works that bid to restore the traditions broken by the Revolution and to garner their author a government appointment.

Still, by privileging exoticism and geographic displacement as formal signs of rupture, Chateaubriand set other worlds, more particularly the New World, at the center of contemporary European literary life and imagination. He made exoticism into the thematic basis for a literary, fictional discourse on otherness, alienation, and origins. This use of the exotic, at once serving rupture and preservation, encoded the reaction to—or recovery from—the French Revolution in a simultaneous absorption and rejection of the ideas considered responsible for its eruption and its violence. The choice of the New World as a worthy theme of European discourse encouraged the use of the exotic by American writers engaged in consolidating their own revolutions and formulating their own cultural worth and identity; there Chateaubriand gained authority by challenging literary traditions, for in legitimating a discourse of the other, he made such a discourse available to the other who breaks

---

[8] In *Mémoires d'outre tombe* Chateaubriand shows an ex post facto consciousness of his role in the development of the romantic sensibility: "In me there began, with the so-called romantic school, a revolution within French literature. . . . when I . . . read fragments of the *Natchez*, of *Atala*, of *René* [to Fontanes], . . . he could not associate these writings with the commonly accepted rules of criticism, but he felt that he was stepping into a new world, that he saw a new nature" (1:482).

away from Europe to assert itself as a self. In effect, the significance of the Old World in the self-perception and self-definition of the New, the determination of the value of the non-European experience for either Europeans or Americans, the varying definitions of the boundaries between nature and culture, the role of Christianity in opposition to variously conceived and evaluated forms of paganism—all these are successfully and legibly formulated in Chateaubriand's works.

As has been seen in the works of Rousseau and Bernardin de Saint-Pierre, by the middle of the eighteenth century, the Americas were no longer identified simply by a catalog of parrots, cannibalism, and naked women, by justifications of conquest and conversion in a discourse of otherness and its domination; they had become available as proof, illustration, and ornamentation of European fictional, philosophical, and political argument. For Montaigne and Rousseau, notions of the Amerindians are integral to the analysis and criticism of European society, common and proven knowledge in need of no special documentation, true in general, if surprising in detail. Still exotic, exoticism had become familiar. Chateaubriand accelerated this familiarization while also reestranging it. His inscription of the New World follows the accounts of early explorers and missionaries and applies Rousseau's theoretical constructs in ways unexpected by the philosopher.[9] It also expresses the newer European concepts of the primitive: the Mississippi Delta becomes a psychological refuge, a place for the expression of passions, rather than for political or philosophical freedom.

Knowledge about the New World had been available to Chateaubriand from his childhood: his father's fortune was based on New World trade (possibly in slaves), and his father's library held the writings of missionaries, traders, and explorers (Painter, p. 135). His friend old Chrétien de Malesherbes, a sponsor of Rousseau and Bernardin de Saint-Pierre and an enthusiast of the Americas, instructed him in his garden of acclimated tropical plants and encouraged him to cross the ocean to find the Northwest Passage. In *Mémoires d'outre tombe*, Chateaubriand claims to have taken quite seriously the idea of beoming an explorer: "If successful, I would have had the honor of imposing French names upon unknown regions, providing my country with a colony on the Pacific coast, taking the lucrative fur trade away from a rival power,

[9] One can imagine Rousseau's astonishment at seeing his ideas incorporated into the constitutions of new American nations, instead of guiding the polities of old Corsica and Poland, just as one can imagine Marx's at seeing a dictatorship of the proletariat installed where there was no history of industrialization like that of Western Europe.

and opening a shorter way to the Indies, controlled by France" (1:287). Thus, when he sailed, Chateaubriand saw in the New World a haven from prerevolutionary France, an opportunity to reaffirm French imperial interests overseas, an occasion to verify Rousseau and Bernardin, recover the adventure of earlier times, assist in the spread of Christianity, and research a novel about the Natchez rebellion with which to make his name in French letters.

This explicit cross-referencing between life and letters is characteristic of Chateaubriand's method of mythmaking. He intended his explorations to be translated directly into glory for himself and for France as he dreamed it; his victories would be neither military nor commercial but spiritual and literary.[10] Thus he read about the Natchez in Guillaume Raynal's book, then voyaged down the Ohio, and finally referred to John Bartram in order to complete the description of the trip and validate the insertion of his own fiction about the Natchez rebellion. The written and the lived validate each other. At the same time the sign of the exotic becomes almost autonomous; the exotic is lifted from its own context and decomposed into individual birds, plants, customs, tribes that may appear anywhere on a map of the New World, each sufficient to call up all the others.

But Chateaubriand himself does not propose this autonomy of the representative sign; he insists on its congruence with the experience of the signified and informs his readers that *Atala* is accurate, since it was written "under the huts of the savages" and since even American readers, who could have said "these are not our rivers, our mountains, our forests" (p. 22), accept its truth.[11] His information as well as his protestations were in fact found convincing across the Atlantic, where Francis Parkman, for instance, classed him among historians (Lombard, "Chateaubriand's American Reception," p. 224). Yet the documentary strength of Chateaubriand's writings on the exotic arises less from their accuracy than from their congruence with what is already known.[12]

---

[10] The elaboration of the myth of Captain Cook, as documented by Gananath Obeyesekere in *The Apotheosis of James Cook,* provides an interesting contrast; the "practical" became enshrined, in the wake of English economic success; Chateaubriand's way faded before it, particularly in the consciousness of the English-speaking world. It is all the more interesting to find the traces of Chateaubriand's discursive strategies in the American literatures of nationality, boosted by an overt privileging of the "cultural" which sometimes hid and sometimes displaced the operations of the "practical."

[11] Unless otherwise noted, citations of *Atala* refer to the Weil edition.

[12] Not all reviewers thought his account accurate. An anonymous review article in the *American Quarterly Review* states that, though Chateaubriand "is evidently willing to

Thus, although Chateaubriand's savage does not accord with Rousseau's theoretical construct of natural man, his Indian protagonists absorb the popular definitions of savage nobility and function as referents to non-European humanity. The reader of Chateaubriand's day found in *Atala, René,* and *Les Natchez* "real world" examples of Rousseau's theoretical natural men, even though Chateaubriand explicitly disavows that figure in his preface to *Atala* and claims to find raw nature ugly (p. 8). The demurral seems more than a little odd made by an author identified with a literature of exotic, primitive nature: in a characteristic double message, Chateaubriand indicates both the origin of his images and the transformation he operates on them; he has turned a sign of opposition to European civilization into one of integration between the exotic and its consumers and has reassured his readers that it is possible to enjoy otherness without engaging in it.

But Chateaubriand also normalizes the strangeness of the New World landscape by assimilating it to the well-defined cultural difference of a primitivism that stands at the origin of the contemporary and civilized: he presents primitives as ancestors and refers ancestry to classical antiquity. He knew the literature of paradise and golden ages lost and the more recent European recovery of its own primitives. He had translated *Paradise Lost* into French, and one of his friends had translated the Ossian poems.[13] Asserting their continuity, he tried to be both modern man and bard: on the tedious Atlantic crossing, he welcomed the excitement of a serious storm by lashing himself to the mast and reciting Homer to the waves, and he whiled away a stop on the island of Saint Pierre by shouting lines from James Macpherson's Ossian epics at the sea from atop a lonely rock.

Chateaubriand's travels in America exist in the flattering twilight between asserted fact and acknowledged fiction, presented in a discursive

---

have it thought, that he had lived long, and traveled much in our wilderness, and among our Indians . . . this cannot be. His descriptions of scenery in Atala and the Natchez, are thoroughly false." Still, the critic praises *Atala* because "the imagery, the feelings, the language, are borrowed from a state of nature" and because it "takes human nature . . . one step higher in its moral history [than *Paul et Virginie* had], and precisely at that point, where the first blending of the influences of society with savage life produces that development of the feelings and passions, which is, perhaps, the most favorable for poetry and fiction." At the end the article invokes classical Greek literature as a yardstick for this writing of the New World, inasmuch as it too was in that liminal state "which gave us the Iliad" ("Works of Chateaubriand," pp. 460, 471).

[13] In the Furnes edition the *Essai sur la littérature anglaise* is followed by the original English and Chateaubriand's prose translation of Milton's epic.

mode in which the ideological component promises to reveal the truth and in which the boundaries between the read and the lived are blurred.[14] Though he tells the trip at least twice, in *Voyage en Amérique* and again in *Mémoires d'outre tombe*, his precise itinerary is still a matter of conjecture and the accuracy of his reporting, a cause of controversy. We know that he avoided the cities, centers of the administrative and intellectual life of the new republic he professed to admire.[15] He did not, when he had a chance, examine what its vaunted civic virtue had achieved; instead, he set off with a guide and two bearskins in the direction of Niagara Falls and then with traders down the Ohio. The rest is vague but exotic; eventually he headed back to the East Coast.[16]

[14] Many studies document Chateaubriand's borrowings; Joseph Bédier's, one of the earliest, concludes that Chateaubriand never set foot in the region where he places the action of *Atala* (*Etudes critiques*, pp. 125–294). Gilbert Chinard finds the sources of Chateaubriand's America in his early readings of Raynal and the missionaries he wanted to imitate, and also in the fiction of exoticism popular at the time, particularly *Paul et Virginie*, credited with introducing into French literature a "modern form of exoticism" to which *Atala* became one of the most notable contributions (*L'exoticisme américain*, p. vi). Armand Weil identifies various passages borrowed from travel literature, including works by Gilbert Imley, Jonathan Carver, Pierre Charlevoix, and John Bartram, the last probably furnishing the name of the Indian hero of *Atala* (Introduction to Chateaubriand, *Atala*, pp. lxix–lxxxiv). Christian Bazin finds the written antecedents of Chateaubriand's America in travel literature; in Marmontel's *Incas*, Voltaire's *Zaire*, Bernardin's *Paul et Virginie*; and in works now completely forgotten, such as *Odéralis: Histoire américaine, contenent une peinture fidelle des habitans de l'interieur de l'Amérique*, an anonymous romance published in Paris in 1795, or Nicolas de la Dixmérie, *Azakia: Anecdotes huronnes* (1765) (*Chateaubriand en Amérique*, pp. 186–87). Chateaubriand did not invent his materials or even pioneer the use of his subjects; he restructured them, making them newly readable.
[15] In *Mémoires d'outre tombe* Chateaubriand is relatively kind to the cities he visited, though significantly he complains not only about materialism and inequality but also about the lack of "monuments" in Philadelphia (1:278). As Michel Riffaterre argues in "Chateaubriand et le monument imaginaire," Chateaubriand associates "monuments" with history and the legitimation of a polity by its connection with the recorded past; his criticism of the new cities is therefore not just aesthetic but implies a judgment of value and a pronouncement on the legitimacy of the civilization they represent.
[16] In many instances Chateaubriand was more interested in the shape of his story than in the accuracy of its details; so his precise itinerary in the United States has been a matter of controversy. Appendix 14 to *Mémoires d'outre tombe* traces the polemic (1:593–98), and provides one map (p. 597) of the itinerary according to Bédier (p. 145), who has Chateaubriand reaching the towns of Natchez, formerly French, and Cuscowilla in Florida; a second, currently more widely accepted route takes the Ohio River to the Mississippi and returns by way of, say, Louisville. Painter concludes that, though most probably Chateaubriand went to Niagara Falls, the southern portion of his trip is less certain, its descriptions showing many traces of previous writings about the regions he claimed to have visited (pp. 200–214). Throwing up his hands in frustration, Painter summarizes: "His commentators agree that [after leaving Niag-

His itinerary and its vagueness indicate that even if the voyage to America was undertaken to validate the literary through the factual, its most important acts were performed for their symbolic load. With his attempted visit to George Washington, to whom he had brought a letter of introduction, Chateaubriand honored, somewhat perfunctorily, the American embodiment of Roman civic virtue and the promise of a return on the American continent to the values of the European past.[17] His pilgrimage to Niagara honored the untrammeled power of nature.[18] The trip down the Ohio honored, by emulation, the early (French) explorers of the continent. His second recounting of the voyage (*Mémoires d'outre tombe* rearranges and summarizes what had been told in *Voyage en Amérique*) incorporates not only the political, mystical, and historico-geographical facets of his experiences, but also samples of other travel writings: the famous incident in which he plays with the "two Floridians," Indian maidens who appear to him while he is resting on a river island, seems to have been inspired by Bartram (Painter, p. 206); the amusing episode of the little French dancing master fiddling in the forest and teaching a minuet to the savages has a counterpart in the travel account R. G. McWilliams identifies as the Penicault Narrative.[19]

---

ara] he cannot have gone where he says he went, even though they are unable to decide where he *does* say he went, or to find evidence that he went anywhere else." Later he declares: "It must be admitted that at this point his itinerary becomes vague, inexplicit, dreamlike, as he turns from the truth of factual realism to the truth of poetic beauty" (p. 191).

[17] Chateaubriand's visit to Washington, which he describes in *Mémoires d'outre tombe* (1:279), comparing the American president to Cincinnatus, has also been a matter of dispute. The actual letter of introduction Chateaubriand took to Washington, from the marquis de la Rouërie, spent a long time buried in the collections of the New-York Historical Society before it was found by E. K. Armstrong and published in *PMLA* (see *Mémoires*, app. 14, 1:607). From the existence of that letter Painter deduces that Washington did receive Chateaubriand, etiquette pertaining to letters of introduction making it imperative that the carrier should call and be received (p. 177). Chateaubriand makes a great effort to discern Roman traits in the New World city of Philadelphia and its inhabitants (*Mémoires*, 1:278–80).

[18] Niagara was a necessary point of pilgrimage in visits to North America, and as Peter Conrad shows in the introductory chapter of *Imagining America*, it is a kind of Rorschach blot where tourists see their own characters, their own expectations or prejudices about the land and the nation they had come to visit.

[19] *Fleur de Lys and Calumet*, Richebourg Gaillard McWilliams's edition and translation of the Penicault Narrative, includes a spirited account of how French visitors to an Indian village near Mobile played their fiddles, moving the Indians to dance, and then demonstrated a minuet to them (pp. 106–7). The coincidence does not prove that Chateaubriand knew that particular story, but Charlevoix was one of the many writers on French America who used the Penicault manuscript as source material (see McWilliams, Introduction), and Chateaubriand had read Charlevoix.

In this writing and rewriting of America, Chateaubriand further transforms the discourse of American exoticism and reincorporates it in the
imagination and literary language of Europe. The intertextual impulse
of his work is strong enough that, although he rejects Rousseau's concept of the natural man—inasmuch as "the natural man of *Du contrat
social* was unqualified to sign the contract which Rousseau imputes to
him" given the limits of his experience (Shackleton, "Chateaubriand
and the Eighteenth Century," p. 16)—Chateaubriand presents his
younger self as emotionally drawn to "primitives," excited by sharing
night camp with a family of Indians and exchanging greetings with a
true representative of natural man or disappointed and "cruelly humili-
ated," in his quality as a "disciple of Rousseau," at the sight of the
dancing master's hopping pupils (*Mémoires*, pp. 301–3, 291). Chateaubriand fleshes out the philosopher's theoretical construct, validating the
original inhabitants of the Americas by the theory rather than testing
the theory against them. When he leaves unsatisfactory Philadelphia
to sleep on his bearskins under the stars, when he restores the Ohio
to an assumedly original solitude that eliminates the trade that allowed
him to sail it, Chateaubriand abstracts the republic he holds up for
admiration from the historical circumstances of its existence and
charges it with representing in fact what Homer or Macpherson can
offer only as myth or fiction. As Barbéris contends, even in writing the
epic of the Natchez, he fixes the event in a half-mythic past, a recovered
European prehistory reassuringly both familiar and remote.[20]

Filtering his experience of America through his reading, his memory,
and his writing, Chateaubriand forged the image that for at least half
a century shaped the way in which the New World was spoken and
thought of in the general European imagination: its place in the opposition between nature and culture, the sensual freedom marking both its
attractiveness and its distance from true civilization, the relation between its own and European history. To the extent that autochthonous
discourse on the Americas came to participate in the ideological and
linguistic universe of the metropoles, moreover, directed at both sides
of the Atlantic—the one guaranteeing its authenticity and the other its
readability—Chateaubriand's Americas come to ground an American
discourse of America, with its own canon of acceptable forms. His memoirs and his fictions made the exotic comfortingly familiar, ready to be

[20] According to Barbéris (*Chateaubriand: Une réaction*, pp. 63–64), although *Natchez*
mentions French political developments of 1715–1725, its comments can also be read
as relevant to the events of 1789–1792.

appropriated with wonder and tranquillity, as a novelty that does not challenge an accustomed distribution of power. His America was authorized by an extensive literature of exploration and empirically verified in his own voyage across the ocean; it was further authorized by his use of the popularized version of Rousseau's vocabulary as well as his rejection of Rousseau's controversial theories; finally, it was authorized by his membership in the intellectual, social, and political elite of his time. Even more than his image of the Americas, it is this authority that the national literatures of the Americas would strive to appropriate.

Chateaubriand's best-known work and greatest success was *Atala*, published in 1801 as an extract from a promised larger epic, *Les Natchez*, and later incorporated in *Le génie du christianisme*. It was from the beginning a blockbuster, spawning, like *Paul et Virginie*, a lively retail trade in prints, lamp shades, and coffee cups, which commercialized and popularized exoticism. The novel was immediately translated into a number of languages, reprinted abroad (there are American editions as early as 1801), imitated and adapted for the theater; it is still taught in schools.[21]

It tells the story of the Indian maiden Atala and her lover Chactas, whose two tribes are enemies and whose love is doomed by the disorder of savage lives as well as by the imposition of Christian values; by the impulse toward an ambiguously valued fusion of American and European blood and civilization, as well as by a fatal cultural diffusion and displacement. Even more clearly than *Paul et Virginie*, *Atala* develops the thematic clusters of a literature about otherness, the commonplace signs of unequal power relations between cultures: sexual contact, history, the complex concept of nature, and writing.

As in *Paul et Virginie*, the marriage plot in *Atala* fictionalizes contact between members of different cultures and the possibility of establishing a new, synthetic unit in terms that mimic an extreme form of exogamy; it then shadows it with a test of the prohibition against endogamy by adapting the common eighteenth-century interest in sibling incest and opposing the fear of the other with the desire for and the taboo against the same. *Atala* also raises the problem of history in the New World, making its absence, as usual, redeem European misdeeds and ensure European superiority. In a still plausible metaphor, it connects cultural with individual development: without history, Americans—

[21] Weil devotes a long section of his introduction to an account of the multiple direct progeny of *Atala* (*Atala*, pp. xxxi–lxi). For American adaptations and imitations, see Lombard, "Chateaubriand's American Reception," pp. 222–24.

Amerindians or colonists—are like children. The introduction of a school edition of *Atala* explains, with the certainty of ideological assertions, that Chateaubriand is an accurate reporter of the condition of New World populations, "whose semi-childish mentality . . . is in close correspondence with historical truth."[22] The assertion justifies continuing European tutelage, but the text can also, with the common perverseness of texts, invite an American cultural work that reads *Atala* as a record of European desire to flee from history into the American wilderness, valued because it escapes that tutelage.

Finally, *Atala* contains a startling codification of the imposition of signs on that same wilderness whose redemptive value depends on freedom from imposed significations. Its landscape, at first sight, occupies a "natural," neutral, and unmarked slot in opposition to a European culture in search of its complement. This neutral and unmarked landscape, however, is also incommunicable until Europe begins to map, that is, to write, the wilderness. The desire for nature as wilderness is revealed as the desire for the void, for nature as absence, which however must become a plenitude if it is to mark the boundaries of Europeanness. *Atala* and *René* oscillate paradigmatically between the oppositions of nature and culture, myth and history, absence and presence.

Atala approaches the questions of marriage, history, writing in well-established ways; insofar as it shapes discourse, its power derives also from its place in the literary and other politics of its time and place of origin. It is not only an exotic love story but also part of the *Génie du christianisme*, Chateaubriand's proposed contribution to restoring the values of order and Christianity battered by Enlightenment philosophers and revolutionary mobs. Resolutely straddling apologetics and entertainment, *Atala* spices the uplifting with the sensational and, like lobster bisque on a day of abstinence, makes religious duty into sensual pleasure. It presents itself to its wide and varied public as a palatable defense of a civilization indisputably valuable in itself, its boundaries

---

[22] Raymond Bernex, Introduction to *Atala*, p. 11. The introduction discusses Chateaubriand's itinerary and after reviewing the literature, comes to definite conclusions (he did not go down the Mississippi; he did go to Niagara Falls), but it also concludes that the precise facts are not that important. "What really matters is their incantation" (quoted from V. – L. Tapie, *Chateaubriand par lui-même*, 34), contributing to the canonical mix of certainty and inaccuracy which characterizes the purely ideological image of the other. This edition also reprints illustrations from various editions of *Atala*, as well as some of the better-known portraits of Chateaubriand, documenting the popular iconography of the novel and its author.

clearly marked by the surrounding barbarism found both in the paganism of the untouched New World and in the blasphemy of a desacralized Old World.

The story of Atala reaches the reader at the end of a chain of narration that transforms an oral account into written history. The narrator arrests the transmission of tales through generations of non-European protagonists now near extinction and translates it into a book for a growing and increasingly literary public, which still remembers with residual familiarity the credibility and verisimilitude of the spoken word. *Atala* thus operates a transition between an ahistorical America and a Europe of the written word; the scribe in the text witnesses the destruction of the narrating voice and preserves its narrative of the destructive encounter between the written and the oral, the historical and the mythic.

But reversing the ascription of power to Europe and decay to conquered America, the exchange of life stories which composes the tale is also designed to cure the disease of civilization from which the young Frenchman René suffers by integrating him into an Indian tribe. The old Indian Chactas tells René of his life and tragic love. Chateaubriand, in another reversal of values, establishes Chactas's authority by describing him as blind like Homer and Ossian, guided by a young girl as Oedipus was guided by Antigone; he is also partly civilized, having been transported to France as a galley slave; there, he had enjoyed the privileges of an exotic specimen—had met with Louis XIV, heard Jacques Bossuet, spoken with Voltaire, attended performances of tragedies by Racine, and befriended Fénelon.[23] Chactas's story is thus placed in a precise, Western (in this case, French: "Western," like "European," is always metonymic) historical context that counterbalances the American ahistoricity of his origin and the narrative chain that acquaints us with him. He had seen France at one of the recognized high points of its civilization, and the respect accorded him by great Frenchmen makes him respectable. His personal history introduces into the text a brilliant European historical past against which to set the value of the American continuous present, and his success at court allows Chateaubriand to sidestep two ideologically troubling matters: the influence of the American Revolution on French history and the moral standing of a European

---

[23] Weil suggests that the outline of Chactas's history is derived from the story of a Hottentot who was raised in Europe but rejoined his people on the first opportunity, told in a note to Rousseau's *Discours sur l'origine et les fondements de l'inégalité* (Introduction to *Atala*, p. lxxii).

society whose civilizing contact with the hero is made by means of his enslavement.

If pursued, the question of Chactas's enslavement—like that of the slaves on the island and Virginie's Parisian education in *Paul et Virginie*—would threaten the allocation of value between his world and that of the Europeans who displace him, between the powerless, desirable exotic and the empowered civilizer. Chateaubriand's strategy for neutralizing such concrete questions of value is to make Chactas successful in both worlds and to particularize the problem raised while generalizing proposed solutions. Chactas's enslavement appears simply as a surmounted obstacle in his individual biography, but his privileged position in the French court and intellectual world holds out a promise to the exotic in general. His experiences allow the old Indian to walk, as we are told, "on the line . . . between society and nature" (*Atala*, p. 9), opening the two sides to each other. Chactas's first words to René and to the reader are "I see in you the civilized man who has made himself into a savage, you see in me the savage man whom the Great Spirit . . . has desired to civilize." But the sequel to Chactas's statement reintroduces the matter of values into the encounter between Europe and America, placing on the protagonists the burden of an unresolvable ethical problem when Chactas asks: "Who of us two has gained or lost more with this change in position?" (p. 35). This question of valuation undermines the strict position of mediation which the first utterance seems to establish, but it opens the space for Chateaubriand's discourse: it is the space in which arise the strategies for self-valuation in the literatures of the New World, the space of choice, where it is implicitly asserted that civilization and barbarism are not givens but subject to change and to the will. His own discourse becomes possible in the apparent decision between them which inscribes civilization on savagery.

This is Chactas's story. As a young boy, he is orphaned in a war between his own and an enemy tribe: Indian politics occasions the first European interference in Chactas's life and allows Chateaubriand to transpose the customary justification for European interference in the affairs of native populations from the political and ideological to the biographical.[24] The noble Spaniard Lopez rescues Chactas from his enemies, teaches him the language, customs, and religion of the whites,

---

[24] Hulme discusses early colonial European politics of interventions, which justified colonists' suppression of both sides by recasting local rivalries in moral terms (*Colonial Encounters*, pp. 47, 53, 76–77).

and lets him return to the wilderness when, "after having spent thirty moons at St. Augustine, [he] was seized with disgust for the life of the cities" (p. 36). Like his listener René, Chactas has fled civilization in disgust. As soon, however, as the de-savaged Chactas is released into the forest, he is captured by the tribe that had orphaned him, tied up, and judged worthy of sacrifice; he is shown as incompetent in the forest but possessed of a generalized Indian nobility. For the reader, inasmuch as his is the unquestioned nobility of nature and his capture is the act of men-in-nature, the differences between them are neutralized, submerging both tribes in one embracing otherness.

That night there comes to the prisoner the most lovely maiden of the enemy tribe, dressed in a long, flowing white gown, and wearing a small cross around her neck. Atala looks like an Indian Virginie, but her stated function as a "bride of the last night" contradicts and completes her presentation as the prototypical virgin of romantic fiction: the symbol around her neck controls the titillating signs of sensuality with which her (exotic) role invests her, but it also draws the acceptable boundaries of her sensuality by subjecting it to European rules and values. Thus the love between Chactas and Atala is organized as an exotic variation on traditional European marriage plots that consider the possibility of unions between protagonists of different social class, birth, or fortune and solve the problem of difference by invoking the leveling potential of personal merit, chance, or an essential similarity hidden through adverse circumstances. Nevertheless, the cross does not erase the exotic, which opens the plot to additional exploration of the possible relations between different cultures. Once again, the central topos of the encounter between Old and New Worlds is encoded in terms of endogamy and exogamy, but though he goes farther than Bernardin, Chateaubriand too avoids an actual limit case, for the Indianness and the Europeanness of the protagonists are incomplete. Chactas's history and Atala's cross invade an anthropologically justified account of "savage" customs; they reveal the extent to which the documentary claims of the novel are subject to European use. This invasion of the native context also prefigures the development of the lovers' relationship, which becomes problematic only through interference from explicit European, Christian rules that forbid its fulfillment without marriage or from implicit rules that ban marriage between members of different groups. It is important in this sense, as will be shown later, that the education of Chactas by Lopez acquires a quasi-genetic character, touching extreme exogamy with incest, establishing an equivalence between physical and institutional channels for the transmission of cultures, and lending to the taboo separating culture from culture the legitimacy of separating culture from nature. Finally, it is precisely the inconsistency of the lovers' definition as either savage or civilized, as separated either by excessive closeness or excessive distance, that makes *Atala* into a seminal text for encoding both the characteristic and the differentiating traits of national identity in the early literature of nationality.

Chactas and Atala fall in love immediately; she offers to free him and, upon his insistence, to flee with him. They escape through a now-benign forest of melodiously named trees, of water buffaloes rising like river gods from streams where crocodiles bellow, of birds and flowers glittering among the foliage in encyclopedic variety. Like a sampler, their paradisiacal wilderness juxtaposes signs denoting a generalized American state of nature in opposition to societies where the cross, the dress, or—Chactas's Indian captors classified for the novice as an oppressive society—the sacrificial stake constrain individual action and thwart desire.

That juxtaposition of signs constructs the exotic within an unequal power relation: the more powerful language creates the "exotic" as it generalizes differentiating traits, imposes its own familiar values on them, and finally, as a condition of acceptance and intelligibility, negates otherness. When Chateaubriand places a semitropical forest on one side of the Mississippi and a prairie on the other, when his crocodiles produce amber under tamarinds, when he arranges nature in spectacle, rather than with the mimetic accuracy explicitly claimed for the descriptive, "factual" presentation of his material (Bart, "Descriptions of Nature," pp. 83–93, esp. 84), he is exercising the privilege of an external, powerful discourse to make the other into the typical, ready for easy consumption. Differentiating signs become interchangeable; the prairie indicates otherness and Americanness as easily as the Spanish moss or the doeskin-clad Indian. The presence of a number of such signs simply reinforces the common reference without introducing either differentiation or complexity. But this exotic picturesque is simply a delicate, inventive sauce. The meat is in the characterization of Atala, where juxtaposition encodes otherness in a culturally more powerful process of normalization: an Indian maiden, she wears the garb of European iconographic representations of the not-yet-sensual and not-yet-assigned feminine, underscored by an iconographic mark of spirituality, but she appears in the story in the role of a sexual partner assigned by alien custom. As the rules governing sexual behavior are most often explained and understood in terms of what is "natural" (or, conversely, "perverse"), differences in their operation are simple, intuitive markers of otherness. In the figure of Atala, Chateaubriand formulates the definition of otherness in terms of the natural and the sexual but does not make explicit the lines of opposition within these fields. The resulting ambiguity appears even in the description of Atala's expression, a composite of the accepted and the devalued, though desired feminine: "On her face there was something virtuous and passionate . . . an extreme sensibility linked to a deep melancholy" (p. 40). The cross she wears indicates the other's acceptance of identity and value from an external power and presupposes an active acquiescence from a recipient ready to erase part of his or her difference and identity. The sensibility in Atala's expression and her flowing white garments (p. 60), on the other hand, mark the other as essentially familiar, reducing the traits of its difference. Thus otherness is assimilated, and empathy shades into the exercise of power. Any residue is then defined as a deficiency, always imperfectly remedied: as we shall see, Atala makes an imperfect Christian.

The flight of Atala and Chactas continues to encode the difficulty of representing true otherness. The forest seems to replace the constrictive—or fatal—determinations of social groups, Spanish and Indian, with the freedom of nature, but the freedom is qualified by its danger to a "natural" distribution of power. Chactas, a man brought up among Europeans, cannot survive in pure American nature and must rely on Atala, who teaches him to feed, clothe, and find himself in the wilderness. Atala could free Chactas because she was the daughter of the chief; she can teach love and living in nature because she is natural, a daughter of the forest. These attributes elevate her above Chactas, imprisoned, incompetent, contaminated with Europeanness. But the promise that her teaching and her help offer Chactas and, by extension, René, refugees from civilization, dissipates under the constraints Chateaubriand imposes on her.

The lovers' flight through the forest also traces the disturbance of the boundary between the natural and the social occasioned by the encounter with the other. In direct contact with nature unmediated by social organization, the lovers necessarily confront the basic social question of sanctioned behavior toward each other, posed in its most striking aspect, sexuality. Any society encodes the limits on its expression in a complex system of rules, from the fundamental taboo against incest to the positive regulations organizing the choice of a mate. Like Bernardin de Saint-Pierre and the first Europeans, who, confronted with their first naked Amerindians, decided that such marked deviation from a European dress code signified complete sexual availability and therefore the absence of any codes of conduct, Chateaubriand must consider the consequence of life "in nature" on a regulated sexuality seen as the mark of "culture."[25]

In the forest, away from restraining social codes, Chateaubriand's young heroes face the possibility of a moral renewal beyond the corrupting forces of civilization. But their freedom makes him nervous, and after a few pages Chateaubriand finds it necessary to reinstitute restraints to the free operation of their passions. His unease is not only psychological but also ideological. Inasmuch as the novel intends to reestablish Christian morality in a society that had experimented with its removal, these rules of sexual conduct must appear "natural," the inescapable moral basis of any viable codification of behavior, operating in the heart of the forest and of the individual, governing the actions of even those who live beyond the boundaries of the encoding culture. Loving and passionate, fleeing from socially prescribed death, free in the forest where only their own natural feeling for propriety guides their actions, Atala and Chactas embrace. What limits, if any, can individual choice impose on this embrace? To what extent does nature, which has made them virtuous, regulate their passions, which, though natural, cannot, if morality is also to be natural, be left to reign unchecked?

Chateaubriand reintroduces the system of checks that must finally characterize even an alternative society in the passage where the growing physical attraction between the two lovers culminates:

"From there on the struggles of Atala became useless; in vain did I feel her raise a hand to her bosom . . . ; already did I hold her tightly in my arms, and was drunk with her breath, having sipped all of love's magic from her lips. With my eyes turned toward heaven, I held my spouse in my arms by the flashing lights of the storm, and in the presence of the Eternal One. It was a wedding feast worthy of our misfortunes and of the greatness of our love: sublime forest that made your domes of verdure and lianas billow in the wind like the curtains

[25] Todorov notes the progression from observations on dress to conclusions about cultural states: "Physically naked, Indians are also, in Columbus's eyes, devoid of any cultural characteristics [such as] mores, rites, religion" (*Conquête*, p. 41).

of our bed, flaming pines that became the torches for our hymeneum, raging flood, bellowing mountains, awesome and sublime nature, . . . could you but hide for one moment, in your mysterious horrors, the happiness of one man.

"Atala offered but a feeble resistance: I was almost touching the moment of bliss, when all of a sudden an impetuous flash of lightning, followed by a burst of fire, cut a line through the thick darkness, filling the forest with sulphur and light, and breaking a tree at our feet. We fled. Oh, surprise! In the silence that followed, we heard the sound of a bell!" (Pp. 75–76)

In romantic fashion, Chateaubriand's raging elements and responsive forest are in sympathy with the lovers: the correspondence between the storm and the approach of "bliss" for Chactas is almost too perfect to be properly "artistic" and signals, instead of the willed construction of the literary artifact, a natural congruence between nature and extra-social humanity. But with great economy Chateaubriand reinstitutes separation with the same movement that posits unity and imposes a natural check on natural impulses. The thunderclap, the lightning, the falling tree are implicit in the storm; the warning against the object of desire is implicit therefore in the very force of desire; the rupture between man and nature is inherent in their relation, in an unresolvable tension that also becomes a stability of man-in-nature and does not threaten the relation of power between him and the man-in-culture who writes him.

But for Chactas and Atala there is another element at play: the necessary excess of Christianity, whose signal, the bell, arises immediately after the tree falls, in the silence that follows naturally upon the violence of the thunderclap. The bell reminds us that Chateaubriand and his readers cannot imagine for his protagonists a freedom not constrained by the civilization that writes them. Atala is part of the dream of a civilization and is intended to be read within its system of values. The fury of the elements is therefore not sufficient to thwart the "natural" outcome of the passion beween her and Chactas; it needs the complement of the rescuing missionary's bell, which reintroduces the limits imposed by civilization identified with Christianity. If Chateaubriand and his public are to write and read savages as human, they must also keep them within culturally determined definitions of the human. At best, then, Chateaubriand offers a sleight-of-hand, the natural within the systems of civilization, like a magic rabbit in a top hat.

Saved by Christian civilization from undisciplined indulgence in "natural" passion, Atala finally enters the exchange of histories which makes up the novel. Readers and characters find out that she has been vowed to lifelong virginity, that her passion may not seek the socially sanctioned and regulated outlet of a chaste marriage. Atala is the illegitimate daughter (by rape?) of an Indian "princess" (savage nobility characterized in terms of European political hierarchy)[26] and a Spaniard. Converted to Christianity by a Franciscan monk, Atala's mother on her deathbed consecrates her daughter to a life without men, using the religion of the conqueror against one of the forms of his conquest and erecting her own barrier to exchange. With the mother's vow Chateaubriand turns a European prohibition against sexual contact into an American rejection of contact and, reassuringly, places the burden of denial on the other. Torn between love and loyalty, Atala poisons herself with her mother's potion and dies amid the consolations of Father Aubry and the groans of Chactas.

The savage groans and Christian consolations with which Chactas and Father Aubry react to the death of Atala reestablish the separation between European and American threatened during the stay in the forest; her death, meanwhile, confirms the interdiction against the lovers' "wedding." But Father Aubry frames the interdiction in completely European terms by transferring to the Americas a religious controversy between Jesuits and Franciscans and placing the cause of the ban not in the intrusion of the bell but in the unreasonable Franciscan sanction of an excessive vow. This explanation further determines the "reading" of the American tragedy in European terms by allowing Chateaubriand, the writer-politician, to intervene in an extratextual French political debate.

If the root of Atala's dilemma is sunk in European politics, its embodiment in the impossible choice between two virtues is the stuff of tragedy and inscribes her "savage" story in a high-culture literary series. Yet this inscription also marks her difference, since one of the terms of her dilemma is an alienating and exotic, rather than cathartic excess. The demands to which Atala cannot reconcile herself are those of a culture half alien to her whose worth she must acknowledge and to whose power she must bow because of her very virtues; loyalty and imperfect knowledge characterize her noble half savagery and force her to honor her mother's decision to accept Christianity as a revenge against Chris-

---

[26] Pocahontas is a "princess"; Oroonoko is an African "prince."

tians. The impulses that conflict with these demands are permitted in the culture of her other half: as the "spouse" of Chactas condemned to death, she would have been obliged to yield to him; her partial yielding in the forest is never held against her in the text. Placed between two cultures she is potentially a mediating character; in effect, however, she exemplifies the impossibility of transition. Chateaubriand claims in the preface that his story is a tragedy, a form with no room for transition or compromise.

This reference to genre deflects attention from the fact that Atala's destruction arises not, as in tragedy, from the contradictions inherent in a single culture but from the conflict between contradictory elements in two cultures, each furnishing her with one of the weapons that kills her. Her mother's vow, with its misunderstanding of Christianity, affirms the positive value of a religion that commonly justified colonization and at the same time implies the inability of the colonized either to receive it in its perfection or to make a return of equal value. Her mother's poison, however, allows Atala to distance herself from Christianity by following a more ancient classical model of European virtue.

Though the different reactions to the death of Atala begin by affirming the incompatibility of culture-characteristic stances and reproduce the rupture between the aims of the lovers and those of the culture that writes them, Chateaubriand finally abuts on a rupture within the European position itself. Father Aubry's consolation, a traditional spiritual discourse of resignation and rejection of the world, modulates to a wholesale and emotional rejection of European civilization. "What would you think then," he asks the dying Atala, "if you had been witness to the ills of society, if, upon setting foot on the shores of Europe, your ears had been assaulted by the long cry of pain that rises from that old land?" (p. 103). The logic of his argument resides outside the text; Chateaubriand's discourse of the Americas is a discourse for Europe, to which America (whose acquiescence is adduced in the author's assertion of accuracy) is allowed as a spectator, like a child allowed to listen to the conversation of an adult dinner party. America is a laboratory for the examination of European problems, where one can isolate matters of fact and value. Because he assigns value to American characteristics, however, Chateaubriand can not only consolidate the discourse of Europe on America but also buttress that of America about itself. American authors use the elements he identifies as valuable— the immediacy of nature, the exemption from history, the purity and strength of emotions, the fiction of a new beginning—because these oppose and correct European characteristics and legitimate American difference. The result is a metonymic spread of positive value to other characteristics considered important in autochthonous literature though not relevant to the metropoles, such as the narrative form given to the subjugation of the Amerindian other in the formation of the American self.[27]

So far we have seen how Chateaubriand encodes the relation of an exotic America to a conquering Europe in a marriage plot that transposes to the personal level the possibility of combining cultures. In *Atala* and in *René*, as in *Paul et Virginie*, the marriage plot also presses into new service the then-common theme of incest and plays it against the more obvious one of exogamy, using religion as the operative difference. Because the psychological and the ideological do not usually meet in critical discourse, the relation of mutual implication between exogamy and incest in the literature of the exotic is not usually noted. In Chateaubriand that relation appears with unusual clarity and consistency. His interest in the incest motif has received critical attention, but its ideological dimension is generally submerged in speculation about the intense relationship between the young Chateaubriand and his sister, Lucille.[28] In *René* the relationship between René and his sister, Amélie, conditions the hero's destructive interest in the Indian maiden Céluta, clearly opposing forbidden incest to impossible exogamy. But the relationship between Chactas and Atala, culturally distant from the author, is even more directly indicative of the thematic importance of the incest motif in the acculturation plot.

Balancing the anxiety of the encounter with otherness and the reassurance offered by the reencountered self, variations on exogamy as acculturation recur in most fictions by Chateaubriand. In *Les martyrs*

[27] This preoccupation appears both in Cooper's treatment of the origins and legitimacy of landownership and transmission from colonizers to the following generations and in the Brazilian José de Alencar's fascination with legends of place, where future generations of Brazilians can seek their national roots.
[28] The precise nature of Chateaubriand's relationship with Lucille has fascinated biographers; they agree that it was intense, exclusive (in the isolation of Combourg, where both spent their adolescence), and important for Chateaubriand's development as a writer. Judgments on the likelihood of "something" having happened between them vary according to the temperament of the biographer. Louis-Martin Chauffier heatedly denies Chateaubriand's "guilt" and especially Lucille's (*Chateaubriand*, pp. 39–40). Painter agrees, but reasons that in the absence of proof, we will never know for sure (pp. 64–66). Barbéris glances at the "erotic madness" of the "friendship with Lucille," without judging or elaborating (*Chateaubriand: Une réaction*, p. 25). André Maurois suggests that the intensity of the relationship depends precisely on the repression of its sexual component (*René*, pp. 33–36).

he pairs Christian man and pagan (Roman) woman, and in *Le dernier Abencérage*, Christian woman and infidel (Muslim) man.[29] In the American fictions the translation of the anxieties of acculturation and cultural replacement into the incest/miscegenation marriage plot receives a treatment that endures in the American literatures of nationality, where the marriage plot, with its companion the incest plot, can function as a multivalent metaphor for the complexities of acculturation.[30] Within it, Atala's "savagery" is not simply ornamental, and her misguided Christianity is not accidental. She completes the series that goes from Chateaubriand's oriental protagonists through Céluta and Chactas to René and Father Aubry in increasing degrees of "Europeanism," erasing lines of absolute difference and tempting with the delights of a crisis of identity whose interest is intensified by the specter of incest. The contortions with which Chateaubriand introduces incest into *Atala* also indicate its importance for the construction of the exotic, for even if his preoccupation with incest is biographical, no biographical necessity would force him to develop it in an exotic setting. If, nevertheless, the incest motif is grounded intra-or intertextually—that is, if it derives from an internal logic of the acculturation motif which operates also in *Paul et Virginie*, especially in its stated preference of the more intense sibling love over a more demanding exogamy—then its presence in *Atala* is a further sign of the importance of exogamy as a grounding metaphor in fiction about the exotic and its relation to a model culture.

Chactas is the first to describe his lover as his sister, when she discloses that she is the daughter not of the Indian chief but of the same Lopez who, like a father, had sheltered and educated Chactas. This equation of the biological and the cultural becomes problematic in the writings of autochthonous American authors too, for it impedes the affirmation of a newly founded, independent cultural identity by demanding payment of a cultural debt to the former metropoles. In *Atala* the equation serves contradictory functions. As a morally positive value,

[29] Chauffier notes the pattern but connects it with the incest motif only by suggesting that in either case Chateaubriand took little trouble to invent new plots (p. 49).
[30] Eric J. Sundquist discusses the role of incest in Cooper's work at some length, though he links it not to the problems of acculturation in the New World but to a later phase in which a patrician class uses it as a method for preserving its privileged position against the pressures of Jeffersonian democracy (*Home as Found*, pp. 11–16). Doris Sommer, in classifying the literatures of nationality as "romance," also foregrounds the marriage motif, more optimistically than it is envisioned when coupled with incest, perhaps because she concentrates on those literatures' concerns with intranational differences.

it proposes a cure for the cultural alienation that plagued the European consciousness by erasing the break between culture and nature, seen as the origin of alienation, the source of solitude, the abyss between self and other. As a negative value, it blocks the marriage plot and alleviates the anxiety of cultural otherness by preserving the self from dissolution into the other, proposing an end to alienation as dangerous as the alienation itself. For alienation can also function as an identifying characteristic of the self, threatened by the exogamous marriage plot, which raises the dangerous possibility of allaying alienation by changing the rules that govern, with the force of nature, the proper allocation of mates. The discourse of the exotic shows the marriage plot on the dangerous boundary between nature and culture, threatened by extrasocial desire immediately rejected as extranatural, as that which cannot be inscribed.

Structurally, the incest theme in *Atala* links Chactas and his interlocutor, René, and both with Chateaubriand himself as the exemplary European in America. Inasmuch as the love between Atala and Chactas remains unconsummated and ends tragically, however, like the marriage of René to Céluta, the New World becomes, as Barbéris observes, a site where marriage, the objective of the bourgeois novel, cannot occur (*René de Chateaubriand*, p. 107). And if marriage, as the seed and microcosm not only of the bourgeois novel but of any social group, cannot occur, the implication may be that the New World cannot be the site for the establishment of a new, hybrid, civilization. Though Barbéris values the impossibility of marriage positively, because through it the New World subverts bourgeois society, it can also be valued negatively, either as denying the possibility of sexual integration on which social integration depends (*René de Chateaubriand*, p. 109), or as denying the possibility of an alternative to that society.

The limitations of *Atala* as a discourse about the other show in plot, narrative focus, and characterization the necessarily paradoxical nature of a discourse by the other emergent as a self within the same linguistic and cultural context. As a discourse of the exotic, *Atala* both offers and denies true alternatives to dilemmas inherent in the dominating culture, brought into relief as it approaches the other; it also shows the naturalness with which evasion can be accepted as synthesis or, conversely, as a point of departure for an opposing discourse.

According to Jean-Pierre Richard, René's inadaptation, like the "ennui" with which he infects (or which he expresses for) a generation of

European youth, is one of the ways in which Chateaubriand introduces "into the bosom of the American destiny . . . the fault, the fatal principle of nonadequation" (*Paysage de Chateaubriand*, p. 37). But by its implied definition, this principle functions only in the juxtaposition of cultures and only from a European perspective. In the combination of morality and titillation offered in the story of Atala and Chactas, incest, as a sign of social inadaptation, complements exogamy and blocks the marriage of the protagonists just as it heightens the emotional charge of their encounter: "It was too much for our hearts, this brotherly friendship visited upon us and adding its love to ours" (*Atala*, p. 75). But exoticism also legitimates passion and incest, by placing them at the origin of the civilization whose high morality promises a formula for adaptation and defines a proper distance from the virtuous prurience of the relationship between the lovers. As Father Aubry explains to Atala: "I will not speak to you of the marriages between the firstborn of men, of those ineffable unions in which the sister was the spouse of the brother, in which love and brotherly affection mingled in the same heart, and in which the purity of the one increased the delights of the other" (p. 104). The exotic neutralizes the culture-bearing function of the incest taboo, but the dangers of incest as well as of exogamy arise only through European intervention. They are imposed on America like Atala's cross and Chactas's enslavement, and these two in turn are defined as receptive vessels for a European definition of America which usurps their voices while confirming them as the only proper representatives of a new, American civilization.

The tragedy of Atala hinges on the double division between nature and culture, operated by the incest taboo and by Christianity. The appearance of the supplementary distinction is called forth by the ambiguous place of the Amerindian in the determination of the boundary between nature and culture. The savage, when noble, embodies the virtuality of culture and disturbs a system of differences between instinct, immediacy, iteration, on one hand, and thought, memory, history, on the other. Noble, he becomes the ancestor, associated with ancient Greeks and Romans and, like the ancients, subject to redemption by Christianity. Savage, he becomes the antagonist, subject to forceful domination by Christianity. *Atala* depends on both views. Chateaubriand's insistence on classifying *Atala* as a tragedy, like Henry Fielding's invention of the literary category "epic poem in prose" aims to derive respectability from the classics but also distances his characters and qualifies their virtue as surpassed by that of his modern readers.[31] Out of a noble and ancient despair, Atala poisons herself to escape the conflict between duty to a vow and the desire of her noble heart. But like a savage, and unlike the tragic hero of classical French theater, she does not know all the rules that govern her field of potential action; she drinks the potion not because, like a hero, she rejects compromise but because, like a savage, she does not know it is possible. "What!" she exclaims, "was there a remedy! Could I have been relieved of my vows!" And Father Aubry comforts her: "Yes, my child," and tells her about the sorry state of Europe (p. 99).

Although Father Aubry's effect on the destiny of the lovers is negative—he blocks their embrace but not Atala's suicide—he is written as the most unambiguously positive character in the tale. Through him European cultural power reaches even into the deepest wilderness. It is not a virtual, metaphoric reach. Like the first missionaries he has set up a village in the middle of the forest and hurried its inhabitants out of "primitive" hunter-gatherer nomadism into the more "civilized" state of the peasantry. Benevolently, he presides over their young polis, still virtuous enough to generate, as in Rousseau's dream, the perfect society. But the good father modifies the Rousseauean model and replaces the consent of the governed, the contract that legitimates authority, with the absolute power of an alien, universalizing system of rules and values.

Blessing, marrying, baptizing, and burying, Father Aubry controls the points at which social organization sanctions and integrates the activities of individuals. But he also blesses "the rock, the tree, the fountain just as, in other times, and according to the book of the Christians, God blessed the uncultivated land, bestowing it upon Adam as his inheritance" (p. 90). This gesture assigns to the conqueror a divine right to the new paradise and places him at the origin of the world, of society, and of history.

But Father Aubry is not only the creator and the legislator; he is also the tutor, who, like his model in Rousseau's *Emile*—or like the state in the newly independent American nations—tries to build the good society on careful and illustrated instructions, parceling out rules and knowledge for his pupils' virtue and happiness.[32] He distributes land

---

[31] Chateaubriand points to the parallel in the Preface to *Atala* (p. 9), when he notes that, like *Philoctète*, his tale has only three characters, and within the text itself, when he introduces Chactas by comparing him to Oedipus and Ossian (p. 32).

[32] Recently there has been considerable critical interest in how the state controls socialization through education. See, for instance, Ross J. Pudaloff, "Education and the

and crops to teach notions of property and "social economy," and to preserve "fraternal charity" (p. 90), but he has also "endeavored, in teaching them the road to salvation, to apprise them of the first arts of life, without, however, taking them too far along, and maintaining these honest people in that state of simplicity which brings happiness," because he "felt the superiority of this stable and busy life over the errant and idle life of the savage" (pp. 82, 91). His program combines criticism of the European fall from virtue with a rejection of the unmodified life of the savage and places all power in the hands of the European tutor. Father Aubry refuses to spell out for the governed the principles that govern them: "I have not given them any law: I have only taught them to love each other, to pray to God and to hope for a better life: all the laws in the world are contained in these" (p. 90). His benevolence is also his power; in his village exotic otherness provides a redemptive alternative to the sophisticated, historical European self, but only by being barred from becoming a covaluable equal. Father Aubry proposes to preserve his ideal society by removing it from history and withholding from it the knowledge of writing, which is the foundation of history as understood by Europe and which promotes the consciousness of the self and its place in the world—both seen to be at the root of European malaise. Father Aubry confirms history and writing as privileges of Europe, which has misused them, to be kept from a New World conceived as a preserve of virtue. Characteristically, Chateaubriand restores, in the relation of power between European and American, a relation of power between the church and public disturbed by the Reformation, the printing press, the Enlightenment, the Revolution and, at the limit, the discoveries that made Father Aubry's alternative society possible.

Father Aubry fails, however. The European imposition of history on "primitives"—the steps from nomadism to settlement, from hunting and gathering to agriculture, from idols to the true God—subjects the original inhabitants of the New World to European history. Father Aubry's ideal village is built, like Marie Antoinette's dairy, on the notion of a primitive simplicity that exists only as a relation not between myth and history but between two social groups of unequal power. The Indian village is destroyed, like the dairy, as the struggle for power erupts. In the Edenic Mississippi wilderness, roving tribes displaced by the

Constitution," and, for verification in the Brazilian case, Marisa Lajolo and Regina Zilberman, *A leitura rarefeita.*

conquerors and caught up in alien disputes for their land, make war against each other, borne along on that current of history which Chateaubriand dreamt they should oppose.

And so we return to Chactas, who is only an admiring spectator of Father Aubry's village. Though an Indian like the missionary's wards, as René's interlocutor he mediates between the two cultures, completely belonging to neither. Atala's death leaves him in an almost antagonistic relationship with Father Aubry and Christianity. "Perish the God who goes against nature," he cries, rolling on the ground and biting his own arms with savage fury, when Atala dies of virginity and poison (p. 96). But after enslavement gives him the opportunity to see secular European civilization, he can accept its spiritual offering and is competent to comfort René. It is an accommodation refused by another Chateaubriand pagan, Aben-Hamet, the hero of *Le dernier Abencérage;* the difference between them distinguishes the Amerindian otherness, conceived as an absence, from the Muslim one, conceived as a cultural opposition. Both are ineffective; neither hero wins his beloved; neither leaves the impress either of action or of posterity on European history.

Chactas is ineffective because Chateaubriand can see America only as a natural world to which the original inhabitants belong like the water buffaloes or the butterflies that adorn it without leaving their mark on it, without making history. Chateaubriand's savages differ from civilized people less in their closeness to nature than in their distance from history. Although René feels alienated because, unlike the Indians he meets, he does not carry the bones of his ancestors on his back, this connectedness he envies is structurally untranslatable for him (p. 123). The Indians' portable history shares the transitoriness of their nomadic life, out of which heroes such as Father Aubry must lead them.[33] It is incomplete, since it does not produce the monuments that provide Chateaubriand with his bearings in time and space, determining the value of what he discovers and describes.[34] Without such monuments

[33] It is interesting to compare this representation with that of the Jesuit relations discussed in Chapter 2. Chateaubriand does not mention anything like the permanent burial grounds to which the bones were taken eventually; the argument for greater piety of Amerindians forcibly confronted with mortality does not occur to him; though he presents the defense of Christianity as central to his literary endeavor, it is the argument about a secular civilization, for which history is not a given, that has his attention.

[34] See Michel Riffaterre, "Chateaubriand et le monument imaginaire." Hermine Riffaterre argues that the monuments can also be literary: Chateaubriand will often explain something he has in front of his eyes by reference to another landscape he has only read about but which carries the cultural weight of classical associations ("L'imagination livresque").

the American wilderness is free from the corruption of time but also inferior to those societies whose ancestors are safely weighed under the heavy, inscribed stones that anchor their descendants to the orderly flow of a historical process. Thus, while he longs for the integration with nature possible in the absence of history, Chateaubriand's hero, defined by a European historical sensibility that alone produces that longing, cannot receive what the exotic promises. Barbéris shows how this disjunction operates by reading *Les Natchez* allegorically, the Indian rebellion figuring a crisis in the reign of Louis XVI, contemporary with its setting, which in turn foreshadows another in postrevolutionary France contemporary with its writing (*Chateaubriand*, pp. 63–64). But these allegories do not clarify events by transposing them to a different level; they repeat events in ever-changing guises and despair of an exit.

This stress on problems of history may seem excessive, inasmuch as *Atala* is not ostensibly a historical novel but a love story to which the Natchez uprising is only peripheral. Yet Chateaubriand begins the prologue with history. "In days of yore," he writes, "France possessed, in North America, a vast empire which stretched from Labrador to the Floridas, and from the shores of the Atlantic to the most remote lakes of Upper Canada" (p. 27). The tale depends on European colonization; its moral conflict arises from a difference between two religious orders about jurisdiction over savage souls. One cannot blame Chateaubriand for deeming European politics a matter of life and death for Americans; one can, however, point out that insofar as *Atala* constitutes a model fiction of and about the Americas, it presents an autochthonous American fiction with a particularly clear statement of the problem of adapting a discourse made acceptable for its ideological charge to a use that must deflect that charge.

Chateaubriand knows that European history can always intrude upon the farther reaches of America. In *Mémoires d'outre tombe* he tells the end of his American voyage. He is a guest at an idyllic mill where fish jump in the brook, birds fly in the air; sitting by the fire, a cat on his knee, he feeds the hearth with scraps of old newspapers, alternately glancing at them and watching a squirrel frolic on the back of a large dog. Suddenly he reads that the Revolution has forced the king of France to flee. He has a vision of himself as a hero of Tasso's in a painting he admired in Naples (years after his American voyage): honor calls him back to aid the Bourbons (1:340).[35] Whatever the real story—maybe

[35] In note 8, on that page, the editor traces Chateaubriand's reference ("A sudden conversion took place in my spirit: Renaud saw the picture of his weakness in the

only that his money was running out—Chateaubriand turns it into a parable about the difficulty of escaping European history, which exerts its pull even in the depth of the wilderness. But before it can be a story about the pull of history, it has to be a story about the desire to escape it. The escape is not toward the abstract, the ineffable, or the mystical but toward the exotic. The exotic does not exist in or for itself, however. It is there in relation to the familiar, to be consumed, reported, inscribed in the play of alternatives to the customary and the normal.

Finally, the exotic is there to be written. Chateaubriand brings home neither the map of the Northwest Passage nor an addition to French glory or territory but a sheaf of papers, which he carries around in war and into exile and credits with saving his life in battle (*Atala*, p. lxiii). That protective text constructs an exotic landscape integrated in the language of the more powerful consumer of exoticism. Its inscription of the wilderness teaches a generation of sensitive and solitary Europeans to rewrite their own mountains and valleys, grasses, birds and skies, and provides a generation of newly independent Americans with a language with which to write their difference as nature into civilization. We learn that yellow roses on islands floating in the Mississippi "rise like small pavilions"; vines and begonias climb the tallest trees, "forming a thousand grottoes, a thousand vaults, a thousand porticoes"; a tree on the opposite bank of the river is like "a joyous hostel . . . an airy castle"; and as "a thousand sighs rose from the vaults and the corridors of that mobile building, never did any of the marvels of the ancient world come close to this monument of the wilderness" (*Atala*, pp. 28, 29, 64). Chactas speaks this last description; Chateaubriand enlists his semisavage voice, indistinguishable in tone, vocabulary, and reference from that of the narrator, assimilates it to a European discourse, and endows it with the universality of sensibility. The transposition of the narrator's language to the Indian protagonist, like the translation of plants into buildings, is not a slip but a consistent strategy, apparent also when Chactas transposes cultural value judgments and asserts that "drunkenness, which lasts a long time among the Savages, . . . is, for them, a kind of malady" (p. 62). With this strategy Chateaubriand separates Chactas from the "savages," familiarizes the strange,

---

mirror of honor in Armida's gardens; though I was not Tasso's hero, a similar mirror showed me a reflection of myself in the middle of the American bower") to a painting of that episode from Tasso which Chateaubriand admired on his trip to Italy in 1804: cultural artifacts color, even anachronistically, his view of American nature and of himself in it.

and bestows value on American nature by translating it into European monuments. Thus, the savage other's consciousness of self is assimilated to the civilizing conqueror's, and the encounter with the other is saved from being an encounter with true otherness.

But familiar judgments and familiar architecture are not all that Chateaubriand superimposes on the wilderness. The same tree described as a castle and a hotel is also encoded as a product of European luxury manufacture: during the day a multitude of butterflies, insects, and birds surround the tree, attach themselves to the mosses hanging from it, and produce the effect of a "tapestry on white wool, where a European worker embroidered brilliantly colored insects and birds" (p. 64). The hand of the European worker legitimates the beauty of the American tree; moreover, translation of a translation, the description matches an actual Gobelins tapestry, based on drawings by travelers to the Americas.[36] This inscription of the American landscape tames the wilderness as it claims to describe it. It ascribes value to the landscape by inserting it into a tradition of European high culture which has already assimilated and forgotten an earlier influx of the exotic, and it ensures Chateaubriand's power to control otherness within a familiar language. It peoples the forest with an Indian youth who is just like a young Greek spirit, a romping "genie of Spring"; with another young Indian sitting upon a rock like a classical marble statue; with the Amerindian version of the myth of Orpheus; or with the Indian lover who completes the recuperation of the European past in the American wilderness by singing to his beloved a "natural" echo of the Song of Songs: "Her breasts are like two spotless fawns, born on the same day from the same mother" (*Atala*, p. 47, 56, 48).

In this context, the most daring figure of inscription becomes almost commonplace. Like a lover at a picnic, defacing trees with hearts and initials, Father Aubry carves into the trunks of centenary oaks outside his cavern the Song of Songs and the epic poems of Homer (*Atala*,

---

[36] The Museu de Arte de São Paulo owns a tapestry titled *Indian Hunter*, based on designs by Albert Eckout, transported to paper boards by François Desportes, and part of a series called *Nouvelles Indes*, the originals of which were sent by Maurice of Nassau as a gift to Louis XIV of France in 1687, and transferred to the Gobelins workshops in the same year; there they were reproduced until 1730, when they wore out. The tapestry at São Paulo shows a pair of trees, composites of palm, cactus, and deciduous forms, carrying, and surrounded by, an encyclopedia of the flora and fauna of the Americas (Carlos Lemos et al., *The Art of Brazil*, p. 45).

p. 84).[37] There Chateaubriand operates a direct transformation of nature into culture which leaves intact the appearance and the essence of both by assimilating the natural to the early and the other to the ancestor, translating the strange language of otherness into writing and history. As directly as that, Chateaubriand transforms the New World into an element in the discourse of the Old.

In time Chateaubriand's encoding of the New World assumed the position of model and adversary for American literatures of national consciousness. He brought the New World into the mainstream of literary discourse in the Old and invested it with contemporary significance. He did so, however, by transforming it into pure raw material to be used in accordance with the syntax of a culture from which the new literatures were striving to differentiate themselves. Their task, then, was to define the autochthonous and affirm its value while rescuing it from the classification of otherness on which identity and value had till then depended. Cultural independence demanded the affirmation of identity without putting the ascription of value into jeopardy, the rescue of the exotic from servitude to the system that defined it as exotic, and its transformation into the domestic without sacrifice of its claim to value. It demanded the recovery of authority from an alien inscription, a daring, critical redefinition of exotic otherness as an element in the definition of the self.

Chateaubriand wrote America for Europe, inscribed Europe on the New World, created a wilderness that, though unable to satisfy it, provided a space commensurate with European desire. Like the voyagers in whose footsteps he wished to walk, he gave the European imagination a geography of escape and transformation. He did it by investing the wilderness—that place without history, without writing, without the

---

[37] Though writing the *Iliad* on trees might seem an overstatement of inscription, a passage in Chateaubriand's later assessment of the contemporary state of the United States shows that he not only saw the process as inevitable, engaged in by Americans themselves in their claim for legitimacy, but also, at least if performed by Americans, as faintly ridiculous, certainly incongruous: "There is, among the Muscogulges, the Seminoles, the Chickasaws, a city of Athens, one of Marathon, another of Carthage, another of Memphis, another of Sparta, another of Florence. . . . In Kentucky one finds a Versailles" (*Memoires* 1:342) The sense of estrangement aroused by these familiar names in unfamiliar settings is present throughout even the laudatory account of the material progress of the United States, the improvements in transportation, and the increase in population, and finally turns to ill-concealed contempt when Chateaubriand considers the literary scene and the works of such as Charles Brockden Brown and James Fenimore Cooper ("Les lettres aux Etats Unis," *Memoires*, 1:344–50).

rules that mark familiar boundaries of culture—with a positive value as an otherness from which Europe could reassume its own history, its own place, its own self. That reassumption, however, imposed on the wilderness, as signs of value, those very boundaries it had existed to deny, subjecting it to European history, inscribing it with European writing, subordinating its social organization to the origins of Europe's. Nevertheless, the new literature of the Americas was able to use the positive evaluation of its defining characteristics as a pivot on which to give the wilderness another spin, to assign it an autochthonous value, and to translate it from an otherness to a mediating self, readable on either shore of the Atlantic.

The nineteenth-century literatures of nationality developed a variety of strategies to recover the wilderness for the definition of a national cultural consciousness. They assimilated European origins to New World histories, affirmed the value of original New World cultures on their own terms, denied the importance of these cultures, and attempted to incorporate New World elements into a definition of national character that at the same time valued them and transformed them. The categories of history, of marriage, of the boundaries between nature and culture have been constants in the development of such national or cultural discourse. Barbéris claims that like Balzac and Beyle, Chateaubriand "taught us to read the modern world" (*Chateaubriand*, p. 352). To participate in this discourse, New World writers had to write against this reading and, therefore, to incorporate it.

6

James Fenimore Cooper
and the Image of America

James Fenimore Cooper was not the first American writer, but he was the first to receive wide national and international recognition— in the form of multiple editions and translations—when he entered the tense dialogue with the European discourse of the New World which underlies the creation of an American literature of nationality.[1] He addressed American concerns and two different publics: New World readers, to whom he gave an assurance of increased cultural power,[2] and European readers, who could legitimate his works with their recognition and approval. The positive reception of Cooper's work was prepared in Europe by the long presence of a discourse of exotic America, from ancient accounts to the hot fictions of Chateaubriand, and in his own land by the desire, or need, to reclaim this discourse.

Cooper is now remembered for only some of his works (in that dark house, Jane Tompkins read *The Deerslayer*, not *Notions of the Americans* or the Littlepage series), and not all he wrote was well received in his

[1] From different angles and to different purposes, both Jane Tompkins, in "What Happens in *Wieland*" (*Sensational Designs*, pp. 40–61), and Emily Miller Budick, in "Literalism and the New England Mind: Charles Brockden Brown's *Wieland* as American History" (chap. 2 of *Fiction and Historical Consciousness*), see Brown's adaptation of the gothic as an instance of literature of nationality. Their reading, which is not endorsed by all critics, argues for pushing the beginnings of a purposeful "literature of nationality" back from Cooper. Cooper's greater popularity, however, gives a clearer view of the interaction between the production and consumption of such works.
[2] As we shall see, Cooper was read as a model in other newly independent parts of the New World.

own time. The ups and downs of Cooper's popularity outline the limits within which a claim for cultural independence can make itself acceptable. The combination of desired information, recognizable language, acceptable ideas and images within which author, text, and audience interact—Hans Robert Jauss's "horizon of expectations" ("Literaturgeschichte," pp. 144–207, esp. 173–89)—functions in an especially interesting form to shape the reception of Cooper's work because of how it interacts with the role of exoticism in the claim for discursive power.[3]

Cooper made it his conscious task to change this horizon, whose limits are, in any case fluid, changeable, says Jauss, by a great work. For Cooper, who of course did not put it in these terms, the task was to expand the horizon till it encompassed the cultural legitimacy of American writing (Wallace, *Early Cooper*, p. 63). The limits of expansion can generally be traced in the record of a work's sales, in what is commonly called its influence, and in the reactions of reviewers and critics, those "accredited judges of art and arbiters of taste" who, in the words of Janet Wolff, "are themselves socially defined and constituted, and bring to bear in their judgments specific ideological and positional values" (*The Social Production of Art*, p. 139), and who therefore tell us as much about their own expectations as about the objects of their discussion. Cooper's case illustrates the tension between a New World literature of nationality and its divided public. The study of their interaction yields information not only about his work but also about its necessary connection with the ideological environment it addresses and expresses.

Cooper became a writer close to half a century after the Revolutionary War, when the nation's political autonomy was well established but its cultural autonomy, the legitimacy of an American idiom, and the viability of an American literature were still debated on both sides of the Atlantic.[4] As his letters and diaries show, Cooper considered cultural independence a necessary complement of political independence and

---

[3] James D. Wallace says that Cooper invented an American reader to go with his newly invented American novel; Wallace agrees with Jauss's notion that a great writer expands the "horizon of expectations" but brackets the question of literary excellence ("Cultivating an Audience," p. 40).

[4] David Simpson, in *The Politics of American English*, discusses the formalization of a recognizably American idiom soon after independence, with special attention to the linguistic work of Noah Webster (chap. 2) and to the literary production of Cooper (chap. 5); he also documents the importance of the question of American English, whether disallowed by English authorities or welcomed by Americans, in arguments about the cultural identity and independence of the new nation.

believed it had to be contested. It is clear from their reactions that Americans valued his novels' affirmation of national identity and readers on both sides of the Atlantic valued his treatment of the history, land, language, and population of the new nation. As James D. Wallace argues, however, and as Cooper's own literary career shows, the horizon of expectations of any readership for American literature was circumscribed by European literary practice, even as it was subject to mounting pressures on "American writers to validate the experiment in democracy with an indigenous democratic fiction" (*Early Cooper*, p. 2). Cooper's novels provided his audience information and interpretation no less estimable than the pleasure they afforded as fictions.

Cooper and his public were not always on friendly terms. The great initial success of *The Spy* and the Leather-stocking books was not repeated with the Littlepage series, for instance, which, instead of flattering his American readers' sense of accomplishment, castigated the nation for abandoning the old republican values. The reception of *The Travelling Bachelor, or Notions of the Americans* (1828), in which Cooper explored the same national concerns as in his earlier novels and whose impulse is laudatory, not adversarial, represents an entirely different form of failure. Robert E. Spiller warns us not to dismiss *Notions*, for "there is every reason to believe that Cooper considered this book the most important of his works up to that date" (*Fenimore Cooper*, p. 126).[5] Nevertheless, critics and the public received it at worst with execration and at best with indifference. This contrast to the reception of the Leather-stocking series delineates a limit to the horizon of expectations of Cooper's public both in the United States and abroad.[6]

[5] Wayne Franklin suggests that Cooper was defensive and uneasy about the book (*The New World*, p. 48), in part because Lafayette had asked him to write an account of his triumphant visit to America in 1824–1825, and he could neither refuse nor enjoy the obligation; however, he agreed with Lafayette on the need for a book to dispel European ignorance about the United States (pp. 49–50).

[6] Cooper wrote *Notions* in France. Having decided to honor Lafayette's request for an account of his visit, Cooper thought he would hang onto the visit a larger "sketch" of the United States as seen by a visitor whose arrival coincides with Lafayette's (letter to Charles Wilkes, Paris, 25 January 1828, in *Letters and Journals*, 1:242–43). As a travel account, *Notions* belongs to a popular genre of its time, two or three books on impressions of trips to America being published every year between 1810 and 1860 (René Remond, *Les Etats Unis devant l'opinion française*, 1:269). Within *Notions* itself, Cadwallader reviews several such accounts, finding them inadequate and unfairly critical. *Notions* was first published in England (London: Henry Colburn, 20 June 1818), appearing in America with an unusual delay of a few months (Philadelphia: Carey and Lea, 14 August 1828); books expected to sell well were often published almost simultaneously in various countries. For the publication data, see Robert E. Spiller and Philip C. Blackburn, *A Descriptive Bibliography*, pp. 56–57. Al-

The problem does not lie in the form of *Notions of the Americans*, an account of travel from Old to New World which fits easily into an established and still-popular genre. The preface asserts truthfulness: Cooper warns his readers that "many orthodox unbelievers will listen to what the author has said of America in this work, with incredulous ears" (1:x), but he assures them that his facts are as correct as possible, that he "hopes that refutation will not easily attack him in the shape of evidence" (1:vii). The book exists because he has realized that "there is, perhaps, no Christian country on earth in which a foreigner is so liable to fall into errors as in the United States of America," where "institutions, the state of society, and even the impulses of the people, are in some measure new and peculiar," so that Europeans who confront it must "unlearn" much before they can begin to "learn correctly" (1:ix). Thus, the preface also defines a relation with its readership: the narrative voice will speak truths not yet fully accepted and ask to be believed even if belief demands changes in perception, interpretation, and evaluation. Cooper addresses himself to reason and promises that accuracy instead of imagination will guide his representation of American reality; he will make pure truth available through a fiction meant to be transparent. He proposes a literary object that is stable and carries reliable meanings, so the public can read correctly and then adapt its opinions and attitudes to the truth that is both foundation and result of that stability. But this agreement between work and public is not necessarily easy. If *Notions* is pedagogical (the public will learn correctly), it is also potentially polemical (in order to learn, the public will have to unlearn). The implied hope is that transparency will correct the ambiguity inherent in fiction, especially in forms derived from the literature of the metropolis, and that truth will prevail over misconceptions both of ignorance and malice.

---

though it was reprinted in the United States, *Notions* did not go through as many editions and reprints as was customary for Cooper. It had only one French edition, by Killian, rather than Gosselin, Cooper's usual publisher, and in a translation by Mlle H. Preble, rather than by Auguste Defauconpret, who had a French version of each Cooper work ready a few months after its English publication. (Defauconpret also translated Walter Scott into French. See Vitorino Nemésio, Introduction to Alexandre Herculano, *Eurico, o presbítero*, p. 19. *Eurico* is one of the two best-known Portuguese historical novels; Nemésio traces its debt to Scott, documenting the circulation of historical novels throughout Europe; in noting the translator, he also indicates the perceived kinship between the Scottish and American writers of romances.) Two German editions of *Notions* appeared, in 1828 and 1829, but unlike the preceding (and many of the following) works by Cooper, "*Notions* did not seem to have been published elsewhere in Europe" (Spiller and Blackburn, p. 57).

Thus, *Notions of the Americans* attempts to change the image of the new American nation, an image Cooper himself had helped establish in earlier works such as the Leather-stocking series. *Notions* counteracts the exoticism of those tales, which, as fiction, bear at best an oblique relation to the new reality Cooper wants known, understood, and valued. One could say that in *Notions* Cooper wants to reverse Chateaubriand, turn his back on Niagara, mothball the bearskins, and concentrate on the advantages of Philadelphia.

In *The Spy, Lionel Lincoln,* and particularly the first Leather-stocking novels Cooper had begun to elaborate a national epos. There other new countries and their populations could see themselves emerging, distinct from the former metropoles, working out elements of their national ideologies (in the sense of sets of beliefs communally held and thought of as "natural"). The task is paradoxical. Cooper had to differentiate the American from the European and also to legitimate the American against the European; he had to stress the difference in nature and the equivalence in value between what was of the New World and what was of the Old. He had to do so in the language of the former metropolis— language taken both in its ordinary sense and as literature, broadly understood as the cultural forms of organizing systems of meaning.

Cooper's first and very successful novels drew on a long European tradition of representation of the alien and the primitive[7] and on a more recent European interest in a fiction of the exotic. Like other writers in the New World, Cooper took up this exotic otherness and, by a small strategic shift, used it in opposition to the metropoles; the European literature of the exotic became a literature to be written against by an American literature of the exotic. Cooper's career as a writer began with a programmatic imitation of British novels in *Precaution*, and his continued use of established European novelistic conventions of plot and character helped trace the boundaries of acceptability for American writing, but in subsequent novels he expanded these boundaries and, as Wallace notes, "transform[ed] both his art and his audience from awkward imitations of the English into something triumphantly American," creating, in the process, a reading public for American writers, both at home and abroad (*Early Cooper*, p. vii).[8] The success of the

[7] The point is made by Clarence Gohdes, *American Literature in Nineteenth-Century England*, p. 128; it also applies to Brazilian literature (Ledo Ivo, "O romance poemático," p. 6).

[8] Wallace stresses Cooper's awareness of and responsiveness to his potential readers' habits and expectations, shown in the clear and specific choices of tone and argument Cooper makes in *Precaution* (*Early Cooper*, pp. 2, 63, vii, and esp. 67).

Leather-stocking series, which surpassed that of Cooper's previous novels, strengthened the authority of their language and exotic materials.[9]
But *Notions* set out to criticize this exoticism and to replace it with a
language that addresses the newness of America in terms valuable on
their own and not tailored to a tradition of defining Europe's civilized
self in relation to American primitivism. Thus, in contrast to the earlier
works, *Notions* offers a revealing insight into the thematic logic and the
success of Cooper's better-known, better-loved, and plain better fiction.

When Cooper wrote *Notions of the Americans* to change the terms in
which his nation would be known and valued, he was already famous
and could rely on a previously earned authority.[10] *The Spy* (1821), *The
Pioneers* (1823), *Lionel Lincoln* (1825), *The Last of the Mohicans* (1826), and
The Prairie (1827), well-accepted fictions that used native American materials, had become a source of nativist pride at home and a source of
information about America both for educated readers and for the
masses abroad (Gohdes, p. 149). Conscious of his position as "the first
of our major writers," Cooper "thought of his novels as public acts"
and "conceived of his duty as public and national."[11] His letters and
prefaces show that he considered it his task to make the new American
republic known to itself and to the world, to argue for the importance

[9] Success is tricky to define. It can mean, in our day, the American Academy and
Institute for Arts and Letters award to Raymond Carver or Robert Ludlum's pro-
tracted presence on best-seller lists or the renewal of a contract for writer number 35
with Silhouette Books. For the present discussion it means steady above-average
sales (and some best sellers), respect from critics lasting beyond a writer's time, and
demonstrable influence on other writers and on the public in general. Cooper was
successful enough to be the first writer in America to live entirely from his writings;
in fact, Wallace argues, financial need was one of the factors that made Cooper start
writing novels in the first place (*Early Cooper*, pp. 78–79). After the surprisingly good
sales of his second novel, *The Spy*, whose second printing of three thousand copies
sold out in two months, leading to a third printing of five thousand, Cooper had
several successes (*Lionel Lincoln, The Pioneers*) and finally what we would call a blockbuster in *The Last of the Mohicans*, whose first five thousand copies sold so fast that
his publisher stereotyped all his subsequent novels, and which was translated into
many languages (James D. Hart, *The Popular Book*, pp. 80–81). French translations of
Cooper's novels generally appeared within a few months of publication in English;
American and British editions appeared as nearly simultaneously as an interpretation
of copyright regulations favorable to Cooper could make them; critics concur that
everybody had read him or at least heard of the Leather-stocking.
[10] Charles Adams reminds us that the novels immediately preceding *Notions* had not
been successful and argues that Cooper "had lost his public" ("The Guardian of the
Law," p. 120), a claim that seems inconsistent with contemporary critics' suggestion
that he should return to the wilderness of his successful novels.
[11] Richard Chase, *The American Novel and Its Tradition*, pp. 43, 47. Charles Adams
claims Cooper identified his own self with the nation's (p. 121).

of its present achievements, and to claim for it the legitimacy conferred on a nation by its history.

To his annoyance, Cooper was often compared with Walter Scott as a writer of historical fiction, and the similarities of plotting and characterization are not difficult to identify. In Cooper's work, however, the past legitimates a new nation rather than naturalizing a tradition; he uses the past to strengthen his country's claim to attention and authority abroad and its self-confidence at home, not to mourn the passing of an old order; his novels endeavor to construct a "usable past."[12] For Cooper's contemporaries these differences are sufficient to make him original. William Gilmore Simms, for example, remarked: "The genius of our countryman, conceived the novel idea of so framing his narrative as to make it illustrate the radical differences in operation and effect, of the policy of the new world, in opposition to the old."[13]

In the Leather-stocking series, these "radical differences," were received enthusiastically by critics and public. In *Notions*, however, where they appear on the political and not the mythical level, they did not please. Cooper wants to convince his readers that the new nation not only promises to redeem the European past but also prefigures a successful future for a polity whose institutions are at the same time derived from the best European political and social thought and independent of its political, cultural, and economic power.

Notions assumes a European audience misinformed about American conditions. It was written, says John P. McWilliams, "to disabuse a foreign audience and counteract adverse publicity" (*Political Justice in a Republic*, p. 167).[14] In its epistolary form, however, it also posits a more

[12] See not only Commager but also Harry Levin's treatment of the concept in "Literature and Cultural Identity," p. 145.

[13] William Gilmore Simms, *"The Writing of Cooper,"* p. 225.

[14] European ignorance of America annoyed Cooper, who spoke of it often in his letters and journals, even when discussing unrelated matters. In one of the *Brother Jonathan* letters, he suddenly interrupts a discussion of Edward Effigham and *Home as Found* to state, "I have lived long enough in Europe, and under circumstances sufficiently favorable too, to know that the accounts published in this country and the opinions that prevail in it, are very little like the facts in the other hemisphere generally" (*Letters and Journals*, 4:267). He expresses similar sentiments in letters to Charles Wilkes (Paris, 25 January 1828, 1:246–47) and to Mrs. Peter Augustus Jay (26 March 1827, 1:209). Cooper also thought of the Leather-stocking tales as carrying factual information, as we can see from the prefaces, which assert the novels' historical accuracy, or, for instance, from his letter to Henry Colburn dated Paris, 17 October 1826, where, in what Spiller and Blackburn judge to be the first mention of the Leather-stocking books as a connected group, Cooper declares that *The Pioneers*, with *Mohicans* and *The Prairie*, "will form a complete series of Tales, descriptive of American life" (p. 224).

limited, though representative company of readers. The recipients of the letters are a select group including a Dutch baron and navy captain, an English baronet, an Italian *abbate*, a French count and retired colonel, a Scandinavian professor, and a Russian prince. None belongs to the highest social or professional rank, but all have leading public positions.[15] As travelers, like the first writers about America, they are sanctioned by an old tradition of reporting on new worlds. Combining respectability and adventurousness, they are sympathetic to the new and credible when they report or evaluate conditions in non-European parts of the world. Given their status, they will be heard in professional associations and among policy makers; their written opinions will count. Presumably, they represent an audience Cooper would particularly like to persuade, because they are reliable carriers of his truths to their own publics.

The Bachelor himself, whose letters constitute the book, is distinguished only by his curiosity and fair-mindedness (Wayne Franklin calls him "an ideal European observer of the West" [*The New World of James Fenimore Cooper*, p. 51]). We learn almost nothing about his history or his person; he is less a character than a neutral conduit, a pane of clear glass through which the new world he visits can be seen truly; he embodies Cooper's belief in the possibility of observing cultural phenomena without prejudice.

To combat prejudice, then, his letters to the bachelors' club contain almost nothing but factual information. They report on the successful military establishment of the United States, on its educational system and democratic government, on the numbers and character of its population, on housing, on the presidency. They are like chapters in a school book, conceived to inform and to form public opinion with data neatly arranged under representative headings. The long letter on public opinion from Cadwallader, the Bachelor's American guide and friend, reveals intratextually how Cooper thinks of the book's extratextual importance; its aim is to correct the distortions about America which the English impress upon the world, distortions that endanger the peace and the very survival of the republic: "I do not believe that two grave and thinking nations will ever enter into hostilities on account of pasquinades; but pasquinades can produce a state of feeling that may render it difficult to overcome serious obstacles to peace" (*Notions* 1:331). Cooper realizes that his task of enlightenment is made difficult by the strong

---

[15] Interestingly, like the unmarried Leather-stocking, they are also all bachelors.

interest that power, even (or especially) waning power, has in maintaining at least the verbal forms of the status quo: "It was an offence
against the geographical sovereignty of England . . . to presume to re-
nounce her dominion at all. It was, and is, a constant offence to aristocracy everywhere, to exhibit an instance of prosperous and happy
democracy. It was a bitter offence against the hierarchical establishment
to demonstrate that religion and order, and morals, could exist without
its aid" (1:318). Cooper wagers that an enlightened people will see in
the New World, not a threat to the Old but a promise to perfect it. He
believes his book can effect change because he equates rational judgment with ideology (in the Barthesian sense of belief disguised as, and
disguising, fact) and assumes that both are equally accessible to logic.
Thus *Notions* defends American difference as a rational improvement
on European values and knowledge, without acknowledging their ideological charge.

The problem, *Notions* implies, is that unlike an exotic tale, which is
familiar and easy to accept, American democracy is an experiment never
tried in Europe (1:236). Democratic institutions shape the nation's character and its people, and Europe distrusts democratic institutions; ignorance causes European fears, and *Notions* will dispel them through
argument and information. Reassuringly, Cooper notes that the economic, political, and moral development of the new nation originates
in the Old World; America's difference grows out of the familiar; it does
not subvert it. *Notions* claims that America is clearly a civilized Western
society and that the rules that organize it broaden but do not challenge
the prevailing distribution of political and cultural power between the
two shores of the Atlantic. No wonder Wayne Franklin concludes that
Notions may have been "Cooper's most daring fiction to date," turning
desire for parity with Europe into fact; Cooper was aware, says Franklin,
that *Notions* glossed over problems treated in the two books bracketing
it, *Pioneers* and *The Wept of Wish-Ton Wish* (*The New World*, p. 52).

In his prefaces, as in *Notions*, Cooper recognizes the rift that these
new rules create between the New World and the Old.[16] In the "Author's
Introduction" to *The Pioneers*, he notes that the new American landowner gives "his name to instead of receiving it from his estates, as in

---

[16] Wallace speaks of *Notions* as similar in genre to the prefaces, though longer and
more detailed (see, for instance, *Early Cooper*, pp. 126–27). To judge from Cooper's
comments on *Notions*, it is probable that he did not draw a strong generic distinction
between it and the novels of American content he had published; *Notions* possesses
a fictional component equivalent to the informational component of the novels.

Europe" (p. 9). In *Notions*, the American Cadwallader tells the Bachelor that "moral feeling with which a man of sentiment and knowledge looks upon the plains of your hemisphere is connected with his recollections; here it should be mingled with his hopes" (1:250). In both statements the easy rhetorical juxtapositions span great differences in the posited world views of American and European, new and old; possession of land and relation to the past are based on fundamentally different principles, so that material, historical, and social conditions, as well as the ideas that explain and justify them, must be reexamined. The passages imply that the relations between history and national or individual identity are different in the Old and New Worlds; they also claim that the New World draws its legitimating power from the future rather than the past. No matter that Cooper contradicts this claim by taking the Leather-stocking series ever deeper into the past. The assertion here is tactical, its purpose to free America from the tutelage of a European past whose value and authority are the ideological guarantees of European power.

Perhaps it was Cooper's hope for a reasonable accord between the old and the new that led him to miscalculate the effect of *Notions* so seriously. After its publication in England, he wrote to his American publishers that he expected "this work will pay . . . a handsome profit, for several Americans who have read it think it will do better at home than abroad." The publishers disagreed: "You are, we think, in error as to the extent of interest the book will excite here. To produce much interest severity is required, & however we may grumble at it, we are more disposed to read a book in wh. we receive castigation than one in wh. we have praise." As if justifying Cooper's assessment of the need for his book, they continue: "The fact too, of it being the production of an American, not the view of a foreigner examining our institutions & our society will be against it."[17] Cooper could only conclude that Cadwallader was right: Americans "saw with English eyes, and judged with English prejudices" (1:312), and therefore, the new republic was not yet fully emancipated. More important, the reaction of his American publishers shows that Cooper had not recognized that part of the relationship between books and readers is the imperfect correspondence between the expressible and the "legible," or acceptable.

Notions misses its audience in more specific ways. The Bachelor is

---

[17] See the correspondence between Cooper and the publishers, Carey, Lea, and Carey, May 1828, *Letters and Journals*, 1:262–63.

only mildly infected with the European misconceptions the book contests. Because he always sees the error of his thoughts so easily, *Notions* lacks intellectual drama and ignores the emotional charge of a shift in power. Furthermore, because Cooper is trying to show that his United States is a most refined and tranquil country, exactly fitting the European notion of the civilized, the Bachelor's travels want even the commonest kinds of mishap to which voyagers are exposed: his hosts are always hospitable; hotels and inns are always clean and comfortable, if not luxurious; the roads are good; the means of transportation faultless; the people helpful, informative, and polite; the countryside rich and well cultivated; the food tasty and plentiful; the laws perfect; the customs officials courteous, reasonable, and nonintrusive. Indeed, the landscape, as Franklin points out, reminds the Bachelor of France (*New World*, p. 57). The orderly and prosperous life of the people mirrors and grounds their prosperity and the order of their institutions. From internal evidence it is difficult to see why the book was written at all and how it differs from a statistical survey that, as Cooper himself says in the preface, would be outdated by the time of publication. A modern reader's sensibility might be strained by how the Bachelor skims over the question of slavery, benevolently hopes the Indian population will be absorbed into the superior civilization of the whites, and admires the situation of American women, who are "protected" from public affairs and even from the management of household finances, but to his contemporary readers Cooper's picture of his country appeared unfailingly flattering.

If this description makes the book seem anodyne, even boring, it is accurate. Critics could have steered the public away from it simply by pointing out what a chore it would be to read it. The passion of the negative reviews it received, however, indicates that *Notions* hit a nerve: English reviewers received this picture of prosperity most ungraciously. The *Literary Gazette* called it "the essence of puff, puff, puff," and "a sickening rodomontade . . . offensive to every reader of taste and discretion," and the *Edinburgh Review*, whose opinion Cooper valued enough to answer, complains of his "ruling, distorting, and coloring real life despotically as a girl deals with her first doll."[18] In this compari-

---

[18] Unsigned reviews from *Literary Gazette* (June 1828): 385–87, and *Edinburgh Review* 49 (June 1829): both reprinted in Dekker and McWilliams, pp. 152, 150, 152. In a letter to Charles Wilkes, Rome, 6 January 1830, Cooper mentions he had answered the article in "The Edinburgh." On 17 February 1830, in Rome, he tells Horatio Greenough that he had sent off the "manuscript of the letter" he wanted published in England and read especially in France. In a note, James Franklin Beard identifies

son of Cooper with a little girl, the critic points to the sore nerve: he expresses the anger of authority (male and parental) defied by a dependent's bid for freedom and rivalry for power. He concludes the review by expressing his confidence that in the future America "will be less and less disposed to pour contumely on the Ithaca whence she sprang, or to break that bow of Ulyssean greatness, which, today, at least, she cannot draw," (p. 152), and by advising that in the meantime the new nation behave with more becoming respect and humility.[19] The reaction seems directed less at the truth than at the effect of Cooper's argument, which would necessitate a reappraisal of transatlantic power relations and of Europe's (in this case, England's) view of itself as unchallenged in its domination. The critic of the *Edinburgh Review* does not mind the idea of a future reappraisal, but he is not yet prepared to accept the new American nation as an equal and is outraged that Cooper thinks he should.

Cooper was astonished. He had hoped his readers would accept his strong, prosperous, and civilized America as an equal among Western powers, just as the bachelors accepted Cadwallader for his good manners, proper conversation, and the education he offers their visiting fellow. Cooper's earlier books had also described the new land favorably, but *Notions* shows the importance of the terms of comparison. Whereas earlier travel or exoticizing literature saw America as a theater for unre-

---

"the letter" as "Cooper's 'Letter to the Editor of *The Edinburgh Review*," adding that it was never published. See *Letters and Journals*, 1:400, 404.

[19] Two British reviews may seem insufficient evidence for an argument about the reception of an American book, but in the case of *Notions* there is some justification and little alternative. British reviews were generally translated and reprinted in other countries; so they influenced more than just their initial public. For instance, the only review *Notions* seems to have had in Germany was a translation of the article in the *Literary Gazette* in *Blaetter fuer literarische Unterhaltung*, 13 January 1829 (Karlheinz Rossbacher, *Lederstrumpf in Deutschland*, pp. 94–95). Furthermore, the very scarcity of reference to *Notions* is a fact of its reception. Though American critics usually give it part of a paragraph in their overviews of Cooper's work, reviews in papers or journals are scarce. *Poole's Index to Periodical Literature* has entries for early reviews of almost everything Cooper wrote but nothing for *Notions;* the compendious Remond does not even mention it in a list of Cooper's works (p. 289); Dekker and McWilliams say only that its reception was on the whole unfavorable and that any praise was defensive. They suggest that the silence of American reviewers indicates "embarrassment over Cooper's outspoken republicanism" and that American reviewers had a better chance than usual for deferring to British opinion, given the delay in the American publication of *Notions* (p. 148). In the "Historical Introduction" to *Notions*, Gary Williams lists thirteen American reviews of the book (p. xlvii, n. 60) and observes that all either repeated the comments of the *Literary Gazette* or complained about American reliance on British judgments. Only one praised *Notions* (p. xxxv).

stricted European activity or a stage for European dreams of renewal, expressed in terms of noble Indians and bountiful land, *Notions* challenges the power relation upon which the exotic depends. It disturbs the discourse of the exotic by depicting a modern state whose new forms of political, economic, and social organization might supplant those of Europe. The promise of renewal in Cooper's earlier works was more acceptable because it threatened neither the integrity of existing power relations nor that of familiar fictional conventions.

Thus the purpose, emphasis, and argument of *Notions of the Americans* reshape the genre of European accounts of travel to the Americas.[20] Whereas in the traditional opposition between primitive and civilized, Americans—original or adventitious—are the "primitives" and Europeans the "civilized," *Notions* presents America not as inhabitable "nature" but as the proper site for civilization carried by its citizens. Summing up his comparison between George Washington and Napoleon, Cooper explains, once again, the difference between his enterprise and the usual exposition of exotic difference: Washington stands not as a corrective to Napoleon but as completely different and superior kind of warrior statesman: a "parallel between these eminent men is impossible; but a comparison is easy indeed" (2:194). A parallel would preserve the oppositional relation and the subordinate position of the American term, while a comparison implies equivalence. And in this way too Cooper distresses both the critic of the *Literary Gazette*, who indignantly sends him back to his "novels and romances," and the critic of the *Edinburgh Review*, who opines that America should be content to be thought a "land of promise" for a vague future.

Among the acceptable "novels and romances" to which the *Literary Gazette* alludes are the first three books of the Leather-stocking series, which, ending with the death of the hero, seemed at the time complete. Though other Cooper novels had been successful, those about the Leather-stocking had caught on most strongly, both at home and abroad, where his adventures had been quickly translated into all major European languages.[21] Unlike the de-exoticizing *Notions*, they write the

[20] Levin, in *The Myth of the Golden Age*, esp. chap. 3, and Hoxie Neale Fairchild before him (*The Noble Savage*) show the dependence of European views of the New World on the well-established genres of travel and exploration accounts, upon which were also built comparisons between the two worlds and arguments about the nature and origin of European civilization.

[21] In 1823 *Pioneers* was published in New York by Wiley, in London by John Murray, and in Paris by Gosselin (translation by Defauconpret), with two more translations in 1835 and 1849; it appeared in German in 1824 and shortly after that in Danish,

New World in the familiar language and narrative conventions of historical and exotic romances. William Kelly says that the preface to *The Pioneers*, the first of the series, "anticipates [the novel's] conclusion and undermines whatever suspense [it] might produce" (*Plotting America's Past*, 5–6) with its description of a peaceful, settled countryside—just like that through which the Bachelor is taken. Suspense is thus transferred to *how* civilization will be imposed, to "the dynamics of American development" (p. 6). This displacement may account for the easier acceptance of a civilized American landscape, but the body of the novel shows us not so much the "beautiful and thriving villages" of the preface as the pristine lakes and wild forests of the traditional image of the New World. Even Geoffrey Rans, who, like Kelly, though by a different route, proposes to rescue the Leather-stocking novels from mythical and transcendent readings, acknowledges that "one of the great puzzles in any rigorous reading [of the series] is how it could ever have stirred the patriotic sense, how the pride taken in the emergence of an American voice could have so completely obscured what that voice was saying, the criticism the series embodies" (*Cooper's Leather-stocking Novels*, p. 4). He implies that Cooper has been consistently misread; but then the misreading, like the misreading of Rousseau through which Uncas and Chingachgook become noble savages, is as important in the history of the novels' reception as are the feminist readings of Annette Kolodny and Nina Baym or the psychological and mythical readings Rans opposes.

When Natty Bumppo is mythologized, his stance toward the wilderness and toward civilization appears either to embody or to resolve the problematic relation between them and the nation. In either case, his progressive transformation into the mythical Leather-stocking is a curious case of interaction between literary creation and the public imagination.[22] When we first see him in *The Pioneers*, wiping his nose on his sleeve (p. 20), he is just a curious character, not a hero. D. H. Lawrence sees the drop on his nose as an index of freedom ("Fenimore Cooper's

---

Swedish, and Spanish. In 1826 *The Last of the Mohicans* was published in Philadelphia by Carey and Lea, in London by Miller, in Paris by Gosselin, and in Germany in separate editions at Braunschweig, Stuttgart, Leipzig, and Frankfurt am Main. It also appeared in Danish (1828), Italian (1829), Swedish (1830–31), Spanish (1832), Dutch (1833), and Portuguese (in Paris in 1838); there were also various reprints and new editions. *The Prairie*, too, was published in America and England and in French and German translations in 1827. (Spiller and Blackburn, pp. 27–31, 42–46, 48–51.)

[22] In "Literaturgeschichte als Provokation," esp. sec. 7, Jauss maintains that reception does not determine production but is neither passive nor isolated from it.

Leatherstocking Novels," p. 70), but it more likely indicates class or
social position. At the end of the novel, Natty proves to have been a
very good servant; his manners are lower-class; his status explains the
mystery of his actions.[23] On many levels, the novel indicates that Cooper intended Judge Temple to be the central character and the central
action to be the taming of the wilderness and the passage from savagery
to civilization, but Natty upstages the judge. He calls forth the more
appealing image of an America just on the brink of civilization and still
exerting the attraction of the wilderness.

Natty's first appearance in *The Pioneers* is not his first appearance in
print: the chapter in which he saves Elizabeth from the panther preceded the novel on the market and presumably stimulated the sale of
thirty-five hundred copies of the book on the first day of publication.[24]
In that episode, Natty is not a toothless old scout, but a knight of the
woods; he knows the ways of the wild and the tools of civilization; his
behavior, as he places his knowledge, his skill, and his life at the service
of young ladies in distress, falls directly within a code that defines the
traditional hero of humble appearance and noble heart. His talents, his
outlook, and his actions are in harmony with the personal needs of
Judge Temple and the collective needs of the settlement; there is hardly
a hint that the rest of the novel will show this harmony to be problemati-
cal.[25] Natty may even, as he saves Elizabeth, gain the advantage over
the judge, whom he puts under personal obligation; he appears on the
side of concrete, man-to-man bonds created in the preservation of a
family, whereas the judge later opts for legal, abstract obligations that
are to benefit the community and underlie the American polity. But the
anticipatory chapter is the model for the later Leather-stocking books,
not for those parts of *The Pioneers* which record how a town was built
and prospered in the wilderness or how it instituted the complicated

[23] Leslie Fiedler calls Cooper "the most class-conscious of American writers" (*Love
and Death in the American Novel*, p. 184).
[24] Rossbacher comments on Cooper's marketing strategies and gives this prepublica-
tion trick as an example of his concessions to public taste (p. 22).
[25] Philip Fisher shows how firmly Natty Bumppo, even at his most isolated and indi-
vidualistic, is connected with the collective, cumulative history of the United States.
He is always "imbedded in the increasingly wasteful solutions of others" (*Hard Facts*,
p. 72), and "the great, central hard facts [are] always . . . incidental to thousands of
other transactions that seem to have nothing to do with them and . . . as if by
accident, resume the configuration of their historical solution" (p. 73). But when he
says that they "seem to have nothing to do with them," Fisher also indicates that
the myth of the Leather-stocking works only because that connection is kept implicit
and mystified.

relationships and compromises necessary in the state of civilization that *Notions* praises. Insofar as it records the establishment, in a wilderness subject to the "law of nature," of a polity subject to human laws derived from reason and will *The Pioneers* is closer to *Notions of the Americans* than their differences in genre, quality, and interest indicate. But the novel's progeny derives from its exotic component familiarized by narrative structure, plot, and characterization.

In *The Pioneers* the Leather-stocking's lower-class status subordinates him to Judge Temple, who represents not only in possession and authority but also in cultivation and reason, the civilization that changes Natty Bumppo's world. The dispute arising at Natty's first appearance touches immediately on the problems of planting civilization in the wilderness and reflects Cooper's doubts about their resolution. These are issues that *Notions* suppresses.[26] In the argument about who may keep the deer shot in that scene, Oliver and the Leather-stocking invoke a "natural" right: the animal is theirs since they have killed it for food on free land. As the judge lays claim to the deer, he invokes property rights first, then his obligation as a magistrate to enforce these rights and regulate the activities that take place on the land, and lastly the mediation of money: property, law, and money effect the passage from the law of nature to the regulations of civilization. As the scene develops, however, the argument shifts to a question of class: because they are lower-class, Oliver and Natty do not need the saddle of venison as much as the judge's household does, even though they earned it by shooting the animal. The problem of property remains unresolved on either level; establishing and applying the law becomes a doubtful proposition, and the judge, generally a sympathetic figure whose efforts to civilize the wilderness are cast in a favorable light, seems slightly ludicrous, if not dishonest. The scene puts the "natural" criteria of ownership to work on the side of the hunters, while Judge Temple's appeal to class devalues the claim of culture over nature by recalling the critique of class (which we saw unraveling in *Paul et Virginie*) as "unnatural" rather than "civilized." In a further deflection of the argu-

[26] The ambiguous and problematic ways in which all important matters—history, contact between races, relation to nature, the nature of empire and civilization—are dealt with in the Leather-stocking novels forms the core of Geoffrey Rans's argument for Cooper's continued importance. His "highest fictional value . . . and greatest political utility" is that he "demystifies ['civilization's'] most prized values. Cooper's . . . incomplete consciousness is irrelevant; it does not impair the opportunity his work offers the reader to reach full consciousness" (*Cooper's Leather-stocking Novels*, pp. 41–42).

ment, when the judge finds he has injured Oliver, the allocation of the saddle becomes less a contest of principle than an exercise in charity and reparation. As the scene develops, the civilizing process becomes problematic as well as arbitrary.

The Pioneers, the least "mythical" work of the series, provides the clearest view of the contradictions and confusions with which an American civilization that emulates and opposes Europe is imposed on American nature. Some critics set this first novel apart from the rest of the series. According to Rans, given what *The Pioneers* "actually tells," even *The Prairie*, where Natty is "more nearly mythic" (p. 101), must be "qualified and demystified," but he is perhaps overestimating the public's memory and desire for logic in fiction. Kelly sees in the novel Cooper's clearest conflation of the personal and the national, his ambivalence toward the power of his father and father-in-law and toward Walter Scott and European civilization (p. 35–43).[27] The difference of *The Pioneers* from the other Leather-stocking novels and Natty's transformation are congruent: mythification takes a specific direction. Unlike the judge, who fumbles in vain for principles that can harmonize community and individual needs, Natty conjures up a world where they are not in conflict; but to do so he must remove one of the elements in the opposition that conditions his creation. For him the only acceptable community is predicated on personal preference and presents no conflict of loyalties. He lives by the "natural" and therefore inviolable laws of the forest, to which he assimilates the wishes and needs of old Mr. Effingham (his employer) and of the Great Serpent and Oliver (his friends). He claims to derive his ethical values from Christian doctrine, but characteristically, he dispenses with prelates or churches; friendship and religion become "natural," functioning in accordance with laws of the heart, inviolable like those of nature. For Cadwallader in *Notions*, the legitimacy of the new nation derives from its excellent institutions, from a man-made framework of laws and customs; for Natty value is grounded in the "laws" of the forest and that other natural phenomenon, the "heart."

When Natty reappears in the following books of the series, he no longer embodies the conflict between society and the individual; he is in flight from civilization, even as he serves it. The traits that marked his social class on his first appearance become individual characteristics,

[27] Kelly surveys the psychological reading of the series, particularly Stephen Railton's *Fenimore Cooper*, as well as Cooper's ambivalent reactions to Scott in letters and in articles (pp. 35, 37, 38).

and no longer place him on the lower ranks of an established social structure; instead, they characterize the sturdy woodsman to whom class is irrelevant and who can, like other beings of the forest, blend into—become one with—the world of nature. Whereas in *Pioneers* his head is "thinly covered with lank" hair, his fox skin cap is "much inferiour in finish and ornaments," his brows are "shaggy," and his neck is "scraggy" (pp. 22–23), in *The Last of the Mohicans* he is "muscular," with a figure "attenuated rather than full"; he wears an emblematic "forest green" shirt, and his features reflect his ambiguous position between white man and Indian, in the "sun-burnt . . . complexion of one who might claim descent from a European parentage," as well as his outstanding moral quality, the "sturdy honesty" of his expression (pp. 28–29). In the third book of the series, *The Prairie*, he appears, unnamed, as the very spirit of the unspoiled American continent, no longer necessarily Christian, hardly even human: "The sun had fallen. . . . In the center of this flood of fiery light a human form appeared, drawn against the gilded background as distinctly, and seemingly as palpable, as though it would come within the grasp of any extended hand. The figure was colossal; the attitude musing and melancholy" (pp. 14–15). All markers of class, race, and personality have dropped away, and Natty has become an emblem, a spirit. Although he still serves settlers and explorers, and although the novel is set at the precise historical time of the Louisiana Purchase, Natty is no longer an actor in a historical process or a marginal element in the sociopolitical makeup of a pioneer village; he has become a romantic loner, who singly (in a double sense) opens the world for settlement and then disappears in a glory. He exists in a fully "primitive" landscape, where human bonds have to be constructed from the beginning, as in the group of Ishmael Bush, and where no laws at all stand between settlers and the land. He dies, finally, among his Indian friends, who honor him as a "valiant, a just, and a wise warrior . . . gone on the path which will lead him to the blessed grounds of his people" and as a "just chief of the palefaces" (p. 386). But this last is exactly what he is not: a chief presupposes a social organization, and though the Leather-stocking bequeaths to those who follow him the immensity of yet-unoccupied America, he is set apart from them; they are building their own country, of which they would never consider Indians the "rightful owners" (p. 27).

The slide of the Leather-stocking from folksy figure to symbol, from a member of society, however reluctant, to a nameless and placeless spirit, has consistently seemed appropriate, if not logical or realistic, to

Cooper's readers. Nevertheless, it runs counter to Cooper's customary emphasis on the virtues of civilization.[28] The melancholy note in the image of the Leather-stocking against the dying sun is a reminder of the inherent contradiction between what attracts settlers to the wilderness and what settlers finally do to the wilderness, a contradiction central to Natty's role as scout and adversary of "civilization." Natty's "honesty" is the mediating term that allows Cooper to sever his character from a society he still serves, for it places the source of ethical judgments in the individual rather than in society and eliminates the potential conflict between the Leather-stocking's white "gifts," of which he is proud and which he never considers relinquishing, and his alliance with the unspoiled land and its original inhabitants.[29] In the Leather-stocking series, the immensity of the land calls for a free figure such as Natty[30] and its conquest also demands the loosening of established social bonds. In this, the Leather-stocking series directly opposes *Notions of the Americans*.

The Leather-stocking's history, his disappearances into the sunset,

[28] Bernard Rosenthal says that Cooper's American readers never took all that mythical stuff very seriously, approving, like the novelist, of replacing Indians with a more advanced civilization. His argument resembles that of Roy Harvey Pearce, who believes that, though the Leather-stocking is "the man of the forest mythically perfected," still "American society sweeps over" him, for he is "not civilized perfection" (*The Savages of America*, p. 204). His "radical inadequacy for civilized life," says Pearce, dooms him, at best, to marginality, together with the Indians whose "savagism" he partially shares (p. 205). Rosenthal does not quite explain why American readers are attracted to the Leather-stocking, but thinks Europeans like him because they miss the point of Cooper's collusion with his American public (*City of Nature*, p. 74). Pearce arranges the Leather-stocking tales in order of the chronology of Natty's life (p. 202), which lets him show Natty decaying from Deerslayer to the marginal figure of *The Pioneers* and Chingachgook taking to drink rather than rejuvenated and restored; that strategy fails to account for either the development or the attractiveness of Natty as a literary figure. Henry Nash Smith does balance the allure of the Leather-stocking's anarchic component with Cooper's ultimate judgment of his unfitness for civilized life (*Virgin Land*, chap 6).

[29] According to Robert E. Beider, the theory of different "gifts" characteristic of different races was current in Cooper's time: "In *Crania Americana* (1839) and subsequent articles, Samuel C. Morton set out to demonstrate that the Indian was a separate species from the Caucasian and therefore possessed different abilities. . . . it was unreasonable to expect Indians to become civilized because they were incapable of advancing out of savagery. Each race had its own inherent gifts" (p. 311). Philip Fisher identifies such generalizations with the "collapse of categories" that eliminated the earlier difference between the Indian as noble and as savage and became part of the justification for the Jacksonian Indian Removal (p. 36).

[30] Whereas Lawrence reads the Leather-stocking's lack of social ties as freedom, Wallace sees it as a sign of exclusion and Natty as one of Cooper's characteristic "marginal heroes" (*Early Cooper*, p. 172).

and his refusal of a permanent home trace the steady westward expansion of the new nation. As a character, in the usual sense of having attributes such as choice, will, or even just preferences, the Leatherstocking is in flight from that expansion, but within the structure and meaning of the Leather-stocking saga, his simultaneous service to and avoidance of culture are both indispensable to his popularity. He can, at the same time, criticize and reassure Cooper's readers. He finds them destructive, but he also protects their ambition and their desire for adventure. He teaches them to cope with the untamed nature for which they think they long and loosens the cultural bonds under which they chafe; yet he preserves the security these bonds offer. He promises both freedom and safety.

Cooper's European admirers relished that sense of freedom, that view of a life unencumbered by the economic difficulties that dogged their ordinary days. Karlheinz Rossbacher shows that in Germany, the Leather-stocking novels (and their many contemporary imitations) became a code, allowing for a certain freedom of speech in the face of imperial censorship (p. 22). What beckons from the Leather-stocking books, however, is not an escape from oppressive European politics to superior American politics, as in *Notions* but an escape to a prepolitical, primitive state through fiction, travelogue, and philosophical argument. Natty's whiteness and his strict code of values, on one hand, the redness of his skin and his woodsman's craft, on the other, characterize him as a mediator between the social and the natural, the village and the forest, the law of society and the law of nature.[31]

His skin makes the Leather-stocking into a mediating figure in yet another sense. If white characters are often uncertain about Natty's race (though the true "primitives" can always tell he is not Indian), it is because Cooper creates him "half-rigged; being neither brig, nor schooner," as Cap puts it in *The Pathfinder* (p. 16), a "hybrid offspring of civilization and barbarism," as one early critic sees it, or, as Balzac,

---

[31] Ross Pudaloff argues that for Cooper American culture, not the natural setting in which it develops, constitutes the nation's contribution to the world: "The culture created by Americans was responsible for the valuable and unique elements of American society" ("Cooper's Genres," p. 720). It is a measure of the force of the public's desire for the exotic that Cooper's rendition of the natural made his defense of American culture so widely read. Note, though, that Pudaloff makes this point precisely about *Notions*. He also finds a split not just in Cooper's rendition of the relation between nature and culture but also within his rendition of American culture, between those parts of his novels that function as historical romances and those that function as marriage novels, those dealing with "politics" and those propounding a "society" (p. 712).

extrapolating from the physical, understands it, "a magnificent moral hermaphrodite, born of the savage state and of civilization."[32] But Cooper did not favor literal hybridism,[33] and though he needed Natty as a mediator, his readers, like his Indians, were never left in doubt that Natty was white.

The white characters' moment of doubt allows Cooper to resolve the tingle of otherness into the safety of the familiar. For a few pages it displaces Cooper's treatment of the encounter with otherness from its customary location in the marriage plot and connects it with the problem of drawing boundaries between culture and nature. Natty's mediating position is the more important because Cooper believes that the rules governing whites and Indians are different by nature. The rules governing whites are codified in Christianity, which establishes a correspondence between the physical and the moral. Explaining why he won't take scalps, Leather-stocking says, "My gifts are . . . such as belong to my religion and color," and "I'll not unhumanize my natur' by falling into ways that God intended for another race" (*Deerslayer*, pp. 75, 76). Religion and race are coupled and together define him. He does not consider the Indians inhuman, and he spends much of *The Deerslayer* either vainly trying to persuade his companions to respect them or suffering the consequences of his own respect; he simply considers them a different kind. The line drawn by color and religion cannot be crossed, especially through marriage.[34] Leather-stocking is the character closest to the white-Indian boundary on the white side, and in *The Deerslayer*, when he is at the age of marriage and helps Chingachgook secure his mate, he must state his position: "I am white—have a white heart, and can't, in reason, love a redskinned maiden, who must have a redskin heart and feelin's" (p. 129). In *The Prairie*, where he has lost

[32] Francis Parkman, "The Works of James Fenimore Cooper," *North American Review* 74 (January 1852): 147–61, reprinted in Dekker and McWilliams, p. 252. Balzac admired Cooper; his review appears in *Paris Review*, July 25, 1840, trans. K. P. Wormeley, *The Personal Opinions of Honoré de Balzac* (Boston, 1899), reprinted in Dekker and McWilliams, p. 196.

[33] See Jane Tompkins's discussion of the Leather-stocking novels in *Criticism* 23 (1981): 24–41, reprinted as "No Apologies for the Iroquois: A New Way to Read the Leatherstocking Novels," in *Sensational Designs* (pp. 94–121).

[34] This aspect of the Leather-stocking saga has been widely studied, especially as it appears in *The Last of the Mohicans*. Fiedler believes that "miscegenation is the secret theme of the world's favorite story of adventure, the secret theme of the Leatherstocking Tales as a whole" (p. 205), and for Nina Baym, Cooper's is not so much an "American" way of facing the question of intermarriage as a "male" position in close and contentious intertextual relation with similar stories by women. See "How Men and Women Wrote Indian Stories."

all the names he had acquired in the other novels, he frequently refers to himself as "a man without a cross," as if that, and not the actions that had made him Deerslayer, Pathfinder, or Hawkeye, were both his final identity and his legacy. Uncas, on the other hand, the noblest of all Cooper's savages and the closest to the boundary on the Indian side, is still made to take a scalp—even if it is just one—so that he is firmly marked as having red "gifts." The readers, if not the characters, "see" the fresh scalp at his belt and learn his true nature. But Uncas can still raise the specter, if not the question (for the line is not in the end questionable), of "crossing." Ordinary lust of Indian men for white women threatens the whites only as would a hungry bear that attacked their camp. Uncas, however, falls in chivalrous love with Cora, who reciprocates. Whereas Alice sees in him only the animal or the aesthetic object, Cora sees in him the man, in the sense in which she is woman.[35] But having conjured up the specter of love between Uncas and Cora, Cooper beats a retreat.[36] He never leaves Cora and Uncas alone together; he never brings himself to comment on their feelings for each other; he makes Cora a nonwhite, giving her an African ancestry, the result of her father's crossing of the line,[37] and finally, he eliminates the problem by killing the lovers. Only the Indian maidens at their funeral, who do not play the game by white rules, sing about the possibility that Uncas and Cora might meet again in the next world (and Leather-stocking is happy that Munro and Heyward do not understand the chant).

Cora, the woman with a cross, straddles the boundary that separates the white, civilized game from the nonwhite one, and for that alone she is doomed. She cannot belong to either side and will not be one of the mothers of the nation. She is not even attractive to any of the white males in the story as the forbidden (Jewish) Rebecca is to Scott's hero Ivanhoe, and the dark, sensuous ladies of romantic fiction can be to heroes they will lose to feeble pale blondes. Uncas, who loves her, is doubly doomed, for not seeing the taint in her and for looking with desire across the line that separates them.

[35] See also Terence Martin, "From the Ruins of History," p. 227.
[36] Fiedler says Cora and Hayward are attracted to each other (p. 206), but though he admires her, Hayward does not think of Cora as a wife. Fiedler also asserts that "Cooper's own contemporaries urged him to let Cora and Uncas be joined in marriage" (p. 207): thus Cooper's horror of this marriage is his own; his tolerance is reserved for the sexless but homoerotically tinged relationship between Natty and the Great Serpent, which becomes a fundamental American myth.
[37] Kelly notes that Colonel Munro was driven abroad because, for reasons of class, he could not marry his sweetheart (p. 54). As in *Paul et Virginie,* class barriers lead

Cora is also Cooper's adaptation of European literary convention to the requirements of a literature of nationality. She belongs to the set of dark, interesting, but doomed heroines, descendants of Mme de Staël's Corinne,[38] who die or enter convents in nineteenth-century novels while their blond, submissive sisters marry romantic heroes. The pale, blond Alice, for whom no critic has anything good to say,[39] will marry and raise the future citizens of the republic. In her, Cooper rejects the exogamous possibility with which Colonel Munro experimented, and Cora, the result of the experiment. The question for Cooper is not, however, one of character. As Nina Baym points out, Cora "is not in any meaningful sense a bad woman. On the contrary, she is very good" ("Women," p. 704). Her darkness does not denote a character flaw, only a "cross", it thus becomes part of the dramatization of the themes of separation and distinction central to a vision of the new land where the establishment of civilization requires that only one stance toward nature, one strand of history, one strain of the population impose themselves. The theme of incest, prominent in texts that confront "crossing" of class or color lines as a real possibility because it provides an alternative as dreaded and desired as marriage to the other, is correspondingly attenuated in Cooper's novels. It flickers briefly over the relationship between Oliver and Elizabeth in *The Pioneers* (as does exogamy in the suggestion that Oliver is a blood relation of Mohegan). It does not disappear, however, and Leslie Fiedler finds it in the love of the same underlying the friendship between others which binds the Leatherstocking and Chingachgook, as well as a string of male friends from different races central in the literature of a culture that steadfastly prefers the absence of issue to hybridism.[40]

It is only in the Leather-stocking himself that Cooper allows for the permeability of boundaries between white and Indian, which come to stand for the realms of culture and nature, and only by isolating him from settlements and barring him from marriage. Natty settles on the

---

to an alternative New World society. In this case, however, migration is deleterious; the alternative is not in any way viable.

[38] See Ellen Moers, "Performing Heroinism."

[39] In "The Women of Cooper's Leather-stocking Tales" Nina Baym calls her "unquestionably the silliest of Cooper's heroines." Because "she is certain to faint whenever any situation of stress arises," she is the character "in which the concept of woman as package becomes literally expressed" (p. 704).

[40] For Fisher, cultural continuity through marriage is coupled with massacre (p. 36); the possibility of hybridism is eliminated by the elimination of one of its elements. In any case, it is dangerous territory.

frontier and becomes its embodiment. But it is part of the impulse of civilization, defined in the terms Europe took to America, that it should keep pushing against the frontier and absorbing nature into itself. Natty's duality keeps him outside the cycle of production and reproduction as surely as Cora's "cross."

But the Leather-stocking is also a hybrid of two literary figures. He is the early adventurer who tells about savage lands and begins to inscribe European history on their emptiness, and he is the inhabitant of these lands, waiting in innocence to redeem Europe from its history. A French critic saw him as "the embodiment of the first dream of Jean Jacques Rousseau,"[41] indicating at the same time one of the curious transformations of the noble savage in common parlance and how a figure such as the Leather-stocking could seem familiar to European readers of tales of discoveries and conquest, of Rousseau and Chateaubriand. In Natty and the Delawares of the Leather-stocking series, the noble savage of a misread Rousseau returns to the American shores, invested with discursive authority but shorn of the characteristics upon which such authority had been built, for Cooper dissociates his creation from the political implications of the Rousseauean primitive. Cooper's primitive is not "original." For Cooper primitivism can be invested under the aegis of nature with the highest personal virtues, but without schooling, without books, without a society, even his "good" primitives cannot give birth to a civilization.

Thus the Leather-stocking usurps the place of native noble savages. The first real Indian to appear in the Leather-stocking books is John Mohegan, sad remnant of a once-powerful tribe, humble at religious services and drunk at the inn, whom Elizabeth tries to console for the loss of family, tribe, land, and culture by promising to buy one of his baskets. He resembles the Indians that the Bachelor describes, the "degenerate specimens" found near settlements or the "few peaceable and half-civilized remains of tribes" (*Notions* 1:245) with whom Cooper himself seems to have been most familiar.[42] These are the last of the "dying

---

[41] F.A.S., "The United States: American Literature, Novels of Mr. Cooper," *Globe* (Paris), 19 June 1827, pp. 173–75, and July 2, 1827, pp. 205–7, trans. J. P. McWilliams, rpt. in Dekker and McWilliams, pp. 125–36, esp. 134.

[42] In "Small Family Memories" Susan Cooper tells of a trip her father took to Washington specifically to meet with a delegation of prairie Indians, Pawnees and Sioux, apparently to gather material, for he "had already decided upon a new romance, connected with mounted tribes on the Prairies" (p. 59). At that time, however, Cooper had already written *The Last of the Mohicans* and transformed John Mohegan into the Great Serpent; the transformation was not a consequence of his meeting with an Amerindian population he had not known before.

race" to whom Karl May refers in the brief but forceful indictment of white conquest and settlement which constitutes the introduction to his *Winnetou*, whose noble Indian hero can escape degeneracy only by dying beautifully before its inevitable onset (pp. xi–xiv).[43]

In *The Last of the Mohicans* Cooper's Indians also take on mythical colors. As the action recedes from the town of *Pioneers* toward a wilderness still untouched by Europe, the problems, conflicts, internal contradictions of settlement fade away. *The Last of the Mohicans* presents itself as literature of nationality and as a historical novel based on documented incidents, but as Cooper transposes history from the domestic of *Pioneers* to the heroic, he easily falls into the traditional European narrative of the Americas, including the split image of the Amerindian as cannibal/noble savage which owes more to his reading than to his observation. This split image recurs in the series, with the evil Magua, Arrowhead, and Mahtoree opposing the noble Mohegan, rejuvenated into the Great Serpent, Uncas, or the Pawnee Hard Heart.[44] But even the noble primitives retain some taint of unacceptable savagery; its emblem is the scalp Uncas takes behind the other characters' backs. Scalping replaces cannibalism as the anticultural mark, and it does so more directly and openly than the danger of "crossing" undercuts the possibility of exchange and the legitimacy of desire for the uncivilized.

As for the Leather-stocking, cut loose from society after *The Pioneers*, he acquires characteristics of that same noble primitive—but christened, white, nonscalping, and nonmarrying. He is as free of savagery as of European spleen and as fit for life in the wilderness as any of its original inhabitants. He is acceptable even to American critics unconvinced by the nobility of Cooper's Indians, such as Francis Parkman, who claimed that Magua resembles real American Indians much more closely than Uncas.[45] A public of Americans and Europeans familiar with fiction about primitives and eager to find regeneration in the New World, however, saw Uncas and Chingachgook as continuous with

---

[43] The novel was first published in 1892, inspired, in part, according to the editor (p. 749), by indignation at the injustices shown in *Uncle Tom's Cabin*. It is also possible to detect the spirits of the Leather-stocking and Chingachgook in the characters of Old Shatterhand and Winnetou.

[44] John P. McWilliams, in "Red Satan," draws an extended comparison between Cooper's Indians and Homer's heroes and, unlike Cooper, writes Amerindians as ancestors of European culture, he also mentions Chactas as one of the models for the virtuous Amerindians (p. 143).

[45] Parkman, in Dekker and McWilliams, p. 255.

Natty and easily recognized their primitive nobility, which consigns the sad Mohegan to oblivion.[46]

The Leather-stocking tales also invoke a view of the New World as the place where the golden age is not a dream of the past but an aspect of contemporary reality, where the ancestral primitive exists in innocence and plenty, uncorrupted by progress or civilization. Natty's "honesty" guarantees a primitive innocence, even though he spends most of the Leather-stocking novels rescuing friends from what are clearly not so innocent primitives; his asceticism assures his readers that in the forests of America there is paradisiacal plenty, safe from the greed of an acquisitive civilization. He invites those readers to think of themselves as capable of the same virtue in the same natural surroundings.

But if they are readers, they exist within writing and history. The innocent perfection of the exotic questions colonization and settlement as well as that second, political perfection of American life and institutions which is the subject of *Notions of the Americans*. In the myth, a golden age precedes government. Logically, it is difficult to write at the same time of a golden age and of the transformation that will make it perfect for the future of political man. Logically, it becomes inevitable, as Cooper thought it had been historically inevitable, that the representatives of the primitive man whose natural habitat is the protohistorical age of gold expire or that the white man who comes closest to embodying primitive virtues clash with villages, governments, laws, and other signs of the workings of a social contract.[47]

[46] Though Uncas fits the pattern of Chateaubriand's fictional virtuous savage, it is not clear whether Cooper had read the French author. Margaret Murray Gibb reports Susan Cooper's assertion (*Pages and Pictures from the Writings of James Fenimore Cooper*, p. 130) that her father had not read *Atala* and would not have liked it if he had (Gibb, *Le roman de bas-de-cuir*, p. 107). Arguably, both women were interested in an entirely original Cooper, eager to stress his "Americanness" by denying any foreign influence over his writing. Although Cooper wrote little about his reading, especially of novels, the first of the Bachelor's letters in *Notions* shows that he kept up with what Europeans wrote about America, for he was always interested in correcting their misconceptions. It is therefore not unlikely that he had, at some point, seen a copy of *Atala*, a blockbuster set in North America and available in an American edition in English in the same year of its French publication (Armand Weil, Introduction to *Atala*). Reluctantly, Marcel Clavel accepts Susan Cooper's statement, noting, however, the availability of three translations of *Atala*, one printed in Philadelphia (*Fenimore Cooper*, p. 381). Cooper mentions that he was lent *Les Natchez* (1826) but did not read it because he did not trust Chateaubriand's descriptions of Indians—his own being the only accurate ones (letter to Charles Gosselin, 1–7(?) April 1827, *Letters and Journals*, 1:211–12).
[47] F.A.S. says that the Leather-stocking series embodies the dream of Rousseau, but without the social contract (Dekker and McWilliams, p. 134). As for Cooper, in *The Prairie* he makes Battius, whose arguments never stand up to reason, defend the "social compact" (p. 148).

Cooper's fictions of national identity accounted for the relation between different populations and between settlement and wilderness in
the synchronic categories of marriage and the division of nature from
culture by means of property and law. He also tries to account for the
diachronic relation between present and past. The new nation's need
to compete with, distance itself from, and gain the approval of the
metropolis whose domination it had escaped so recently and incompletely grounds his search for terms in which colonial history can be
told and legitimated. His tales attempt to make up for the weight of
European centuries and to find for a nation with a short history what
the Brazilian critic Antônio Cândido calls the "depths of legendary
time."[48]

For Philip Fisher *The Deerslayer*, last in writing, earliest in chronology
of the tales, illustrates Cooper's notion that American history begins
with the arrival of Europeans who bring their time to the New World
and for whom discovery and settlement are chapters of European history. Though Cooper thinks his books should contribute to the "just
appreciation . . . of the wonderful means by which Providence is clearing a way for the advancement of civilization across the whole American
continent" (*The Pathfinder*, p. viii),[49] he also wants to dissociate his nation
from the "cold and selfish policy of the distant monarchs of Europe"
(*Mohicans*, p. 15) and rescue from European indifference or greed the
feats of American heroes.[50] One of his strategies of dissociation is his
search for New World equivalents to characteristics upon which Europeans (more specifically, the English) base their claims to superiority:
if Europeans look down on the former colony for not having any history
to speak of, Cooper will speak of American history. He states at the
beginning of *The Deerslayer*: "On the human imagination events produce
the effects of time. Thus, he who has traveled far and seen much is apt
to fancy that he has lived long, and the history that most abounds in
important incidents soonest assumes the aspect of antiquity. In no other

---

[48] Antônio Cândido, *Formação da literatura brasileira*, 2:221. Harry Levin, echoing Commager, speaks of American writers' "search for a usable past" ("Literature and Cultural Identity," p. 145).
[49] We are on the familiar ground claimed by Raleigh at the very start of colonization.
See Chapter 2.
[50] See the author's note in *The Last of the Mohicans* on George Washington, whose
name "does not occur in any European account of the battle which he had won for
the British against the French and the Indians," even though "all America rang with
his well-merited reputation" (p. 17).

way can we account for the venerable air that is already gathering around American annals" (p. 9).

His strategy is to rescue American history by setting it in a kind of psychological time, similar in a way to Rousseau's notion of the primitive as introspection, measured in actions rather than in eons; he retells many such actions and devotes to minutiae the time and attention normally granted to important events: "When the mind reverts to the earliest days of colonial history, the period seems remote and obscure, the thousand changes that thicken along the links of recollections throwing back the origin of the nation to a day so distant as seemingly to reach the mists of time" (*Deerslayer*, p. 9). Emphasis and attention to detail make American history seem as long as European history, the founders as long-lived as biblical patriarchs, their peopling and civilizing of the New World as weighty as the birth of European nations. He is careful not to extend these "mists of time" beyond the moment at which colonization started, however, for the other premise of his account is that the European colonizers created the New World out of nothing. Cooper separates national, historical time from the unrecorded events that preceded colonization and, unarticulated, are as if consigned to the realm of nature. Cooper calls the rock at the end of Lake Glimmerglass "a seat that held many a forest chieftain during the long succession of unknown ages in which America and all it contained existed apart in mysterious solitude, a world by itself, equally without familiar history and without an origin that the annals of man can reach" (*Deerslayer*, p. 139). History and writing become synonymous in this formulation; unwritten origins, events that are not retrievable from annals or books, cannot be part of the definition of a national self. When the Leatherstocking series, which Cooper presents, among other things, as history, recreates events on Lake Otsego or on the prairies beyond the lakes, it rescues the heroic enterprise of colonization from the fate of the meetings by the great chieftains. Cooper's tales bring his America out of mysterious solitude and into Western consciousness, provide it with an origin inscribed in "the annals of men," make it a part of Western discourse. Inscribing the feats of Greeks and Trojans on American woods, as Father Aubry does, is the European solution to the absence of American writing; Cooper's is to turn the feats of woodsmen into books. At the same time he banishes the original Americans from history altogether, except as written into colonization.

But Cooper also provides the myth in which a proper history begins, by metamorphosing the Leather-stocking from the scruffy character of

The Pioneers into the legendary figure of *The Prairie* or *The Deerslayer*, D. H. Lawrence's favorite. It is significant and characteristic that even there he avoids the taint of otherness and makes a legend not of the Indians who preceded the settlers but of one of the colonizers, because, James Grossman believes, "Cooper's sober views as a social historian are not those of a literal believer in the Noble Savage." Instead, "Cooper regarded Indian civilizations as vastly inferior to Christianity, and when he undertook, in his later novels, a realistic rendering of Indian character his subjects were 'bad' Indians" (*James Fenimore Cooper*, p. 46). The disappearance of the Mohicans and the Pawnees differentiates these Indians from romantic, primitive, redemptive man; the ahistorical form of primitivism is superseded by the accomplishments of civilization.[51]

The Leather-stocking allows Cooper to encode this supersession not as a confrontation between European and Indian but as a natural process. Natty's knowledge of Indian languages and customs and his love of the land do not estrange him but make him the necessary instrument for the transformation of New World nature into the equivalent of Old World culture. Georg Lukács thinks "Cooper's greatest artistic achievement" was "his singular development of Scott's middle-of-the-road hero" (*The Historical Novel*, p. 64) into a Leather-stocking, who, like the central characters in Scott's historical novels, can further the march of history. But for all that, the Leather-stocking's progress casts doubt on the process in which he is engaged, whether providentially or historically directed. His color, his "white gifts," and his cultural loyalties make him the scout for a historical process that he basically distrusts and finally disapproves, but neither his distrust nor his disapproval affect his decisions to stand by the characters charged with the future of the society for which Cooper writes.

Thus the Leather-stocking series is also doubly oppositional: it tells how a new society was formed against that of the former metropolis, based on the rule of law and in close contact with nature, through a central character who criticizes the project he furthers and who will not accept the law that conditions its functioning.[52] In *The Pioneers* the Leather-stocking demonstrates that the law opposes nature and allows its destruction. In this double movement, the series also criticizes the discourse of the exotic on which it depends, since the discourse cannot

---

[51] Says McWilliams: "If, on the frontier, the white man can preserve the virtues of Christian civilization, Cooper's assumptions about the progress that accompanies the passing of the Indian will be justified" (*Political Justice*, p. 242).
[52] See Wayne Fields, "Beyond Definition: A Reading of *The Prairie*," pp. 93–111.

accommodate the civilization for which it asks recognition. And so we see the need for *Notions of the Americans*, which can accommodate civilization, at the cost of the recognition granted the exotic.

As he records the happy result of an inevitable, melancholy process, Cooper is caught in a dilemma. He agrees with his European predecessors in the literature of the exotic that earthly paradises and golden ages must end. The paradises are profaned; the gold of antiquity turns to the bronze and iron of modern times; the heroes die. Projected into the future, the golden age means death. D. H. Lawrence, for whom the development of the Leather-stocking saga into myth constitutes an accretion of beauty, does not fail to note its concomitant drift toward death and killing, seeing this bloodshed, in fact, as the essence of the myth (pp. 86, 92). But Cooper does not suffer from either preromantic or early twentieth-century nostalgia; in the Leather-stocking books he explains why the golden age must end but attempts to show that its ending leads to something better; the sadness that something good should be destroyed and the horror at the evil within the good that destroys it are counterbalanced by the possibility of desired renewal. The death of Uncas becomes bearable because it brings victory over Magua and marriage between Alice and Hayward; the savagery of the lumbering Bush family gives way to their acceptance of some organized form of justice. In the Leather-stocking series the languages of the golden age and the noble savage make accessible to the reading public something that even the author might not have known how to think of in other terms. In this appropriateness lies part of the qualitative advantage of the series over *Notions*. But the reception of *Notions* and Leather-stocking series also indicates the limits imposed upon Cooper by the discourse of the exotic.

In the Leather-stocking series, that discourse allowed Cooper to collaborate with his readers, using what they knew to tell them something new.[53] The differences in quality and reception between the Leather-

[53] Rossbacher (who, though Austrian, participates in a general German-language culture) is particularly aware that "all those who . . . expected of America renewal and regeneration and of Cooper's novels that which was entirely new, an escapist transcendence, could only respond to those novels insofar as they presented what was already known. . . . thus the Indians were read not only as images of opposition, but also as familiar figures" (p. 87). At the time, as Rossbacher notes, German reviewers almost uniformly commented on the informational value of Cooper's novels (pp. 39, 41). In fact, they knew exactly what he was qualified to write about: in a review of *The Pathfinder*, the critic of *Europa: Chronik der gebildeten Welt* (1840) congratulates Cooper on going back to writing about the things with which he is most familiar: the natural world of America (see Richard Dilworth Rust, "Historical Introduction"

stocking saga and *Notions of the Americans* come from Cooper's misapprehension of how his writing functioned: he thought it wrapped factual information about America in palatable form. His public shared
this misapprehension. Young Germans, dreaming of immigration, read
his novels as if they were Baedeker guides for their new land, and critics
such as those of the *Edinburgh Review* praised Cooper for the truth of
his Leather-stocking novels but condemned *Notions* because it did not
present facts they liked in that intelligible language of the American
myth. As Cooper tries to make a case for an America that, like Cadwallader, can sit as an equal in the closed club of European nations, he
disturbs the comfortable relationship these nations had built with an
America defined as not yet ready for the assumption of power and
maturity; his bid for parity chips away at their sense of identity by
changing the established definition of the New World, threatening to
reduce the importance of the nations to which *Notions* was addressed.

The approval of English critics for a national literary production was
sought not because American critics were snobs or cowards but because
Europe was necessarily the source of values and of the language in
which Cooper and his contemporaries had to think of themselves.
When Cooper raged at the dependence of American critics on their
European colleagues and wrote books and articles to prove them
wrong, he was chafing at a disparity in cultural power. His books contributed to the formation of American literature and to its acceptance
as autonomous at home and abroad and therefore gave it the power to
determine other discourses of exoticism. He too was compelled to create
a national image by depending on previously established models,
mythic and literary. The persistent and well-known myths of the primitive to which so much in the Leather-stocking saga refers give it the
validity and truth value that facts and statistics could not confer on
Notions; these myths, this discourse of the exotic, give the saga an interest that *Notions*, for all its smooth roads and comfortable houses in a
wilderness, could not approach.

The truly new quality of Cooper's New World could be accepted and
valued only as it referred to what was already well known; yet his works
also give glimpses of something non-European. In *Notions* as well as in
the Leather-stocking saga, Cooper proposes renewal through political

---

to *The Pathfinder,* p. xx). Rosenthal says Europeans accepted Cooper's novels as sources
of factual information because they wanted to believe him, because his fiction conjured perils that were easily and predictably contained" (p. 56), and therefore, he
was a reassuring guide.

institutions, rather than through a mystical primitivism. The books promised that the new nation would be able to realize Europe's projection of a wonderful future, rather than satisfy its nostalgia for a wonderful past, to implement its political thought rather than its mythic dreams. A readership owes no obligation to logic, however, and so *Notions* offended because its defense of an effectively subversive government deliberately left out the process of establishing that subversion; in its reach for legitimacy it erased the delicious whiffs of illegitimacy which could make the Leather-stocking's defiance of Judge Temple so attractive. *Notions* praises the American people for striving to build a just society of civilized, educated, informed citizens and is silent about the pleasure called up by the image of an individual in a world of pure potentiality, where the rules of social and political conduct which confine his reader do not apply and where his heroes must establish new rules. At the same time as *Notions* describes the comfortable roads and inns and fields, it is silent about the violence that made them possible and forever tainted them.

Notions assimilated the American experience to what Europeans knew and valued about their own and left out, as problematic, the assimilation of Europeans to the otherness of the New World. The Leather-stocking, by contrast, mythic and dreamlike, was more easily assimilated into a fiction of renewal and freedom than were the hard facts and cheerful prospects observed by the enlightened Bachelor. And thus, despite the problematic nature of the return offered by the Leather-stocking series, despite the clumsiness of its language and the creakiness of its plots, despite Cooper's difficulty settling for any particular mode of owning the land or organizing a new society on it, despite the constant reminders that the idyllic life of the Leather-stocking is not possible once any group of people occupies the land or organizes a new society on it, the attractiveness of his world prevailed and gained Cooper millions of readers in dozens of languages, making him the first representative of an internationally respected New World literature. Thus he also became a pioneer for all New World writers in the difficult endeavor of representing the otherness of the New World in understandable terms and in reconciling the expected exotic faces of their new nations with the respectable, acceptable, valid faces they desired.

7

Nationality and the "Indian" Novels of José de Alencar

Cooper's Leather-stocking series was read most attentively and fruitfully not in Europe but in other parts of the Americas, where a collection of Spanish colonies and the single Portuguese one were pupating into nations and, like the United States, creating national literatures. They too, looking for autochthonous subjects, found the opulent scenery and the original inhabitants sanctioned by the European discourse of the exotic and began to fashion from them a way of representing a non-European identity. Cooper showed that it could be done and was admired for it.[1] His works were aligned with European examples of how to use exotic materials and seen as patterns for adapting a discourse of the exotic to the production of an American literature of nationality.

The Cooper with whom other American literatures of nationality established an intertextual relationship was strictly the creator of the Leather-stocking. Neither his sea novels nor those in which he conducts an acerbic argument with his contemporaries were taken as models. Certainly the choice in *Notions of the Americans* to assert national identity by opposing exoticism, its assumption that the power relation on which

[1] According to Doris Sommer Cooper's "Latin-American heirs . . . reread and rewrote him" (*Foundational Fictions*, p. 52). The Argentinian Domingo Faustino Sarmiento, indeed, "copied" Cooper (p. 65).

186

the exotic rests can be renegotiated through a shortcut that avoids it, does not enter the repertoire of these other literatures of nationality. The material these literatures do absorb, moreover, is organized differently from the Leather-stocking series, just as *The Last of the Mohicans* treats cultural material differently from *Les Natchez*.[2] The variety of possibilities the literatures actualize indicates at the same time their contingency and their dependence on protonational cultures already being elaborated during colonial times. Thus the "Indian" novels of the Brazilian José de Alencar illustrate a different use of the exotic from Cooper's, arising from a different polity, engaged in different internal and external power relations, and shaping a different national image.

Unlike Cooper, who for most of his life was a private, though well-known citizen, José de Alencar (1829–1877) lived as a public figure: he was a journalist, state representative, minister of justice for two years under the Brazilian emperor Pedro II, and an active participant in the public life of the new independent Brazil. As a shareholder in one of the country's first railroads (Alceu Amoroso Lima, "José de Alencar," pp. 55–56), he had a direct interest in Brazil's internal and external economic affairs, and he rounded out his participation in public life as a novelist, dramatist, polemicist, and critic, who, like Cooper, considered it a civic duty to found a recognizably Brazilian literature.[3] Brazilian critics agree that he succeeded; regardless of how each judges Alencar's works, nearly all describe him as preeminently, primarily, radically the writer of a literature of nationality.[4] Like Balzac, he decided to cover the

---

[2] For example, though the series sees civilization as Christian, Natty rejects churches and religious organization, preferring the forest as the best place of worship—a far cry from *Atala's* defense of Jesuit colonization, the only form of social organization the novel details.

[3] Alencar explains his motives in *Como e porque sou romancista* (Why and how I am a novelist) and "Bênção paterna" (A father's blessing).

[4] See, among others, Afrânio Coutinho: "Alencar created Brazilian fiction, propelling it in the right direction, that of a search for the expression of the nationality" (*A tradição afortunada*, p. 99); T. A. Araripe, Jr. "The undecided novelist determined then to be Brazilian" or "*Iracema* is the most Brazilian of our books" (*José de Alencar*, pp. 18, 194); Machado de Assis: "[*Iracema*] is also a model for the cultivation of an American poetry that, please God, will be reinvigorated by works of such superior quality" (Review of *Iracema*, p. li). Fábio Freixeiro, quotes the obituary for Alencar in the *Diário oficial*, a publication whose main function is to record government business and activities, to the effect that he was "the first Brazilian man of letters" (*Alencar*, p. 36). Nelson Werneck Sodré links Alencar's success in his enterprise to his continuous popularity (*A ideologia do colonialismo*, pp. 43–59) and adds, "Alencar always intended to create a Brazilian literature, and to that end he wanted to change the process of literary composition in form and content, by choosing Brazilian motifs" (p. 53).

nation's history and geography with his novels; he wrote plays for a stage still mainly dependent on imports,[5] he proposed to create an appropriate variant of the Portuguese language for a truly Brazilian literature, which he justifies in his "Carta ao Dr. Jaguaribe."

For examples and justification, he looked abroad, adapting and transplanting themes and structures developed in other dramatic, novelistic, even operatic traditions by writers such as Alexandre Herculano, Chateaubriand, Cooper, Balzac, Dumas, and Rossini.[6] Resorting to a common strategy for claiming authority, the critic Décio de Almeida Prado inserts Alencar in a literary series that extends from contemporary European works back, "in the specific case of comedy, at least as far as ancient Rome," and he identifies him as the "perfect" author in whose work to trace "Brazilian thought concerned with urgent local problems" (p. 27). Alencar's novels do not present great literary or philosophical problems; they are an American offspring of Montaigne and Rousseau, Chateaubriand and Bernardin de Saint-Pierre. They improve on the works of "Indianists" such as Gonçalves de Magalhães and Gonçalves Dias—Alencar's harsh criticism of Magalhães notwithstanding—and they elaborate literary ideas made popular in Brazil by the visiting French critic Ferdinand de Dénis, who, a generation before Alencar, had written that "every nation, so to speak, secretes a literature in accordance with the genius of its people" (Antônio Cândido, Formação 2:315). Prado is not looking for the direct influence of particular authors or works on Alencar, though Alencar himself called upon Plautus, Aristophanes, and Molière in defense of his choice of characters.[7] Nevertheless, insofar as he adapted European forms to the culture around him, Alencar became the definer, chronicler, defender, and at times critic of some of the central cultural tenets of his own nation. He justified the creation of a literature of nationality by appealing to a European literary

[5] For a discussion of Alencar's formulation of a national identity in works for the stage, see Flávio de Aguiar, A comédia nacional.

[6] In the autobiographical sketch Como e porque sou romancista, Alencar says he learned French so he could read Balzac; he also read Chateaubriand (p. 30). He looked for models abroad and set himself the task of creating national equivalents.

[7] Specifically, he defended his choice of a slave as the central (comic) character of O demônio familiar, for which, among other things he was attacked by the abolitionist Joaquim Nabuco (see Afrânio Coutinho, ed., A polêmica Alencar-Nabuco, pp. 135, 120; quoted by Prado, "Os demônios familiares," p. 48). Flávio Aguiar studies the role of Alencar in the creation of a Brazilian theater. Both Aguiar and Prado address Alencar's treatment of what Prado calls "the central problem of nationality," slavery (p. 46), abolished only in 1889. It is a vast and important subject, beyond the scope of the present work.

tradition and to theories about literature as an expression of national character proposed, as we have seen, by Schlegel and other German historians and philosophers.

To a large extent Alencar followed the early romantic program, as Antônio Cândido outlines it, "the establishment of a literary genealogy, the analysis of the creative capacity of autochthonous races, and [the use of] local aspects as stimulants to the creative imagination" (*Formação* 2:317). In the series of newspaper articles in which he criticizes Magalhães's Indianist epic *Confederação dos Tamoios (Cartas sôbre "A confederação dos Tamoios")*, Alencar develops the directives he then followed in writing the first of his "Indian" novels, *O Guarani*. He planned the novel to be more than an adventure romance along the lines of *Atala* or *The Last of the Mohicans* and assigned it the dual program of showing how one writes the true Brazilian national epic and how the new nationality differs from the European civilization where it originated and from which it received its language and ideas. According to Antônio Cândido, Alencar fulfills his purpose; he defines

> the literary universe of the Brazilian writer, and classifies three families of themes, which correspond to three moments of our social evolution: the life of primitive man; the historical formation of the colony, characterized by the contact between Portuguese and Indian; contemporary society, which in turn comes under two aspects: the traditional life of rural zones and the life of the big cities, where the vivifying contact with the leading peoples of Western civilization frees us from the narrowness of our Portuguese heritage. (*Formação* 2:362)

This summary attends to the necessary implication of a literature of nationality, that it arises in relation to other, extranational cultural formations; it also marks one difference between the North American and Brazilian cases. Brazilian literature arises in a multiplicity of relations—with Portugal, a colonial power devalued itself relative to other European cultures; with those other cultures themselves, England, France, Germany; and with the United States, a postcolonial culture still under construction. These multidirectional relations coincide with, though they may not cause, a Brazilian tendency to bypass (or co-opt) dualistic oppositions one of whose terms must be eliminated. Yet this eclecticism may also be seen as an early and constitutive example of the characteristically Brazilian creation of a national cultural identity out of a patchwork of "influences" that refuses nothing and transforms everything.[8]

Meanwhile, at a time when the ability to adopt and adapt cultural forms from the metropolis was considered a sign of increasing national cultural competence, the unusual congruence between how Alencar saw himself and how he was seen by his public and most of his critics allowed him to function as a kind of cultural prism, refracting the light of his place and age. This is not an idle image, though I do not use it as those contemporaries might have wished, for the character of any given time is made up of differences and contradictions, their interaction more representative than any individual trait. The work of Alencar, like that of many writers who receive both popular and critical approval, has such incongruities.

In most of his novels and plays Alencar fictionalizes the present or the recent past of the nation, in the city or the backlands, but in the three Indian novels—O Guarani, Iracema, and Ubirajara[9]—the question of nationality occupies a central position. At issue is not how the nation presents itself to itself but what constitutes its core and its difference.[10] Almost inevitably, Alencar alights on what was already becoming the commonplace definition of national character—that Brazilians are the unique and fortunate combination of three races. Silviano Santiago calls the notion the "value of hybridism" ("Roteiro," p. 5), and it winds its way through any examination of national history, culture, or letters, any attempt to define a distinctive Brazilianness. Envisioning a Brazilian national literature, Alencar asks: "What can it be other than the soul of the fatherland, which migrated to this virgin soil with an illustrious race, was impregnated with the American sap of the land that sheltered

[8] Roberto Schwarz proposes such a view in "Nacional por subtração," where he urges us to look for a Brazilian culture not in what remains after subtracting what is not "original" (especially considering the destabilization of that concept by Derrida or Foucault, whose ideas are also imports to Brazil) but in the relationship it establishes among the elements that constitute it.

[9] Critics have disputed the classification of Alencar's novels. Wilson Martins prefers to see O Guarani classed with the historical works rather than with Iracema and Ubirajara, the Indianist ones (História da inteligência brasileira, 3:65). I agree with Martins that O Guarani is a "novel of nationality" (3:60), but I group it with those that have Amerindian protagonists (calling it Indian rather than Indianist), for all three address the question of national character and foreground history, endogamy/exogamy, and the relation between story and book, oral and written.

[10] David Haberly says that Alencar's "Indianism was simply a logical and effective strategy in the struggle to create a meaningful and complete national history, to establish a consciousness of national separateness and worth, and to defend that new identity against powerful cultural pressures from abroad" (Three Sad Races, pp. 32–33).

it, and becomes richer by the day as it makes contact with other peoples and suffers the influx of civilization?" ("Bênção paterna," p. 697).[11] The idea appears in literary criticism as well as in literature: in the section on romanticism of his *História da literatura brasileira*, Sílvio Romero explains that the purely white Brazilian, an ever rarer phenomenon, would be hard to tell from his or her European ancestor; to preserve the distinction from that ancestor, "it is indispensable to agree that the *type*, the perfect incarnation of the genuinely *Brazilian* person, as produced by biological and historical selection is, for the time being, in the vast class of mestizos of all kinds, in the immense variety of their colors" (p. 214). The notion informs the work of Gilberto Freyre, whose success at home and abroad indicates the acceptability, if not the truth, of his formulation: "There arose in tropical America a society whose structure was agrarian, whose economic development was based on slavery, and whose population was a hybrid of white and Indian at first, with the subsequent adjuncture of Negroes." He traces this tendency toward the interpenetration of populations back to the Portuguese, "an undefined people, between Europe and Africa" (*Casa grande e senzala* 1:5, 6). Thus the difference between Brazilian and European lies in a similarity between Brazilians and one kind of European, and the discontinuity of American history is continuous with a sector of European history; it is as if differences, like color, exist only in the form of gradation. Like Romero, he concludes that "every Brazilian, even the whitest, blondest, has in his soul and in his body . . . the shadow, or at least the hint of Indian or Negro."[12]

It is necessary to stress for a North American culture that has been placing ever greater value on the distinctions between populations of different origins (or "ethnicities") that these remarks by Freyre, Romero, and scores of others are neither derogatory nor exculpatory. Just as practice is often at odds with national ideals of justice and equality for all in the United States, however, a national ideology that makes every Brazilian embody the harmonious conjunction of all human races does not necessarily guarantee social, political, or economic equality and harmony.[13] The dicta of Romero and Freyre, statements of both essence

---

[11] The figure is not quite coherent, but it is unusual: the land is virgin, as one can by now expect, but it is the European soul that is "impregnated."

[12] See Freyre, 2:395. This view of Brazil is current outside the country as well. Pereira mentions almost two decades' worth of UNESCO-sponsored studies of "our interethnic experiences" (*Côr, profissão e mobiliade*, p. 17).

[13] Pereira's study, for instance, documents racial discrimination even in one of the most "open" fields of activity, radio broadcasting. In general, the view of Brazilian

and value, say what Brazilians like to think about themselves and what they see as good about themselves. The belief in the positive value of hybridism, implying a distaste for definite distinctions and a search for the harmonious combination of heterogeneous elements, constitutes one of the great arguments in the literature of and about Brazil. The vicissitudes of the belief create tensions in literature and thought, and its setbacks are viewed with sadness, as evidence that it is difficult to achieve ideals in an imperfect world, or viewed with indignation, but not seen as a reason to abandon the ideal. Similarly, in North American literature, liberty, and individuality remain ideals that determine action and ground judgment no matter how often they are defeated. The great image of Ahab tied to the whale or of Jim tied up at the Phelpses warn against oversimplification or self-satisfaction but do not convey despair.

As Alencar went about translating into literature the gamut of Brazilian life, earning the epithet "our little Balzac" from Antônio Cândido,[14]

society as racially harmonious is under challenge by sociologists, historians such as Emilia Viotti da Costa, and literary critics such as Robert Schwarz or Flávio Aguiar. Many point out the harm done to the Brazilian polity not only by the institution of slavery but also by the consistent masking of its debilitating effect on Brazilian culture and economy. The record of the actual relations between settlers and original inhabitants shows, as it does in the rest of the Americas, the destruction of autochthonous cultures. There has recently been a spate of studies on cultural contact in Brazil, with particular emphasis on the African contribution, much of it implicitly or explicitly opposing the ideology of racial harmony with the facts of African slavery and the enslavement or purposeful destruction of Amerindian populations. But even the most indignant studies often end up documenting not only the common brutality of conquest and slavery but also the difference of the Brazilian experience, particularly in the extent to which non-European elements have been integrated into a general Brazilian culture. A good sample of such studies appears in the essays of *Escravidão e invenção da liberdade,* edited by João Reis, which deals with the history and presence of Africa in the state of Bahia. But one should also heed warnings about an equation between mixing populations and mixing cultures: as Rodolfo Stavenhagen maintains in "Siete tesis equivocados sobre América Latina," the wide distribution of cultural traits from different populations within American nations does not necessarily entail either harmonious or equitable relations between their representatives. As for relations between Portuguese and Indian in Brazil, it is, in effect, an unusual legal feature that the marquis of Pombal granted "special benefits . . . to white settlers marrying Amerindians." See A. J. R. Russell-Wood, "Preconditions and Precipitants," p. 9. Russell-Wood also states that "miscegenation became a characteristic in the evolution of Brazilian society" but notes the difference between policies toward Indians and those toward the population of African origin, barred from official positions by "purity of blood" regulations (p. 11).

[14] Antônio Cândido, *Formação,* 2:229. See also José Montello, "Uma influência de Balzac." Haberly, referring to Alencar's own assessment (in José de Alencar, *Romances ilustrados,* pp. 165–67), notes that "during the last years of his life, Alencar wanted to believe that he had set out from the very beginning to create the Brazilian novel, working in four subgenres: the aboriginal novel, the historical novel, the novel of urban life, and the novel of rural life" (*Three Sad Races,* p. 35).

he wrote not only about how his country explained itself to itself but also how it contradicted this self view in enunciation or in practice. Discussing Alencar's urban novels, Roberto Schwarz observes that Brazilian literature displays a certain characteristic incoherence, a discontinuity between thought and plot, a lack of cohesion that results when writers try to incorporate the latest ideological trends of the more powerful and more developed nations into national literary works and social and political analyses, twisting and bending national reality. Writers influenced from abroad either radically misread the national situation or, Schwarz sees it, develop an almost inevitable critique of foreign ideas. Thus, for instance, Brazilian literature came to present European liberalism as one among several possible stances toward reality rather than, following the European view, as the most correct way of interpreting the world and organizing empirical data. In Europe liberalism concealed the conditions of burgeoning capitalism, but in Brazil, where the economy depended on slavery and work could not therefore represent an ethic, liberalism did not conceal a thing; it did not address an existing situation but simply became an idea to dress the fashionable.[15]

Schwarz's account turns an incongruity into an advantage.[16] The radical criticism of Western ideologies entailed in their misapplication turns into farce the tenets that gave European romanticism and realism their high seriousness. Similarly, Augusto Meyer notes another discontinuity of the inevitable "existential" stance of Brazilian literature in general, Alencar's in particular, which arises from the realization of the tenuousness of all efforts, including the literary to recover the vast emptiness of the nation with words and fictions (*A chave e a máscara*, pp. 45–58). For Meyer, something like Schwarz's necessary incoherence is a necessary estrangement: like Iracema in Alencar's eponymous novel, all Brazilians are strangers in their own country—the Indians made so by contact with the Europeans, the Europeans and Africans made so by contact with the land. Antônio Cândido, dealing with the same phenomenon, observes the development of a "literature of roguery" ("Dialética da malandragem") defined by discontinuity in characterization, in which a "realistic" set of familiar secondary characters is peculiarly at odds

---

[15] See Roberto Schwarz, *Ao vencedor as batatas*, esp. chap. 1, "As idéias fora do lugar" (Ideas out of their places), pp. 13–28. He specifically mentions the ideas contained in the Declaration of the Rights of Man, transcribed into the 1824 Brazilian Constitution (p. 14).

[16] In "nacional por subtração," Roberto Schwarz notes the advantage of this reasoning for nationalistic psychology and pushes beyond it. In the end America stands again as a redeeming criticism of Europe.

with the more modern, "realistic" protagonists of nineteenth-century novels, who appear ridiculous and out of place as they wrestle with the problems that give their European counterparts the look and feel of real life.[17] Thus while changing some of the traditional value judgments about Alencar's work, and recontextualizing some of its thematic material, the newer Alencar criticism aligns itself with the old in considering his works an accurate expression of Brazilian reality, if only because incongruities within and outside the text appear in such close correspondence. The incongruity hypothesis of this newer criticism also gives an unexpected twist to the old argument about how much an American literature of national definition owes to foreign formal and thematic models. The hypothesis makes it possible to accept the power of European cultural forms in the creation of a national literature while denying the subjection of the latter to the former, casting doubt not on the power itself but on its effectiveness. Accepted, the dominant discourse proves inadequate, and its inadequacy in turn sanctions a national discourse. In fact, this sanction applies to the point of greatest threat to cultural independence, namely, to the difficulty of transforming the awkward "copy" into another "original." The exotic can then become an instrument of appropriation while declaring its independence from a defining external discourse.

This argument for appropriation could also be made about Alencar's Indian novels, where the novelist toils not in Balzac's but in Chateaubriand's fields, where he deals with the past and not with the contemporary urban scene on which Schwarz bases his analysis. There Alencar creates myths of national origin. Cooper foregrounds the occupation of the land, the clearing of forests and building of towns, the relation between the natural world and that of culture, and his most memorable character functions first in his capacity as "scout" on the borderlands between the two. Alencar, however, foregrounds the relation between populations, addressing the problems of hybridism, not of separation. In that choice, he reverses both Cooper and Chateaubriand, introducing an incongruence in the logic of their fictions at the precise point where they affirm the ultimate victory of the European and the impossibility of compromise. Recounting the first phase of colonization—when Portuguese scouts took Indian women and established relations with their tribes, persuading some to settle around the new forts and trading

---

[17] Schwarz, in *Ao vencedor*, chap. 2, builds on Antônio Cândido's analysis in *Formação*, 2:218–32.

posts to help defend them against French and Dutch incursions—
Alencar links it with the European view of the unspoiled inhabitant of
the New World as a hope for redemption of a cruel and decadent
civilization.[18]

When he addresses the second phase of the history of white-
Amerindian contact, the implications of his treatment veer away from
those of his models. In the second phase the Portuguese began to settle
into farming communities, enslaving the original inhabitants of the land
and killing them when they resisted.[19] The Amerindians died in captivity, refused to work, and fled into the dense, distant forests. Later,
at least in settled parts of the newly independent nation, where few
Amerindians were left, the stresses of contact were attenuated. It was
possible to take Amerindians for heroes of nationality: their refusal of
slavery became a prefiguration of independence. It was as if they too
had signed with their blood and sealed with countless bodies the "Independence or Death!" the first emperor, Dom Pedro I, is supposed to
have shouted as he declared an end to the ties linking Brazil and Portugal.[20] Historical events thus reinforce the literary tradition but also trouble it, for they couple with death the heroism that should bring the
new nation and its people to life, and they make responsible for that
death those who should have been redeemed in the new nation.

With European ideas and Brazilian historical facts Alencar's Indian

[18] Freyre speaks of Portuguese "use of native populations, especially women, not only
for work but also as an element in the constitution of families" (1:23). The "taking"
of Amerindian women and the "persuasion" of tribes were mostly but not always
forceful; there are reports of women who allied themselves with the settlers of their
own volition or to signify their tribe's alliance, and since certain tribes were traditionally inimical to others, they could make common cause with the other's enemy. Conversely, every Brazilian schoolchild learns about João Ramalho and other pioneers
who went to live with Indian tribes, became prominent among them, and facilitated
contact between them and later settlers. Pedro Calmon documents the story of Martim Soares Moreno, the historical settler who appears as the hero of Alencar's *Iracema*
and who was caught by a Portuguese expedition, together with the Indians Poti and
Jacauna, and not immediately recognized as being non-Indian since he was "naked
and painted like them" (*História do Brasil*, 2:36).
[19] This was not, of course, the only way in which Amerindians were approached, but
the Jesuits' attempt to settle them into autonomous agricultural communities did not
play a significant role in the literature of nationality, which concentrated on the
secular aspects of colonization.
[20] Cavalcanti Proença writes in *José de Alencar:* "There is no point in asking . . . why
Indians never became slaves. . . . they fled, died, rebelled, or were incompetent
slaves. . . . The nationalist spirit saw in this only the love of liberty and an example
that it took to heart when it severed ties with the metropolis, making it into a lesson
and into the heritage of the native land" (p. 50).

novels help define and strengthen a national ideology of identity and value. His assertion that this new and valuable Brazilian identity is a composite of European and Amerindian is accepted. His Indian protagonists still give their names to newborn citizens, and *Iracema* has gone through more than one hundred editions in the first hundred years since its publication.[21] But as it develops, the idea of a heroic nation formed by a great but decadent European people revitalized by American purity becomes less clear and simple.[22] It has to incorporate the violence against the land and the rejection of the real Amerindian, and it has to make itself readable in a world that does not automatically see as good the harmonious blending of heterogeneous elements. Each of the three novels under discussion centers on the beneficial marriage of different nations, but the conditions for these unions and their unhappy consequences deny the overt message that the merging is possible or desirable. The dream of virtue and differentiation from Europe in Alencar's novels becomes fuzzy under scrutiny. This fuzziness gives some of the incongruity Schwarz notices in the urban novels even to his Indian novels, and their use of historical and social data makes them less a veil over nothing than a complex record of the interaction between a mythical and a historical definition of a nation.[23]

Like histories, Alencar's Indian novels tell myths of origin. As in the Leather-stocking series, their order of composition is at odds with their chronological order, as Santiago mentions, though he ascribes the nonchronological composition to Alencar's increasing knowledge about Indian life, language, and customs ("Roteiro," p. 5). *O Guarani*, first published as a serial in 1857, is set at the beginning of the seventeenth century, when towns were beginning to grow and whole families, rather

---

[21] Plínio Doyle, "Pequena bibliographia de *Iracema*." Freyre reprints a drawing of "A Fonseca Galvão, whose father, out of nativism, changed the family name to Carapeba" (1:cxiii). Proença, illustrating both Alencar's popularity and the common resort to Indian associations to signify identification with the land, mentions a list of daughters of immigrants called, for instance, Ingeborg Iracema Rann, Iracema Mueller, Iracema Jaeger, etc. (see "Transforma-se o amador na coisa amada," p. 238). A well-known São Paulo family of German origin called itself Muller Carioba, the Indian word Carioba signaling their commitment to the land of immigration and their desire for acceptance.
[22] "'To regenerate is the destiny of America within the destinies of humanity,' said José de Alencar" (quoted by Proença in *José de Alencar*, p. 42).
[23] Some such evaluation underlies even negative assessments of Alencar's achievement: the anonymous author of "José de Alencar," in *Movimento brasileiro*, objects to Alencar's excesses but agrees that "America . . . has to continue on this path of fusion of cultures and infuse the resulting amalgam with its known new spirit." The writer concedes that Alencar's "falsified Indian becomes an ideological reality" (p. 5).

than just isolated settlers, began to establish residence in the new colony; it is an action-packed, fairly traditional romantic novel in the vein of Scott, mixing historical and fictional characters.[24] *Ubirajara*, the last of the three, published in 1874, is set in the time before the arrival of the Portuguese. With its elaborate footnotes reflecting Alencar's extensive reading about Indian customs and language, it claims factual accuracy, and conducts a running polemic against old travelers and chroniclers who, Alencar charges, misunderstood and misrepresented what they had seen; yet both its action and its characters are fictitious. *Iracema*, published in 1865, is set around 1603, when the Portuguese were founding the first forts and villages in what is now the state of Ceará. Subtitled a "legend," it is also a myth of place, telling how certain topographical accidents received their names—what stories give them meaning—and expressing a "Brazilianness" rooted in the land, its beasts, flowers, and voluptuous fruits, its seductive force and frailty. As in *O Guarani*, some of the characters of *Iracema* are historical, but they are better known than those of the first novel; indeed, the white settler and the Indian hero of the war against the Dutch are familiar to every schoolchild. These permutations of the historical and fictional, the variations on known literary formulas and the invention of new ones, and the backward movement in time are some of the more explicit ways Alencar deals with the disjunction between ideology and historical or social fact. These incongruities provide the tension and help guarantee the appropriateness of the three novels.

A moment's return with new knowledge to the large armchair where Jane Tompkins read Cooper (and I read Alencar) in summers long past might bring to light an opposition between the conventional and the problematic in the two authors' works, apparent in the difference between what memory retained and what present attention reveals. Thus, of the description of the Paquequer River which opens *O Guarani*, one remembers the water "leaping from waterfall to waterfall" into "a lovely basin, formed by nature . . . under curtains of lianas and wild flowers," and "virgin forests stretched along the banks of the river, which flowed amid arches of verdure, their capitals the fans of palm trees" (p. 32). Closer attention shows, however, that what was remembered as a reference to unmodified nature actually refers continually to cultural codes that inform the work. Not only is the forest both temple and boudoir, reminiscent of Chateaubriand's transposition of forest into architecture,

---

[24] For a comparison of Alencar and Scott, see Araripe, pp. 46–47.

but as the river flows down the page, it is divided into three parts. At
its head it is free and wild, like a coiled serpent, a running tapir, and
a leaping tiger—conventional indicators of wilderness and nature, the
snake recalling an ambiguously valued Eden, the tiger a generic non-
European wildness to be found indifferently in India or among Indians,
and only the tapir a specifically Brazilian nature. At midcourse the river
is received into the lovely basin like a groom into a bridal bed canopied
with lianas and wild flowers. At its mouth, where it enters the Paraiba
River and comes closest to the colonial settlement of Rio de Janeiro, it
is a vassal of the larger river, a "slave" who submissively suffers "the
whip of its lord" (p. 31).[25] The river runs from positively valued but
nonhuman freedom to the negatively valued civilization at an outpost
of the metropolitan government; from the purely natural sphere, which
at least in the figures of serpent and tiger is hostile to human influence,
where there is neither time nor story, to the sphere of Europe-imposed
indignity, which the new nation has just escaped. At the basin is the
middle ground: there a Portuguese gentleman has built his house; there
Peri, the Indian, becomes a member of the household, and there he
turns the bedroom of Ceci, daughter of the house, into a nest decorated
with native feathers and plants, creating a space that parallels as nature-
in-civilization the civilization-in-nature implied in the images of the
river as groom, the basin as bed. From the very opening of the novel,
Alencar prefigures the breach in the boundary between civilization and
nature which in his culturally acceptable figuration defines the newness
of the new land; created out of something like a chemical reaction, the
new is the result of combination of heterogeneous materials. In his
universe boundaries of place and even being are forever being crossed:
the Paquequer leaps over the waterfall a tiger and lands in the basin a
groom; Peri goes from forest to house, Ceci from house to forest when
she flees with him at the end of the novel. The contact between the
social order brought by the settlers and the order of nature they found
gives rise to free elements that cannot be properly classified in accordance with either, which are the start of a new order.[26]

[25] Silviano Santiago, in "Liderança e hierarquia em Alencar," calls attention to the
same metamorphosis of the river but sees it as a change in relationship rather than
in being. All the same, he considers the change an illustration of how Alencar engages
in the task of both creating and codifying a "national consciousness" (p. 10).

[26] Santiago contends that Alencar uses Indians as free elements because they are
outside the hierarchical system of European origin imposed upon the new land,
although one could also argue that their marginal position was unstable, threatened
by enslavement, which would classify them at once at the bottom of the hierarchy;
war, which would moot the question; or absorption.

But we also remember Cooper's Lake Glimmerglass, with its pristine, Edenic aura. Leather-stocking gasps when he first sees it, "so placid and limpid that it resembled a bed of the pure mountain atmosphere compressed into a setting of hills and woods." But here "bed" no more connotes culture than it would if Cooper were speaking of a bed of basalt or sedimentary rock: the simile does not take Glimmerglass out of the inanimate world. Any flights of fancy would in any case be quelled by the next sentence: "Its length was about three leagues, while its breadth was irregular, expanding to half a league," and so on through measurements and points of the compass (*Deerslayer*, p. 27). The description removes the lake from any metaphorical transformation, anchoring all expression indicative of feeling toward it ("sweep of the outline," "gracefully," "solemn solitude and sweet repose") to its presentation simply as an object in itself, with form, dimension, and direction.[27] At the end of the passage, after it has delighted, within reason, the object is said to instruct: "This is grand!—'Tis solemn!—'tis an education of itself, to look upon!" the Leather-stocking exclaims (pp. 27, 28). That is, 'tis a teaching aid. It is a useless one, too, for Leather-stocking does not need that education, since his moral stand and his attitudes toward the land, the forest, the Indians are set and immutable throughout the series. Contrasting to him in disposition but equally impervious to the lake's lessons is Judith Hutter, who, from living there, "ought to be a moral and well-disposed young woman," yet, as Hurry Harry puts it, "has the vagaries" (p. 28). The lake neither suffers nor effects change. The political meaning attached to it is as slight as its moral influence. Only once is it included in political discourse, when we are told it may belong to the king, who, however, lives too far away to determine what really goes on around there; for all practical purposes Tom Hutter has possession of the place (p. 30). As Cooper's readers well and proudly know, the irregularity of ownership dissociated from possession will be set straight by historical developments. Within the novel, however, the lake will clearly not be affected by any of these historical events. In the course of the tale it is grave, temple, battlements, highway, and larder, but the transformations are always con-

---

[27] Shirley Samuels finds in *The Last of the Mohicans* several such transformations of people and landscape into geometric and measurable abstractions; the effect is a violent blurring of the boundaries between the categories of the human, the natural, and the technological—the first and last falling into that of the cultural. Thus the novel becomes not a record of the impossibility of transposing (negatively expressed as blurring) boundaries but a dire warning against it.

nected with its use, never metaphorical; it never crosses any boundary into life, history, or culture.

Along the river in *O Guarani*, as around the lake in *The Deerslayer*, characters gather to enact a drama of national origins.[28] The noble Dom Antônio de Mariz has established himself, with his lares and penates, on lands a couple of days' travel from Rio de Janeiro granted him for faithful service by the king of Portugal. In the wilderness, on the natural rampart of a rock beside a river, he has built a house for his family and retainers and lives like a feudal lord. He had moved from Portugal so he could be politically, if not economically independent of the colonial power, whose legitimacy he considers doubtful, the crown then being, for dynastic reasons, in the hands of the Spanish king. Alencar thus creates an ingenious compromise between loyalty to the metropolis and independence.

Dom Antônio has a stiff wife, a noble son, a beautiful blond, blue-eyed daughter, and an illegitimate daughter by an Indian woman. As the story begins, he receives into his house a noble young man, Álvaro, an appropriate suitor for his legitimate daughter Ceci. Attached to the household is the Indian Peri, who once saved Ceci's life and has since abandoned his tribe and his family. Peri is treated as a friend by Dom Antônio and Ceci, as an imposition by Mrs. Mariz and the half-Indian Isabel. With Álvaro, there also arrives a classically gothic Italian villain, the former monk Loredano, who, having shed his cassock and got hold of the map to a silver mine around the Mariz property, insinuates himself into the household and immediately starts subverting Dom Antô-nio's vassals, plotting his destruction, and lusting after the gentle Ceci.

The situation is eminently recognizable. Noble lords, heroic youths, helpless sweet maidens, and defrocked Italian villains are common-places of the European imagination, and novels featuring them enjoy the artistic status of, say, paint-by-numbers canvases. A good part of Alencar's achievement lies in the oddities he introduces into the com-monplace, which suddenly acquires a double reference as it is used to make the new intelligible and familiar by clothing it in an old language and concepts. This is another way of viewing the incongruities that slip into works featuring transplanted cultural idioms. Dom Antônio is not just a noble lord: he is also both a loyal Portuguese subject and a rebel, having crossed the ocean to avoid bowing to the Spaniard on the Portu-

[28] Cf. Philip Fisher's "fixed geography and small set of characters" of *The Deerslayer* (p. 73).

guese throne. His independence depends on and is protected by the new land, since he could not claim such freedom anywhere else. In this mixture of loyalty and autonomy one can read, with the hindsight of the novel's first public, a prefiguration of the great independence compromise, when the legitimacy of blood ties offset the illegitimacy of severing political links with the metropolis, when the son of the king of Portugal became the first ruler of a country newly independent form Portugal.

Alencar's characters embody some of the same established fictional elements as Cooper's—the dark and the blond maidens, the noble Indian, the concerned father, the romantic hero, the defining role of Christianity—but Alencar arranges them quite differently. Álvaro, the heroic youth, is just the sort James Fenimore Cooper likes to marry to his heroines, and at the beginning he is assigned to Ceci, tacitly accepted by her father, but then he falls in love with the dark and intense half-Indian Isabel, who feels for him the consuming passion only dark heroines can muster. The lovers are doomed to die their separate lovers' deaths, in accordance with convention, but it is not conventional that their relationship should replace the one between the blond heroine and the romantic hero or that their passion should meet with the approval of other characters or of the narrative voice. Ceci, for instance, who should be the injured party, is all blushing smiles and serious concern for their happiness when she learns about their love. Thus, while in one sense Isabel is like Cora, for she is of mixed ancestry, is unhappy, and must die, in another sense she is most unlike her. The accepted link with Álvaro indicates that the woman with a cross is not to be excluded a priori from the roster of those who will originate the population of the new nation. Her death, however, indicates that the conditions for her inclusion in the line of ancestors have not yet been created. The bitterness Isabel derives from her ambiguous position in the household and the death of the lovers are part of the pessimistic countercurrent to Alencar's racial optimism, though only Alencar would have permitted Isabel to die happy in reciprocated and finally guiltless love.

The blond maiden, Cecilia (called Ceci by Peri because in his language *ceci* means "to hurt," and by Alencar because he can then join in one name Christian saint and Indian sensibility), also seems a stock figure of sentimental fiction: her coloring, unusual and unexplained, is the first indication that her origin is in literature. She "was the goddess of this little world, which she lit up with her smiles, and cheered with her playfulness and her charming fancies" (p. 39). But Alencar modifies the conventional purity of the stereotype by surrounding her with signs of voluptuousness and sensuality which hint at the link to be established between her and the fruitful land, and at the function she will ultimately fulfill. Here is how the villain of the story finds her:

> Cecilia slept wrapped in pure white sheets; her little blond head lay on the finest lace, over which were spread her lovely golden ring-lets, , , . Her shift had fallen open, half-showing a neck of the purest lines, whiter than the cambric around it, and the slight movement of her breath revealed, under their diaphanous veils, her delicate breasts. All of this was framed like a painting by the billows of a blue damask coverlet whose wide folds molded the girl's pure and harmonious out-line on the transparent whiteness of the linen sheets. (P. 243)

Her innocence, underscored by the Virgin's colors of the blue coverlet and white sheets, is strong enough to stay the villain's hand for a crucial moment, but at the same time the overt sensuality of the tableau pre-pares the later scene in which she accepts and desires Peri as a man, thus making it plausible that she should, with him, populate the land.[29] The sensuousness is, however, but a small oddity in the characteriza-tion, not unprecedented. The great oddity is the development of Ceci's relationship with Peri, which constitutes Alencar's first and most opti-mistic statement on the theme of hybridism as the defining trait of the new population in the new land.

Only the hero and the villain, Peri and Loredano, are not character-ized in terms of the theme of hybridism. They are of a piece, unmiti-gated and relentless in their heroism and villainy. Their oddity lies not in their characterization but in the contexts they establish and in the oppositions they construct. Loredano's evil and Dom Antônio's or Álv-aro's nobility are defined within an Old World context, according to the criteria of an old culture; their models are the Christian knight and the renegade monk of romantic fiction if not of medieval reality. But Peri, who is as intensely good as Loredano is intensely evil, is a product of the wilderness, where he is king. Appearing "like the beneficent genius of the Brazilian forests" (p. 136), he is the unspoiled natural man, and

---

[29] Alencar rewrites the gothic in his characterizations of the villain as well as the passive and innocently sensuous heroine; it is not by chance that both Cooper (as Henry Nash Smith has shown in *Virgin Land*, chaps. 7–9) and Alencar have originated popular forms in their own literatures; they built on the historical novel and the gothic, which already addressed and reached a mass public.

in this context he is opposed to the Aimorés (counterparts of Cooper's Mingoes), barbaric, savage Indians (pp. 269, 291) that besiege Dom Antônio's house and represent the other, menacing face of nature. In other words, if Peri himself is of a piece, the opposition to him is a composite of the European and the Amerindian. Unlike Uncas, who, alone, stood up only to Magua, Peri is a worthy foe to both barbaric nature and depraved civilization. In each cultural construct, the elements from which self and other are constructed may be the same and arise from similar operations on similar data: like Cooper's, Alencar's good and bad Indians are only partly the product of direct study of Amerindian cultures; mostly they derive from patterns into which elements of early accounts were organized in Western imagination. Similarly, his heroes and villains echo many of the most accessible works of European fiction. But in his manipulation of the relations of characters with one another, Alencar attempts to broaden or, in any case, to modify these patterns and to create an as yet unexplored combination of elements, claiming it as characteristic of a nation that would and would not be part of the Western world.[30]

After a suspenseful sequence of events (Alencar knows how to end chapters just as the villain raises his hand to touch the sleeping virgin) in which Peri and the noble whites save one another's lives several times, the novel arrives at its grand crisis: the Aimorés can no longer be turned back; Álvaro dies in Isabel's arms after being wounded in a sortie against the besiegers; Isabel (imitating Atala's gesture) poisons herself with curare inherited from her mother; and Peri is at his wits' end because his scheme to defeat the Aimorés by poisoning himself, letting himself be captured and eaten, and thereby poisoning them has been thwarted. Peri (like Chactas, but for practical, not for spiritual reasons) finally decides to be baptized so that at least he will be able to carry Cecilia away and save her. Dom Antônio performs the sacrament by touching him on the shoulder: Peri is now Christian and a knight not only in substance but in form.[31]

[30] Affonso Romano de Sant'Anna describes the patterns into which Alencar organizes his characters in a detailed structural analysis of O Guarani (see Análise estrutural de romances brasileiros, chap. 3) but does not link them to models outside the work.

[31] According to Wilson Martins, Peri is identified with Dom Antônio at this point and becomes "a Portuguese, Christian gentleman, without ceasing to be Brazilian and Indian," in his person the perfect cultural hybrid and henceforth worthy of Ceci (3:67). Martins recognizes that the other Indian-white unions in the novels do not work out but does not conjecture about the reasons, saying only that they just did not take place at the "appropriate historical moment" (3:69).

He escapes in a boat with the sleeping Ceci, just as the Aimorés scale the defenses of Dom Antônio's stronghold, and as the fugitives float down the river, the girl's father, the ruler of the Portuguese enclave in the Brazilian wilderness, shoots his gun into a powder keg and blows up the house and everyone in and around it. The successful white-Indian pair does find the necessary conditions for their relationship to succeed, which turn out to be the destruction of both white and Indian societies: Ceci's father allows her to flee with Peri only because there is no chance that he or any of the inhabitants of his house will be able to survive the attack of the Aimorés. Though hybridism is not preferable to death, death is the condition that makes it possible. This is the case even though the tone of the novel, the effort made to win the readers' sympathies for Ceci and Peri, and the sympathies the readers do accord them make their flight away from her house and into one another's arms seem not a desperate last resort but a desirable conclusion, the tragedy at their back almost worth it for the sake of the brightness and purity of their future. It is not the adolescent reader but only the older critic who asks whether Alencar, too, had his doubts when he wrote this *Romeo and Juliet* in which the lovers are preserved but the social structure around them must perish.[32]

In the forest Ceci sees her friend with new eyes, "the eyes of the soul." In her father's house he had been "an ignorant Indian, born of a barbarous race . . . a friend, but a slave friend." Her perception of his nobility had been contaminated by his subjection; but as he regains his freedom, he is "the king of the desert," and nature bestows on him the insignia of power: "The tall mountains, the clouds, the waterfalls, the rivers, the century-old trees were his throne, his canopy, his cloak and his scepter" (p. 378). She also sees him as the male and, implicitly, the possible mate; her innocence is no longer that of a child but that of a young woman; her unconscious attraction to him, which had damp-ened her enthusiasm for Álvaro, begins to show itself even to herself. She blushes and flutters and finally, in a displacement of meaning that once more introduces the suggestion of incest into the representation of extreme exogamy, calls herself his "sister." As for Peri, once he is back in the forest, he recovers all the power that had been his before he moved into the house of the Portuguese settler. He has also made an exchange, however: he has won the white woman and will become

---

[32] On the similarities and differences between Cooper's and Alencar's treatment of love between youths of different ancestries, see also Haberly, *Three Sad Races*, p. 44.

the founder of a people, but his conversion to Christianity radically separates him from the tribe he used to lead.

On their second day away from the destroyed house, a great flood comes rolling down the river which, according to the original plan, would have carried Peri and Ceci to the city and civilization. Ceci unties their boat and sets it adrift, out of reach, because, she explains, "she had been raised in the desert" and "was a Brazilian virgin, not a girl of the court" (p. 389). As the waters rise, the girl and the Indian climb a palm tree; in its crown he lets his breath touch her face and she swoons, in one of those pretty scenes that suggest sexuality without shocking gentle female readers. He also tells her the story of Tamandaré, an Indian Noah, who survived a flood by climbing into the crown of a palm tree and who, once back on dry land repopulated the earth.[33] She says they will die and meet in heaven with the little angels. As the book ends, he has uprooted the tree in a superhuman effort to free it from the rising waters, and they float toward the horizon. Though in her final speech Ceci mentions death and an eternity as Peri's sister, generations of readers and critics have disregarded the possible variant interpretation and resolutely read the ending as a promise and a definition of the new nation in the new world, child of Europe and America.

This preferred reading of the ending holds that Peri will be the second Tamandaré, that the issue of his union with Ceci will populate the new land, and that this union removes the flaws of both forest and civilization, since its precondition is the death of Loredano and the Aimorés, as well as Ceci's affirmation of her Brazilianness and Peri's Christianization.[34] Their union promises improvement by differentiation and makes the New World, specifically Brazil, into the ideal place for achieving a harmony between differences which had always eluded other nations. Even leaving aside the ambiguity of the ending and the

[33] Thomas Gladsky notes the similarity between the heroes charged with guaranteeing "the orderly transition of society from one generation to the next" ("The Beau Ideal," p. 46), all of them representing a "beau ideal" of the Jeffersonian "natural aristocrat" (p. 44), and laments that it was the figure of the Leather-stocking that prevailed, since this preference deprived Cooper of the opportunity to create a popularly accepted model of the beau ideal for America (p. 46). But the power of the writer to "create" a "model" is circumscribed by the available material, and its acceptability does not depend on the artist alone. Accepted or not, however, the representatives of the beau ideal are in effect charged by Cooper with founding an American society, and they stand in strong contrast to the Indian Peri—or Iracema—who receives the same charge, though on ambiguous terms, from Alencar.

[34] See Araripe, p. 5: "Alencar's inspiration reaches its highest point . . . in Ceci's resolution to become Brazilian, a daughter of the desert."

dependence of this univocal interpretation on the same national ideology that the ending reinforces, however, one should note that the promised regeneration by combination of races takes place not in house, city, tribe, or any other European or Indian social organization but in the forest, which underlies social organization, and Christianity, which transcends it—and at the price of a catastrophe that eliminates barbarism together with civilization.

Alencar uses the forms of romantic fiction, the stereotypes of plot and characterization, to set up and then tame a radical utopian scenario in which harmony is predicated on destruction. He uses historical figures, such as Dom Antônio de Mariz, and the techniques of historical fiction to replace the narrative of history with that of desire: the only dead Indians are the bad Indians; the forest wins because even Dom Antônio, who is good but Portuguese, dies; but the good Dom Antônio wins too because his heroic death eliminates all the villains and because his child and his religion live on and form an alliance with the land where his independence led to his death. In searching for a proper expression of the originality and value of the new nation for which he writes, Alencar uses and transforms history and literature, creating a myth of things as they must have been to become what they are not, even in his day, and finding a language for his readers' real dreams.

In *Iracema*, subtitled *A Legend*, Alencar gives a second account of the formation of the new people and the nationality. The title signals this purpose: Iracema, the name of the heroine, is a word Alencar invented following rules of word formation in the predominant Indian language along the Brazilian coast (p. 237 n. 2) but it is also an anagram of America.[35] The work uses highly figurative and stylized language. The opening phrases—"Verdes mares bravios da minha terra natal, onde canta a jandaia nas frondes da carnauba" ("Wild green seas of my native land, where the jandaia sings in the fronds of the carnauba")—are the language of a literature that attempts to reproduce the rhythms and accents of the oral tradition, that strives for the distinctive poetry said to be the natural expression of the "primitive." Thus the novel inscribes itself in the curious tradition marking the point in European literary history when civilization gave form to its civilized desire to be primitive, and the written word that aimed to be intelligible across communal

[35] Silviano Santiago makes this point in "Liderança" p. 8; he refers to Afrânio Peixoto for the observation but gives no further details. Martins thinks it is ridiculous to attribute meaning to the anagram (3:220). Whatever Alencar's intentions may have been, now that the anagram has been identified, it is part of the reading.

borders tried to recover its origin in, and assert its kinship with, a communal tradition that relied on speech and memory for self-definition and preservation. But *Iracema* also tries to address the new problem of how to tell the story of the encounter between Europe and what is truly non-European in a way that justifies both and devalues neither.

For his hero, Alencar chooses Martim, once again a historical figure, the founder of the first viable Portuguese settlement in what is now the state of Ceará, where Alencar was born. The tale itself is loosely based on historical events. A series of footnotes that anchor the poetic text to a reality of archives, annals, chronicles, and anthropological observations recounts and documents events, figures, and information about the original population of the region. But Alencar also rearranges the truths of these documents. For instance, the historical model of Martim disappeared for a few years into an Indian tribe: he was next seen, naked and painted, when he was captured with his tribal companions by a Portuguese expedition. It was only after this episode that he went back to the king's service as settler. Alencar knows about the incident (he refers to it in *Ubirajara*, p. 240 n. 16), in the course of which a historical meeting between Martim and an Indian woman may have taken place, but by excluding from the legend the capture by the Portuguese and by making Martim's adoption into Indian culture, paint and all, take place as a more or less private event involving only Iracema and his friend Poti, he emphasizes the difference between Indian and European. It is as if, although he was defending hybridism, Alencar did not want to consider the possibility of a protagonist's complete loss of cultural identity. The cultural identity he envisaged for his actual readers could then, within the freedom of fiction, encompass the presence of disparate elements without any of the possible conflicts generated by disparity.

Martim's character and adventures are only the frame of the tale, however; the focus is Iracema, and the argument her encounter with him. He surprises her asleep in the forest; startled, she shoots an arrow at him, which grazes his cheek; they are attracted to each other. She is described entirely in terms of native plants, birds, and animals: she is slender and pliant like the palm tree; her voice is like the murmur of the hummingbird; the touch of her body is sweet like the wild amaryllis and soft like the hummingbird's nest (p. 44); she obeys her man's summons like the native doe and suffers like a whole series of tropical plants pierced for their sap or torn from their bulbs. She is also the daughter of the tribe's medicine man and the virgin who guards the sacred wood and knows the secret of ritual narcotic and hallucinogenic plants. In her self, her knowledge, and her ritual function, in her demand for a pledge of blood before she can be known, she combines strength and powerlessness, passivity in her sleep, aggression in shooting the arrow. She can act to induce sleep and dreams that subject Martim to her will, but in subjecting him, she becomes subject to the demands and logic of his story. She represents the land and signifies the harmony between her people and the natural world; in her, the land takes its toll from the invaders. The pull she exerts over Martim is the pull of the new land, and his disruption of that harmony is the disruption that settlement brings.

Iracema is pure (like every acceptable nineteenth-century romantic heroine), but her purity does not come from the suppression or the absence of passion. She is the "brown virgin of ardent love," in opposition to the "blond virgin of chaste affection," Martim's childhood sweetheart (p. 266). The "blond virgin" never becomes an active character in the novel, but it is a sign of Alencar's debt to established plot structures that he evokes her as a shadow to Iracema, completing the blond-dark pair of heroines characteristic of romantic fiction; once again, as he had in O Guarani, he transposes to the tropics the Rowena-Rebecca pair of Scott's Ivanhoe. Once again, he reworks the implications of the pairing: Iracema's relationship with the hero is desirable and fruitful. Nevertheless, history and ideology trouble the positive meaning at first ascribed to their union.

Having seen Martim and fallen in love with him, Iracema sets about seducing him with the characteristic generosity that centuries of accounts had ascribed to the land. She gives him a green potion to make him dream, intending it as a gift that would take him home to his blond beloved. At first it has that effect, but then, because it works to satisfy his true desire, it brings him back to the forest and Iracema. Later, on the last night he spends as a guest under her father's roof, he demands another potion, hoping it will again bring him Iracema, whose chastity he respects as much as he does her father's hospitality: he is a gentleman. She gives him the draught; he sleeps; he calls her name; she goes to him. She rises, as Alencar puts it, his spouse: there is a natural marriage, the consequence of desire, the effect of the powerful attractions and secret substances of the land. Neither of the spouses' social groups sanctions the marriage. Iracema's father had said that if she made love to the foreigner she would die, and Martim has to be unconscious when they make love because otherwise he would be violating the code of conduct that makes him a worthy representative of his own people and justifies his presence among Iracema's. The wording of the passage, however, does not even hint at any authorial disapproval of either Iracema's or Martim's action. In part Alencar may wish to absolve Martim from the guilt of possession; in part the sequence of events expresses a male dream of perfect feminine compliance. Within the overt context, however, the "marriage" of Martim and Iracema defines and sanctions the genesis of the new man and woman of the tropics, born of nature and civilization but free of constraint.

The portrayal of Iracema's sexual availability brings together a complicated cluster of ideological implications. It accords with the earliest views of Amerindian women's freedom from the strictures of European sexual morality of which their nakedness is the scandalous sign. From the earliest accounts the scandal is counteracted in two diverging ways: by seeing nakedness as a sign of innocence or by noting that it is less seductive, and therefore less immoral, than the suggestive clothing of European women.[36] At the same time, Iracema's initiative relieves the Portuguese settler of responsibility for a union that eventually leads to her destruction. Her action, positively valued by the narrative voice, promises a new encoding of behavior which avoids the constraints organizing sexual contact in the colonizer's society and purifies it by force of nature and truth. Nevertheless, Alencar cannot write outside of the system of signs, meanings, and values within which he and his audience live. So Iracema suffers a fate homologous to that of the passionate, dark heroines of romantic fiction: pregnancy and death. Her passion proves incapable of asserting itself against the demands of "man's work"—war and nation building—which take Martim away from her. Yet, there is a mediating term between these oppositions: the son of the doomed union between Iracema and Martim is not doomed, and the tale charges him with the future, both genetic and ideological, of the new nation.

In a recent discursive and critical turn, as consistent with present

---

[36] Jean de Léry declares: "But I will say that, despite opinions to the contrary, as to concupiscence provoked by the presence of naked women, the complete nudity of women is much less attractive than is commonly imagined. The adornments, cosmetics, falsies, frizzed hair, lace collars, bustles, overskirts and other fripperies with which women here among us embellish themselves and of which they can never get enough, cause incomparably more harm than the habitual nakedness of Indian women, who, however, yield to none in the matter of beauty" (p. 121). Montaigne echoes Léry's reasoning in his essay "Des cannibales."

ideological needs as past readings were with the needs of their times, *Iracema* has been viewed not as telling the story of the creation of a distinctive and independent Brazilian culture but as justifying and naturalizing the imposition of the metropolitan, Western, patriarchal culture on female, non-Western (more precisely, extremely western) persons of the new nation. In its more radical form, this reading strips the heroine of any power and authority Alencar had granted her and denies the differentiating role he had ascribed to her, once again assimilating Brazilian culture to the ideological structures from which Alencar sought to distinguish it.[37] Nevertheless, this reading highlights another of the incongruities inherent in Alencar's project: the interplay between the valuation of difference with which to characterize a separate, independently valuable Brazilian culture and the suppression of difference required by the ideological climate within which this aim is to be accomplished.[38]

The marriages between white and Indian at the core of both *Iracema* and *O Guaraní* seem to imply not only a relaxation of social constraints but also a weakening of all boundaries of being. The integration of Dom Antônio's house into the rock where it stands fits into this pattern, as does Ceci's decoration of her room with Peri's gifts of feathers, straw, flowers, and stuffed birds, which turn it into a tropical nest; so, too, do the substitution, at the end of the novel, of the palm tree for the canoe and the constantly threatened absorption of Iracema into the natural world. Similarly, the lines between masculine and feminine become blurred: specifically, the men become feminized. Strangers in the realms where they are led by their women—Peri in the house, Martim in the forest—they go through a period of disorientation and lose some of the qualities that defined them in their own worlds. Both recover, so to speak, but with different results, since Peri's reassumption of the title of king of the forest allows him to win and protect Ceci, whereas Martim abandons Iracema for the "masculine" pursuits of warfare and coloniza-

[37] Glossing over differences, Ria Lemaire invokes Helen of Troy and the *Aenead* to establish continuity between *Iracema* and a misogynist classical Western literary tradition; she uses the proven tactic of reference to the classics to make of *Iracema* simply another retelling of the same old "awful reality" of real mistreatment of women ("Rereading *Iracema*," p. 71).

[38] Regina Zilberman, in *Do mito ao romance* (chap. 9, pp. 141–52), stresses the absorption of Iracema into the context of the colonizer as emblematic of the fate of the "natural" elements of the new nation but does not deny the book's continuing presence in the formation of the "myths" upon which Alencar, like other authors engaged in the same task, constructs a sense of national identity.

tion; the loss does not determine the destiny of the characters who suffer it.[39] It is as if, with this blurring of differences, Alencar were toying with the creation of a true alternative to European culture, one that would fulfill the promise of renewal but would also demand a restatement of established distinctions between nature and culture, male and female. As is probably inevitable, these distinctions, which permeate the language, also invade the tale and limit the imagination. It is a difficulty inherent in the task Alencar originally set himself of writing history, of creating a usable past.

In *O Guarani* the preconditions for the marriage that should signal victory for the ideal of renewal are catastrophic. In *Iracema* the marriage does not destroy two peoples (though it triggers a war between the traditionally inimical tribes of Martim's spouse, Iracema, and his friend Poti), but Martim and Iracema can live with each other only as long as they live apart from their cultures. The world they build together cannot last.[40] It does for a while: they live idyllically in a cabin by the sea, and when she tells him she is carrying his child, he kneels at her feet and otherwise shows his delight. But she knows, and Alencar knows, that their sacrifices are not symmetrical—only the explosion of Dom Antô- nio's powder keg could produce such symmetry—that she has become a stranger in her own land, whereas he can always go back to his job. She senses his restlessness and at one point counts the ways he no longer loves her:

When you walk in the high fields, your eyes avoid the fruit of the jenipapo and search for the cactus flower; the fruit is sweet but it has the color of the Tabajaras; the flower is white like the face of the white virgin. When the birds sing, your ears refuse to listen to the melodious notes of the graúna, but your soul opens to the call of the japim,

---

[39] One should note that Alencar proposes the value of exogamy by the creation of two complementary pairings: Indian man and very white woman in *O Guarani;* Indian woman and Portuguese man in *Iracema.* Ignoring the earlier novel, Lemaire notes the paradigmatically oppressive pairing of the Portuguese man and the helpless Indian woman (p. 71 n. 4). Since Peri does not die, his relationship with Ceci might have strengthened Lemaire's contention that male power is presented as overwhelm- ing even racial difference. At the same time, that example would complicate her argument about the uniform subjection of the non-European.

[40] Darcy Damasceno points out that the novel is not as idyllic as it seems, since all the encounters between Iracema and Martim include a moment of fear or rejection and most take place in a context of danger for the couple ("Alencar e *Iracema*").

because it has golden feathers like the hair of the one you love!
(p. 294).[41]

She knows too that she will die like the abati, a plant that withers as
soon as it has borne fruit. Her first surmise is wrong, since Martim
longs for work, not for a woman; but by the time her son is born, she
is completely alone, and she calls him Moacir, "son of my sorrow."[42]
Soon after his birth she dies of loneliness and a broken heart in the
arms of Martim, who has turned up to see how she is doing and who
takes the son to be raised abroad.

But if Iracema has lost, that does not mean Europe will keep the
spoils forever. In an epilogue set four years later, we learn that Martim
returns to Ceará, filled with bitterness at his loss and longing for the
beaches and breezes of the land where he had been happy (p. 303). He
touches the earth where his wife lies buried, his sorrow melts into
abundant tears, and his soul is made whole. He has come with an
expedition, and they build a village, erecting a church near Iracema's
grave. The coastal Indians transfer their huts to the new settlement,
and Martim's friend Poti is baptized and given the name under which
he becomes the hero of history books, the defender of the Portuguese
colony against foreign invaders, operating the passage from Indian legend to white history—something Iracema could not do and Peri did
not need to do.

At this perilous point of transition, contemporary discussion of a
literature of exoticism heats up. Insofar as the relationship between
Martim and Iracema reflects a power contest between colonizer and
colonized, between written and nongraphic cultures, between the European self and the Amerindian other, it is possible to read Martim's
regret, Iracema's persistence in the name and settlement of the land,
and Poti's alliance with the Portuguese against the Dutch as so many

[41] The Tabajaras are an Amerindian tribe. The graúna is a black bird. "Hair as black
as the wing of the graúna" has become a poetic cliché, a capsule parody of Alencar's
style. There is no indication in the text that Martim longs for his former sweetheart;
in this expression of Iracema's jealousy Alencar reinforces the metonymy that allies
her with Brazil by the implied metonymy with which she allies the blond girl with
Europe.
[42] Proença, in Estudos literários, points out that Iracema's words at the birth and nam-
ing of her child echo those of Rachel giving birth to Benjamin (p. 53). Lemaire thinks
the child's name refers to Genesis and "the anathema God pronounced against Eve
when she was expelled from Paradise." (p. 72 n. 5). Alencar often finds classical and
biblical parallels to Indian customs, forcing a revaluation of the Indian in relation to
the classical and biblical ancestry of European peoples.

ways in which the non-European is repressed, buried, wrenched from its autonomous existence to become, at best, an appendix to colonization. In the actual novel, however, Martim's regret indicates not only a more or less uncritical view of Iracema's fate and his responsibility for it, an unwillingness to consider alternatives to his behavior toward her, but also a positive evaluation of her person, culture, and contribution. If Iracema's seduction of Martim relieves the conqueror of responsibility for her fate and makes her responsible for the destruction of her people and eventually of herself, it also assigns her the power to act and refuses to place her in the briefly comforting role of absolute victim, from which the logical path to action and responsibility is difficult. If Moacir/Sorrow is brought up by his father in Europe, rather than by his mother in the New World, his survival at the foundation of the new town affirms the presence of the Amerindian other in the constitution of a Brazilian self, at the same time as it attentuates and controls this presence. Finally, the introduction of the Dutch invaders of the Portuguese colony brings into play other dichotomies, which complicate the original one between European self and American other by splitting the European into two camps, just as the Amerindian side had earlier been split between Iracema's Tabajaras and Poti's Potiguares. These divisions open a sphere of freedom for Poti's actions, which are neither determined by the pressure of an overwhelming Portuguese power nor open to the accusation of treason to a uniform Amerindian interest. Just as Cooper made a point of placing the war against the French in the political center of *The Last of the Mohicans*, reminding his readers of the challenges to British power, so Alencar reminds his public of the limitations to Portuguese power: the subjection of the Portuguese crown to the Spanish and the invasion by the Dutch make adherence to the original colonizers' cause a matter of choice rather than coercion and raise the possibility of the colonizers' military and cultural defeat by another, greater force, that of the nation arising from their absorption of and into the new land.

O Guarani and *Iracema* uphold the value of hybridism, which functions as the mechanism by which the power and the distinctiveness of the new nation are achieved, but both novels in the end draw up an account of its cost. In *O Guarani* that cost is buried in a whirlwind of action: Ceci needs only a few minutes of prayer beside the river to reconcile herself to the loss of her entire family and get ready to depart with Peri into the forest. In *Iracema* attention to the cost is deflected by the language, the highly stylized poetic idiom Alencar invented: short sentences, short paragraphs, great density of imagery, incantatory rhythms, and repetition of Indian names within an almost classical syntax carry out the combination of American and European elements, accomplishing what the plot shows to be only imperfectly possible. In the process, Martim's loss of Iracema is translated into the acquisition of an important distinction between the colonial power and the new nation: the characteristic expression of their new land's history in its own language. The feelings of nostalgia and melancholy aroused by the language gloss over the conditions of its creation, even though Alencar does not exclude these conditions from his tale. the reality of domination, conquest, and death remains hidden mainly because of the ideology of harmony that the text conveys, in an elaborate game of hide-and-seek set up with all apparent good faith.

Though the promise of hybrid offspring in O Guarani and the founding of the Portuguese-Indian village at the end of Iracema seem to bode well for the formation of the hybrid society that Gilberto Freyre discusses as characteristically Brazilian, the love stories in both novels suggest that only essential—not social—man or woman can freely choose to marry someone who has skin of a different color, worships different gods, obeys different laws. Iracema and Martim are happy only when they are alone together and no duties to king or medicine man occupy them; on such a vacation from society their child is conceived. But Moacir is "the first Cearense" (p. 303), and with him, Alencar shows that harmonizing heterogeneous elements is unequivocally possible only on the ideological level. Freyre's hybrid society appears in O Guarani in a world of the imagination, swept clean of the civilizations that mark the difference between the heterogeneous elements to be conjoined; it appears in Iracema after the heroine, representing the natural world, becomes a memory, her son goes to Europe, and the Indians, now baptized, merge into the official history of the country founded by the Portuguese. Finally the hybrid society becomes a sign, among others, of the reality and the difference of the Brazilian enterprise, with the sign's peculiar independence from the thing signified.

Years after Iracema, in Ubirajara, Alencar returned to Amerindians for the third and last time. The novel has the earliest setting, before the Portuguese arrived on Brazilian soil. It tells the story of Ubirajara, a young warrior of the Araguaia tribe who goes out into the world to make a name for himself—literally, since in the course of the story he changes names in accordance with his feats and purposes. In fair combat he vanquishes the most renowned warrior of the enemy Tocantins, then goes to live with them as a stranger, wins the hand and heart of their most desirable virgin, and finally, by marrying both her and the young girl whom he had loved in the village of his birth, effects the union of the tribes, peace between them, and prosperity for all.

There is a hybrid marriage in this novel too, but the terms have changed; Ubirajara's Tocantim wife is alien not in her color but in her dress and in belonging to a tribe that is the hero's traditional adversary. When the young virgin of the Tocantins first sees Ubirajara, she recognizes him as an Araguaia by the red feather in his headdress: her tribe's color is blue. At the end of the novel, uniting the two tribes, Ubirajara wears both colors. The union benefits both sides and, far from leading to the destruction of either the partners or their societies, ensures the tribes' survival in a kind of golden age up to the time, known but not mentioned in the story, when the conquerors arrive.

But Alencar does not entirely eliminate the European element. It exists, of course, in the book's language, charged with European meanings even while it strives to express what it conceives as Indian thought. Most clearly, however, it appears in a veritable cotext of footnotes, where Alencar more or less directs the reading of his story and conducts a running argument with earlier historians and chroniclers of Indian customs, specifically opposing the common and contradictory notions that Amerindians were tabulae rasae, eager for European inscription, and yet, because they were savage or anticivilized, they provoked European aggression. His Araguaias and Tocantins are protocivilized, in the sense in which nongraphic civilizations can be seen as protographic; and they resemble in some ways medieval Europeans and in others the Greeks, Romans, and Jews of classical and biblical times. If Alencar's view of Amerindians as Hercules, Jacob, Cato, or Lancelot in feathers seems odd, it reveals how any confrontation with otherness dislocates meanings and shifts contexts. In context, this translation performs the double task of inserting Indians in history and providing Brazil with an autochthonous past as respectable as that of the former colonial power.[43] Both the text and the footnotes of Ubirajara argue the value of the Indian component of the new tropical nation. The story does it for the individual by creating a hero; the footnotes do it for the Amerindians in general by drawing parallels between their culture and Western civilization. Yet

[43] For Antônio Cândido, Alencar's heroic Indians "express the Brazilians' deep desire to perpetuate the convention that provides a country of crossbreeds with the alibi of a heroic race, and a nation of short history with the depths of legendary time" (Formação, 2:221). Martins avers that Alencar's "implicit purpose [in O Guarani] was to confer nobility and prestige on Brazilian origins" (3:66).

the division of the text keeps in abeyance the violence of their historical encounter. The European element is close at hand but harmless, interpreting from outside the story. In *Ubirajara* Alencar can present the ideology of mingling untainted, its utopian consequences unclouded by memories of destruction and guilt.

The violence that occurs in the novel is always ritual. Even cannibalism is presented and justified as ritual, structurally akin to the Christian Eucharist (*Ubirajara*, p. 356 n. 37)[44]—that is, motivated, predictable, and controlled. Thus, while the text details feasts and flights, its anthropo logical and critical cotext attempts to rescue Amerindians from a couple of centuries of bad press that painted them as the "savage" other to the victorious European self. The notes liken any number of defining European customs to those of the Brazilian Tupis. They scold historians and colonizers for declaring Amerindians to be atheists and for identifying the universal entity of religion with its particular signs in altars and idols (p. 337 n. 22). They translate Tupi theology into ancient Greek terms, and they point out that, as descendants of the barbarian Goths, Gauls, Franks, and Celts, Europeans had little call to be upset by the religious practices of a different sort of barbarian. They note that in questions of honor the Tupis were at least as particular as any knight (p. 353 n. 36). And one especially long note to the chapter titled "The Nuptial Combat" makes sure the reader gets the point of the medievalizing language by explaining that "these games in which there was fighting, combat, and races, presided over by women who judged the valor of the champions and bestowed prizes on the victors, are showcases of as much gallantry as any joust could have exhibited"(p. 381 n. 61). Finally, in his most daring approximation, Alencar tackles cannibalism: "The remains of the enemy thus became something like a sacred host, which strengthened the warriors. . . . [Cannibalism] was not revenge, but a kind of communion of the flesh." The words of the warrior who is to be sacrificed echo those in which the sacrament of Communion is said to have been instituted: "This flesh you see is not mine, but yours; it is made up of the flesh of the warriors I sacrificed, your fathers, sons, and relatives. Eat it, for you will be eating your own flesh" (p. 356 n. 37).

---

[44] Hulme sees this homology as conditioning European fantasies about American cannibals, used to estrange Amerindian populations and make them unacceptable (*Colonial Encounters*, pp. 81–84); Alencar sees the same homology but uses it to deestrange cannibalism. The similarity had occurred to Jean de Léry, who used it to attack his Catholic companions' belief in transubstantiation; they would want to "eat

The notes also assimilate ancient Brazilian history, defined as the time before colonization, to an ancient European history of Greek heroes, biblical patriarchs, and in tune with fashionable medievalism, medieval knights. In Silviano Santiago's words, Alencar "correctly guessed . . . our past in accordance with values that were becoming dominant and ideologically correct within the independence-stressing thought of the nineteenth century" (p. 8). Unlike Cooper, who postulates the creation of historical, or Western, time in America ex nihilo, Alencar sees the writings of the first chroniclers of the discovery and settlement as the record of a prehistory, acceptable within European ideological structures because it so closely resembles European history. *Ubirajara* thus provides the new country with a legitimating chronological depth.

Also unlike Cooper, who excludes Native Americans from history, Alencar sees Amerindians as proto-Christians and shows Europeans as old barbarians made heroic by legends homologous to those he tells. This homology of pasts conditions the convergence of two histories on American soil. Just as he had made different cultures and populations permeable to each other, he makes into a permeable membrane the historical boundary between former metropolis and former colony. If Amerindians had their own forms of holy communion and created their own versions of medieval jousts, then the "annals of men" can be extended to transform the synchronicity of ethnography and anthropology into the diachronicity of a familiar historical discourse. In Alencar's Indian novels the newness of the present American civilization resides not in the various breaks that separate colonizer and colony, but in what they postulate as the characteristically Brazilian capacity to see knight and Indian blend into a composite figure that extends the Brazilian past to European depth.

Alencar's Indian novels both state and criticize the ways his readers see themselves. His voyages back in time represent successive stages in his dramatization of this tropical civilization for which he had set out to construct a language and to formulate an ideology. This civilization defines itself as European and of the New World, heir to European dreams of starting afresh but unencumbered by old guilts and failures; it sees itself as respectful of the new land's ancient population, heir to its regenerative innocence and generous with its saving gift of Christianity; and it prides itself on arising from this process of mutual regen-

---

the flesh of Jesus Christ not only spiritually but materially, in the manner of the savage *guaytaka*, who chew and swallow raw flesh" (*Viagem*, chap. 6, p. 94).

eration and salvation, original in its double source, distinct from the European past and projected into a model future. But the first novel concludes that such newness costs the destruction of the past, except for the minimum number of individuals needed to create a future. The second novel envisages a distressing compromise: the Indian part is sacrificed, its continuing regenerative influence ensured by its absorption into the blood or the history of the new settlers. In the third novel the primitive survives on its own and prospers, but the other term of the hybridizing process moves to a different level of discourse, from plot to commentary. Together, the novels write the dream of the nation, valued for creating an "and/and" in a world that finds it difficult to think in any terms but either/or. They allow the imagination to extend the limits of acceptable reality in the name of its own distinctive good.

The differences between Cooper and Alencar show how different ideological constructs can arise from similar goals and materials. Both authors measure the distance between the desire for a new, redemptive American beginning and the reality of a continent where nature is destroyed and the primitive is either derided or exterminated or both. Both authors, while claiming historical and anthropological accuracy of representation, produce myths. And both show that though their mythical creations seem part of the positive fantasies of peopling a new land or starting history anew, they carry in themselves the same seed of dissolution and destruction that prompted their reactive creation.

In Alencar's work this vision of destruction appears in the very implications of the harmony he establishes. His books are neither tired reiterations of European fantasies of Eden nor even blueprints for the harmonious conjunction of differences but radical tracts in which a utopia no more than adumbrated costs the destruction of both nature and civilization. Bracketing the violence implicit in *his* choice,[45] Cooper proposes a less radical integration of European and American which leads to a continued march through the seemingly endless American wilderness, as Leather-stocking both flees civilization and opens trails along which it can implant itself. As Annette Kolodny points out in an entirely different context Cooper's myth is finally sterile; his heroes leave memories but no descendants (*The Lay of the Land*, pp. 105–9). Chingachgook and Leather-stocking embody noble savage and noble white but they

---

[45] Recall Philip Fisher's dramatic statement of the abrogation of agency and responsibility by writers of a North American literature of nationality: "and on the way to the marriage . . . there was a massacre, there was a massacre, there was a massacre" (p. 73).

are discontinuous with the succession of American history; they stand alone, outside tribe or village, fantasy figures in opposition to historical developments. If Huck Finn is a descendant of Natty Bumppo it is because, in the end, he too rejects the civilization and history of the new nation.

Cooper and Alencar wrote histories of hope and disappointment and created myths of opposition which, unlike most myths, do not explain what is but tell what was dreamed or wished but is not. In the end, these myths do not account for the identity of the people who invented them but represent an otherness against which they sometimes measure themselves, to which at other times they aspire. They show the new nations split against themselves from the beginning, arising from contradiction. In ways their authors probably did not intend, the new nations become old, begin to acquire the depth of mythical time (with concomitant historical disillusionment) that they so desired as they began to exist on their own.

The cultural material from the New World, then, suffered another transformation; as it was adapted to the formulation of an American national consciousness, it lost the pure notation of otherness it had carried in the first accounts, as well as the sign of alterity in nature and origin it had gained in the eighteenth century. It was integrated into history and shaped into the notion of a distinct national self, which arose from negotiating, with varying results, the line that separated it from its source and opponent on opposite sides of the Atlantic. These variations fragmented a transatlantic non-European self and instituted new oppositions, which in turn could reproduce, as inequalities of power established themselves among American polities, the patterns of acceptance and conflict which had once obtained between former colonies and former metropoles.

8

Nationality Redefined,
or Lazy Macunaíma

Cooper and Alencar provide representative examples of how, in the nineteenth century, a literature of national identity began to be built in two new American nations. By the beginning of this century, affirming difference and defining nationality had become less critical for the United States as the nation's cultural and economic power grew. The early literatures of nationality in the United States and Brazil are easily comparable because the power relations between the United States and England, on one hand, and between Brazil and Portugal, on the other, were similar; so were the new nations' tasks of affirming national identity and claiming cultural parity with the former metropoles. In time, however, power relations between the United States and England (or Europe) changed. When the United States began to be a world power, its economic, military, and cultural influence was added to that which Europe (mainly France and England, but Portugal as well) still exercised on Brazil. The modernism of Mário de Andrade was therefore a continuation of the romanticism of Alencar in a way in which that of Ezra Pound, T. S. Eliot, or Gertrude Stein was not a continuation of Cooper's. The new literary idiom of Brazilian modernists expressed relations of power in terms similar to those of its predecessors in the previous century and continued to concern itself with defining nationality in reference to a powerful other.

But as before, these cultural products from the margin can also play a role in the ideological economy of the dominant cultures. The so-

220

called Boom of Latin-American literature reproduces within the Americas the relationship between more and less powerful but interconnected polities that obtained a century before between the two shores of the Atlantic. Mario Vargas Llosa and Gabriel García Márquez, translated into English or French, reach a wide public to whom they seem elemental and fresh; their realism is magical, in contrast to the humdrum variety grown domestically in Europe or the United States, and the primitive violence they write of is almost redemptive. They offer instant and automatic "estrangement" by using the language of power idiosyncratically.

In redefining nationality against external pressure, however, a work can also idiosyncratically subvert the schemes of interdependence in its own cultural environment. *Macunaíma* (1928), by the Brazilian Mário de Andrade, problematizes the relation between national identity and foreign influence by estranging the exotic itself and blocking its formulation of national identity. The other against whom the self-definition becomes necessary is divided: an enviable and unavoidable political and economic power resides in England and the United States; France and Italy, as intellectual and artistic models, stimulate the creation of a language in which the confrontation can take place; and a German ethnologist provides the science, the raw data upon which the image of a national self is built.

Six years before the publication of *Macunaíma*, Andrade had taken part in the "Week of Modern Art," held in the Municipal Theater of São Paulo. In that most conventional plush, red-and-gilt forum hired for the occasion by an editor of the respectable and widely circulated daily *Jornal do comércio,* there was bedlam. A full house chanted the refrains of unruly poetry by Manuel Bandeira, whistled and stomped at the dissonant music of Heitor Villa Lobos, gasped at disturbing paintings by Fernand Leger's student Anita Malfatti, and listened to Graça Aranha and Oswald de Andrade demolish established poets and literary figures.[1] For the people involved in modern art, the Week was the culmination of years of experimentation and contacts with European movements such as dada, futurism, surrealism and with the works of Guillaume Apollinaire, Paul Verlaine, Stéphane Mallarmé, Emilio Mari-

---

[1] See Raul Bopp, *Movimentos modernistas no Brasil,* especially chapter 1, "Movimento modernista de 1922," for an eyewitness account of the week and further developments.

netti, Emile Verhaeren, and others.[2] In those few days the São Paulo rebels became the established avant-garde. Their works were published not only in little magazines brought out by themselves but in the literary pages of large newspapers such as *Correio da manhã*. Editors were sympathetic to these efforts to transform and renew artistic expression in Brazil and hoped they would propel the country out of its provincial corner into the larger world. Taking models from France and Italy, the Brazilian modernists were to transform expression to voice cultural and economic transformations modeled on those in England and the United States.[3] In their work an authentic spirit of Brazilian nationality was to find a language characteristic of the nation and "legible"—if just barely—within the syntactic and semantic rules of the models. The task was possible because the models themselves were then open to that particular kind of renewal and willing to encourage it. French artists looked to African and other "primitive" art for inspiration, and the economically dominant nations were investing in "primitive" markets, whose rapid urbanization was seen, paradoxically and inevitably, as a desired sign of progress.

Macunaíma draws up an account of these changes. It is written in the city of São Paulo, as coffee begins to enrich the state of São Paulo, attracting floods of national migrants and foreign immigrants and challenging older centers of national political power. In a history told from the point of view of progress, this change is seen, on the whole, as desirable. But *Macunaíma* tries to find the continuity between modernization and a primitive substratum. It is a sophisticated act of trans-

---

[2] Meeting in Paris in 1913 with Tristão de Athayde and Rodrigo Otávio Filho, Graça Aranha urged them to renew Brazilian literature: "Do something new. Do something crazy." In 1922 Aranha was invited to give the keynote address at the Week. Members of the cultural and economical elite of São Paulo took regular trips to Paris and were acquainted with the artistic innovations of the time (Bopp, pp. 17n, 16). Mário de Andrade refused to join these pilgrims of culture and never left Brazil, but he had an enormous library and subscribed to a number of French journals, particularly *L'esprit nouveau*, of which he had the complete collection (see Gilberto Mendonça Teles, "L'avant-garde européenne," p. 106). Andrade's library, now in the care of the Instituto de Estudos Brasileiros of the Universidade de São Paulo, is being catalogued under the direction of Telê Ancona Lopez; from the catalog Nites Therezinha Feres documents Andrade's reading in contemporary French texts (*Leituras em francês*).

[3] Luis Alberto Moniz Bandeira, in *Presença dos Estados Unidos no Brasil*, documents the efforts of the United States to supplant England as the most important economic presence in Brazil. See chap. 28 in particular, for a discussion of the years when modernism was at its peak. See also Elizabeth Lowe, *The City in Brazilian Literature*, especially chap. 1, for a discussion of the relation between urbanization and modernist literature in Brazil.

culturation which at first garnered mixed reviews for its difficult, idiosyncratic language. Some readers were sympathetic, but even those who did not like it praised it for being "talented nonsense."[4] Later the book entered popular culture. In 1974 Portela, one of the main "samba schools" in Rio de Janeiro, made it into the theme of its presentation in the great Carnival parade; a movie based on the novel was successful domestically and shown in Paris and New York; *Macunaíma* became a play in 1977.[5] Despite its formal daring and its association with a movement that is often identified with a predominantly intellectual acceptance of "modern" social, economic, cultural phenomena, *Macunaíma*, like other texts in literatures of nationality, is a critical adaptation that integrates an external discourse into the fabric of national life. Its reworking into other media and other levels of discourse shows that it has not become, like other modernist texts, just the symbol of a historical moment.[6]

Macunaíma may be acceptable because it is as nationalistic in its reference as it is modernistic in its referent, answering one more time, under new conditions of economic and cultural dependence, the newly urgent need for a literature of nationality. Like the romantic texts of José de

---

[4] Haberly stresses the negative reception (*Three Sad Races*, p. 145), but he also shows the importance of the text and its positive contemporary reception (p. 146). "Talented nonsense" are the words of João Ribeiro, one of the friendly early readers (see "*Macunaíma: Herói sem nenhum caráter*–por Mário de Andrade," in Mário de Andrade, *Macunaíma*, p. 345).

[5] See *Macunaíma*, pp. 428–37, for reproductions of paintings, of the theme song from the carnival parade, of an ad for the movie in Paris, of production and casting of the movie, of a photograph from the theatrical production.

[6] Neil Larsen analyzes the relation of *Macunaíma* as literary text to its various adaptations to mass media and its relation to European modernism, on one hand, and a Brazilian popular substratum, on the other. Popularization is problematic because, though it uses the colloquial language register of the book to crack open a difficult text that left alone would "keep the masses at arm's length," it risks a "'romanticization' of the mass consumer" (criticized by Theodor Adorno) and opens the way for the "commercialized exoticisms" of Brazilian movies produced under the state-supported Embrafilme (*Modernism and Hegemony*, p. 90). The relation to European modernism is problematic because although Andrade, according to Larsen, escaped the double bind of a "dependent" discourse, which must claim independence and separate identity in terms supplied and controlled by the dominating culture, he might have just run into a blind alley. In *Macunaíma*, says Larsen, Andrade "seeks to undermine the very categories of an estranging, ethnographizing Reason—race, natural environment, level of technical development, and such—whereby cultural domination is made to appear rational," by asserting, in a discourse taken from ethnography, "the informant's worldliness" and, in a wily maneuver, by "appropriating the entire discursive field" (p. 85). But as we shall see, his success is in a way indirect, negative. For an analysis of the movie, see Robert Stam, *Subversive Pleasures*, chap. 4, pp. 122–56.

Alencar, whom Andrade saw as his forerunner, the modernist *Macunaíma* accomplishes a revaluation of "national subject matter."[7] It integrates a tradition of opposition to literary forms associated with external
domination internally accepted. If the romantics, writing within half a
century of their country's independence, saw themselves as opposing
the (Portuguese) colonial power, which till then had determined the
political, economic, and cultural life, the modernists opposed a different
and more diffuse source of domination and adduced different elements
as characteristic of a national identity.

The concern with national identity was not abandoned in Brazil between the romantics and the moderns; it was part of the adaptation of
other literary movements to the Brazilian scene, accompanying national
and international shifts in political and economic power. Aluísio
Azevedo's novel *O cortiço* (The tenement, 1890), which finds the primeval mud where Zola's human masses arise on the outskirts of an expanding Rio de Janeiro, is not only a study in the accumulation of
capital, but also a meditation on the viability of what it posits as characteristically Brazilian features—sensuality, hybridness (of African, Amerindian, and European), and closeness to nature—within a global
economy. In Lima Barreto's *Triste fim de Policarpo Quaresma* (Sad end of
Policarpo Quaresma, 1911) the hero is placed in an insane asylum for
trying to live like one of Alencar's ancestral Amerindians, then tries to
develop Brazilian agriculture with North America machines and techniques, and is finally defeated by a characteristically national combination of insects and politicians. Both novels give greater play than
Alencar to the African element in national identity. In both novels a
pessimistic strain, present, as we have seen, even in Alencar, proposes
a problematic view of national difference and reminds the reader of
continued dependence on an external economic and cultural power.
This awareness of outside pressure on the assessment of its nature and
its value leads to a certain instability in the determination of national
character, persistently redefined in oppositional terms.

When Mário de Andrade took Macunaíma for his hero, the primitive—preferably African—had been fashionable in Paris for about a
decade, in terms similar to that of the exotic American one century
earlier. African carvings and bronzes were admired in Parisian muse-
ums; prominent Frenchmen traveled to the tropics with their baggage

---

[7] See Proença, *Roteiro de "Macunaíma,"* pp. 43–46, on common features of Alencar
and Andrade.

of French culture and carried back the tropical exotic. Raul Bopp tells about Paul Claudel's diplomatic visit to Rio in 1917, in the company of the composer Darius Milhaud. Delighted with the tropical city, they filled the embassy with exotic plants and parrots given them by their astonished Brazilian friends, and Milhaud made the popular song "O boi no telhado" (for which he paid no royalties) into "Le boeuf sur le toit," charming with catchy rhythms and playful dissonances. Soon, Bopp reports, both sides of the Atlantic "narrated an imaginary Brazil with colorful landscapes, like a land of utopia," and "the Brazilians who went to Paris on their vacations began to like that cordial 'Brazil' in all its primitive freshness" (*Movimentos modernistas*, pp. 14–15). When they returned, these travelers brought back a new valuation of "national" characteristics that had been treated with great distrust by those who, like Azevedo, implied that it was precisely its preference for the pleasure of the senses over their control and its proximity to unmediated nature which kept the nation economically and culturally dependent. At the Week of Modern Art, then, much of the work presented and of the theory behind it was concerned not only with the renewal of artistic forms which was part of modernism but also with a rethinking of the meaning of nationality and a revaluation of its distinctive characteristics.

The specifically literary movement the young modernists fought against and replaced, "paranassianism,"[8] had proposed regularity in literary form and universality in subject so Brazilian artistic production could merge into production from elsewhere. Even when they treated patriotic subjects, the paranassians took the classic literary language of Portugal as a model.[9] Their bid for parity employed tactics of camouflaged and infiltration rather than confrontation.

[8] The name of the movement is taken from that of a group of French poets "whose works were collected in anthologies called *Le Parnasse contemporain*, issued in three phases, in 1866, 1871, and 1876," among them Théophile Gautier and Lecomte de Lisle, who opposed the romantics with a neoclassical poetics of rigorous, "perfect" forms (Afrânio Coutinho, *Introdução*, pp. 203–4). The French movement petered out by the 1880s, but its influence continued into the new century in Brazil (Haberly, *Three Sad Races*, p. 100).

[9] Pierre Hourcade notes that the paranassian movement was very concerned with linguistic purity, meaning conformity to standards set by Portugal, and that it had "no true national content" (Reflexions sur la poésie," pp. 62–63). Not quite so. The sonnet—of course—"Língua portuguesa" (Portuguese language) by Olavo Bilac, strongest of the paranassians, defines the language as the "last flower of Latium" and mentions only Camões as having written great works in it but, between these two high-culture references, calls nothing but natural phenomena to describe it, except for one comparison to a tuba and a lyre, products of human ingenuity, and

But the moderns used other means for other ends. Oswald de Andrade was, at the time, the most notorious of the rebels. His "Manifesto antropófago" (Anthropophagist manifesto), published in the same year as Mário de Andrade's *Macunaíma*, for a while defined the aims and methods of the movement. The manifesto, says Bopp, presented itself as "a descent to the genuine, still pure origins of the nation, which would capture the germs of renewal, repossess the subjacent Brazil . . . and strive to reach a specific cultural synthesis, with greater emphasis on national consciousness" (p. 64). Oswald de Andrade returns to an identification of contemporary Brazilian national character with the Amerindian past, but he uses it in a new way to oppose the imposition of a European culture on Brazil: instead of rejecting European culture, he proposes to incorporate it, literally, as cannibals did Europeans. Rather than identify cannibalism with Christianity, as Alencar did, or place cannibalism at the opposite pole to civilization, as did the conquerors, Oswald de Andrade proposes to solve the problem of the other as self by forcing an identity between them. He also tries in this way to wrench the consumable exotic—the Brazilian, the Amerindian— away from the centers of consumption by consuming the consumers.[10] So, with monumental jokes, he debunks or demythifies grandiose concepts of nationalism based on a Europeanizing culture: he proposes as a patron saint for Brazil the—historical—Bishop Pero Sardinha (Sardine), eaten by coastal cannibals when his ship sank off the shore of Pernambuco, and as the most important national holiday October 11, the day before Columbus's landing and the last day of freedom for the Americas.

---

one invocation of a mother's voice speaking in it to her child. He even claims that the language has the "aroma / of virgin forests," an odd way of celebrating the language of an admired *European* civilization. Such observations, however, have no place in a polemic discourse that aims to disengage a new literary movement from the one that precedes it. As Haberly notes, "The Modernists loathed Olavo Bilac's Parnassian verses," though, as he adds, they intended to "accept his vision" of Brazil's characteristic ethnic composition, in the famous phrase, the mingling of its "three sad races" (*Three Sad Races*, p. 129). On the other hand, Mário de Andrade himself recalled that, ecstatic over the paintings of Anita Malfatti, exhibited during the Week of Modern Art and bringing news of cubism to a group of young intellectuals who knew the French impressionists but had somehow missed Cézanne, he penned "a sonnet in a most parnassian form" celebrating a work titled *The Yellow Man*. See "O movimento modernista," in *Aspectos da literatura brasileira*, pp. 231–55, 232.
[10] Larsen sees "Antropofagia" as an attempt, frustrated in the end, to define for a dependent economy a form of "consumptive production," a narrative form that "suppl[ies] the representational conditions for the practice of 'language' that dissolves all texts—all productions—in the identity of its own process as continuous consumptive production" (p. 84).

He not only accepts the need for a patron saint, however, he also, in his earlier call for "a literature for export," accepts the concept of literature as a consumer product: nationalism, and even the eventual return to the cannibals, should produce something desired by the rejected European culture and must, therefore, consider the tastes of a target market.[11]

Mário de Andrade was not one of the anthropophagists, but critics and the reading public quickly connected his novel, in which an Indian antihero represents Brazilian authenticity with the literary manifesto that took cannibals as models for intellectual endeavor, ancestors of present-day Brazilians, and sources of a desired difference from other cultures. Despite disclaimers and a growing disaffection between the two writers, Mário de Andrade often found himself working in the same vein as Oswald, since he too was embarked on the production of a recognizably Brazilian literature defining a recognizably Brazilian character at a particular historical moment. Reappraising the movement twenty years later, Mário de Andrade himself characterized it as an effort to create a national culture: "Manifesting itself particularly in the arts, but also staining established social and political customs with violence, the modernist movement announced, prepared, and to a great extent created a national state of mind." The new literature was to address not only the Brazilian situation but also the changes it reflected in the rest of the world, brought about by "new political ideas, the new speed of transportation, and a thousand and one other international causes . . . the internal progress of technology and education," and so on (*Aspectos*, p. 231).

Thus, a common perception of the need to define national culture within a world economy—expressed in various forms of discourse— led to different strategies. Oswald de Andrade placed national literature on the international market, while Mário de Andrade turned toward an internal audience and, like Macunaíma (who refused to ask the government for a grant to study art in Paris), made it a point never to leave Brazil. Yet even if he was less concerned about the insertion of Brazilian literature into the class of phenomena called world literature (compris-

[11] The call for a literature for export appeared in the "Manifesto da poesia pau-brasil" (Brazilwood poetry manifesto), *Correio da manhã*, 18 March 1924. The "Manifesto antropófago" (Anthropophagist manifesto) was first printed in the *Revista de antropofagia*, year 1, no. 1 (May 1928). Andrade datelines it "'Piratininga' [the Indian name of São Paulo], Year 374 of the Swallowing of Bishop Sardinha." Both manifestos are reprinted in Oswald de Andrade, *Obras completas*, 6:5–10, 13–19.

ing those works that are "legible" outside the boundaries of cultures where they are produced), he looked to the international literary movements of his time for a language to frame a definition of nationality. Despite differences in methods and personalities, Mário and Oswald de Andrade's choice of the American Indian to signify Brazilianness is, in the end, a traditional gesture among national authors.[12] Once again, also, they are not only defining an internal phenomenon but also purveying exotic fare, for which outside interest has opened the internal market. Those Brazilian friends of Claudel's who provided him with tropical plants and parrots and those traveling Brazilians who, in Paris, became enamored of their own primitive, unspoiled, redemptive, and hopeful country, were participating in a recurring exchange of cultural goods and values between the less and the more powerful.

Mário de Andrade was aware that primitivism is not a representation of reality but a language. In a letter to the critic Tristão de Athayde, he explains that he uses the "primitive" not because he wants to recreate a state he cannot authentically claim, since he is a cultivated man, and not because he wants to use it specifically as a marker of difference but because he is at the beginning of a process: that of defining a Brazilian culture distinct even from that of countries such as Russia, in which an exportable literature is relatively new: "I am primitive because I belong to a beginning phase."[13] Primitivism, in this argument, becomes a value-free category, purely descriptive. He also claims that his technical innovations are attempts to systematize what has already been formed in Brazil, that they do not create but reflect a reality (linguistic and other) of which writers and other intellectuals have not yet become entirely aware because they have been too preoccupied with whether Brazilian productions measure up to or are sufficiently distinctive from European ones. In other words, he claims for his work an independence from current literary trends which parallels the independence he wishes for his country but which his very intellectual development, his library, his friends' trips to Paris for inspiration and verification must deny.

With his primitive heroes, his revolutionary language, and his claims

[12] Antônio Cândido, in "Literature and the Rise of Brazilian National Identity," notes that regardless of the literary school they belong to, Brazilian writers have always considered it part of their function to address the problem of national identity. See also Haberly, *Three Sad Races*, 129–30, on the modernists' return to the Amerindian as emblem of national identity.
[13] See in *Cartas de Mário de Andrade*, the letter of 23 December 1927, pp. 16–17, 22.

of isolation and independence Andrade creates a useful fiction from within which he can speak his nation; it is a little like the useful fictions of isolation which allow scientists to study certain phenomena in their laboratories. Rather than turn his eyes on the world and try to adapt its offerings to a Brazilian reality defined as insufficient and incomplete, he looks on what Brazil has to offer in isolation. He claims that this entity Brazil, which he tries to capture, has already produced a typical idiom to express a typical reality and that he is just tapping a flourishing and till-then neglected popular culture, not out of a desire to abandon his intellectual formation but in order to give a more accurate account of the level at which the differentiating elements of nationality are to be found. His explanations privilege the linguistic element, which is programmatically subjected to reevaluation: "When I started to write wrong Portuguese, didn't I immediately announce that I was making a Brazilian grammar, with which announcement I simply intended to show that I was not improvising, but doing something thought out and systematic?" (*Cartas*, p. 21). In his reasoning, the opposition right/ wrong appears with its values reversed and comes to stand for the political dichotomy between national and alien, as well as for the logical dichotomy between random and systematic: the positive value of ratio- nality is attributed not to traditional criteria for judging literature and language but to their revaluation.

His reversals of customary evaluation do not affect all dichotomies in the same way—system and rationality are positive, as is "wrong" grammar—and this may be one reason why Mário de Andrade had to spend so much effort dissociating himself from the more anarchic procedures of Oswald de Andrade and his group, who favored a more straightforward concept of primitivism, of its authentic presence in Bra- zil, and of how well it represents Brazilian culture. In the end, Mário de Andrade's work on language and on the integration of popular cul- ture into learned discourse had the same abrasiveness and destructive- ness as that of the anthropophagists; at the time, however, it too could be mistaken for a fall into chaos rather than an attempt at a new, subver- sive order.

Meanwhile, both authors appropriated the European rebellion against received forms and turned it into a sign of nationalistic affirmation. As a rebellion, it promised a language free from compromise with estab- lished internal or external powers, in which to redefine national reality. But it also depended on those same structures to establish the scope and orientation of its opposition. In *Macunaíma* Mário de Andrade attempts to evade the dilemma: he uses Indians and the language of exoticism to characterize Brazilianness, but his work redefines the enterprise by changing the way in which the customary signifiers of nationality are used. He recodifies the relation between an authentic national expression and the language of exoticism, to confront the problematic relation between a national character, defined as unique, and the ethical or aesthetic paradigms, which, though not unique, guarantee the intelligibility and legitimacy of such a definition because they are current and established.

But the enterprise proves problematic once again, insofar as exoticism is a category in the discourse of power. If, as Oswald de Andrade proposes, exoticism is not only the way in which the more powerful speak of the less powerful but an opportunity for the latter to enter the international cultural market, it is not, for all that, free of market pressures. In a sense, Mário de Andrade cannot define primitivism to suit his purpose, because, beyond the reach of his ability to reform Brazil's literary language, primitivism as the exotic has been enrolled in a more powerful discourse. One could say that he attempts to do from within the language of exoticism what Cooper, in *Notions of the Americans* tried to do from without, that is, to appropriate a language. But that language was not innocent, and he could not avoid the problem of how to articulate difference or identity, even for internal consumption, within an already established set of meanings and values.

So in *Macunaíma* Mário de Andrade turns exoticism on its head. By following very closely the collection of tales about Macunaíma, a trickster figure of the Taulipang people, published by Theodor Koch-Grünberg in *Vom Roroima zum Orinoco,* he models his discourse on the discipline of ethnology, which claims to be scientific and thus objective and value-neutral. His Indian protagonist appears not as a representative of primitive virtue who will redeem a tired and corrupt civilization—like Alencar's heroic Indians—not, that is, as the carrier of values arbitrarily imposed from the outside but as a malicious innocence redefined into enlightened provocation to make a tired and corrupt civilization more aware of itself. His values, if any, are not derived from an extraneous discourse to fulfill an extraneous need. Macunaíma is free of the European-imposed and Brazilian-accepted load of virtue of villainy which burdened previous literary Indians; he is the prototype for a recognizable national character that defines itself not as either in conformity with or in opposition to some European model but as characteristically undefinable. As Darcy Ribeiro implies, continuing in the subversive vein mined by Andrade, *Macunaíma* results from a centuries-old "game of blindman's buff," during which "the strange people seen by Columbus and Americo [Vespucci] turn into" diverse American nationals, while those who remained there—on the other side of the Atlantic—"cobble together new-worldly utopias" with elements of "our healthy and gentle savagery." In turn "we ape them and they mimeticize us," until all definitions of identity are destablized; at that point Macunaíma becomes a universally recognizable privileged representation of that nonidentity (*Utopia selvagem*, p. 31).[14] A "hero without any character," as Mário de Andrade calls him in the subtitle, Macunaíma subverts any ontological, moral, psychological, or literary order. At the same time, the refusal to define character as centralized subject, whether psychological or social, and the introduction of immotivation into the vocabulary available for the presentation of literary characters are distinctively modernist strategies of opposition to their predecessor texts. Once again, as in the case of the early novelists of nationality, one can invoke the zeitgeist and mention not only French enthusiasm for the primitive but also that Robert Musil's *Mann ohne Eigenschaften* was being written at the same time as *Macunaíma*.[15] What distinguishes Mário de Andrade, however, is that instead of denying influence, he showed that acceptance, even incorporation, can be a form of criticism; if the foreign must be used to define the national, acknowledging transposition can become a form of nationalization and can indicate that the affirmation of nationality is itself a traditional and characteristic Brazilian activity, inevitably paradoxical.

In part this conjunction of the new and the traditional in Mário de Andrade's work was as important for its acceptability as the author's personal position in a group of artists who, well placed in the local social hierarchy, exercised their recognized and accepted role as revolutionizers and revitalizers of the intellectual landscape. They prepared the way for the intellectual acceptance of the change from an agrarian

[14] In this "fable," Ribeiro tells the adventures of a hapless, cheerful, sensual mulatto soldier in a fantasy Brazil, both historical and futuristic, with variations on themes from *Macunaíma*. The hero ends up in an Indian tribe on a flying island (there are enough mentions of Swift to place its identification beyond conjecture), ruled by a Caliban and two ecumenical nuns; readers are also treated to the blueprint of a utopian government in a Brazil ruled by a multinational computer called Prospero.

[15] According to Haberly, Mário de Andrade was trying to formulate not the absence but the excess of qualities, the juxtaposition of racial and cultural components in himself and in the Brazilian national character which precluded the coherence and unity necessary for an intelligible definition of nationality (*Three Sad Races*, 137–38, 146).

to an industrial economy, the growth of the cities and shift of population, the influx of immigrants. All these promised to reopen the possibility, probably not as visible since independence, of Brazil's assumption
of a more prominent position in the international concert of nations.
This integrative function operates whether Mário de Andrade is for
or against the changes it entails: because *Macunaíma* incorporates the
phenomena of change and raises the problems they cause, it is pivotal
in the development of Brazilian literature and, more generally, in the
development of a language in which the country can speak of itself in
its new garb.

The thread from which Macunaíma's adventures loosely hang is his
voyage from the small Indian village where he was born to São Paulo
and back, in a loop whose squiggles and curlicues cover most of the
Brazilian territory. At first he is simply fleeing hunger, like so many
inhabitants of rural Brazil; later he is on a quest for the magic stone
given him by the woman he married, which he has lost. The flight,
when Macunaíma and his brothers abandon their home, beset by famine and discord, eventually becomes subsumed in the quest, enabling
Andrade to transport his hero from north to south without making him
a refugee: what he seeks is valuable, but what he abandons is not
valueless. Throughout, Andrade refuses to establish hierarchies. Macunaíma lives in a world of leveled values which embraces all the regions
of the country, all their people and stories, all events and decisions.

Macunaíma marries a spirit of the forest. After giving him much
pleasure and a child who dies, she is sucked dry by a snake and climbs
into heaven. The magic stone she had given him ends up in the hands
of a capitalist and adventurer who cooks spaghetti sauce with human
meat, carries the vaguely Slavic-Italo-American name of Venceslau Pietro Pietra, and like many immigrants, lives in the industrial city of São
Paulo. But Pietra is also the giant Piaimã of Amazonian Indian mythology, and he becomes a synchretic figure, a Euro-cannibal who erases
the long-elaborated essential difference between the civilized and the
barbaric.

In his quest for the stone, Macunaíma is like a traditional hero of epic
and folktale,[16] except that he does not have the usual heroic qualifica-
tions. At the inception or climax of any action, bellicose or romantic he

---

[16] In an extended analysis of *Macunaíma* in the terms Vladimir Propp used to study
Russian folktales, Haroldo de Campos demonstrates Andrade's fidelity to the form
of the Taulipang myth. See *Morfologia do "Macunaíma."*

is as likely as not to yawn, "I feel sooo lazy," and go to sleep.[17] He lacks
the spirit of enterprise that promises progress: he pursues his enemy
only fitfully, and does what he can to avoid meeting him "man to man"
by dressing up as a French prostitute or by sending in a surrogate
(chap. 6). When he meets a monster, he flees, sensibly but most unhero-
ically. He eats too much and is cheerfully incapable of resisting any
temptation of the flesh. When forced to fight, he resorts to ruses, but
even so, he is one of the more vincible figures in literature. He is a
trickster of flickering cleverness and innocent malice, charming, guile-
ful, unpredictable, irresponsible, stubborn, lewd. One could not derive
from him anything like a traditional literary character, or from his motives and actions anything like a code of preferred behavior. On the
contrary, he negates the steadiness, reliability, and goal orientation necessary to achieve the kind of success that depends on hard work and
delay of gratification, and so his laziness becomes a challenge to the
power that has imposed work and accumulation on those who did not
want it or think they needed it. Macunaíma is of many minds, and
follows them all, challenging also traditional notions of character, plot,
causality, and verisimilitude. He throws into question the qualities
needed for success as defined in the world that calls him primitive. At
the same time, his subversion of literary and conceptual categories falls
into a known category. He is a modern antihero, though he has been
transposed into the primitive mode. The primitive, however, is once
again being defined as the known category thought to capture the essence of the New World.

In this double characterization as primitive and modern, Macunaíma
is not a model but an instance; he redefines the primitive as neither
noble nor redemptive; he is not Adam before the Fall but the unsayable
id. He also dribbles past more recent associations attached to the antihero, for he is not in opposition to well-known literary figures but an
alternative to them. He is not an anti-Peri; he leaves Peri behind. He is
not the hope of a tired and disillusioned civilization that can find renewal, because it can still find itself, in denial; he denies the point of
that civilization. His antics do not foreground the problems of good

---

[17] Larsen notes that this refrain "not only 'proves' that [Andrade] . . . has read Paulo
Prado's *Retrato do Brasil*, but invites speculation that all such texts, however vainly
they may insist on their own 'scientific' detachment, are really nothing more than
the same *pensée sauvage* that they deludedly believe they have domesticated" (p. 85).
Paulo Prado's (1926) is one of the many books that seek to identify the causes of
Brazilian backwardness. See Larsen, p. 110 n. 14.

and evil, of conformity to tradition or freedom acquired by experimentation on the borders of the acceptable or imaginable; they evade those problems. Macunaíma does not do what is good or evil, what will make him progress or remain backward; he does what will get him into or out of trouble, what will bring him pleasure, cause him pain, or throw him into danger.

He is born as aware of his surroundings as Oskar in *The Tin Drum;* with just as little childlike innocence, he seduces his sister-in-law by turning himself from an insufferable brat at home into a gorgeous young man in the forest (she gladly suffers beatings from her husband to protect her pleasure with little Macunaíma). Later, when he is wandering in the forest with his brothers, he kills, more or less by chance, a monster who is threatening a young maiden.[18] When the monster's head pursues him to offer its everlasting magical services, he flees ignominiously and never hears the offer. Macunaíma is not noble and courageous; he is not a defender of helpless women, though some random action of his may have the random effect of protecting one of them; he does not uphold the values of the family; he is not even alert enough to profit from magic help when it turns up. Yet because his actions are so random that occasionally they have the same results as those of the noble hero or produce the same rewards, they break the symmetry of opposition; they configure an attempt to define otherness as independent of an extraneous, self-defined self. The remedy Macunaíma would offer to a tired Western civilization is not recourse to its own neglected virtues; he brings to the growing metropolis of São Paulo no higher morality of a simpler life. Quite simply, he will not be used.

The episode with Vei, the sun (chap. 8), contextualizes Macunaíma's otherness in literary and ideological terms. He finds himself in one of the classic fairy-tale trial situations: he is promised wealth and one of the sun's daughters for a wife if he stays on a little island off Rio and keeps away from women for one whole day while the sun goes on her round. He complies for a while, then becomes restless, goes out to explore the city and falls in, and into bed with, a Portuguese fishwife, recently immigrated. Caught, he loses his chance of making something of himself, of harnessing the tropical sun. From there on, the sun punishes him and, at several other points in the tale, mercilessly burns his back. The passage can be read allegorically: incapable of delaying

---

[18] This episode can also be read as a lethal parody of Peri's transformation from subjugated domestic to king of the Brazilian forest and protector of Ceci.

gratification, innocent in the pursuit of sensual pleasure, ready to yield to the appeal of the best but also the most undemanding that the former colonial power can offer him, Macunaíma shows some of the most charming and also some of the most destructive traits generally attributed to the Brazilian character. Therefore, he forfeits the opportunity to become as successful as (geographically and sensually) temperate heroes, who are so ready to question the values of alternative (and tropical) cultures. Macunaíma loses his chance to make the tropical sun work for his advancement and justifies the association of the tropics with irresponsible backwardness. In this reading, the conjunction of the Iberian heritage and the merciless sun condemns him to a hand-to-mouth existence, narrated in his eventual return from the developed city of São Paulo (whose development is thus also thrown into question) to the Amazonian forest, where he dies.[19] The allegorical reading, however, disregards the surface texture of the tale. The wit of the writing; the image of Macunaíma covered with bird droppings, washed and put to dry by Vei on the island off Rio; the zest with which the hero explores the city and "plays" with the fishwife; and the implication that the condition imposed by the sun is unreasonable counterbalance the regret at the lost opportunity and confirm the value of Macunaíma's refusal to play the game of "order and progress."[20] The chapter seems to deny that this positivistic motto, which graces the Brazilian flag, expresses either the reality or the authentic aspirations of the nation.

Macunaíma subverts the usual order of things not only by shuffling hierarchies and values but also by blurring the boundaries that help organize thought and identity. In line with Brazil's traditional view of itself as a place of exemplary race relations, where differences in color are absorbed into a multihued national culture,[21] *Macunaíma* blurs the

[19] Telê Ancona Lopez gives a very similar allegorical interpretation in "A margem e o texto," pp. 40–41. For reasons slightly different from mine, Haroldo de Campos rejects this reading (p. 239).

[20] The motto "order and progress" reflects the convictions of the young army officers who in 1889 deposed Emperor Pedro II and proclaimed the republic. It has become shorthand in a long ideological debate about the principles that define national identity and the goals and methods that should rule the nation.

[21] Once again there is reference to this pervasive view of race relations in Brazil, best known at this time in the formulation of Gilberto Freyre's *Casa grande e senzala* and contested in more recent sociological studies of racial relations in Brazil, such as Octavio Ianni's *Raças e classes sociais no Brasil*. Haberly says that Andrade casts doubt on the optimistic view from the vantage point of his own "racial multiplicity" (*Three Sad Races*, p. 143). For present purposes it is important only to note the presence of an ideology of racial harmony.

distinctions between the races. Unlike the earlier novels of national identity, however, *Macunaíma* does not treat the subject of contact within the marriage plot. Though the affair with his sister-in-law touches the incest motif of the other fictions and his various couplings with the Portuguese woman and the Polish girl who receives the African god Exu in a trance touch the vexed question of exogamy (since the hero belongs to all races, all his couplings are radically exogamic), these matters appear fleetingly. Macunaíma is lusty, but his only marriage dissolves, and his only child dies. The creation of a future population is none of his concern; he belongs to a population already there and already mixed.

Macunaíma is born black, "son of the fear of the night" (p. 7), into an Indian village; his first adventures take place in the forest, amid Indian myths. Then a bath in a magic pool makes him white and turns his brother Jiguê's skin copper-colored, but his second brother, Maanape, remains black because the other two used up all the magic water (chap. 5). In *Macunaíma* the races that make up the population have the same family origin; differences, though consequential, are accidental. Interactions, even if not peaceful, are matter-of-fact: it is with the help of the African spirit Exu, temporarily inhabiting the young Polish woman, that Macunaíma wins his first victory over the giant Piaimã (chap. 7). In this episode Andrade completes the cycle through which his hero is made to encompass all races: the scene presents a characteristically Brazilian religious syncretism that integrates contributions from all populations. Macunaíma's ritual transformation refers to a characteristically casual treatment of race and reaffirms one of the most emphatically stressed Brazilian values. One notes, however, that when he bathes in that magic pool, Macunaíma becomes not just white but tall and blond, as is the woman receiving the African spirit: Andrade's text registers the common Brazilian self-characterization as a nation where all races are equal and equally respected, while the details of his representation contradict this central privileged message. By illustrating the ideology of racial harmony, *Macunaíma* accords with part of the reality of the composition of Brazilian national consciousness; in the choice of terms expressing this accord, however, Andrade incorporates observable data that contradict the ideological representation. The clash between ideal and reality is as much as part of what is characteristically national as are the clashing elements. At the same time, this layering of contradictory references functions like the figure of Pietra-Piaimã, to deconstruct exoticism by removing it from system of simple oppositions between primitive and European.

In Alencar's work the violence of the contact between different people in the Americas becomes a rhythmic throb in the background, like the noise of kettledrums in a romantic symphony; in the foreground, like the strings, are virtuous and heroic Indians. When Macunaíma goes to Exu, however, he does not show or acquire virtue—just effectiveness. Violence surges and then turns into satire. A description of extraliterary reality changes into a tool of literary expression. When Exu, the African trickster god, possesses the young woman of Polish origin, Macunaíma feels a great urge to take part in the rite. He "plays" with the woman while she is in a trance and thus becomes the "son" of Exu. Then he joins the line of petitioners asking favors of the god in the woman: a butcher wants customers to buy his tainted meat (granted), a lover asks that his girl be given a teaching job so they can marry (granted), a farmer wants his farm freed of ants and malaria (not granted), a doctor asks for the ability to write elegant Portuguese (not granted). The witty formulation of these matters just barely keeps under the control of satire the cruelty of rape and dishonesty.

This leveling of values, demythification of the hero, and deromanticizing of the exotic coalesce when Macunaíma asks Exu to make Venceslau Pietro-Pietra/Piaimã suffer. The trickster god transports the giant into the medium's body, where he is thrashed and tortured till Exu himself cries out and the woman lies half dead on the ground. At intervals, the narrator repeats: "It was horrible." Finally, a modified, vaguely sacrilegious recital of the Lord's Prayer restores Exu and the woman to health, while the giant lies on the floor of his palace, howling, gored and beaten, burned and cut, bleeding and foaming at the mouth. Exu leaves, and Mário de Andrade, who had once attended such a ceremony with friends, puts a list of their names in the book and replaces his own with Macunaíma's.[22]

Blurring boundaries between races, religions, literary and extraliterary reality, author and creature, Mário de Andrade tries to characterize an independent otherness. The violence he invokes at these boundaries makes it difficult to accept this otherness as redemptive of the discomforts of the familiar; it also re-estranges the exoticism of a romanticized New World, unmasking it as a familiarized and tamed otherness. The specific ingredients of the anarchic stew he concocts are a recognizable part of everyday Brazilian life, and the satire that spices it serves to link it to a reality with which readers are familiar and of which they can be

[22] See interview with Antônio Bento, *Macunaíma*, p. 375.

expected to disapprove. But the violence of the incidents described and their satirical intention also work against the movement toward internal exoticism which Bopp mentions, and make the typical into a source of discomfort more than a reason for pride. Thus *Macunaíma* questions even the affirmation of national identity which underlies its own creation.

A similar estranging integration results from the "degeographication" of which Mário de Andrade speaks in his prefaces to *Macunaíma*.[23] The hero's origins and adventures make geographical boundaries irrelevant to the definition of national character. Macunaíma is born somewhere in the Guianas, and his opponent Piaimã is from somewhere else: in the Taulipang myth his name means "stranger." The spirits who help and annoy the hero are from anywhere in South America or Africa. His heritage, as promised by Vei (but not delivered), is, as in the Brazilian saying used to deconstruct sophistication, Europe, France, and Bahia ("Oropa, França, e Bahia" [*Macunaíma*, p. 67]). The language of his tale contains many words of Amerindian origin, Africanisms, Gallicisms, Anglicisms, and regional expressions from everywhere in the country in such a linguistic riot that a reader, while recognizing all as Brazilian and delighted at finding childhood words that were lost in the homogenization of schools and standardized writing also finds it difficult to read the specialized vocabulary of his fellow Brazilians' childhood words. The three great spheres of Macunaíma's activities—the forest, the countryside, the city—are independent of national boundaries. They coexist, as in the domain of the giant Piaimã, whose house is an urban palace in the middle of a rural sylvan grotto developed by an English company in the city of São Paulo.

On one hand, degeographication is an expansive force that allows Macunaíma to chase and be chased throughout Brazil, from forest to town to field in one paragraph, madly galloping through the folktales, customs, and idioms of the entire country. On the other hand, it is centripetal, showing the possibility—at a time when the first great push for industrialization was concentrating in São Paulo a mad jumble of people from the entire world and from all levels of technological development—of an integration of disparate elements, creating a modern version of the traditional view of Brazil as a place where integration is possible.

---

[23] These prefaces were written at the time of the book's publication but not published until they were collected by Marta R. Batista et al., in *Brasil*, pp. 289–95.

But this sort of unification is also corrosive, since, closing the circle opened with the invention of the nation one century before, it refuses to base its notion of nationality on the easy patriotism that derives pride and identity from more or less arbitrary national borders. At the only clearly official, patriotic gathering Macunaíma attends, he displaces the designated orator, tells an Indian tale immediately accepted by the public, and subverts the occasion by replacing univocal, official symbols such as the flag with "natural" multivalent signs such as the constellation of the Southern Cross (which, however, also appears on the positivist Brazilian flag). Though from the official point of view the abolition of geographical boundaries and the subversion of patriotic occasions introduce disorder into the body politic, within *Macunaíma* the dissolution of these expected distinctions begins to establish a more appropriate basis for a feeling of national affiliation. The play with political boundaries also calls into question the position of the nation in the world: relations, including (or especially) relations between nations, depend on boundaries, and unstable boundaries, like Macunaíma's laziness, disconcert power.

More tellingly, Andrade blurs the accustomed boundaries between nature, as in the New World, and culture, as in the developed West. He deromanticizes the primitive, which becomes emphatically not a redeemer of the discontents of the civilized world but an ill-mannered claimant to the voice and power of "civilization." The primitive Macunaíma guards against the excesses of government power or the evils of a nationalism that turns more or less accidental geopolitical boundaries into matters of pride and criteria for definition; he reinforces the ideals of racial equality on which his nation had always prided itself and through which it had claimed a moral superiority to those nations that based their sense of superiority on preserving the races distinct and legitimated their economic domination by it. Macunaíma integrates the national territory as no other literary creation had done and offers a way out of the fragmentation of national literature by competing regionalisms, each claiming to be representative. His motives and actions are always both savage and ignoble.

Given this superoppositional otherness of Macunaíma, it remains to be seen how the urban primitivism he inaugurates redefines urban modernity. In his treatment of the relation between Macunaíma and technology, Andrade conflates some of the terms in which other works in this vein trace the boundaries between nature and culture, on one hand, and between history and myth, on the other. What will Macunaíma do when confronted with the superior technological sophistication of those who affirm their power over the new nations by providing them with guns, internal combustion engines, and telephones as necessities of civilized life?

He might have remained pure by refusing them, but refusal is a solution generally chosen by refugees from civilization, not by those with whom they take refuge. In São Paulo, Macunaíma meets with technological progress at the center of economic power and sees the signs of economic development which Brazil will have to take on as it claims parity with and affirms its difference from a world that would define it. Unwilling to deny the reality of Brazil's desire for parity and unable to force the truth by denying the desirability of the products of technology, Andrade undermines their importance by attacking them at the point of production and making their magic accessible to Macunaíma as magic. When Macunaíma finds out about taxis and telephones and the need for money other than the load of cacy (cocoa) he had brought with him from the Amazon, he takes possession of this new world by turning his brother Jiguê into whatever gadget he happens to need at the moment: "He turned Jiguê into the machine telephone, called up the giant Piaimã and called his mother names" (p. 44). He turns his brother into the "machine taxi" when he needs transportation, or conversely, he looks up to the "machine moon" in the sky. Just as he can technologize nature, he naturalizes technology and asks the Englishmen who own the whiskey, gun, and ammunition orchards to give their trees a shake for him (chap. 5). Magic and nerve provide Macunaíma with the products of civilization. By making primitive magic produce telephones and trees produce guns, Andrade abolishes distinctions between nature and culture and erases the history that mediates between the son of the forest and the giant of the industrialized São Paulo.

But there is a rub. Despite his magic and his ability to make the Englishmen shake guns and whiskey out of their trees for him, those trees are still not his, and in the end the episodes do not abolish history but recall it. He too is incapable of resisting the lure of European weapons and firewater. Thus he remains outside of a historical process in which he could, at least to some extent, dictate the language that speaks him. All that remains open to him is the power of use over those artifacts.[24] By subjecting machines to Indian magic and referring to the

[24] Larsen posits consumption as affirmation, but magic is not part of a Marxist vocabulary. Mário de Andrade is as perceptive as Larsen sees him, but bitterer.

"machine moon," he eliminates the distinction that had defined his position within the realm of the powerless and demands a revaluation of the world. Since he cannot require that revaluation from the powerless position he occupies, however, Macunaíma becomes a fantasy of possibility, rearranging the world through the imagination. The anarchy that is his medium proves incapable of functioning as a principle of government and interpretation, unable to anchor an order of political and epistemological meanings, though it can remind its readers that the arrangements they are asked to take for granted are not facts of nature, and it can make differences imaginable. Macunaíma subverts by the imagination; he has the nerve to posit a different arrangement from that which makes him perpetually exotic.

At the end of the book Macunaíma finally beats the giant in a Rabelaisian scene that ends with him swinging madly from a liana in the giant's entrance hall and the giant falling into his own spaghetti sauce, where he melts with a multitude of other ingredients into a unified soup. Macunaíma wins back his stone and returns to the place of his birth, but his victory is no apotheosis. Back home his friends are gone, he is hungry, the sun beats on his back. His brothers and his women die. He knocks on the doors of various forest spirits seeking shelter and company and is refused until one of them finally takes pity on him and turns him into a constellation, an arbitrary design imposed on amorphous eternity.

There remain telling and writing. Chapter 8, close to the middle of the book, consists of a "Letter to the Icamiabas," written by Macunaíma, who titles himself emperor, to his "subjects" who in São Paulo are known by the more classical Hellenic name of Amazons. The letter is written in an archaizing Portuguese whose satiric intention is given away by a phonetic Brazilianism in the title (*pra* instead of *para* as it is officially written and pronounced), and it inverts the conditions under which Caminha's letter to the king of Portugal was sent. Like Caminha, Macunaíma describes the charms of the women he encounters, but they are the women of the big city, French prostitutes who demand lobster and champagne and deplete his treasure, forcing him to appeal to his subjects for more cocoa to be changed into money at a very unfavorable rate. The diction, which imitates classical Portuguese, jumbles together the centuries between the discovery and the present; it is punctured with anachronisms and Brazilianisms that question its adequacy to the present and to a separate Brazilian culture by shifting back and forth between classical antiquity and Amerindian myths, presented as equivalent but not synonymous. The letter thus questions all four centuries of writing the New World, beginning with the first document of discovery and colonization. With its description of industrial São Paulo to the Icamiabas and with its demands for products of forest extraction to pay for French prostitutes in the most developed economic center of the nation, the letter also inverts the discoveries and restates relations of economic dependency. It translates disparities in economic and cultural power between Brazil and Europe into disparities between the "savage" and the "civilized" wherever they appear, but it promises that the helpless subjection of the savage leads to the inevitable subversion of the civilized. At the end, Macunaíma observes that the people of the city have the strange habit of speaking a barbarous but vital language but writing a different, "Camonian" one, the language he is using in his own missive. But the missive is a parody, and since the Icamiabas may be illiterate, it is destined not to be read, breaking the loop of American writing upon which from the times of the first accounts, both subjection and independence had been predicated.

There remains at the end of *Macunaíma* a storytelling parrot who wanders off into the distance, on the shoulder of a man to whom it spins the tale of Macunaíma, transposing language from the realm of culture into that of nature so the story can be told to us. This is the innovative, revolutionary language Mário de Andrade invents for his work, incorporating the vocabularies of the many nations that form Brazil, respecting a popular native syntax and, because he is a cultivated man, as he always admitted, transforming it into a new, flexible, expressive, recognizably Brazilian literary language recovered for writing.

In the trajectory from parrot to narrator to text, *Macunaíma* asserts cultural independence from the former colonial power, which till then had dominated the former colony's mode of expression, if not its economy, and opens the way for the possibility of expressing a critical view of the world which subverts the customary perception of national reality. Like Alencar, who began by forging a "Brazilian" language, Mário de Andrade finds in language the final and lasting affirmation of his work. In it man and parrot, culture and nature, join in the creation of the anarchic Macunaíma, who, if he does not solve the problems of exoticism, of domination, of economic and cultural dependency, finally becomes part of what is understood as Brazilianness by creating a different articulation of all these problems. He enters a national mythology in this now-basic text of Brazilian literature not only by redefining national identity in terms of disjuncture and incoherence but also by positing a

different relation between the discourses of a powerful self and an other
defined as dependent. In this novel the absence of power proves subversive and destablizes the discourse of power without replacing it. In this
way, it affirms the interdependence of definer and defined, center and
margin, neither term of which is intelligible without the other. Essential
to this decentralization and deconstruction is Andrade's refusal to make
an exception for his own discourse: a parrot is a doubtfully adequate
symbol for oppositional or differentiating speech.

Having mounted his radical attack on the discourse of power, however, Andrade feels free to inhabit it, and just as Cooper and Alencar
used the forms of romantic fiction to challenge the distribution of
discursive power between former metropoles and former colonies, so
Andrade uses the modernist idiom for a similar and still necessary
challenge. The result of the adaptation he performed was not the affirmation of an identity whose contradictions battled an overarching vision of national identity as coherent and stable; it was, rather, a vision
of all identity as fragmented, all structure as unstable, that is, fictitious,
and of a Brazilian national identity finally relevant within the discourse
of power only insofar as it embodies the destruction that this discourse
suspects it carries within itself. Bakhtin called this relation between
stability and corrosion, center and margin Carnival.[25] Having carni-
valized their own carnival into a huge tourist attraction for the developed world, Brazilians are amused. Macunaíma, rewriting Chactas,
would probably roll on the ground with laughter.

---

[25] Robert Stam refers to Mikhail Bakhtin's "Forms of Time and of the Chronotope in
the Novel" in his analysis of Brazilian film. The movie *Macunaíma* and Brazilian
film in general, he contends, carnivalize Americanization, especially Hollywood. See
Subversive Pleasures, pp. 122–56.

9

Conclusion:
Exoticism as Strategy

The relations of power between the United States and Europe, on one hand, and the United States and Brazil (extrapolating, the United States and Latin America), on the other, changed in the course of the nineteenth century, as did the various American literatures; the elements isolated in the literatures of independence (the treatment of history, of place, of otherness) took on different configurations. In Brazil and Latin America such elements tended to persist; in the United States they became residual in mainstream literature and more characteristic of regional or "minority" writing.

Outside of the Americas, literatures of exoticism which serve definitions of national or cultural identity continue to be written and to declare inequalities in the distribution of power between interconnected self and other. We see the complex relation between power and identity, writing and power when Antônio Cândido examines the links among the French Enlightenment, Portuguese literature, and a fledgling, nationalist Brazilian literature at the end of the eighteenth and the beginning of the nineteenth century (*Formação*, chap. 1) or the connection between literary movements in France and the United States and a Brazilian literature suddenly caught in a shift from an exoticism of hope to one of "underdevelopment" ("Literatura e subdesenvolvimento"), or when Kwame Appiah, in "Out of Africa," examines how contemporary Africa writing is often read as a representation of African identity against a powerful and defining European (or Euro-American) culture.

Appiah sees cultural identity too (like nationality at the beginning of the nineteenth century) as constructed. Thus "African" culture is an abstraction whose manifestations in any number of very different populations have in common only that they are called African by those who do not belong to any of them. This "Africa" could argue against the powerful cultural discourse that determines it only in the very terms, positive or negative, of that discourse.[1] European elaborations on African customs (such as their codification into what is called Ashanti law) can at the same time preserve and distort them, turning a flexible and contingent aggregate of judgments (orally transmitted) into a (written) monument then seen by Africans as in authentic opposition to European legal institutions. Yet, in Appiah's view, the impulse to elaborate a definition of cultural identity is all but inescapable when unequally powerful cultural discourses come into contact. Though it often yields an "ersatz exoticism," it can also operate what Antônio Cândido sees as an adjustment "in depth" which turns "dependence" into "interdependence." He calls attention to a vast movement, beginning (for Latin America) in the thirties, which promised the creation of a "cultural interdependency" between the centers and the peripheries of cultural power ("Literatura e subdesenvolvimento," p. 155). Cultural identity can develop as a difference that rejects "demonization and subjection" and realizes that the difficulty is "not that [ideologies, like cultures,] exist antagonistically, but that they *only* exist antagonistically" (Appiah, "Out of Africa," p. 175).

The preceding chapters followed the formation of a European discourse of the Americas and then saw how that discourse was used to contest power, define an American identity, and claim power in turn. Cooper and Alencar showed how the initial discourse about the Americas was variously adapted in the Americas and that its different forms still circled questions of the division between nature and culture, the contact with difference, the importance of history and writing. In Mário de Andrade's work we see not only a reformulation of this discourse from the periphery but also a sign that the centers from which the discourse of power emanates have been relocated.

With parody, deflation, demythification Macunaíma decenters a Brazilian discourse of power as proposed by Alencar. His world is openly

---

[1] "Indeed," Appiah writes, "the very invention of Africa (as something more than a geographical entity) must be understood, ultimately, as an outgrowth of European racialism; the notion of Pan-Africanism was founded on the notion of the African, which was, in turn, founded not on any genuine cultural commonality but on the very European concept of the Negro." ("Out of Africa," p. 164).

fragmented: cultural elements refuse to coalesce into a definite narrative shape and even the narrative itself shows the disjunction between the cultural elements and the technological and economic world in which and for which they exist. For Mário de Andrade this harlequin world is the true representation of Brazilianness, and coherence is not necessary for identity.[2]

But whereas this incoherence is still determined by its contact with a center of power (the English owners of the gun and whiskey orchards, the French proponents of modernism, the German scientists who research Macunaíma), a different form of decentralization takes place in the United States as it begins to impose its own cultural power on the world it had once challenged. One hundred years after independence, when Henry James finished *The American*, the United States had become, as in Cooper's *Notions of the Americans*, a prosperous, economically and militarily powerful nation. Nevertheless, for James the question of its cultural power was still open, still important enough to place at, or close to, the center of several novels and stories. In *The American*, Christopher Newman has amassed a fortune (in bathroom appliances), but has not acquired the cultural and historical depth denoted by paintings, castles, cathedrals, and a wife from the old French nobility. Between his success and his failure lies the distance separating the new nation from the cultural power it had tried to claim for a century. Yet Newman's moral victory over the corrupt Bellegardes, themselves defeated in the marriage market and in politics, sounds the familiar themes of European decadence and American redemption.[3]

Like his predecessors, James treats questions of history and cultural power through the marriage plot, where, in reverse gender assignment but traditional gender function, New (American) man attempts to conquer himself a wife from the Old World. John Carlos Rowe, carefully highlighting all the historical connections and implications Newman misses in his siege of the Bellegardes, contends that the prototypical American New Man fails because, deprived by birth in the New World of the equivalent of historical depth, he cannot see where the European cultural fort was best defended or where it could be breached ("Politics

[2] Notions of disjunction, maladjustment, or incoherence are central to Roberto Schwarz's analyses of Brazilian literature and culture. (How central can be seen in the interview reprinted as "Cuidado com as ideologias alienígenas," in *O pai de família*, pp. 115–22).

[3] For a discussion of how marraige, market, and power are related in *The American*, see Carolyn Porter, "Gender and Value in *The American*."

of Innocence"). Implicitly, the novel rejects Cooper's strategy of simply positing a historical depth for the new nation; it also rejects the more general New World strategy of choosing among various ways to establish historical depth. *The American* battles for authority on the opponent's field and confronts European history head on, even at the cost of the marriage itself. Just as Valentin refuses the historically authorized advantage of class in the duel with Kapp, marking his essential nobility and sealing his defeat, so Newman refuses the advantages of money and will, signaling that he deserves to marry Claire, and that he will be unable to do so. His burning of the document that incriminates the Bellegardes is more than equivalent to Valentin's shooting wide of the mark, more than a sign of the curious kinship between the death-seeking nobleman and the energetic Newman: it turns back against Europe the historical inscription of the Americas by Europe. The new man forgives the crime of the European family whose acceptance he had desired and burns the written record of that crime. Like the English owners of the whiskey trees, however, Mme de Bellegarde does not care. James links history with the marriage plot to probe the possibility of an alliance between a historically constituted European self—the Bellegardes and their circle never doubt that Newman is other—[4] and a historically innocent representative of the New World. The impossibility of the marriage is a direct consequence of historical innocence: Newman doesn't "get" the historical context that conditions the Bellegardes and so he also doesn't "get" how to use the written record of their history.[5]

James produces one last twist, however: his own claim to parity, based on the writing of that cultural object *The American*. Newman may be naive and incapable of reading the terrain on which he battles for parity, but Henry James, who creates the novel and its hero, is quite capable of making it contain both Newman's abortive claim and the historical

[4] Inspecting him through her "antique eyeglass, elaborately mounted in chased silver," as if he were a latter-day Chactas or one of the Hurons examined by Montaigne, old Mme de la Rochefidèle, who had always "wanted greatly to see an American," decides, against her expectations, that Newman is not very unlike other human beings (*The American*, p. 145).

[5] The theme of incest, expected in a novel about marriage between differences, appears, attentuated and almost unexpected, in Valentin's protestations that he will not marry because he loves Claire: "I arrange it [not marrying] by adoring you, my sister,' said Valentin ardently" (p. 169). In one revision of the novel, as well as in the last act of the play made from it, there is the intimation that Mme de Bellegarde had an affair with M. de Cintré, Claire's deceased husband (Royal A. Gettman, "Henry James's Revision," p. 474; Leon Edel, "The Revised Ending of the Play," pp. 487, 488).

sophistication Newman lacks.[6] And as his stature grew, nationally and internationally, James provided some of the early signs that the battle for parity might have been won.

After World War I, when the United States established itself as a world power, the question of defining national consciousness retreated from the center of its literature. Even when it arises, as in *The Great Gatsby*, with F. Scott Fitzgerald's evocation of Manhattan as the first Europeans might have seen it, the question takes on a new guise. Newly rich, Gatsby aspires to history and privilege, but his model is the American East. His America still looks up to Oxford, but Oxford is now within reach of an American nobody victorious in the war. Appropriately, Gatsby now imitates (almost farcically) the original successful American abroad—Benjamin Franklin—with his list of steps to self-made success. His ambitions and strategies recapitulate efforts to claim cultural parity explored in an earlier literature of national identity, but the centers of cultural exchange in the novel are now the American West and the American East. The confrontation between nature and culture, the question of marriage between members of the same world (Daisy and Tom) or of different worlds (Daisy and Gatsby) are not asked about Europeans and Americans, however defined, but about different kinds of Americans. Unlike the young men whom Cooper charges with forming and preserving American society, Tom does not represent an ideal of civilization derived from Europe. He is a thoroughly American cad, and the opposition between him and Gatsby or between him and the narrator, Nick, is an intranational affair.

Fitzgerald reshapes the traditional framework in which an earlier American literature of national and cultural definition claimed cultural competence, still including the attempt both to acquire historical depth and to deny its importance (probably the most-often-quoted exchange in the novel is that in which Gatsby asks incredulously why it should be impossible to replay the past, to negate history).[7] Emily Miller Budick therefore places Fitzgerald in a line of development that leads to William Faulkner in one direction and reaches back through Emerson and the transcendentalists to Cooper and Brown (pp. 143–58). But Fitzgerald

---

[6] According to Gettman, Newman is not "obtuse" in the first version of the novel, and the 1907 edition revises certain passages to make his "awareness of the attitudes and motives of others" more evident (pp. 470, 471).

[7] "I wouldn't ask too much of her" says Nick; "'You can't repeat the past.' 'Can't repeat the past?' [Gatsby] cried incredulously. 'Why of course you can!'" (*The Great Gatsby*, p. 111).

does not simply rewrite his predecessors; by examining cultural fault
lines within the United States, he documents one consequence of acquiring discursive power: the awareness of differences at the source of
that discourse, so that it is no longer necessary to forge a single, coherent image of national identity.

Meanwhile, across the Atlantic, Ernest Hemingway's Americans roam
the world as part of a cosmopolitan set: there is no question that they
belong to whatever informal structure has replaced Cooper's international Bachelors' Club; they are as tainted and decadent as their
European companions. The Atlantic no longer separates purity and
redemption from decadence. Blocked marriages between Americans
and Europeans no longer stand for the impossibility of crossing the
boundary between nature and culture, American and European, self
and other—categories now rearranged along different axes. Male and
female are irreconcilable on either side of the ocean; decadence is
American or British; redemption is found in a Spanish arena or a river
in the primeval Upper Peninsula of Michigan. Still discrete, the signi-
fieds of the earlier discourse of difference are separate from the places
that once had seemed to define them, uprooted, as in Rousseau's elaboration of the concepts of nature and society.

Thus, questions of cultural identity in the traditional sense become
diffuse, and the confrontation between an American self and its European definition as other loses urgency. They retreat into the literature
of American regions or subcultures, where disparities of power make
themselves felt. The problems of identity and value once raised in a
literature that, though set in locales as specific as the Hudson Valley or
the Susquehanna, made them stand for the nation as a whole, appear
in Faulkner's work within a southern society that sees itself as distinct
from and devalued by the powerful industrial North. This claim of
distinctiveness does not imply the relinquishment of a claim to be representative, however: eventually the imaginary Yoknapatawpha wants to
stand not only for the South but for the entire nation.

Hemingway diffuses, expatriates, dislocates Americanness, but Faulkner traces the consequences, internal and external, of the shift in cultural power. Faulkner relocates the relevant oppositions of history and
myth, self and other, nature and culture in a divided America. The
complicated role of race in the history of the United States in general
and the American South in particular and Faulkner's preoccupation
with the definition of a southern self and its place in a wider American

culture,[8] make the theme of intermarriage and its satellite, incest, central to his work. But as Eric Sundquist sees, Faulkner's is not the usual optimistic presentation of a literature of cultural definition and consciousness. Neither writer nor critic holds up the hope of the South's (the New World's) redemption and avoidance of the North's (the Old World's) failings; that hope breaks up on the shoals of slavery. Slavery and spoliation remove the New World difference of innocence and in the end join with the increase of cultural and economic power to reduce the distance between the two sides of the Atlantic.

When Sundquist says that "Faulkner did not set out to be a historical novelist in the strictest of terms" (p. ix) and proposes that his work rests on "the twin themes of incest and miscegenation" (p. 21) he seems to negate the connections between the affirmation of historical depth, the separation of culture from nature, and the marriage plot in the literature of cultural identity. The problem seems to be psychological, for the American South is fatally "caught between two proscriptions": incest guarantees purity and the inviolability of a self defined in the shifting terms of race, but it violates the taboo that founds culture; miscegenation makes civilization possible, but it threatens the integrity of (in Leather-stocking terminology) a racially "uncrossed" self (pp. 19–23). Intermarriage appears as the return of the repressed, which must be brought to the surface lest it poison not only the suppressed South but also the entire nation. One thinks of "The Bear," with its difficult reconstruction of the blood links among three races in the New World, the past of a tri-racial Yoknapatawpha County, metonym for the South and for the nation. History reappears as genealogy and juxtaposes a social hierarchy based on race to the despoliation of nature. Through the Indian Ikkemotubbe, Faulkner links the problematic present of the North American South to a pre-Columbian past whose virtue is not synonymous with innocence. Ike's respect for the original nature and people of America makes him into one more American mediator between past and present, nature and culture, but he is also as incapable of participating in the familial, social, economic, and legal structures that mark Europe's presence on these shores as Cooper's Leather-stocking was before him.

Other works approach these questions from different angles. As André Bleikasten shows, *Light in August* translates the matter of race into

[8] Eric Sundquist links both when he speaks of "the single and most agonizing experience of his region *and nation* . . . the crisis and long aftermath of American slavery" (*Faulkner*, p. 6, my emphasis).

ideological terms for which notions of newness or opposition to definition from the outside are no longer necessary. Thus the origin of Joe Christmas's dual conflict "resides not at all in actual race differences but in fantasies—both public and private—about race," for "there is no factual evidence for his mixed blood," which has been fairly invented by the "rabid racist" Doc Hines ("*Light in August,*" p. 83). But the novel also posits the relation between a white—and male—self and a black— or female—other, inextricably intertwined, as central to the definition of a southern and, by implication, American cultural identity. If the play with the idea of hybridism in *Light in August* is reminiscent of that in *The Pioneers*,[9] it cannot be removed in the later novel as it was in the earlier one, and it becomes lethal. Faulkner's South belies Cooper's West. In a similarly upended quotation, Faulkner demands recognition of historical depth, carried by characters who occupy the positions of what Weisbuch calls "lateness," relative to the corresponding "earliness" of Cooper's (*Atlantic Double-Cross,* chap. 8). Quentin of *The Sound and the Fury* stands in for Chateaubriand's decadent Europeans, who came to the New World to be cured of their excessive civilization. Faulkner's southerners, then, claim a historical depth based on suffering which reverses the usual association between historical depth and political, economic, and cultural power. Faulkner dismembers the triad and claims (history and) culture against money or politics. But Faulkner's South also offers its history and culture as a ballast to the power it contests, and its confrontation with the foundational crime of slavery as a more complex, more honest basis for a national claim to prominence. This literature of southern identity lacks the self-affirmation of the earlier literature of nationality but sees itself as representative because it remembers experiences ignored at its peril by a dominant culture of which by rights it ought to be a better-integrated part. As he relocates the contest for discursive power within the United States and claims the power of self-definition for the South, Faulkner reproduces the discourse of the older contest between the Americas and colonial powers, and, like the older writers, institutes a literature of the (now southern) exotic.

The reception of Faulkner's work corroborates the sense that it mediates between the definition of a regional and a national identity. As Lawrence Schwarz shows, especially after receiving the Nobel Prize in

[9] Oliver evokes the possibility of intermarriage, but his "Indianness" is socially constructed and, in the end, does not count.

1950, Faulkner was seen less as a southern writer than as an American contributor to a general Western canon of geniuses which includes Joyce and Proust. This recognition reversed initial opposition to southern critics who had argued for Faulkner's relevance to a general American culture (*The Making of Faulkner's Reputation*, pp. 22–23, 26), though, as Schwarz also points out, acceptance of Faulkner as spokesman for American culture also depended on the publishing boom of the war and postwar eras, as well as on the climate of the Cold War, in which his focus on cultural rather than economic marginality provided a welcome alternative to the *engagée* literature of the thirties. Formally innovative, his work could be read into international modernism, and its often gloomy tone allowed it to vault straight from southern particularity to a generalized Western angst.

Faulkner was also read early on as part of an American intertextual series that includes Edgar Allan Poe, Nathaniel Hawthorne, and Stephen Crane and forms an autochthonous literary history independent of European models or ancestry. In contrast, though Jean-Paul Sartre and André Malraux granted Faulkner's literary status without apology, the praise of other foreign critics (mostly French) focused on his exotic American otherness: Marcel Aymé speaks of Faulkner's "savage religiousness" and looking for terms to describe his characters, "hesitate[s] between *degenerate* and *primitive*." He concludes, as one could have bet he would, that American primitivism is a welcome alternative to European pessimism, anomie, and other civilized ills.[10] European praise for Faulkner's formal sophistication was taken by American criticism as supererogatory; national cultural competence did not need legitimation from the outside. Nevertheless, such praise made it easier for Faulkner criticism to privilege formal analysis; New Critics who had begun their careers as members of the agrarian movement in the South were happy to adjust their subject and their critical stance as intellectual times came to prefer formal experimentation to a thematic focus on the problems of American identity.[11] Thus one finds rearranged in Faulkner's work and in Faulkner criticism the elements that characterize a literature of nationality, reflecting the position of these writings both inside and outside of dominant cultural discourse.

[10] Aymé, "What French Readers Find in William Faulkner's Fiction," p. 4, quoted in Schwarz, *The Making of Faulkner's Reputation*, p. 3.
[11] Sundquist notes that Faulkner criticism has been mostly formal, in keeping with the novelist's own statements about his writings; he has been adopted into the camp of early twentieth-century modernism, closely tied to the New Critics. Sundquist's

Literature by writers who identify themselves as descendants of the originally African component of the American population also display the characteristics of literatures of national definition and propose a reallotment of cultural power. In Ralph Ellison's *Invisible Man* identity is the central, named, problem of its unnamed protagonist; as Houston Baker, Jr., sees it in the Trueblood episode of the novel, history is a part of identity, and both are tested in a complex dialogue between the culture denied its identity and the culture denying it.[12] It should be no surprise that these matters of identity and history appear together in an episode about incest, about the boundaries between nature and culture and also, for good Foucauldian measure, between sanity and madness. Trueblood and the "lunatics" that the civilized Mr. Norton meets after meeting him, are almost inescapably an exotic—and in this case a frighteningly other—spectacle, teasing the wealthy white northerner with knowledge he would rather deny about the world and about himself.

Invisible Man is also more overtly allegorical than the novels I have considered till now. Ellison jettisons the marriage plot, whose function of carrying the argument about contact between self and other had been naturalized in earlier novels. *Invisible Man* does not ask whether contact can take place but whether it will continue to be denied, whether blackness will continue to be viewed as other while it resides within the same source of power that defines it as other—in the white paint that covers the land or in the bowels of the factory that produces the paint.

Though European recognition for Faulkner, Hemingway, and other American writers sounds a distant echo of the old European cultural power over the United States, it counts less than it did a century before. Faulkner, Ellison, and other "southern" or "ethnic" writers use the modernist—later, postmodernist—idiom that places them within a more general "Western" sphere of cultural power. Domestically, however, Faulkner, Ellison, and others display a cultural disunity that is another mark of cultural power, for uniformity arises under the pressure of alien power. Within the United States the production of fictions of cultural definition claiming cultural power is displaced to the margins of fictional discourse (however well-received, these productions present themselves

---

focus on Faulkner's treatment of what he calls his most important subject, race, appears, then, to challenge this critical tradition.
[12] Baker identifies some of the same oscillations between self-definition and definition by others which we have seen in literatures of cultural identity.

as marked by marginality), while the center itself now holds the cultural power to be disputed both within and outside national borders.

In the rest of the Americas the older relations of cultural power still obtain. Rehearsing once again the claim to parity of the less powerful, Carlos Fuentes remarks at the beginning of his study of the "new Hispanic-American novel" that "Thomas Mann . . . is the last great writer who can justifiably invoke the categories of his culture as universal categories." After Mann, "Europeans know that their culture is no longer central; power is displaced toward the eccentric poles foreseen by Tocqueville: the United States and Russia." Within this new distribution of cultural power the Latin-American novel of which Fuentes speaks stakes its own claim to attention (*La nueva novela*, p. 22).

In yet another run of literature and criticism around themes of national and cultural identity, the writers of the so-called Boom in Latin-American fiction achieve the ideal combination of treating national matters and attracting international attention which made Cooper's work so remarkable in his time, and keeps it interesting for ours.[13] Adapting the conventions of a modernism triumphant in Europe and the United States, just as Cooper adapted the conventions of romantic nature-writing and fictionalized history, these writers once again tackle urgent "cultural work" that is felt to be a necessary complement to economic and political "development." They break through the impasse represented in *Macunaíma*'s parody of Caminha in the "Letter to the Icamiabas." Declining parody, the novelists of the Boom appropriate the stream of written words that covered the New World from the beginning and use it to affirm and to debate the relation between word and identity, word and world, in a way that questions some of the assumptions of Euro-American writing.

Twentieth-century literature of national identity in Latin America does not repeat all the strategies of its nineteenth-century predecessor, but it develops the same material in some of the same forms. Thus the interrogation of history brings a characteristic disturbance into the

[13] Some critics hate the term, "Boom," both for its financial connotations and for the implication that the literature came out of nowhere rather than being the logical development of a long and respectable history of Latin (or Spanish) American writing. In *Transculturación narrativa en América latina*, Angel Rama, courteous and erudite, addresses the continuities in the literatures that gave rise to the Boom and its innovations with his notion of "transculturation," the process by which not only the urban, generally culturally progressive elites but also those parts of the continent less affected by internationally current patterns of thought, commerce, and writing, adapt, transform, and assimilate cultural change.

hierarchical arrangement of histories and stories and the assessment of their truth values. As Retamar notes in "Some Theoretical Problems of Spanish American Literature" (pp. 84–94), this interrogation disturbs the usual arrangement and modifies the original hierarchy of genres. One sign of the process is the recovery of American colonial literature in which sermons, histories, captivity narratives receive critical attention and are made to carry a cultural weight formerly attributed only to more "literary" forms. Roberto González Echevarría analyzes the importance of the European and Euro-American discourses of late nineteenth-century science and anthropology in a twentieth-century literature in which Latin America defines national and cultural identity by appropriating, contesting, or subverting discourse that at first had classified it as other (*Myth and Archive*, pp. 12–13).

Like their predecessors, Latin-American authors of this latest burst of self-definition on a world stage stress the exoticism of their settings. Responding to a shift in power, this exotic world exists now in opposition not just to Europe but also to the United States. Thus the protagonist of Alejandro Carpentier's novel *The Lost Steps* is torn between his desire and need for personal renewal in contact with nature and his ability to be an artist in decadent but civilized New York. Appropriately, his predicament boils down to the problem of finding enough paper on which to write down the music that gushes from him when he leaves the city and its semieducated women for the jungle and an unlettered earth mother, Rosario.[14] For Echevarría, the protagonist's need for paper and writing, like all the other instances of writing in the novel, gloss the position of the written word at the foundation of a Latin-American history and identity, carved from the first documents of conquest and colonization which simultaneously deny the historicity of the pre-Columbian past and bring it into the Western world (pp. 1–4, 10–15). In the jungle village the composer finds the point where modern America begins, and where it breaks away from its origins. His notebooks, ceded to him by the civil authority of the village, had been intended for archives: in their civil function they belong to the same series of documents as the marriage contract the composer imposes on Rosario, who

[14] Carpentier orginated the "magical realism" that is one of the hallmarks of the Boom, all of whose participants acknowledge his primacy in setting the terms of a common attempt to develop a literature of cultural definition across national borders. His books have an international readership; even biographically, he mediates between the more powerful cultures of Europe and the United States and the less powerful ones of Latin America.

wants to live with him but not marry him, the code of law that excludes and punishes a leper who disturbs the peace of the Edenic village, and even the mark on the tree which indicates the entrance of the path leading to it through the jungle. In the unlettered village with Rosario the composer gains access to the sources of his creative power, and he also becomes incapable of living without writing. The violence of that primitive world, expressed in disease, rape, and murder, his realization that a threnody is at the origin of the music that makes his life meaningful, and that his music forcefully imposes form on barely distinguishable humanity oozing into death, deprives the primitive of the allure civilization had given it and draws the composer back to New York. His choice cannot be happy though, for the happiness promised by the call of origins, of myths, of the unwritten, remains on the incommunicable side of a clear boundary between past and present, myth and history, story and document, art and archive. The novel refuses to be limited by such boundaries; it argues that these oppositions not only depend on each other but invade each other. In this sense *The Lost Steps* proposes not the usual revaluation of the terms in which cultural definition is stated but a change in how their relationship is posited, an alternative to the usual oppositional structure in which they are said to operate. It is in this sense that one can think of the recent New World novel not as a forum where national or cultural identity is once again asserted by drawing boundaries around myth and tradition and laying claim to history and writing but as a form that questions the need to draw such boundaries. One can ask with Echevarría whether "the coeval births of the novel and the history of Latin America [are not] related beyond chronology" (p. 6) in something like a perception that it may not be possible to distinguish between them.

Carlos Fuentes's *Death of Artemio Cruz* and his massive *Terra nostra* also adapt the historical novel to an examination of national and cultural identity, but of all the novels that came out of that flourishing Latin-American literature of the sixties and seventies, it was Márquez's *One Hundred Years of Solitude* that received the most attention and was considered the most representative. It is also the one that most clearly integrates history, incest, and writing to assert cultural identity and difference. Alfred Kazin spotted this function in Márquez's work and its rejection of definition by a more powerful culture when he reviewed *Leafstorm and Other Stories* for the *New York Times Book Review* in 1972. He wonders "if the outbreak of creative originality in Latin America, coming after so many years of dutifulness to Spanish and French models, doesn't resemble our sudden onrush of originality after we had decided really to break away from the spell of England."[15] Other critics prefer to stress Márquez's debt to early accounts of the New World such as Pigafetta's or Columbus's, where the encounter between two worlds produces epistemological shocks best rendered in the author's trademark deadpan surrealism, which turns a block of ice into magic and views finding a galleon in the jungle as a normal event.[16] Others emphasize the faithfulness of Márquez's apparently fanciful rendition of Colombia's history, including the disappearance without a trace of an entire village's worth of plantation workers and recorded, though not publicized, details illustrating the pressure of extranational economic and political power over the nation and culture where the novel arises.[17]

It is possible to account for or even to discount the strangeness of Márquez's novel through reference to recorded events, but the device by which it ends intertwines writing and event, present and past, in a way that makes such accounting problematic. Like the rest of the novel, its end is a reading: the mysterious text left behind by the magus Melquíades, which is also the text of *One Hundred Years of Solitude*, is deciphered by the last of the family whose history—mirror and microcosm of Colombia and, by extension and implication, of Latin America—is told in that same text; this reading interlocks functions whose separation had founded the concept of American otherness. It reminds us that the novel is a written document and all its characters are fictional, that we are reading a modernist text, classed and valued within a literary series that includes Faulkner but also Franz Kafka or Vladimir Nabokov (whose works make their own cases for the centrality of writing from the margins). It establishes the novel as a history, drawing on the historical documents that underlie episodes in its fictional space and also drawing attention to its kinship with the writing of history, which is a part of the foundation of the polity with which it aligns itself. In this way, like M. C. Escher's drawing of a hand that draws itself, it stands for the connection, implicit in previous fictions of nationality, between

[15] Reprinted in George R. McMurray, ed., *Critical Essays on Gabriel Carcía Márquez*, pp. 26–29, 27.
[16] Humberto Robles, "The First Voyage"; Michael Palencia-Roth, "Prisms of Consciousness."
[17] McMurray quotes Lucila Ines Mena, *La funcíon de la historia*, to the effect that many "fantastic" events in the novel are solidly based on the political and historical realities of Colombia (Introduction to *Critical Essays*, p. 8). Echevarría refers to Iris M. Zavala ("*Cien años de soledad*") and to Selma Calasans Rodriguez ("*Cien años de soledad*") for Márquez's debt to the chronicles of conquest and colonization (pp. 3, 11, 22).

writing and the very existence of the New World. The text also refers
to a modern view of the relation between word and world, however,
and thus calls into question the definition of the New World as other.

As in other novels of national identity, incest shadows *One Hundred
Years of Solitude*. It presides over the origin of the Buendías and falls on
writing, history, and nature in the novel's implicit definition of national
and cultural identity. The incestuous, monstrous offspring of the last
of the Buendías is eaten by that natural tropical scourge, ants, as the
last of the Buendías finishes deciphering the manuscript that gives him
being and takes his life.[18] All the strands developed in one hundred
years of an American literature of national definition and cultural consciousness come together in the last pages of *One Hundred Years of Solitude*.[19] This internationally recognized, exotic novel[20] once again places
a work claiming cultural parity in a market—or within a horizon of
expectations—against which, and with the cooperation of which, such
claims have been presented and granted since the American nations
were established.

The Boom during which writers of Latin America broke into the
international cultural market shows us once again the necessary component of exchange in the literatures of national definition. The debt of
this literature to the innovations of European and American modernism
echoes earlier American debts and once again makes cultural independence depend on cultural contact. The role of the United States as a
source of cultural pressure and as a market for exoticism is a reminder
of the relation between exoticism and power. Faulkner, provider of exoticism for internal consumption, becomes a source of inspiration for a
Latin-American literature of national identity, legitimating the exotic
from inside the discourse of power in a way reminiscent of Chateaubriand's for the earlier American literature of independence. Just as
romantic disaffection opened the way for the affirmation of an exotic

---

[18] According to Echevarría, "the self-reflexiveness of the novel is implicitly compared
to incest" (p. 27). There seems to be more to it, however, than comparison.
[19] Emir Rodriguez Monegal uses his analysis of these last pages to place the novel in
the history of a continental Latin-American literature and link it with works as apparently different from it as those of Borges ("*One Hundred Years of Solitude*: The Last
Three Pages").
[20] D. P. Gallagher recommends the novel as "funny, eccentric, full of dotty characters
described in a straightforward way" ("Gabriel García Márquez," pp. 114–15), as "ex-
otically tropical" (p. 115), and details its relation to topical truth, its presentation of
Macondo as linked, through Melquíades with the depth of history, and as representing as in other Latin-American novels, the overwhelming impact of tropical nature,
whose cycles "invalidate historical development" (p. 124).

self against its European definition as other, so do fissures in cultural coherence within the former English colony open the way for a similar affirmation in the southern part of the New World.

But history does not repeat itself exactly, nor is there a necessary pattern to the differences. The more recent literatures of national identity are akin to those of the past, but they rethink and reformulate the characteristics that connect them in their own ways. At the same time, they exert their own influence, fostering an exotic renewal within established American literary forms, offering some of the technical and subject-matter innovations that would be taken up by writers such as Robert Coover or Thomas Pynchon.[21] Whether these innovations will become an integral part of a dominant cultural discourse depends on the contingencies of history and on the future distribution of political, economic, and cultural power.

Literatures of cultural or national identity are born of the confrontation between cultural entities of unequal power. The product of an interaction, they raise questions of history and writing, of the relation between culture and nature which defines a culture, of the relation between self and other. For themselves and for the other that confronts them, they bring to the fore the problematic character of these distinctions. Their existence is a criticism, not always welcome, of their own and the other's basic assumptions about history, about self, about origin, dressed in the acceptable guise of the exotic.

[21] John Barth's deconstruction of American history in *The Sot-Weed Factor* (1960) precedes *One Hundred Years of Solitude*. I have not seen Barth mentioned among U.S. writers who inspired Latin-American writers.

Bibliography

Abreu, Capistrano de. *Capítulos de história colonial, 1500–1800.* Preface and notes by José Honório Rodrigues. Belo Horizonte: Itatiaia; São Paulo: Editora da Universidade de São Paulo, 1988.

Acosta, José de. *De procuranda indorum salute: Pacificación y colonización.* Eds. Luciano Pereña et al. Corpus hispanorum de pace, 23. Madrid: Consejo superior de investigaciones científicas, 1984 [1588].

——. *Historia natural y moral de las Indias.* 2d ed. Ed. Edmundo O'Gorman. Mexico City: Fondo de cultura económica, 1962 [1590].

Acuña, Cristóbal de. *Descubrimiento del Amazonas.* Colección Buenos Aires. Buenos Aires: Emece, 1942.

Adams, Charles Hansford. *"The Guardian of the Law": Authority and Identity in James Fenimore Cooper.* University Park: Pennsylvania State University Press, 1990.

Adams, Percy G. *Travelers and Travel Liars, 1660–1800.* New York: Dover, 1980.

Adorno, Rolena. "Arms, Letters, and the *Mestizo* Historian in Early Colonial Mexico." Talk presented at the University of Michigan, March 1989.

——. "*La ciudad letrada* y los discursos coloniales." *Hispamerica* 16.48 (December 1987): 3–24.

——. *Guaman Poma: Writing and Resistance in Colonial Peru.* Austin: University of Texas Press, 1986.

——. "Literary Production and Suppression: Reading and Writing about Amerindians in Colonial Spanish America." *Dispositio* 11.28–29 (1986): 1–25.

Aguiar, Flávio de. *A comédia nacional no teatro de José de Alencar.* São Paulo: Ática, 1984.

Ahmad, Aijaz. "Jameson's Rhetoric of Otherness and the 'National Allegory.'" *Social Text* 17 (Fall 1987): 3–25.

Aldridge, A. Owen. *Franklin and His French Contemporaries*. New York: New York University Press, 1957.

Alencar, José de. "Bênção paterna." Preface to *Sonhos d'ouro*. In *Obra completa* 1:691–702. 4 vols. Rio de Janeiro: Aguilar, 1959.

———. "Carta ao Dr. Jaguaribe." Appended to *Iracema*. In *Obra completa* 3:305–20. 4 vols. Rio de Janeiro: Aguilar, 1959.

———. *Cartas sôbre "A confederação dos Tamoios:" Por Ig*. Rio de Janeiro: Empresa tipográfica nacional do diário, 1856. Reprinted, with documents of complete polemic, in *A polêmica sôbre "A confederação dos Tamoios*, ed. José Aderaldo Castelo. Coleção textos e documentos, 2. São Paulo: Faculdade de filosofia, ciências, e letras, Universidade de São Paulo, 1953.

———. *Como e porque sou romancista*. Rio de Janeiro: Leuzinger, 1893.

———. *Iracema*. In *Obra completa* 3:223–320. 4 vols. Rio de Janeiro: Aguilar, 1959.

———. *O Guarani*. In *Obra completa* 2:27–406. 4 vols. Rio de Janeiro: Aguilar, 1959.

———. *Romances ilustrados*. 6th ed. 7 vols. Rio de Janeiro: José Olímpio, 1967.

———. *Ubirajara*. In *Obra completa* 3:321–404. 4 vols. Rio de Janeiro: Aguilar, 1959.

Anchieta, José de. *A província do Brasil*. Rio de Janeiro: Serviço de documentação do Ministério de educação e saúde, 1946 [1585].

———. *Poesias*. Transcriptions, translations, and notes by M. de L. de Paula Martins. Belo Horizonte: Itatiaia; São Paulo: Editora da Universidade de São Paulo, 1989.

Anderson, Benedict. *Imagined Communities: Reflections on the Origin and Spread of Nationalism*. London: Verso, 1983.

Anderson, Warwick. "Climates of Opinion: Acclimatization in Nineteenth-Century France and England." *Victorian Studies* 35 (Winter 1992): 134–155.

Andrade, Mário de. *Aspectos da literatura brasileira*. São Paulo: Livraria Martins, 1972.

———. *Cartas de Mário de Andrade*. Ed. Lygia Fernandes. Rio de Janeiro: Livraria São José, n.d.

———. *Macunaíma*. Critical edition by Telê Ancona Lopez. Rio de Janeiro: Livros técnicos e científicos, 1978.

Andrade, Oswald de. "Manifesto antropófago." In *Do pau-brasil à antropofagia e às utopias. Obras completas*. 6:11–19. Introduction by Benedito Nunes. 11 vols. Rio de Janeiro: Civilização brasileira, 1978.

———. "Manifesto da poesia pau-brasil." In *Do pau-brasil à antropofagia e às utopias. Obras Completas*. 6:3–10. Introduction by Benedito Nunes. Rio de Janeiro: Civilização brasileira, 1978.

Appiah, Kwame Anthony. *In My Father's House: Africa in the Philosophy of Culture*. Oxford: Oxford University Press, 1992.

———. "Out of Africa: Topologies of Nativism." *Yale Journal of Criticism* 2 (Fall 1988): 153–78.

Araripe, T. A., Jr. *José de Alencar*. 2d ed. Rio de Janeiro: Fauchon, 1894.

Arciniegas, Germán. *America in Europe: A History of the New World in Reverse.* Trans. Gabriela Arciniegas and R. Victoria Arana. San Diego: Harcourt Brace Jovanovich, 1986.

Assis, Machado de. Review of *Iracema. Diário do Rio de Janeiro,* 23 January 1866. Reprinted in José de Alencar, *Iracema,* xiv–li. Ed. Gladstone Chaves de Melo. Rio de Janeiro: Imprensa nacional, 1948.

Aymé, Marcel. "What French Readers Find in William Faulkner's Fiction." *New York Times Book Review,* 17 December 1950, p. 4.

Baczko, Bronislaw. *Rousseau: Solitude et communauté.* Trans. Claire Brendel-Lamhout. Paris: Mouton, 1974.

Baker, Felicity. "La route contraire." In *Reappraisals of Rousseau: Studies in Honour of R. A. Leigh,* ed. Simon Harvey et al., pp. 132–62. Manchester University Press, 1980.

Baker, Houston, Jr. "To Move without Moving: An Analysis of Creativity and Commerce in Ralph Ellison's Trueblood Episode." *PMLA* 98 (October 1983): 828–45.

Bakhtin, Mikhail M. "Forms of Time and of the Chronotope in the Novel." In *The Dialogic Imagination: Four Essays,* pp. 84–258. Ed. Michael Holquist. Trans. Caryl Emerson and Michael Holquist. Austin: University of Texas Press, 1981.

Bandeira, Luis Alberto Moniz. *Presença dos Estados Unidos no Brasil.* Rio de Janeiro: Civilização brasileira, 1973.

Banta, Martha, ed. *New Essays on "The American."* Cambridge: Cambridge University Press, 1987.

Barbéris, Pierre. *A la recherche d'une écriture: Chateaubriand.* Paris: Tours, 1974.

——. *Chateaubriand: Une réaction au monde moderne.* Paris: Larousse, 1976.

——. *René de Chateaubriand: Un nouveau roman.* Paris: Larousse, 1973.

Barleu, Gaspar (or Caspar Barlaeus or Caspar Baerle). *História dos feitos recentemente praticados durante oito anos no Brasil.* Trans. and notes by Cláudio Brandão. Preface and additional notes by Mário G. Ferri. Belo Horizonte: Itatiaia; São Paulo: Editora da Universidade de São Paulo, 1974 [1647].

Bart, B. F. "Descriptions of Nature in Chateaubriand." In *Chateaubriand Today,* ed. Richard Schwitzer pp. 83–93. Madison: University of Wisconsin Press, 1970.

Barthes, Roland. "La voyageuse de nuit." Introduction to René de Chateaubriand, *La vie de Rancé,* pp. 9–21. Paris: Union générale des éditions, 1965.

Batista, Marta R., et al., eds. *Brasil: Primeiro tempo modernista, 1917–1929: Documentação.* São Paulo: Instituto de estudos brasileiros, 1972.

Baym, Nina. "How Men and Women Wrote Indian Stories." In *New Essays on "The Last of the Mohicans,"* ed. H. Daniel Peck, pp. 67–86. Cambridge: Cambridge University Press, 1992.

——. *Novels, Readers, and Reviewers: Responses to Fiction in Antebellum America.* Ithaca: Cornell University Press, 1984.

——. "The Women of Cooper's Leatherstocking Tales." *American Quarterly* 23 (1971): 696–709.

Bazin, Christian. *Chateaubriand en Amérique.* Preface by Michel Poniatowski. Paris: La Table Ronde, 1969.

Bédier, Joseph. *Etudes critiques.* Paris: Colin, 1903.

Beider, Robert E.. "Anthropology and History of the American Indian." *American Quarterly* 33 (1981): 309–26.

Benavente o Motolinia, Fray Toribio de. *Historia de los Indios de la Nueva España: Relación de los ritos antiguos, idolatrias, y sacrificios de los Indios de la Nueva España y de la maravillosa conversión que Dios en ellos ha obrado.* Critical study, appendixes, notes, and index by Edmundo O'Gorman. Mexico City: Porreía, 1969.

Benjamin, Walter. *Ursprung des deutschen Trauerspiels.* Frankfurt: Suhrkamp, 1982 [1928].

Bercovitch, Sacvan. *The American Puritan Imagination: Essays in Revaluation.* New York: Cambridge University Press, 1974.

Berkhofer, Robert F., Jr. *The White Man's Indian: Images of the American Indian from Columbus to the Present.* New York: Knopf, 1978.

Bernardin de Saint-Pierre, Jacque Henri. See Saint-Pierre, Jacques Henri Bernardin de.

Bhabha, Homi K., ed. *Nation and Narration.* London: Routledge, 1990.

Biard, Pierre, "Relation de 1611." In *Relations des Jésuites, contenant ce qui c'est passé dans les missions des pères de la Compagnie de Jésus dans la Nouvelle France* 1:1–76. 3 vols. Quebec: Augustin Coté, 1858.

Biggar, Henry Percival, ed. *A Collection of Documents relating to Jacques Cartier and the Sieur de Roberval.* Ottawa: Public Archives of Canada, 1930.

Bilac, Olavo. *Poesias.* 28th edition. Rio de Janeiro: Alves, 1964.

Bleikasten, André. "*Light in August:* The Closed Society and Its Subjects." In *New Essays on "Light in August"* ed. Michael Millgate. pp. 81–102. Cambridge: Cambridge University Press, 1987.

Bloom, Harold, ed. *Gabriel García Márquez: Modern Critical Views.* New York: Chelsea House, 1989.

Boellhower, William. "New World Topology and Types in the Novels of Abbot Pietro Chiari." *Early American Literature* 19 (Fall 1984): 153–72.

Bopp, Raul. *Movimentos modernistas no Brasil, 1922–1928.* Rio de Janeiro: Livraria São José, 1966.

Bové, Paul. *In the Wake of Theory.* Hanover, N.H.: University Press of New England; Middletown, Conn.: Wesleyan University Press, 1992.

Bowlby, Rachel. "Breakfast in America: *Uncle Tom's* Cultural Histories." In *Nation and Narration,* ed. Homi K. Bhabha, pp. 197–212. London: Routledge, 1990.

Braudel, Fernand. *Civilization and Capitalism, 15th to 18th Century.* Vol. 1: *The Structures of Everyday Life;* Vol. 2: *The Wheels of Commerce.* Trans. Siân Reynolds. New York: Harper and Row, 1986 [1985].

——. *The Structures of Everyday Life: The Limits of the Possible.* 3 vols. Trans. from the French revised by Siân Reynolds. New York: Harper and Row, 1981.

Brébeuf, Jean de. "Relation de ce qui s'est passé dans le pays des Hurons en l'année 1636." In *Relations des Jésuites, contenant ce qui c'est passé dans les missions des pères de la Compagnie de Jésus dans la Nouvelle France* 1:100–139. 3 vols. Quebec: Augustin Coté, 1858.

Breitwieser, Mitchell Robert. *American Puritanism and the Defense of Mourning: Religion, Grief, and Ethnology in Mary White Rowlandson's Captivity Narrative.* Madison: the University of Wisconsin Press, 1990.

Budick, Emily Miller. *Fiction and Historical Consciousness: The American Romance Tradition.* New Haven: Yale University Press, 1989.

Burns, E. Bradford. *A History of Brazil* 2d ed.. New York: Columbia University Press, 1980.

Calasans Rodriguez, Celma. "Cien años de soledad y las crónicas de la conquista." *Revista de la Universidad de México.* 38.23 (1983): 13–16.

Calmon, Pedro. *História do Brasil.* 7 vols. São Paulo: Nacional, 1941.

Cameron, David. *The Social Thought of Rousseau and Burke: A Comparative Study.* London: Weidenfeld and Nicolson, 1973.

Caminha, Pero Vaz de. *A carta de Pero Vaz de Caminha.* Introduction and analysis by Jaime Cortesão. Rio de Janeiro: Edições Livros de Portugal, 1943.

Camões, Luís de. *Os lusíadas.* Ed. and Introduction by J. D. M. Ford. Cambridge: Harvard University Press, 1946.

Campos, Haroldo de. *Morfologia do "Macunaíma."* São Paulo: Perspectiva, 1973.

Cândido [de Mello e Souza], Antônio. "Dialética da Malandragem." *Revista do Instituto de estudos brasileiros* 8 (1970): 66–89.

——. *A educação pela noite e outros ensaios.* São Paulo: Ática, 1987.

——. *Formação da literatura brasileira: Momentos decisivos.* 2 vols. São Paulo: Livraria Martins, 1962.

——. "Literatura e subdesenvolvimento." In Cândido, *A educação pela noite e outros ensaios,* pp. 140–62. São Paulo: Ática, 1987.

——. "Literature and the Rise of Brazilian National Identity." *Luso-Brazilian Review* 5 (1968): 27–43.

——. "O olhar crítico de Angel Rama." In Cândido, *Recortes,* pp. 140–47. São Paulo: Schwarcz, 1993.

——. *Recortes.* São Paulo: Schwarcz, 1993.

Carvalho, Ronald de. *Pequena história da literatura brasileira.* Preface by Medeiros de Albuquerque. 10th revised ed. Rio de Janeiro: F. Briguiet, 1955.

Casal, Manuel Aires de. *Corografia brasílica, ou Relação histórico-geográfica do reino de Brasil.* Preface by Mário Guimarães Ferri. Belo Horizonte: Itatiaia; São Paulo: Editora da Universidade de São Paulo, 1976 [1817].

Certeau, Michel de. *Heterologies: Discourses on the Other.* Trans. Brian Massumi. Foreword by Wlad Godzich. Collection Theory and History of Literature, 17. Minneapolis: University of Minnesota Press, 1986.

——. *The Writing of History.* Trans. Tom Conley. New York: Columbia University Press, 1988.

Charvet, John. *The Social Problem in the Philosophy of Rousseau.* London: Cambridge University Press, 1974.

Chase, Richard. *The American Novel and Its Tradition.* Baltimore: Johns Hopkins University Press, 1956.

Chateaubriand, René de. *Atala*. Critical edition by Armand Weil. Paris: José Corti, 1950.

——. *Atala*. Edited and with an introduction by Raymond Bernex. Paris: Bordas, 1968.

——. *Atala. René. Le dernier Abencérage*. Introduction by Emile Faguet. Paris: Flammarion, 1936.

——. *Essai sur la littérature anglaise: "Le paradis perdu" et poèmes traduits de l'anglais*. Paris: Furnes, 1964.

——. *Mémoires d'outre tombe*. Ed. Maruice Levaillant. 4 vols. Paris: Flammarion, 1964.

——. *La vie de Rancé*. Introduction by Roland Barthes. Paris: Union générale des éditions, 1965.

Chauffier, Louis-Martin. *Chateaubriand*. Paris: Seghers, 1969.

Chaunu, Pierre. *L'expansion européenne du XIIIème au XVème siècle*. Paris: Presses universitaires de France, 1969.

Cherpak, Clifton. "*Paul et Virginie* and the Myths of Death." *PMLA* 90.2 (1975): 247–55.

Chiavenato, Julio José. *O negro no Brasil: Da senzala à guerra do Paraguai*. São Paulo: Brasiliense, 1987.

Chinard, Gilbert. *L'exotisme américain dans l'oeuvre de Chateaubriand*. Paris: Hachette, 1918.

Clark, Robert, ed. *James Fenimore Cooper: New Critical Essays*. London: Vision Press, 1985.

Clavel, Marcel. *Fenimore Cooper, sa vie et son oeuvre*. Aix–en-Provence: Imprimerie universitaire de Provence, 1938.

Colombo, Cristóvão. *Diários da descoberta da América*. Trans. Milton Persson. Introduction by Marcos Faerman. Notes by Eduardo Bueno. Porto Alegre: L&PM, 1984. Columbus, Christopher. *The Journal of Christopher Columbus*. Trans. Cecil Jane. Revised and annotated by L.A. Vigneras. Appendix by R. A. Skelton. London: Orion Press, 1960.

Commager, Henry Steele. *In Search of a Usable Past and Other Essays in Historiography*. New York: Knopf, 1967.

Conrad, Peter. *Imagining America*. New York: Avon, 1982.

Cooper, James Fenimore. *The Deerslayer, or The First Warpath*. New York: Signet, 1963.

——. *The Last of the Mohicans: A Narrative of 1757*. Albany: State University of New York Press, 1983.

——. *Letters and Journals of James Femimore Cooper*. Ed. James Franklin Beard. 6 vols. Cambridge: Harvard University Press, 1964.

——. *The Pathfinder, or The Inland Sea*. Ed. Richard Dilworth Rust. Editor in chief Richard Beard. Albany: State University of New York Press, 1981.

——. *The Pioneers, or The Sources of the Susquehanna: A Descriptive Tale*. Albany: State University of New York Press, 1980.

——. *The Prairie: A Tale*. Albany: State University of New York Press, 1984.

——. *Precaution: A Novel*. New York: A. T. Goodrich, 1820.

——. *The Travelling Bachelor, or Notions of the Americans*. 2 vols. New York: Stringer and Townsend, 1852.

Cooper, Susan. *Pages and Pictures from the Writings of James Fenimore Cooper.* New York: W. A. Townsend, 1861.

——. "Small Family Memories." In *Correspondence of James Fenimore Cooper,* 1:7–72. Ed. James Fenimore Cooper (grandson of the novelist). 2 vols. New Haven: Yale University Press, 1922.

Coronil, Fernando. "Discovering America Again: The Politics of Selfhood in the Age of Post-colonial Empires." *Dispositio* 14.36–38 (1989): 315–31.

Coutinho, Afrânio. *Introdução à literatura no Brasil.* Rio de Janeiro: Livraria São José, 1959.

——. *A tradição afortunada: O espírito da nacionalidade na crítica brasileira.* Rio de Janeiro: José Olímpio, 1968.

—— ed., *A polêmica Alencar-Nabuco.* Rio de Janeiro: Tempo brasileiro, n.d..

Cowan, Bainard. "The Unreadable Translation—toward Thinking American Writing." In *Theorizing American Literature: Hegel, the Sign, and History,* ed. Cowan and Joseph G. Kronick, pp. 1–29. Baton Rouge: Louisiana State University Press, 1991.

Cowan, Bainard, and Joseph G. Kronick, eds. *Theorizing American Literature: Hegel, the Sign, and History.* Baton Rouge: Louisiana State University Press, 1991.

Cranston, Maurice. *Jean-Jacques: The Early Life and Work of Jean-Jacques Rousseau, 1712–1754.* New York: Norton, 1983.

Cudina. *Beschreibung des portugiesischen Amerika vom Cudina.* A Spanish ms. in the Wolfenbüttel Library. Ed. Counselor Lessing. Notes and Addenda by Christian Leiste. Braunschweig: in der Buchhandlung des Fürstlichen Weisenhauses, 1780.

Cueva, Mario de la, ed. *Presencia de Rousseau.* Mexico City: Universidad nacional autonoma de México, 1962.

Damasceno, Darcy. "Alencar e *Iracema:* Uma articulação literária." *O estado de São Paulo: Suplemento cultural,* 11 December 1977, 7–9.

DeJean, Joan. "The Law(s) of the Pedagogical Jungle: La Fontaine Read by Rousseau." *Semiotica* 51, 1–3 (1984): 181–96.

Dekker, George, and John P. McWilliams, eds. *Fenimore Cooper: The Critical Heritage.* London: Routledge and Kegan Paul, 1973.

Derathé, Robert. "Les Réfutations du *Contrat social.*" In *Reappraisal of Rousseau: Studies in Honour of R. A. Leigh,* ed. Simon Harvey et al., pp. 90–110. Manchester: Manchester University Press, 1980.

Derrida, Jacques. "Introduction to the 'Age of Rousseau.'" In *Of Grammatology,* pp. 97–100. Trans. Gayatri Chakravorty Spivak. Baltimore: Johns Hopkins University Press, 1976.

Díaz del Castillo, Bernal. *The Conquest of New Spain.* Trans., with an Introduction by J. M. Cohen. Baltimore: Penguin, 1963.

Dickens, Charles. *Hard Times.* London: Penguin, 1969.

Dimock, Wai-chee. *Empire for Liberty: Melville and the Poetics of Individualism.* Princeton: Princeton University Press, 1988.

Dippel, Horst. *Individuum und Gesellschaft: Soziales Denken zwischen Tradition und Revolution: Smith, Condorcet, Franklin.* Göttingen: Vandenhoeck und Ruprecht, 1981.

Dobyns, Henry F. *Their Number Became Thinned: Native American Population Dynamics in Eastern North America*. Knoxville: University of Tennessee Press, 1983.

Doyle, Plíno. "Pequena bibliografia de *Iracema*." In José de Alencar, *Iracema*, pp. 273–94. Ed. Manuel Cavalcanti Proença. 2d ed. São Paulo: Editora da Universidade de São Paulo, 1979.

Drimmer, Frederick. *Captured by the Indians: 15 Firsthand Accounts, 1750–1870*. New York: Dover, 1985.

Dunning, William Archibald. *A History of Political Theories, Ancient and Mediaeval*. 3 vols. New York: Macmillan, 1920.

Echevarría, Roberto González. *Myth and Archive: A Theory of Latin American Narrative*. Cambridge: Cambridge University Press, 1990.

Edel, Leon. "The Revised Ending of the Play." In Henry James, *The American*, pp. 477–92. Ed. James W. Tuttleton. New York: Norton, 1978.

Fairchild, Hoxie Neale. *The Noble Savage: A Study in Romantic Naturalism*. New York: Columbia University Press, 1928.

Faoro, Raymundo. *Os donos do poder: Formação do patronato político brasileiro*. Rio de Janeiro: Globo, 1958.

Faulkner, William. "The Bear." In *Go Down, Moses, and Other Stories*. London: Penguin, 1970 [1942].

Feres, Nites Therezinha. *Leituras em francês de Mário de Andrade*. São Paulo: Instituto de estudos brasileiros, 1969.

Fernández Retamar, Roberto. "Caliban: Notes toward a Discussion of Culture in Our America." In *Caliban and Other Essays*, pp. 3–45. Trans. Edward Baker. Foreword by Fredric Jameson. Minneapolis: University of Minnesota Press, 1989.

——. "Some Theoretical Problems of Spanish American Literature." In *Caliban and Other Essays*, pp. 74–99. Trans. Edward Baker. Foreword by Fredric Jameson. Minneapolis: University of Minnesota Press, 1989.

Fiedler, Leslie. *Love and Death in the American Novel*. New York: Anchor Books, 1992 [1966].

Fields, Wayne. "Beyond Definition: A Reading of *The Prairie*. In *James Fenimore Cooper: A Collection of Critical Essays*, ed. Fields, pp. 93–111. Englewood Cliffs, N.J.: Prentice Hall, 1979.

Fisher, Philip. *Hard Facts: Setting and Form in the American Novel*. Oxford: Oxford University Press, 1985.

Fitzgerald, F. Scott. *The Great Gatsby*. New York: Scribner's, 1953 [1925].

Flaubert, Gustave. *Madame Bovary*. Trans. Paul de Man. New York: Norton, 1965.

Foucault, Michel. *Discipline and Punish: The Birth of the Prison*. Trans. Alan Sheridan. New York: Pantheon, 1977.

——. *The Order of Things: An Archaeology of the Human Sciences*. New York: Random House, 1980.

——. *Power/Knowledge: Selected Interviews and Other Writings*. New York: Pantheon, 1980.

Franco, Affonso Arinos de Mello. *O Indio brasileiro e a Revolução francesa: As origens brasileiras da theoria da bondade natural.* Rio de Janeiro: José Olímpio, 1937.

Franklin, Wayne. *Discoverers, Explorers, Settlers: The Diligent Writers of Early America.* Chicago: University of Chicago Press, 1989.

———. *The New World of James Fenimore Cooper.* Chicago: University of Chicago Press, 1982.

Freixeiro, Fábio. *Alencar: Os bastidores e a posteridade.* N.p.: Ministério da educação e cultura, coleção estudos e documentos, 1977.

Freyre, Gilberto. *Casa grande e senzala: Formação da família brasileira sob o regime da economia patriarcal.* 2 vols. Rio de Janeiro: José Olímpio, 1961

Frieiro, Eduardo. *O diabo na livraria do cônego.* Belo Horizonte: Itatiaia; São Paulo: Editora da Universidade de São Paulo, 1981 [1957].

Fuentes, Carlos. *La nueva novela hispanoamericana.* Mexico City: Joaquín Mortiz, 1969.

Funke, Hans Günter. "Die Utopie der französischen Aufklärung: Formen, Themen, und Funktionen einer literarischen Gattung." *Romanistische Zeitschrift für Literaturgeschichte* 12.1–2 (1988): 40–59.

Gallagher, D.P. "Gabriel García Márquez." In *Critical Essays on Gabriel García Márquez,* ed. George R. McMurray, pp. 113–28. Boston: G. K. Hall, 1987. Reprinted from *Modern Latin American Literature,* pp. 144–63. London: Oxford University Press, 1973.

Gandavo, Pedro de Magalhães. *Tratado da terra do Brasil and História da província de Santa Cruz.* Introductory note by Afrânio Peixoto. Bibliographical note by Rodolfo Garcia. Introduction by Capistrano de Abreu. Belo Horizonte: Itatiaia; São Paulo: Editora da Universidade de São Paulo, 1980. Translated as *The Histories of Brazil.* Trans., annotations, and introduction by John B. Stetson. New York: Cortes Society, 1922.

Gates, Henry Louis, Jr. "The Blackness of Blackness: A Critique of the Sign and the Signifying Monkey." In *Black Literature and Literary Theory,* ed. Gates, pp. 285–321. London: Methuen, 1984.

Gettman, Royal A. "Henry James's Revision of *The American.*" In Henry James, *The American,* pp. 462–77. Ed. James W. Tuttleton. New York: Norton, 1985.

Gibb, Margaret Murray. *Le roman de bas-de-cuir: Etude sur Fenimore Cooper et son influence en France.* Bibliothèque de la Revue de Littérature Comparée, 30. Paris: Librarie ancienne Honoré Champion, 1927.

Ginzburg, Carlo. *Il formaggio e i vermi.* Milan: Einaudi, 1976.

Giordano, Michael. "Re-reading *Des Cannibales:* 'Véritable Tesmoignage' and the Chain of Supplements." *Neophilologus* 69 (January 1985): 25–33.

Gladsky, Thomas. "The Beau Ideal and Cooper's *The Pioneers.*" *Studies in the Novel* 20 (Spring 1988): 43–54.

Gohdes, Clarence. *American Literature in Nineteenth-Century England.* Carbondale, Ill.: Southern Illinois University Press, 1944.

Goulemot, Jean-Marie. "L'histoire littéraire en question: L'exemple de *Paul et Virginie.*" In *Etudes sur "Paul et Virginie" et l'oeuvre de Bernardin de Saint-Pierre,* ed. Jean-Michel Racault, pp. 204–14. Paris: Didier; Université de la Réunion, 1986.

Grimsted, David. "Anglo-American Racism and Phillis Wheatley's 'Sable Veil,' 'Length'ned Chain,' and 'Knitted Heart.'" In *Women in the Age of the American Revolution*, ed. Ronald Hoffman and Peter J. Albert, pp. 338–444. Introduction by Linda K. Kerber. Charlottesville: University Press of Virginia, 1989.

Grossman, James. *James Fenimore Cooper*. London: Methuen, 1950.

Gutwirth, Madelyn. "The Engulfed Beloved: Representations of Dead and Dying Women in the Art and Literature of the Revolutionary Era." In *Rebel Daughters: Women and the French Revolution*, ed. Sara E. Melzer and Leslie W. Rabine, pp. 198–227. New York: Oxford University Press, 1992.

Haberly, David. "The Mystery of the Bailiff's List, or What Fagundes Varela Read." *Luso-Brazilian Review* 24 (Winter 1987): 1–13.

———. *Three Sad Races: Racial Identity and National Consciousness in Brazilian Literature*. Cambridge: Cambridge University Press, 1983.

Hamerow, Theodore S. "Exotic Revolutionism and the Western Intelligentsia." *Modern Age* 36 (Spring 1992): 203–13.

Hart, James D. *The Popular Book: A History of America's Literary Taste*. New York: Oxford University Press, 1950.

Heerallal, Vasanti. "Ouverture et clôture dans *Paul et Virginie*: Essai d'analyse comparative des séquences initiale et finale." In *Etudes sur "Paul et Virginie" et l'œuvre de Bernardin de Saint-Pierre*, ed. Jean-Michel Racault, pp. 83–118. Paris: Didier; Université de la Réunion, 1986.

Hegel, Georg Wilhelm Friederich. *Vorlesungen über die Philosophie der Geschichte*. Vol. 12 of *Werke*. Frankfurt am Main: Suhrkamp, 1970.

Hein, Raymond. *Le naufrage du St. Géran: La légende de Paul et Virginie*. Paris: Fernand Nathan, 1981.

Herder, Johann Gottfried von. "Über die Wirkung der Dichtkunst auf die Sitten der Völker in alten und neuen Zeiten." In *Sämtliche Werke* 8:334–436. 18 vols. Hildesheim: Olms. 1967.

———. "Von deutscher Art und Kunst." In *Sämtliche Werke* 5:157–257. 18 vols. Hildesheim: Olms. 1967.

Hernlund, Patricia. "The Maps in *Gulliver's Travels*." Unpublished paper, delivered at Wayne State University, 5 April, 1990.

Hervé, François, ed. *Madame Toussaud's Memories and Reminiscences of France*. London: Saunders and Otley, 1838.

Holanda, Sérgio Buarque de. *Visão do paraíso: Os motivos edênicos no descobrimento e colonização do Brasil*. Rio de Janeiro: José Olímpio, 1959.

Hourcade, Pierre. "Reflexions sur la poésie moderniste au Brésil." *Europe* 599 (1979): 61–71.

Hudde, Hinrich. *Bernardin de Saint-Pierre: "Paul et Virginie," Studien zum Roman und seiner Wirkung*. Munich: Wilhelm Fink, 1975.

Hulme, Peter. *Colonial Encounters: Europe and the Native Caribbean, 1492–1797*. London: Methuen, 1986.

Ianni, Octavio. "O Negro na literatura Brasileira: Intervenção." In *Seminários de literatura brasileira: Ensaios*. Proceedings of the 3d Bienal Nestlé de literatura brasileira. Rio de Janeiro: UFRJ, 1990.

——. *Raças e classes sociais no Brasil*. Rio de Janeiro: Civilização brasileira, 1966.

Ivo, Ledo. "O romance poemático." *O estado de São Paulo: Suplemento cultural*, no. 61, 11 December 1977.

James, Henry. *The American*. Ed. James W. Tuttleton. New York: Norton, 1978.

Jameson, Fredric. *The Political Unconscious: Narrative as a Socially Symbolic Act*. Ithaca: Cornell University Press, 1981.

——. "Third World Literature in the Era of Multinational Capitalism." *Social Text* 15 (Fall 1986): 1–25.

Jauss, Hans Robert. *Literaturgeschichte als Provokation*. Frankfurt am Main: Suhrkamp, 1970. Translated by Timothy Bahti as *Toward an Aesthetics of Reception*. Minneapolis: University of Minnesota Press, 1982.

——. "Literaturgeschichte als Provokation der Literaturwissenschaft." In Jauss, *Literaturgeschichte als Provokation*, pp. 144–207. Frankfurt am Main: Suhrkamp, 1970.

Jay, Gregory S. "Hegel and the Dialectics of American Literary Historiography: From Parrington to Trilling and Beyond." In *Theorizing American Literature: Hegel, the Sign, and History*, ed. Bainard Cowan and Joseph G. Kronick, pp. 83–122. Baton Rouge: Louisiana State University Press, 1991.

Jehlen, Myra. *American Incarnation: The Individual, the Nation, and the Continent*. Cambridge: Harvard University Press, 1986.

Jennings, Francis. *The Invasion of America: Indians, Colonialism, and the Cant of Conquest*. New York: Norton, 1976.

"José de Alencar." *Movimento brasileiro* 1.3 (1929): 4–7.

Kamen, Henry. *European Society, 1500–1700*. London: Hutchinson, 1984. This book is rewritten from *The Iron Century*, 1971.

Kazin, Alfred. Review of *Leafstorm and Other Stories*. *New York Times Book Review*, 20 February 1972, 1, 14–16.

Kelly, William P. *Plotting America's Past: Fenimore Cooper and the Leatherstocking Tales*. Carbondale, Ill.: Southern Illinois University Press, 1983.

Kestler, Frances Roe, comp. *The Indian Captivity Narrative: A Woman's View*. New York: Garland, 1990.

Kislink, Ingrid. "Le symbolisme du jardin et l'imagination créatrice chez Rousseau, Bernardin de Saint-Pierre et Chateaubriand." *Studies on Voltaire and the Eighteenth Century* 185 (1980): 297–418.

Koch-Grünberg, Theodor. *Vom Roroima zum Orinoco: Ergebnisse einer Reise in Nordbrasilien und Venezuela in den Jahren 1911–1913*. Vol. 2: *Mythen und Legenden der Taulipang und Arekuna-Indianer*. Stuttgart: Strecker und Schroeder, 1924.

Kolodny, Annette. *The Lay of the Land: Metaphor as Experience and History in American Life and Letters*. Chapel Hill: University of North Carolina Press, 1975.

Laclau, Ernesto, and Chantal Mouffe. *Hegemony and Socialist Strategy: Toward a Radical Democratic Politics*. Trans. Winston Moore and Paul Cammack. London: Verso, 1985.

Lafitau, Jean-François. *Moeurs des sauvages ameriquains, comparées aux moeurs des premiers temps*. Paris: Saugrain l'aîné, 1724.

Lajolo, Marisa, and Regina Zilberman. *A leitura rarefeita: Livro e literatura no Brasil*. São Paulo: Brasiliense, 1991.

L'Allemant, Father Charles. "Lettre de Charles l'Allemant à Hiérome l'Allemant, son frère." 1626. In *Rélations des Jésuites, contenant ce qui c'est passé dans les missions des pères de la Compagnie de Jésus dans la Nouvelle France* 1:1–9. 3 vols. Quebec: Augustin Coté, 1858.

Larsen, Neil. *Modernism and Hegemony: A Materialist Critique of Aesthetic Agencies*. Minneapolis: University of Minnesota Press, 1990.

Lawrence, D. H.. "Fenimore Cooper's Leatherstocking Novels." *Studies in Classic American Literature*. New York: Thomas Seltzer, 1923.

Leite, Serafim, S. J., ed. *Novas cartas jesuíticas: De Nóbrega a Vieira*. São Paulo: Nacional, 1940.

Lemaire, Ria. "Re-reading *Iracema:* The Problem of the Representation of Women in the Construction of a National Brazilian Identity." *Luso-Brazilian Review* 26 (Winter 1989): 59–73.

Lemos, Carlos, et al., eds. *The Art of Brazil*. Introduction by Pietro Maria Bardi. Essay by Oscar Niemeyer. New York: Harper and Row, 1979.

Léry, Jean de. *Viagem à terra do Brasil*. Trans. and notes by Sérgio Milliet. Bibliography by Paul Gaffarel. Colloquium in the Brazilian language and notes on Tupy by Plínio Ayrosa. Belo Horizonte: Itatiaia; São Paulo: Editora da Universidade de São Paulo, 1980.

Leverenz, David. "Frederick Douglass's Self-Refashioning." *Criticism* 29 (Summer 1987): 341–70.

Levin, Boleslao. *Rousseau y la independencia argentina y americana*. Buenos Aires: Editorial Universitaria de Buenos Aires, 1967.

Levin, Harry. "Literature and Cultural Identity." *Comparative Literature Studies* 10 no. 2 (1973): 139–56.

——. *The Myth of the Golden Age in the Renaissance*. Bloomington: Indiana University Press, 1969.

Lévi-Strauss, Claude. *Les structures élémentaires de la parenté*. Paris: Presses Universitaires de France, 1949.

——. *Tristes tropiques*. Paris: Plon, 1955.

Lewis, C. S. *The Voyage of the "Dawn Treader."* New York: MacMillan, 1970.

Lima, Alceu Amoroso. "José de Alencar, êsse desconhecido?" In José de Alencar, *Iracema*, pp. 35–72. Ed. Augusto Meyer. São Paulo: Instituto nacional do livro/MEC, 1965.

Lima, Luiz Costa. *The Dark Side of Reason*. Trans. Paulo Henrique Britto. Foreword by Hans Ulrich Gumbrecht. Stanford: Stanford University Press, 1992.

Lindoso, Dirceu. *A diferença selvagem*. Rio de Janeiro: Civilização brasileira, 1983.

Locke, John. *Two Treatises*. Cambridge: Cambridge University Press, 1960.

Lombard, Charles. "Chateaubriand's American Reception, 1802–1870." In *Chateaubriand Today*, ed. Richard Schwitzer, pp. 221–28. Madison: University of Wisconsin Press, 1970.

Lopez, Telê Ancona. "A margem e o texto: Contribuição para o estudo do *Macunaíma*." In *Boletim bibliográfico*. São Paulo: Biblioteca municipal Mário de Andrade, 1970.

Lovejoy, Arthur O. "The Supposed Primitivism of Rousseau's *Discourse on Inequality*." In Lovejoy, *Essays in the History of Ideas*, pp. 14–37. New York: George Braziller, 1955.

Lowe, Elizabeth. *The City in Brazilian Literature*. Rutherford, N.J.: Fairleigh Dickinson University Press, 1982.

Lowe, Lisa. *Critical Terrains: French and British Orientalisms*. Ithaca: Cornell University Press, 1991.

Lukács, Georg. *The Historical Novel*. Trans. Hannah Mitchell and Stanley Mitchell. Boston: Beacon Press, 1963.

Lusch, Wilhelm. *Chateaubriand in seinem Verhältnis zu Bernardin de Saint-Pierre*. Heidelberg: Gebrüder Huber Nachfolger, 1912.

McMurray, George R., ed. *Critical Essays on Gabriel García Márquez*. Boston: G. K. Hall, 1987.

McNeill, William H., *Plagues and Peoples*. New York: Doubleday, 1974.

McWilliams, John P. *Political Justice in a Republic: James Fenimore Cooper's America*. Berkeley: University of California Press, 1972.

———. "Red Satan: Cooper and the American Indian Epic." In *James Fenimore Cooper: New Critical Essays*, ed. Robert Clark, pp. 143–61. London: Vision Press, 1985.

McWilliams, Richebourg Gaillard. *Fleur de Lys and Calumet*. Baton Rouge: Louisiana State University Press, 1953.

Marmontel, Jean François. *Les Incas, ou La destruction de l'empire du Pérou*. Berne: Société typographique, 1777.

Martin, Terence. "From the Ruins of History: *The Last of the Mohicans*." *Novel* 2 (1969): 221–29.

Martins, Wilson. *História da inteligência brasileira*. 7 vols. São Paulo: Cultrix; Editora da Universidade de São Paulo, 1977.

Mather, Cotton. *Magnalia Christi Americana, or The Ecclesiastical History of New-England; from its first planting, in the year 1620, unto the year of our Lord 1698*. With an introduction and occasional notes by the Rev. Thomas Robbins, and translations of the Hebrew, Greek, and Latin quotations by Lucius F. Robinson. 2 vols. Hartford: S. Andrus and Sons, 1853–55 [1792].

Mather, Increase. *Remarkable Providences Illustrative of the Earlier Days of American Colonisation*. Originally titled "An Essay for the Recording of Illustrious Providences." With introductory preface by George Offor. London: Reeves and Turner, 1890 [1684].

Matos Mar, José. "Dominación, desarrollos desiguales y pluralismos en la sociedad y cultura peruanas." In José Matos Mar et al., *El Perú actual (sociedad y política)*. Mexico City: Universidad nacional autónoma de Mexico, 1970.

Mattoso, Kátia M. de Queiroz. *Presença francesa no movimento democrático baiano de 1798*. Salvador: Itapuã, 1969.

Maurois, André. *René, ou La vie de Chateaubriand*. Paris: Grasset, 1938.

Maxwell, Kenneth R. "The Generation of the 1790s and the Idea of Luso-

Brazilian Empire." In *Colonial Roots of Modern Brazil*, ed. Dauril Alden, pp. 107–44. Berkeley: University of California Press, 1973.

May, Karl. *Winnetou: A Novel*. Ed. Erwin J. Haeberle. Trans. Michael Shaw. New York: Seabury Press, 1977.

Melzer, Sara E., and Leslie W. Rabine, eds. *Rebel Daughters: Women and the French Revolution*. New York: Oxford University Press, 1992.

Mena, Lucila Ines. *La función de la historia en "Cien años de soledad."* Barcelona: Plaza y Janés, 1979.

Merquior, José Guilherme. *De Anchieta a Euclides: Breve história da literatura brasileira*. Rio de Janeiro: José Olimpio, 1979.

Merrim, Stephanie. "Aridane's Thread: Auto-bio-graphy, History, and Cortés' *Segunda carta relación.*" *Dispositio* 11.28–29 (1989): 57–83.

Meyer, Augusto. *A chave e a máscara*. Rio de Janeiro: O Cruzeiro, 1964.

Mignolo, Walter. "Signs and Their Transmission: The Question of the Book in the New World." Paper presented at the John Carter Brown Library conference "The Book in the Americas," 18–21 June 1987.

Millgate, Michael, ed.. *New Essays on "Light in August."* Cambridge: Cambridge University Press, 1987.

Moers, Ellen. "Performing Heroism: The Myth of *Corinne.*" *Harvard English Studies* 6 (1975): 319–50.

Montaigne, Michel de. "Des Cannibales." In *Essais*, pp. 239–53. Ed. Albert Thibaudet. Paris: Gallimard, 1950.

Montello, José. "Uma influência de Balzac: José de Alencar." In José de Alencar, *Perfis de Mulher: Lucíola, Diva, Senhora*, pp. xii–xxi. Rio de Janeiro: José Olímpio, 1977.

Nemésio, Vitorino. Introduction to Alexandre Herculano, *Eurico, o presbítero*. São Paulo: Difusão européia do livro, 1963.

Nóbrega, Manuel da. "Cartas." In *Novas cartas jesuíticas: De Nóbrega a Vieira*, ed. Serafim Leite, S.J., pp. 23–129. São Paulo: Companhia editora nacional, 1940.

Obeyesekere, Gananath. *The Apotheosis of James Cook*. Princeton: Princeton University Press, 1992.

Oliveira, José Osório de. *História breve da literatura brasileira*. São Paulo: Martins, 1946.

Pagden, Anthony. "The Savage Critic: Some European Images of the Primitive." *Yearbook of English Studies* 13 (1983): 32–45.

Painter, George D. *Chateaubriand. A Biography*. New York: Knopf, 1978.

Palencia-Roth, Michael. "Cannibalism and the New Man of Latin America in the 15th-and 16th-Century European Imagination." *Comparative Civilizations Review* 12 (Spring 1985): 1–27.

———. "Prisms of Consciousness: The 'New Worlds' of Columbus and García Márquez." In *Gabriel García Márquez: Modern Critical Views*, ed. Harold Bloom, pp. 243–56. New York: Chelsea House, 1989. Reprinted from *Critical perspectives on Gabriel García Márquez*, ed. Bradley A. Shaw and N. G. Vera-Godwin, pp. 15–32. Boulder, Colo.: Society of Spanish and Spanish-American Studies, 1986.

Parry, J. H. *The Age of Reconnaissance*. Berkeley: University of California Press, 1981 [1963].

Pearce, Roy Harvey. *The Savages of America: A Study of the Indian and the Idea of Civilization*. Baltimore: Johns Hopkins University Press, 1953.

Peck, H. Daniel, ed. *New Essays on "The Last of the Mohicans."* Cambridge: Cambridge University Press, 1992.

Peixoto, Afrânio. *Noções de história da literatura brasileira*. Rio de Janeiro: Francisco Alves, 1931.

Pereira, João Baptista Borges. *Côr, profissão e mobiliade*. São Paulo: Pioneira; Editora da Universidade de São Paulo, 1967.

Pérez Galdós, Benito. *Doña Perfecta*. Trans. and Introduction by Harriet de Onís. Woodbury, N.Y.: Barron's Educational Series, 1960.

Perron, Paul. "Toward a Semiotics of Manipulation: Jesuit-Huron Relations in Seventeenth-Century New France." *Semiotica* 74.3–4 (1989): 147–40.

Plattner, Marc. *Rousseau's State of Nature: An Interpretation of the "Discourse on Inequality."* De Kalb: Northern Illinois University Press, 1979.

Poole's Index to Periodical Literature. New York: Peter Smith, 1938.

Porter, Carolyn. "Gender and Value in *The American*." In *New Essays on "The American,"* ed. Martha Banta, pp. 99–129. Cambridge: Cambridge University Press, 1987.

Prado, Décio de Almeida. "Os demônios familiares de Alencar." *Revista do Instituto de estudos brasileiros* 15 (1974): 27–57.

Proença, Manuel Cavalcanti. *Estudos literários*. Preface by Antônio Houaiss. Rio de Janeiro: José Olímpio, 1969.

——. *José de Alencar na literatura brasileira*. Rio de Janeiro: Civilização brasileira, 1966.

——. *Roteiro de "Macunaíma."* São Paulo: n.p., 1955.

——. "Transforma-se o amador na coisa amada." In José de Alencar, *Iracema*, pp. 217–71. Ed. Proença. 2d ed. São Paulo: Editora da Universidade de São Paulo 1979.

Pudaloff, Ross. "Cooper's Genres and American Problems." *ELH* 50 (Winter 1983): 711–27.

——. "Education and the Constitution: Instituting American Culture." In *Laws of Our Fathers: Popular Culture and the U.S. Constitution*, ed. R. B. Browne and J. G. Browne, pp. 23–41. Bowling Green, Ohio: Bowling Green State University, 1986.

——. "One Subject at a Time: Gender and Race in Early American Captivity Narratives." Unpublished paper, 1992.

Quinn, David B., ed., with the assistance of Alison M. Quinn and Susan Hillier. *New American World: A Documentary History of North America to 1612*. 5 vols. New York: Arno, 1979.

Racault, Jean-Michel, ed. *Etudes sur "Paul et Virginie" et l'œuvre de Bernardin de Saint-Pierre*. Paris: Didier; Université de la Réunion, 1986.

Railton, Stephen. *Authorship and Audience: Literary Performance in the American Renaissance*. Princeton: Princeton University Press, 1991.

——. *Fenimore Cooper: A Study of His Life and Imagination*. Princeton: Princeton University Press, 1978.

Rama, Angel. *A cidade das letras (La ciudad letrada).* Introduction by Mario Vargas Llosa. Prologue by Hugo Achugar. Trans. Emir Sader. São Paulo: Brasiliense, 1985.

——. *Transculturación narrativa en América latina.* Mexico City: Siglo veintiuno, 1982.

Rans, Geoffrey. *Cooper's Leather-stocking Novels: A Secular Reading.* Chapel Hill: University of North Carolina Press, 1991.

Reis, João José, ed. *Escravidão e invenção da liberdade: Estudos sobre o Negro no Brasil.* São Paulo: Brasiliense, 1988.

Relations des Jésuites, contenant ce qui c'est passé dans les missions des pères de la Compagnie de Jésus dans la Nouvelle France. 3 vols. Quebec: Augustin Coté, 1858.

Remond, René. *Les Etats Unis devant l'opinion française, 1815–1852.* 2 vols. Cahiers de la Fondation nationale des sciences politiques, 116–17. Paris: Librairies Armand Colin, 1962.

Renan, Ernest. "What Is a Nation?" Trans. Martin Thom. In *Nation and Narration,* ed. Homi K. Bhabha, pp. 8–22. London: Routledge, 1990.

Ribeiro, Darcy. *Aos trancos e barrancos: Como o Brasil deu no que deu.* 2d ed. Rio de Janeiro Guanabara Dois, 1986.

——. *Utopia selvagem: Saudades da inocência perdida—uma fábula.* Rio de Janeiro: Nova fronteira, 1982.

Ribeiro, João. "*Macunaíma:* Herói sem nenhum caráter—por Mário de Andrade." Journal do Brasil (Rio de Janeiro), 31 October 1928. Rpt. in Mário de Andrade. *Macunaíma.* Critical edition by Telê Ancona Lopez. Rio de Janeiro: Livros técnicos e científicos, 1978.

Richard, Jean-Pierre. *Paysage de Chateaubriand.* Paris: Seuil, 1967.

Riffaterre, Hermine B. "L'imagination livresque de Chateaubriand." *Revue belge de philologie et d'histoire.* 50.3 (1972): 768–76.

Riffaterre, Michel. "Chateaubriand et le monument imaginaire." In *Chateaubriand Today,* ed. Richard Schwitzer, pp. 62–81. Madison: University of Wisconsin Press, 1970.

Robles, Humberto E. "The First Voyage around the World: From Pigafetta to García Márquez." In *Gabriel García Márquez: Modern Critical Views,* ed. Harold Bloom, pp. 183–202. New York: Chelsea House, 1989. Reprinted from *History of European Ideas* 6.4 (1985): 385–404.

Roddier, Henri *Jean-Jacques Rousseau en Angleterre au XVIIIe siècle: L'oeuvre et l'homme.* Paris: Boivin, 1950.

Rodriguez Monegal, Emir. "*One Hundred Years of Solitude:* The Last Three Pages." In *Critical Essays on Gabriel García Márquez,* ed. George R. McMurray, pp. 147–52. Boston: G. K. Hall, 1987. Reprinted from *Books Abroad* 47 (Summer 1973): 485–89.

Romero, Sílvio. *História da literatura brasileira.* 5 vols. Rio de Janeiro: José Olímpio, 1943.

Rosenthal, Bernard. *City of Nature: Journeys to Nature in the Age of American Romanticism.* Newark: University of Delaware Press, 1980.

Ross, Andrew. "Uses of Camp." *Yale Journal of Criticism* 1 (1988): 1–24.

Rossbacher, Karlheinz. *Lederstrumpf in Deutschand: Zur Rezeption James Feni-more Coopers Beim Leser der Restaurazionzeit.* Munich: Wilhelm Fink, 1972.
Rousseau, Jean-Jacques. *La découverte du nouveau-monde.* In *Oeuvres complètes* 2:811–47. Ed. Bernard Gagnebin and Marcel Raymond. 4 vols. Paris: Galli-mard, 1964.
——. *Discours sur l'origine et les fondements de l'inégalité.* In *Oeuvres complètes* 3:109–237. Ed. Bernard Gagnebin and Marcel Raymond. 4 vols. Paris: Gallimard, 1964.
——. *Du contrat social.* Introduction by Ronald Grimsley. Oxford: Clarendon Press, 1972.
——. *Emile, ou Traité de l'éducation.* Introduction, bibliography, and notes by François Richard and Pierre Richard. Paris: Garnier, 1964.
——. *La nouvelle Héloïse.* In *Oeuvres complètes* 2:5–745. Ed. Bernard Gagnebin and Marcel Raymond. 4 vols. Paris: Gallimard, 1961.
——. *Oeuvres complètes.* Ed. Bernard Gagnebin and Marcel Raymond. 4 vols. Paris: Gallimard, 1964.
Rowe, John Carlos. "The Politics of Innocence in Henry James's *The Ameri-can."* In *New Essays on "The American,"* ed. Martha Banta, pp. 69–98. Cambridge: Cambridge University Press, 1987.
Russell-Wood, A. J. R. "Preconditions and Precipitants of the Independence Movement in Portuguese America." In *From Colony to Nation: Essays on the Independence of Brazil,* ed. Russell-Wood, pp. 3–40. Baltimore: Johns Hopkins University Press, 1975.
——, ed. *From Colony to Nation: Essays on the Independence of Brazil.* Baltimore: Johns Hopkins University Press, 1975.
Sahagún, Fray Bernardino de. *Historia general de las cosas de Nueva España.* 5 vols. Introduction by Wigberto Jiménez Moreno. Mexico City: Pedro Robredo, 1938 [1569].
Said, Edward W. *Orientalism.* New York: Vintage, 1979 [1978].
Saint-Pierre, Jacques Henri Bernardin de. *Paul et Virginie, suivi de La chau-mière indienne.* Paris: Nelson, 1937 [1784].
——. *Voyage à l'Ile de France: Un officier du roi à l'île Maurice, 1768–1770.* Introduction and notes by Yves Bénot. Paris: Maspéro, 1983.
Samuels, Shirley. "Generation through Violence: Cooper and the Making of Americans." In *New Essays on "The Last of the Mohicans"* ed. H. Daniel Peck, pp. 87–114. Cambridge: Cambridge University Press, 1992.
Sant'Anna, Affonso Romano de. *Análise estrutural de romances brasileiros.* Pe-trópolis, Brazil: Vozes, 1973.
Santayana, George. "Genteel American Poetry." In *George Santayana's America: Essays in Literature and Culture,* pp. 147–49. Introduction by George Barlow. Cambridge: Harvard University Press, 1967.
Santiago, Silviano. "Liderança e hierarquia em Alencar." *O estado de São Paulo: Suplemento cultural,* 18 December 1977, pp. 7–11.
——. "Roteiro para uma leitura intertextual de *Ubirajara.*" In José de Alencar, *Ubirajara,* pp. 5–9. São Paulo: Ática, 1980.
Scammell, G. V. "The New Worlds and Europe in the Sixteenth Century." *Historical Journal* 12.3 (1969): 389–412.

Schmidel, Ulrich. *Wahrhaftige Historien einer Wunderbaren Schiffahrt.* Graz: Akademische Druck- und Verlagsanstalt, 1962.

Schopenhauer, Arthur. *Die Welt als Wille und Vorstellung.* Vol. 1 of *Sämtliche Werke.* Ed. Wolfgang Freiherr von Löhneysen. 5 vols. [Stuttgart]: Cotta, 1960.

Schor, Naomi. *Breaking the Chain: Women, Theory, and French Realist Fiction.* New York: Columbia University Press, 1985.

———. "Triste Amérique: *Atala* and the Postrevolutionary Construction of Woman." In *Rebel Daugters: Women and the French Revolution,* ed. Sara E. Melzer and Leslie W. Rabine, 139–56. New York: Oxford University Press, 1992.

Schulze, Joachim. "Das Paradies auf dem Berge: Zur literarischen Ikonographie Bernardin de Saint Pierres *Paul et Virginie.*" *Romanistisches Jahrbuch* 25 (1974): 123–38.

Schwarz, Lawrence. *The Making of Faulkner's Reputation: The Politics of Modern Literary Criticism.* Knoxville: University of Tennessee Press, 1988.

Schwarz, Roberto. *Ao vencedor as batatas: Forma literária e processo social nos inícios do romance brasileiro.* São Paulo: Duas Cidades, 1977.

———. "Cuidado com as ideologias alienígenas." In Schwarz, *O pai de família e outros estudos,* pp. 115–22. Rio de Janeiro: Paz e terra, 1978.

———. "Nacional por subtração." In Schwarz, *Que horas são? Ensaios,* pp. 29–48. São Paulo: Companhia das letras, 1987.

Schwitzer, Richard. *Chateaubriand.* New York: Twayne, 1971.

———, ed. *Chateaubriand Today.* Madison: University of Wisconsin Press, 1970.

Shackleton, Robert. "Chateaubriand and the Eighteenth Century." In *Chateaubriand Today,* ed. Richard Schwitzer, pp. 15–28. Madison: University of Wisconsin Press, 1970.

Shelley, Mary. *Frankenstein.* New York: New American Library, 1965.

Shklovsky, Victor. "L'art comme procédé." In *Théorie de la littérature,* ed. and trans. Tzvetan Todorov, pp. 76–97. Preface by Roman Jakobson. Paris: Seuil, 1965.

Simms, William Gilmore. "The Writing of Cooper." *Magnolia* (1842): 129–39. Reprinted in *Fenimore Cooper: The Critical Heritage,* ed. George Dekker and John P. McWilliams, pp. 218–27. London: Routledge and Kegan Paul, 1973.

Simpson, David *The Politics of American English, 1776–1850.* New York: Oxford University Press, 1986.

Skidmore, Thomas. *Black into White: Race and Nationality in Brazilian Thought.* New York: Oxford University Press, 1974.

———. "Brazil's American Illusion: From Dom Pedro II to the Coup of 1964." *Luso-Brazilian Review* 23 (Winter 1986): 71–84.

Slotkin, Richard. *Regeneration through Violence: The Mythology of the American Frontier, 1600–1860.* Middletown, Conn.: Wesleyan University Press, 1973.

Smith, Henry Nash. "Symbol and Idea in *Virgin Land.*" In *Ideology and Classic American Literature,* ed. Sacvan Bercovitch and Myra Jehlen, pp. 21–35. Cambridge: Cambridge University Press, 1986.

——. *Virgin Land: The American West as Symbol and Myth.* Cambridge: Harvard University Press, 1950.

Sodré, Nelson Werneck. *A ideologia do colonialismo: Seus reflexos no pensamento brasileiro.* 2d ed. Rio de Janeiro: Civilização brasileira, 1965.

Sommer, Doris. *Foundational Fictions: The National Romances of Latin America.* Berkeley: University of California Press, 1991.

Souza, Antônio Cândido de Mello e: see Cândido, Antônio.

Souza, Márcio. *Mad Maria.* Trans. Thomas Colchie. New York: Avon, 1985.

Spell, Jefferson Rea. *Rousseau in the Spanish World before 1833: A Study in Franco-Spanish Literary Relations.* Austin: University of Texas Press, 1938.

Spencer, Benjamin. *The Quest for Nationality: An American Literary Campaign.* Syracuse: Syracuse University Press, 1957.

Spiller, Robert E. *Fenimore Cooper: Critic of His Time.* New York: Minton, Balch, 1931.

Spiller, Robert E., and Philip C. Blackburn. *A Descriptive Bibliography of the Writings of James Fenimore Cooper.* New York: R. R. Bowker, 1934.

Spivak, Gayatri Chakravorty. *In Other Worlds: Essays in Cultural Politics.* London: Routledge, 1988 [1987].

Staden, Hans. *Brasilien: Die wahrhaftige Historie der wilden, nackten, grimmigen Menschenfresser-Leute.* Ed. with an Introduction by Gustav Faber. Trans. from early high German (Frühneuhochdeutsch) by Ulrich Schlemmer. Tübingen: Erdmann, c. 1982.

Staël, Madame (Anne-Louise-Germaine) de. *Corinne, ou L'Italie.* Paris: Garnier, 1931.

Stam, Robert. *Subversive Pleasures: Bakhtin, Cultural Criticism, and Film.* Baltimore: Johns Hopkins University Press, 1989.

Starobinski, Jean. "La mise en accusation de la société." In *Jean-Jacques Rousseau: Quatre études de Jean Starobinski et al.* Neuchâtel: La Baconnière, 1978.

Stavenhagen, Rodolfo. "Siete tesis equivocadas sobre América latina." In Stavenhagen, Ernesto Laclau, and R. M. Marini, *Tres ensayos sobre América latina,* pp. 9–42. Barcelona: Anagrama, 1973.

Stepan, Nancy. *"The Hour of Eugenics:" Race, Gender and Nation in Latin America.* Ithaca: Cornell University Press, 1991.

Sundquist, Eric. *Faulkner: The House Divided.* Baltimore: Johns Hopkins University Press, 1983.

——. *Home as Found: Authority and Genealogy in Nineteenth-Century American Literature.* Baltimore: Johns Hopkins University Press, 1977.

Sussman, Henry. "An American History Lesson: Hegel and the Historiography of Superimposition." In *Theorizing American Literature: Hegel, the Sign, and History,* ed. Bainard Cowan and Joseph G. Kronick, pp. 33–52. Baton Rouge: Louisiana State University Press, 1991.

Tanner, Helen, ed.. *Atlas of Great Lakes Indian History.* Norman: Published for the Newberry Library by the University of Oklahoma Press, 1986.

Tapie, V.-L. *Chateaubriand par lui-même.* Paris: Seuil, 1965.

Teles, Gilberto Mendonça. "L'avant-garde européenne et le modernisme brésilien." *Europe* 599 (1979): 96–117.

Terrasse, Jean. *Jean-Jacques Rousseau et la quête de l'âge d'or.* Brussels: Académie royale de langue et littérature françaises, 1970.

Tetley-Jones, Ines. "Sentimentalism versus Adventure and social Engagement: A Study of J. F. Cooper's Leatherstocking Tales." Ph.D. diss., University of Heidelberg, 1970.

Thévet. André. *Le Brésil et les brésiliens.* Paris: Presses universitaires de France, 1953.

——. *Les singularités de la France Atlantique.* New edition with notes and commentary by Paul Gaffarel. Paris Maisonneuve, 1878.

Thom, Martin. "Tribes within Nations: The Ancient Germans and the History of Modern France." In *Nation and Narration,* ed. Homi K. Bhabha, pp. 23–43. London: Routledge, 1990.

Tocqueville, Alexis de. *Democracy in America.* The Henry Reeve text as revised by Francis Bowen, now further corrected and edited with a historical essay, editorial notes, and bibiographies by Phillips Bradley. 2 vols. New York: Random House, 1945.

Todorov, Tzvetan. *La conquête de l'Amérique: La question de l'autre.* Paris: Seuil, 1982. *The Conquest of America: The Question of the Other.* Trans. Richard Howard. New York: Harper and Row, 1984.

——. *Frêle bonheur: Essai sur Rousseau.* Paris: Hachette, 1985.

Tompkins, J. M. S. *The Popular Novel in England, 1770–1800.* Lincoln: University of Nebraska Press, 1961.

Tompkins, Jane. *Sensational Designs: The Cultural Work of American Fiction, 1790–1860.* New York: Oxford University Press 1985.

Vallois, Marie-Claire. "Exotic Femininity and the Rights of Man: *Paul et Virginie* and *Atala,* or the Revolution in Stasis." In *Rebel Daughters: Women and the French Revolution,* ed. Sara E. Melzer and Leslie W. Rabine, pp. 178–97. New York: Oxford University Press, 1992.

Ventura, Roberto. "'Estilo tropical': A natureza como pátria." *Ideologies in Literature* 2 (Fall 1987): 145–58.

Villegagnon, chevalier de. *Copie de quelques letres sur la navigation du Chevallier de Villegagnon es terres de l'Amérique oultre l'Aequinoctial, iusques soubz le tropique de Capricorne: côtenant sommairement les fortunes encouroues en ce voyage, avec les moeurs et façons de vivre des Sauvages du pais: envoyées per un des gens dudict Seigneur.* Paris: Chez Martin le jeune, 1557.

Wallace, James D. "Cultivating an Audience: From *Precaution* to *The Spy.*" In *James Fenimore Cooper: New Critical Essays,* ed. Robert Clark, pp. 38–54. London: Vision Press, 1985.

——. *Early Cooper and His Audience.* New York: Columbia University Press, 1986.

Waller, Margaret. "Being René, Buying *Atala:* Alienated Subjects and Decorative Objects in Postrevolutionary France." In *Rebel Daughters: Women and the French Revolution,* ed. Sara E. Melzer and Leslie W. Rabine, pp. 157–77. New York: Oxford University Press, 1992.

Weisbuch, Robert. *Atlantic Double-Cross: American Literature and British Influence in the Age of Emerson.* Chicago: University of Chicago Press, 1986.

Weston, Peter J. "The Noble Primitive as Bourgeois Subject." *Literature and History* 10 (Spring 1984) 59–71.

Williams, Gary. "Historical Introduction" to James Fenimore Cooper, *Notions of the Americans: Picked up by a Travelling Bachelor.* Ed. James Franklin Beard. Albany: State University of New York Press, 1991.

Winthrop, John. *Journal, "History of New England," 1630–1649.* In *Original Narratives of Early American History,* ed. James Kendall Hosmer, 1:266–68. 2 vols. New York: Charles Scribner's Sons, 1908.

Wolff, Janet. *The Social Production of Art.* London: Macmillan, 1982.

"Works of Chateubriand." *American Quarterly Review* 4 (December 1827): 458–82.

Zavala, Iris M. "*Cien años de soledad:* Crónica de Indias." *Insula* 286 (1970): 3–11.

Zilberman, Regina. *Do mito ao romance: Tipologia da ficção brasileira contemporânea.* Caxias do Sul: Universidade de Caxias do Sul; Escola superior de teologia São Lourenço de Brindes, 1977.

Index